# State, Society and the Market in Contemporary Vietnam

Lively debates around property, access to resources, legal rights, and the protection of livelihoods have unfolded in Vietnam since the economic reforms of 1986. Known as *Doi Moi* (changing to the new), these have gradually transformed the country from a socialist state to a society in which a communist party presides over a neoliberal economy.

By exploring the complex relationship between property, the state, society, and the market, this book demonstrates how both developmental issues and state–society relations in Vietnam can be explored through the prism of property relations and property rights. The essays in this collection demonstrate how negotiations over property are deeply enmeshed with dynamics of state formation, and covers debates over the role of the state and its relationship to various levels of society, the intrusion of global forces into the lives of marginalized communities and individuals, and how community norms and standards shape and reshape national policy and laws.

With contributors from around the world, this book will be of great interest to students and scholars of East and Southeast Asian studies, including politics, culture, society, and law, as well as those interested in the role of the state and property relations more generally.

**Hue-Tam Ho Tai** is the Kenneth T. Young Professor of Sino-Vietnamese History at Harvard University, USA.

**Mark Sidel** is Doyle-Bascom Professor of Law and Public Affairs at the University of Wisconsin-Madison, USA.

## ASIA'S TRANSFORMATIONS

Edited by Mark Selden
Cornell University, USA

The books in this series explore the political, social, economic and cultural consequences of Asia's transformations in the twentieth and twenty-first centuries. The series emphasizes the tumultuous interplay of local, national, regional and global forces as Asia bids to become the hub of the world economy. While focusing on the contemporary, it also looks back to analyse the antecedents of Asia's contested rise.

This series comprises several strands:

***Asia's Transformations***

Titles include:

1 **Debating Human Rights***
Critical essays from the United States and Asia
*Edited by Peter Van Ness*

2 **Hong Kong's History***
State and society under colonial rule
*Edited by Tak-Wing Ngo*

3 **Japan's Comfort Women***
Sexual slavery and prostitution during World War II and the US occupation
*Yuki Tanaka*

4 **Opium, Empire and the Global Political Economy***
*Carl A. Trocki*

5 **Chinese Society***
Change, conflict and resistance
*Edited by Elizabeth J. Perry and Mark Selden*

6 **Mao's Children in the New China***
Voices from the Red Guard generation
*Yarong Jiang and David Ashley*

7 **Remaking the Chinese State***
Strategies, society and security
*Edited by Chien-min Chao and Bruce J. Dickson*

8 **Korean Society***
Civil society, democracy and the state
*Edited by Charles K. Armstrong*

9 **The Making of Modern Korea***
*Adrian Buzo*

10 **The Resurgence of East Asia***
500, 150 and 50 year perspectives
*Edited by Giovanni Arrighi, Takeshi Hamashita and Mark Selden*

11 **Chinese Society, second edition***
Change, conflict and resistance
*Edited by Elizabeth J. Perry and Mark Selden*

12 **Ethnicity in Asia***
*Edited by Colin Mackerras*

13 **The Battle for Asia***
From decolonization to globalization
*Mark T. Berger*

14 **State and Society in 21st Century China***
*Edited by Peter Hays Gries and Stanley Rosen*

15 **Japan's Quiet Transformation***
Social change and civil society in the 21st century
*Jeff Kingston*

16 **Confronting the Bush Doctrine***
Critical views from the Asia-Pacific
*Edited by Mel Gurtov and Peter Van Ness*

17 **China in War and Revolution, 1895–1949***
*Peter Zarrow*

18 **The Future of US–Korean Relations***
The imbalance of power
*Edited by John Feffer*

19 **Working in China***
Ethnographies of labor and workplace transformations
*Edited by Ching Kwan Lee*

20 **Korean Society, second edition***
Civil society, democracy and the state
*Edited by Charles K. Armstrong*

21 **Singapore***
The state and the culture of excess
*Souchou Yao*

22 **Pan-Asianism in Modern Japanese History***
Colonialism, regionalism and borders
*Edited by Sven Saaler and J. Victor Koschmann*

23 **The Making of Modern Korea, second edition***
*Adrian Buzo*

24 **Re-writing Culture in Taiwan***
*Edited by Fang-long Shih, Stuart Thompson, and Paul-François Tremlett*

25 **Reclaiming Chinese Society***
The new social activism
*Edited by You-tien Hsing and Ching Kwan Lee*

26 **Girl Reading Girl in Japan***
*Edited by Tomoko Aoyama and Barbara Hartley*

27 **Chinese Politics***
State, society and the market
*Edited by Peter Hays Gries and Stanley Rosen*

28 **Chinese Society, third edition***
Change, conflict and resistance
*Edited by Elizabeth J. Perry and Mark Selden*

29 **Mapping Modernity in Shanghai**
Space, gender, and visual culture in the Sojourners' City, 1853–98
*Samuel Y. Liang*

30 **Minorities and Multiculturalism in Japanese Education**
An interactive perspective
*Edited by Ryoko Tsuneyoshi, Kaori H Okano and Sarane Boocock*

31 **Japan's Wartime Medical Atrocities**
Comparative inquiries in science, history, and ethics
*Edited by Jing-Bao Nie, Nanyan Guo, Mark Selden and Arthur Kleinman*

32 **State and Society in Modern Rangoon**
*Donald M. Seekins*

33 **Learning Chinese, Turning Chinese***
Becoming sinophone in a globalised world
*Edward McDonald*

34 **Aesthetic Constructions of Korean Nationalism**
Spectacle, politics and history
*Hong Kal*

35 **Popular Culture and the State in East and Southeast Asia**
*Edited by Nissim Otmazgin and Eyal Ben Ari*

36 **Japan's Outcaste Abolition**
The struggle for national inclusion and the making of the modern state
*Noah Y. McCormack*

37 **The Market and Temple Fairs of Rural China**
Red fire
*Gene Cooper*

38 **The Role of American NGOs in China's Modernization**
Invited influence
*Norton Wheeler*

39 **State, Society and the Market in Contemporary Vietnam**
Property, power and values
*Edited by Hue-Tam Ho Tai and Mark Sidel*

***Asia's Great Cities***

Each volume aims to capture the heartbeat of the contemporary city from multiple perspectives emblematic of the authors own deep familiarity with the distinctive faces of the city, its history, society, culture, politics and economics, and its evolving position in national, regional and global frameworks. While most volumes emphasize urban developments since the Second World War, some pay close attention to the legacy of the longue durée in shaping the contemporary. Thematic and comparative volumes address such themes as urbanization, economic and financial linkages, architecture and space, wealth and power, gendered relationships, planning and anarchy, and ethnographies in national and regional perspective. Titles include:

1 **Bangkok***
Place, practice and representation
*Marc Askew*

2 **Representing Calcutta***
Modernity, nationalism and the colonial uncanny
*Swati Chattopadhyay*

3 **Singapore***
Wealth, power and the culture of control
*Carl A. Trocki*

4 **The City in South Asia**
*James Heitzman*

5 **Global Shanghai, 1850–2010***
A history in fragments
*Jeffrey N. Wasserstrom*

6 **Hong Kong***
Becoming a global city
*Stephen Chiu and Tai-Lok Lui*

***Asia.com*** is a series which focuses on the ways in which new information and communication technologies are influencing politics, society and culture in Asia.
Titles include:

1 **Japanese Cybercultures***
*Edited by Mark McLelland and Nanette Gottlieb*

2 **Asia.com***
Asia encounters the Internet
*Edited by K. C. Ho, Randolph Kluver and Kenneth C. C. Yang*

3 **The Internet in Indonesia's New Democracy***
*David T. Hill and Krishna Sen*

4 **Chinese Cyberspaces***
Technological changes and political effects
*Edited by Jens Damm and Simona Thomas*

5 **Mobile Media in the Asia-Pacific**
Gender and the art of being mobile
*Larissa Hjorth*

***Literature and Society***

*Literature and Society* is a series that seeks to demonstrate the ways in which Asian literature is influenced by the politics, society and culture in which it is produced.
Titles include:

1 **The Body in Postwar Japanese Fiction**
*Douglas N. Slaymaker*

2 **Chinese Women Writers and the Feminist Imagination, 1905–1948***
*Haiping Yan*

*Routledge Studies in Asia's Transformations*

*Routledge Studies in Asia's Transformations* is a forum for innovative new research intended for a high-level specialist readership.
Titles include:

1 **The American Occupation of Japan and Okinawa***
Literature and memory
*Michael Molasky*

2 **Koreans in Japan***
Critical voices from the margin
*Edited by Sonia Ryang*

3 **Internationalizing the Pacific**
The United States, Japan and the Institute of Pacific Relations in war and peace, 1919–1945
*Tomoko Akami*

4 **Imperialism in South East Asia***
'A fleeting, passing phase'
*Nicholas Tarling*

5 **Chinese Media, Global Contexts***
*Edited by Chin-Chuan Lee*

6 **Remaking Citizenship in Hong Kong***
Community, nation and the global city
*Edited by Agnes S. Ku and Ngai Pun*

7 **Japanese Industrial Governance**
Protectionism and the licensing state
*Yul Sohn*

8 **Developmental Dilemmas***
Land reform and institutional change in China
*Edited by Peter Ho*

9 **Genders, Transgenders and Sexualities in Japan***
*Edited by Mark McLelland and Romit Dasgupta*

10 **Fertility, Family Planning and Population Policy in China***
*Edited by Dudley L. Poston, Che-Fu Lee, Chiung-Fang Chang, Sherry L. McKibben and Carol S. Walther*

11 **Japanese Diasporas***
Unsung pasts, conflicting presents and uncertain futures
*Edited by Nobuko Adachi*

12 **How China Works***
Perspectives on the twentieth-century industrial workplace
*Edited by Jacob Eyferth*

13 **Remolding and Resistance among Writers of the Chinese Prison Camp**
Disciplined and published
*Edited by Philip F. Williams and Yenna Wu*

14 **Popular Culture, Globalization and Japan***
*Edited by Matthew Allen and Rumi Sakamoto*

15 **medi@sia***
Global media/tion in and out of context
*Edited by Todd Joseph Miles Holden and Timothy J. Scrase*

16 **Vientiane***
Transformations of a Lao landscape
*Marc Askew, William S. Logan and Colin Long*

17 **State Formation and Radical Democracy in India**
*Manali Desai*

18 **Democracy in Occupied Japan***
The U.S. occupation and Japanese politics and society
*Edited by Mark E. Caprio and Yoneyuki Sugita*

19 **Globalization, Culture and Society in Laos***
*Boike Rehbein*

20 **Transcultural Japan***
At the borderlands of race, gender, and identity
*Edited by David Blake Willis and Stephen Murphy-Shigematsu*

21 **Post-Conflict Heritage, Post-Colonial Tourism**
Culture, politics and development at Angkor
*Tim Winter*

22 **Education and Reform in China***
*Emily Hannum and Albert Park*

23 **Writing Okinawa: Narrative Acts of Identity and Resistance**
*Davinder L. Bhowmik*

24 **Maid in China***
Media, mobility, and a new semiotic of power
*Wanning Sun*

25 **Northern Territories, Asia-Pacific Regional Conflicts and the Åland Experience**
Untying the Kurillian knot
*Edited by Kimie Hara and Geoffrey Jukes*

26 **Reconciling Indonesia**
Grassroots agency for peace
*Birgit Bräuchler*

27 **Singapore in the Malay World***
Building and breaching regional bridges
*Lily Zubaidah Rahim*

28 **Pirate Modernity***
Delhi's media urbanism
*Ravi Sundaram*

29 **The World Bank and the post-Washington Consensus in Vietnam and Indonesia**
Inheritance of loss
*Susan Engel*

30 **China on Video**
Smaller screen realities
*Paola Voci*

31 **Overseas Chinese, Ethnic Minorities and Nationalism**
De-centering China
*Elena Barabantseva*

***Critical Asian Scholarship***

*Critical Asian Scholarship* is a series intended to showcase the most important individual contributions to scholarship in Asian Studies. Each of the volumes presents a leading Asian scholar addressing themes that are central to his or her

most significant and lasting contribution to Asian studies. The series is committed to the rich variety of research and writing on Asia, and is not restricted to any particular discipline, theoretical approach or geographical expertise.
Titles include:

1 **Southeast Asia***
A testament
*George McT. Kahin*

2 **Women and the Family in Chinese History***
*Patricia Buckley Ebrey*

3 **China Unbound***
Evolving perspectives on the Chinese past
*Paul A. Cohen*

4 **China's Past, China's Future***
Energy, food, environment
*Vaclav Smil*

5 **The Chinese State in Ming Society***
*Timothy Brook*

6 **China, East Asia and the Global Economy***
Regional and historical perspectives
*Takeshi Hamashita*
*Edited by Mark Selden and Linda Grove*

7 **The Global and Regional in China's Nation-Formation***
*Prasenjit Duara*

*Available in paperback

# State, Society and the Market in Contemporary Vietnam

## Property, power and values

**Edited by Hue-Tam Ho Tai and Mark Sidel**

Routledge
Taylor & Francis Group
LONDON AND NEW YORK

First published 2013
by Routledge
2 Park Square, Milton Park, Abingdon, Oxon, OX14 4RN

Simultaneously published in the USA and Canada
by Routledge
711 Third Avenue, New York, NY 10017

*Routledge is an imprint of the Taylor & Francis Group, an informa business*



*British Library Cataloguing in Publication Data*
A catalogue record for this book is available from the British Library

*Library of Congress Cataloging in Publication Data*
State, society and the market in contemporary Vietnam/
[edited by] Tai, Hue-Tam Ho, Mark Sidel.
p. cm. – (Asia's transformations)
Includes bibliographical references.
1. Real property–Vietnam. 2. Right of property–Vietnam.
3. Vietnam–Economic policy. 4. Vietnam–Commerce.
I. Tai, Hue-Tam Ho, 1948– II. Sidel, Mark.
III. Series: Asia's transformations.
HD890.5.Z63S73 2012
323.4'609597–dc23 2012011257

ISBN: 978-0-415-62625-5 (hbk)
ISBN: 978-0-203-09831-8 (ebk)

Typeset in Times New Roman
by Sunrise Setting Ltd

MIX
Paper from responsible sources
FSC www.fsc.org FSC® C004839

Printed and bound by CPI Group (UK) Ltd, Croydon, CR0 4YY

# Translation of cover image

Real Estate Services

4 × 20 meters
4 × 15 meters (Valid Documents)
4 × 10 meters

Vehicle Leases Available

4.15.25.40 seaters

Well Drilling

Contact Mr. Nguyen Tu Telephone: 7181137

Mobile: 0908385920

# Contents

# Figures

# Tables

# Contributors

**David Biggs** is Associate Professor of History at the University of California at Riverside. His research examines connections between environmental issues and politics in modern Vietnam. His first book *Quagmire: Nation Building and Nature in the Mekong Delta* (Washington 2011) examines these issues in the wetlands and waterways of the Mekong Delta. He is presently working on an environmental and social history of a former American military base near Hue.

**John Gillespie** is Professor of Law and Director of the Asia Pacific Business Regulation Group, Department of Business Law and Taxation, Monash University. He teaches and publishes widely about legal change in East Asian legal systems, and applied legal transplantation and regulatory theory. His most recent books are *Legal Reforms in China and Vietnam: A Comparison of Asian Communist Regimes* (Routledge 2010, with Chen) and *Transplanting Commercial Law Reform* (Ashgate 2006).

**Erik Harms** teaches anthropology at Yale University. He has conducted extensive fieldwork in and around Ho Chi Minh City since the late 1990s and is the author of the recent ethnography, *Saigon's Edge: On the Margins of Ho Chi Minh City* (Minnesota 2011).

**Ken MacLean** teaches a range of inter-disciplinary courses at Clark University. He specializes in topics at the intersection of history, anthropology, politics, and geography, and regularly publishes on Burma in addition to Vietnam.

**Nguyen Vu Hoang** is a member of the staff of the Vietnam Museum of Ethnology in Hanoi. He studied social and cultural anthropology at the Vrije Universiteit, Amsterdam and is a doctoral student at the University of Toronto. He has written extensively on urbanization and environment in Vietnam.

**Oscar Salemink** teaches Anthropology at the University of Copenhagen. From 1996 through 2001 he was the Ford Foundation program officer responsible for grant portfolios in higher education, arts and culture, and sustainable development in Vietnam and Thailand. His recent book-length publications include *Colonial Subjects* (Michigan 1999), *Vietnam's Cultural Diversity* (UNESCO 2001), *The Ethnography of Vietnam's Central Highlanders* (Hawaii 2003), *The Development of Religion, the Religion of Development* (Eburon 2005), and *A World of Insecurity: Anthropological Perspectives on Human Security* (Pluto 2010).

**Mark Sidel** is Doyle-Bascom Professor of Law and Public Affairs at the University of Wisconsin-Madison. He has worked in and written extensively about law, non-governmental organizations, and philanthropy in Vietnam, China, India, and the United States. His books include *Law and Society in Vietnam* (Cambridge 2008), and *Regulation of the Voluntary Sector: Freedom and Security in an Era of Uncertainty* (Routledge 2009). Earlier, Sidel served with the Ford Foundation in Beijing, Bangkok, Hanoi, and New Delhi.

**Thomas Sikor** is Reader in International Development at the University of East Anglia. His research examines changes in resource institutions and governance in Vietnam and other postsocialist countries, and has written on property, land reform, resource governance, and rural transformations. His recent books include *The Politics of Possession: Property, Authority, and Access to Natural Resources* (Wiley-Blackwell 2010, with Lund), and *Forests and People: Property, Governance, and Human Rights* (Routledge 2011, with Stahl).

**Hue-Tam Ho Tai** teaches Vietnamese history at Harvard University. Her areas of interest include social and cultural history. She is the author *of Millenarianism and Peasant Politics in Vietnam* (Harvard 1983), *Radicalism and the Origins of the Vietnamese Revolution* (Harvard 1992), and *Passion, Betrayal and Revolution in Colonial Saigon* (California 2010). She also edited *The Country of Memory: Remaking the Past in Late Socialist Vietnam* (California 2001).

**C. Michele Thompson** teaches Southeast Asian history at Southern Connecticut State University. Her research focuses on history of science and medicine in Vietnam specifically and in East and Southeast Asia more generally, and in the languages and writing systems used to transmit medical and scientific knowledge.

**To Xuan Phuc** is the Southeast Asia Analyst for the Forest Trends Trade and Finance Program, based in Hanoi, Vietnam. His work examines the politics of forest management in Vietnam, with particular attention to the dynamics of access to and control over forestland and resources. His research includes three in-depth studies of Dao villages in Vietnam's northern mountains.

**Nhung Tuyet Tran** teaches Southeast Asian and Vietnamese history at the University of Toronto. Her intellectual interests lie at the intersection of gender, law, and religion in early modern Vietnam. She is currently working on a cultural history of Vietnamese Catholicism. She co-edited *Vietnam: Borderless Histories* (Wisconsin 2006, with Reid), and is the author of *Vietnamese Women at the Crossroads of Southeast Asia: Gender, State and Society in 17th and 18th Century Viet Nam* (Hawaii forthcoming).

# Acknowledgements

We are grateful to all of the participants at the workshop on property and property rights in Vietnam, who convened at Harvard University in May 2009; John Whitmore for participating in the workshop and providing helpful comments; Nguyen Quoc Vinh, for his much-appreciated work on the glossary and bibliography; Stephanie Rogers, Leanne Hinves, Hannah Mack, and other colleagues at Routledge, for their enthusiastic and careful work with us on this volume; and Mark Selden, the Asia's Transformations series editor at Routledge, for his encouragement and cogent comments on this volume as it developed.

# Property and values

## State, society and market in Vietnam

*Hue-Tam Ho Tai and Mark Sidel*[1]

What constitutes property? Who may have rights to property? Are these rights absolute or partial? Are they individual, shared, or communal? How do existing social and cultural patterns, some of which pre-date the socialist period, affect property and property rights in an era where the abstract, impersonal forces of the market are privileged over many other kinds of arrangements? How does globalization affect property rights and access to resources? What is the role of the state in regulating rights to, and adjudicating disputes over, property? How do people themselves – in addition to, or separate from, the state – work out their property disputes? How are disputes over property resolved in often very different urban and rural environments?

Questions such as these form the core of lively debates that have unfolded in Vietnam since the economic reforms of 1986. Known as *Doi Moi* (changing to the new), these have gradually transformed the country from a socialist state to a society over which a communist party continues to preside but in which it plays a lesser role as markets, capital, and private property assume greater salience. Conducted both in the mass media and academic venues, the debates encompass the meaning and value of property; legal rights to property and other kinds of rights such as housing or access to resources; the appropriate balance between new infrastructures and the protection of livelihoods and lifeways; and the relationship between society, the market, and the state.

While central to the direction of economic and social development in Vietnam, such debates are by no means confined to Vietnam. Concerns over the kind of issues debated in Vietnam can be found well beyond its borders. Vietnam, however, presents an excellent site for exploring the relationship between property, the state, society, and the market. It is a developing country in more ways than one. While the country's infrastructure of roads, bridges, and buildings is being expanded and upgraded at a frenetic pace, so is its legal and administrative infrastructure. Administrative units, too, are constantly changing, partly as a result of urbanization. In this context, property is continuously in the making rather than fixed, and the relationship between property and authority is changing rapidly as well.

Property is among the most important spheres within which a host of conflicts are played out: the values of the market and social values; legal rights and community norms; protecting livelihoods while also ensuring local and national prosperity through infrastructure development; the relationship between social and cultural traditions and the marketization of property rights; and the relationships between equity and fairness, poverty, and market incentives. The debates are thus about the role of the state and its relationship to various levels of society, about the intrusion of global forces into the lives of marginalized communities and individuals, and about the ways in which community norms and standards shape and reshape national policy and laws.

As Thomas Sikor argues, "property is about relationships among social actors with regard to the use of and control over valuable resources, such as land, material assets, labor, and symbolic values."[2] "Use" refers to the many ways in which social actors derive material and immaterial benefits from resources. "Control" is about how politico-legal institutions, including but not limited to the state, affect the use of resources by social actors. While the rapid pace of change has made the relationships to which Sikor refers unpredictable, it has also made them more visible than in settings where the property regime is more stable and taken for granted. As Sikor points out in the epilogue to this volume, property and authority are mutually constitutive and property disputes are intimately tied to contestations over the state. Uncertainty and unpredictability foster contestations that in turn highlight the nature and limits of both property and authority, the power of the state, the claims of society, and the role of the market. And, sometimes contrary to a standard notion of state versus market (property), he argues that states encourage definitions/laws of property as a means of strengthening its controls.

Although the issues addressed in the following essays have acquired new urgency since *Doi Moi*, they are by no means new. In this introductory chapter, we provide a brief historical overview of various regimes of property that have obtained in Vietnam as well as the changing relationship between market, state, society, and global forces.

While much of the literature on property rights has focused on real estate and land disputes, the definition of property is broader, and so is the concept of property rights. Traditionally, property in Vietnam encompassed not only land, but also labor, knowledge, and skills. During the early dynasties of independent Vietnam (then known as Dai Viet), especially the Ly (1010–1225) and Tran (1225–1400), property was largely royal, aristocratic, monastic, or communal in nature. Rulers allocated prebendary estates in lieu of salaries to their officials. Recipients drew their income from the fruits of the labor (usufruct) of the peasants farming those lands during their tenure in office, at the end of which the estates reverted to the throne. Prebendary estates were also awarded to those who had rendered extraordinary service to the state and were thus considered to be meritorious subjects (*cong than*). Thus, we learn that Ly Thuong Kiet (1019–1105) was rewarded with prebendary land that included ten thousand individuals (*khau*) as reward for successfully repelling the Song invasion of 1075. The social status of these individuals is not made clear in the records; they could have been free peasants, bondsmen or slaves, the three main categories of persons found in Vietnam at the time besides aristocrats and Buddhist monks. Free peasants lived in villages on lands belonging to members of the aristocracy or to the court or on prebendary lands held during their lifetime by officials and meritorious subjects. Bondsmen were individuals who had fallen into debt and worked to pay off what they owed; their status was thus just above that of slaves, who were captured prisoners of war or criminals or their offspring.

In Ly and Tran Vietnam, much land in the Red River Delta belonged to Buddhist monasteries as a result of lavish donations by emperors, aristocrats, and commoners. Ly emperors, in particular, ordered the building of pagodas to serve as symbols of the reach of the state, as centers of communal life, and as resting places for weary travelers. According to the Van Phuc stele in Tien Son district (present-day Bac Ninh), in 1057 "the emperor ordered the building of more than one hundred pagodas in this area and donated more than one hundred plots of land [to them]."[3] The 1209 stele of Bao An pagoda in Me Linh district, Hanoi, records that a man named Nguyen donated land to the pagoda, "totaling 126 *mau*, to provide for the monks, three *mau* for the pagoda warden, and the rest to provide for the people, for maintaining the temple, for holding feasts and festivals and for wandering ghosts."[4] Not only were monastic properties exempted from taxation, but so were the slaves and tenants who cultivated the lands attached to the monasteries. Additionally, they were able to avoid performing compulsory labor (*corvée*) and military service. Many free peasants who sought to avoid discharging these obligations, especially in times of economic crisis or war, were driven to become tenants on monastic lands; this strategy increased the economic pressure on the remaining free peasants, reduced the revenues available to the state and created growing friction between the court and the monastic communities. In 1192, the scholar Dam Di Mong claimed that fully half of able-bodied males in the realm had disappeared from the tax rolls by taking refuge on monastic lands.[5] No doubt, his statement contained a degree of hyperbole. Nonetheless, it reflected not only the increasing wealth of the *sangha* (Buddhist monkhood) during this period and the constraints on the resources of the state but also the fact that, for the majority of ordinary peasants, whether free, bondsmen, or slaves, their major asset was labor, not land. That labor was heavily mobilized for production, construction or warfare by monks, officials, lords or rulers; peasants thus did not have full control over their own labor and bodies.

Under the Tran dynasty, new land was claimed out of the lower Red River Delta. Much of this new land seems to have been transformed into princely estates as the royal clan sought to keep as many of the resources of the realm under its control as possible. Despite the ravages of the repeated Mongol invasions in the second half of the thirteenth century, the economy became more commercialized and the state was able to tax a wider array of goods. During the last few decades of the fourteenth century, Ho Quy Ly (1336–1407), a royal kinsman with dynastic ambitions, sought to curb the power of the royal clan by limiting the size of the princely estates and the number of slaves in the possession of individual owners.

His usurpation of the throne in 1400, however, eventually brought the Ming into Vietnam for a twenty-year long occupation (1407–27).

A major transformation of the regime of property rights took place immediately after the overthrow of the Ming occupation forces. The legal code of the new Le dynasty (1428–1788) codified the growing privatization of land. Potentially, the law gave equal rights of inheritance to men and women as inheritance was based on the will of the deceased property owner and was thus, from a strictly legal point of view, gender neutral.[6] Extant historical documents do not permit us to ascertain whether the law reflected practices on the ground and whether gender equality actually obtained in the disposition of property. Under the Confucianizing emperor Le Thanh Tong (reigned 1460–97), new laws reflecting a more patriarchal outlook were inserted in what became known as the Le Code. Promulgated in the early decades of the Le dynasty, it remained the official legal code of Vietnam until 1788, although much modified and supplemented by other legal documents. The Nguyen legal code which came into effect in 1812 was almost a verbatim copy of the Qing code; it further reduced the rights of women, including the rights to possess and to dispose of property.

In 1839, Emperor Minh Mang (reigned 1820–40) attempted to reverse the privatization of communal land by village elites in Binh Dinh province which had been the base for the Tay Son Uprising (1771–1802). Like the Land Reform of the 1950s in northern Vietnam, Minh Mang's policy had both economic and political goals. According to Phan Phuong Thao,

> As a whole, the equalization campaign did not improve the welfare of Binh Dinh inhabitants and contributed practically nothing to the state's finances .... [But] the outcome – which reflects the undeclared objectives of Minh Mang's policy in Binh Dinh – was a reduction of private landholdings and a restoration and augmentation of state ownership, in this case, of communal fields and lands, accomplished by expropriating half of all private lands, including those previously taken over by the peasants during the Tay Son Uprising.[7]

The scope of this program and the return of private land to communal status caused many middle peasants to lose their land while poor peasants received none. Since village elites sat on village councils, they were in a position to dictate to whom communal land would be allocated – usually their own kin.

With the French conquest that began in 1858 in southern Vietnam and was completed by 1883 with the Harmand Treaty, Vietnam was divided into three separate regions: in the south French Cochinchina, a colony, and further north two protectorates, Tonkin and Annam. The greatest impact of conquest was on the south, where, in 1854, the Court had launched an ambitious program of land reclamation and resettlement. This program had been intended to deal with the ravages of the cholera epidemic of 1849 that had left 600,000 dead. It consisted largely of setting up agricultural plantations under military (and thus state) control in areas that had been abandoned or were previously uncultivated. Peasants recruited to work on these state-sponsored plantations were individuals made landless by calamity and criminals and rebels banished to the south from other parts of the country. The settlements were intended to form the nuclei of new civilian villages; the peasants employed on them would gain title to the land they had cleared and become smallholders. French conquest disrupted this program of land reclamation and transfer of ownership. The colonial authorities laid claim to crown property in the south, including all military-agricultural settlements. Estates that had belonged to "rebels," namely those who had opposed conquest, were also seized. The military-agricultural settlements and the seized "rebel" estates formed the basis of unprecedentedly large tracts that were put to auction and turned into private plantations where Vietnamese and Khmer peasants tilled the soil either as tenants (*ta dien*) or wage laborers for French landlords and local elites who collaborated with them.

The issue of property rights continued to be a vexed question all through the colonial period in the south, as land continued to be reclaimed from the salty marshes of the area, especially in the area known as Transbassac (Hau Giang). The traditional practice by Vietnamese and Khmer peasants of requesting title to the land only after it had been brought into cultivation and thus proven to be a reliable source of livelihood made them vulnerable to expropriation by corrupt officials and land speculators who colluded to withhold titles from them. Such was the background to the Ninh Thanh Loi incident of 1927 described in David Biggs' essay in this volume. In Tonkin and Annam, where land registers were better kept, the temptation to speculate on land was checked by the large number of small owners who would need to be dispossessed in order to cobble together large estates.

Although the colonial state officially eliminated *corvée* and raised taxes in order to pay workers, it continued to rely on conscripted labor for its many large-scale construction projects until the very end of its rule. As the many instances of unrest among plantation workers and others employed on construction projects show, the loss of their own labor was a form of expropriation that could plunge their families into dire poverty while the workers themselves toiled in appalling conditions for starvation wages. As both the chapters by David Biggs and Ken MacLean show, labor continued to be one of the most important forms of property for many peasants.

In both the socialist North and the (relatively) free-market South following independence from French rule in 1954, labor figured prominently as a form of peasant property, to be appropriated, mobilized, compensated – or not. In the North, the state sought to prevent further devastating famines, promote social and economic equality, and provide for peasant livelihood and protection from floods by instituting a program of land redistribution and launching massive projects of dike repairs and dam building. As Ken MacLean shows, these goals overlapped and were sometimes at odds with one another; the mobilization of their labor for the construction projects had the effect of reducing peasants' ability to work on the plots they still possessed after land redistribution, leading many to fall prey to usury and to lose their land. Consequently, state appropriation of one form of property – namely labor – led to the loss of another form of property, namely land.

In post-independence South Vietnam, attempts to address the problems of rural poverty while expanding the economy took different forms. As David Biggs shows, some of these efforts were a continuation of colonial policy; in many ways, they also echoed the Nguyen court's program of military-agricultural settlements. His essay traces the genealogy of debates that occurred in both the colonial press and scientific community about how to conceptualize the causes of, and formulate solutions to, rural poverty. The common perception throughout most of the twentieth century was that, unlike in the long-settled Red River Delta and mountainous center, there was much land still available in the South, though it needed to be reclaimed through large projects of canal digging and draining of salt marshes. During the colonial era, much of the labor needed for these projects came from both local landless peasants and immigrants from the overpopulated North. Both the colonial and postcolonial state in the South sought to avoid alienating landowners by turning landless peasants into either pioneers opening up new settlements or a rural proletariat – albeit one that would enjoy better working conditions and wages than the miserable coolies working on private plantations.

Land reclamation, however, could not adequately address either economic or political issues confronting both peasants and the state in South Vietnam. After the first Indochina War ended in 1954, the Republic of Vietnam was faced with not only resettling one million refugees from North Vietnam but also with countering the popularity of the Viet Minh assertion that labor, rather than capital, was the basis of property claims. While it upheld the claims of landowners (many of whom had fled to cities and had not collected rents during the war years) on legal grounds, it also undertook several attempts at redistributing land. The last and most successful redistribution program, "Land to the Tiller," was launched in 1970. Like previous programs (1956 and 1960), it involved paying landlords at state-established rates and selling it to peasants who were already tilling the land. This program is credited with boosting rice production and reducing the appeal of the National Liberation Front,[8] but was implemented too late to halt Communist advances. The fall of the Republic of Vietnam in 1975 once again altered property rights in the South.

Much has been said and written about Vietnamese peasants' attachment to their village and reluctance to leave behind their ancestral tombs. Yet, throughout the twentieth century (and even during the nineteenth century), various schemes to reduce poverty, increase security, and redress perceived social inequality have frequently involved confiscation, displacement, and resettlement. While the exodus following the Geneva Accords in 1954, in which one million Vietnamese moved from the socialist North to the (relatively) free-market South, is the best known case of mass resettlement in Vietnam, the famine of 1945 caused the Tran Trong Kim government (9 March 1945 to 2 September 1945) to plan for sending one million people southward. (This plan was eventually abandoned because of an outbreak of cholera along the way.)[9] Beginning in the 1960s, migration to the uplands was encouraged by the state to relieve population pressure in the Red

River Delta, but this disrupted traditional patterns of property rights among ethnic minorities as well as their access to local resources. This pattern of migration was not entirely new. The founder of the Le dynasty (1428–1788) was the grandson of a man who had moved to the uplands of Thanh Hoa from the already overpopulated Red River Delta. The New Economic Zones of the late 1970s and 1980s, which were designed to bring back land into cultivation by returning to the countryside peasants who had fled to the cities, have antecedents in the polder projects of the colonial state and, before that, the military-agricultural settlements of the nineteenth century.[10] Another phenomenon was not new: the use of conscripted labor for large-scale projects that interfered with the agricultural cycle, as documented by Ken MacLean for the 1960s in northern Vietnam, was a feature of French colonial policy since the 1890s.[11] While the French introduced long-term labor contracts in order to undertake large-scale projects, wage labor remained insufficient, and conscripted labor was used until the very end of colonial rule.[12]

Divergent perceptions and dreams are an important dimension of debates about the meaning of property and of rights. Where individuals may see shelter, access to livelihood, ties to the past, and means of preserving their lifeways and traditions, planners and other outsiders may see roads to modernity with high-rise buildings replacing modest huts, sources of raw materials for a global market, or electricity for downstream urban centers, wildlife refuges, or dams. Erik Harms points out in his chapter that in many cases, tensions are not necessarily about loss of property *per se* or about urbanization and modernity. The issue often boils down to retaining access to resources such as market, field, or job opportunities, and to defining social justice and the meaning of fair compensation. As Harms suggests, discussions about the market value of property become discussions of social values.

For members of minority communities, the issues surrounding property and property rights are even more vexatious. Not only are notions of property more complex than in the lowlands inhabited by the majority *kinh* (ethnic Vietnamese) population, but rights to the products of the land, whether it be wet rice fields, swidden plots or forestland, are likely to be temporary and shifting as well as held collectively with other members of the community. In this context, minority communities are easily displaced by states whose modernist visions do not accommodate property rights that are distinct from those of outright ownership, possession, or rental, and where boundary lines between different properties are defined by tradition and convention rather than legal documents. As in the case of Java, as described by Nancy Peluso in *Rich Forests, Poor People*,[13] ethnic minority people in Vietnam can be stripped of their traditional access to forestland and thus their livelihood by timber companies to whom local authorities have ceded rights of exploitation to land "without owners." This land can also be turned into preservation land for wildlife or for dams that will generate electricity for the people living downstream in the lowlands and the cities. As To Xuan Phuc's essay documents, in the process, local minority people are stripped not only of their livelihood but also of their traditional way of life, turned reluctantly into modern but propertyless subjects.

It is not only the state or timber companies that deprive upland minorities of their rights to both property and livelihood. In the name of wildlife preservation, scientists operating at both the national and international levels can act together to deprive them of their traditional access to forest resources, as Michele Thompson points out in her essay on the *saola*, the "Asian unicorn." While local minority people provide information about the *saola* with whom they have shared their habitat for centuries, their connection to the *saola* is elided in most discussions of this old, but only recently "discovered" animal. By classifying it and giving it a scientific name, scientists operating on a global stage have made the *saola* "their" property. In the name of protecting this "newly discovered" endangered species, officials have expanded the scope of the Vu Quang Nature Park and prohibited not only hunting, but also the gathering of food and medicinal materials upon which local people depend for their survival. Thus, local people have been expelled from their usual hunting grounds, marginalized in international scientific discourse, and stripped of both livelihood and traditional way of life.

The sundering of property from its social and historical context is by no means unique to rare species. It extends as well to intangible property such as cultural performances, as Oscar Salemink makes clear in his discussion of the process whereby the gong culture of minority peoples living in the Central Highlands of Vietnam became listed as an "intangible cultural heritage" by UNESCO. As this musical genre moved through the process of UNESCO adoption, like the *saola*, it became the property of officials operating at levels increasingly removed from the local context in which gong culture was traditionally enmeshed: provincial, national, international. Rather than an artistic and religious performance that was an integral part of the life of the community, it became a commodity used to market Vietnam's ethnic diversity in the globalized marketplace for tourism, albeit one that did not carry a price tag.

Although it is only in the last decade or so that Vietnam signed an international copyright agreement, the concept of intellectual property was not totally alien to premodern Vietnamese, not all of whom made a living from tilling the soil. In some villages, peasants specialized in a single craft. The skills that went into making specific products were not bought or sold and were considered to be communal property, to be jealously guarded against potential competitors. But, as shown in the essay by Nhung Tuyet Tran on the musical genre *ca tru* – newly recognized by UNESCO as a form of intangible cultural heritage – exclusive rights to artistic performances could be bought and sold in the late eighteenth century. As often as not, since the performers were usually women, access to their bodies accompanied the purchase of their performing talents. This case of transfer of communal performance to private entertainment seems to have entailed other rights of citizenship within the village community as well.

Land, labor, houses, bodies, names . . . The essays make clear that debates about property highlight different perspectives on the same objects, and ascribe different meanings and values to these objects. The actors move in different circles, operate in different contexts, and bring to discussions and negotiations their own terms of reference, target audiences, goals, and experiences.

While it is easy to frame disputes over property rights in terms of a state willing to countenance the expropriation of hapless peasants and hunters in the name of progress and profit, the situation on the ground is more complex. Peasants are not entirely helpless against the state or multinational juggernauts. They can delay, or occasionally even halt or force the modification of, large-scale projects, sometimes seeking better compensation. Some, though by no means all, in fact subscribe to the same modernist vision as urban planners. What they want is fairness and access to resources in order to maintain their livelihood. Others, however, are fighting an uphill battle to maintain their claims to their traditions and preserve their lifeways.

Many conflicts do not reach the courts. In his 1965 study entitled *Village in Vietnam*, Gerald Hickey, noted the role of village councils in South Vietnam in resolving disputes ranging from marital problems to conflicts over land and irrigation. In disposing of the cases brought to the council, the presiding elder sought to balance community norms and compassion with legal rights.[14] Despite the growth of the judicial sector, most disputes continued to be resolved locally by administrators rather than independent judges. In the Socialist North, the notion of an independent judiciary did not exist. Even today, when Vietnamese talk of lodging a complaint (*kien*), they do not necessarily mean bringing a legal suit; instead, they may mean writing petitions to the authorities seeking redress for a variety of wrongs.[15] Besides appealing to the authorities and, increasingly, making use of the media as both Erik Harms and Nguyen Vu Hoang describe in their chapters, more and more cases involving property rights do come in front of the courts. Negotiations and litigation over property reveal that while individuals and whole communities may be at a disadvantage in dealing with outside forces and be stripped of their property – be it tangible or intangible – by provincial, national, and even international bodies, community pressure and norms often act to shape the eventual disposition of cases in a way that undermines legal predictability.

As John Gillespie and Mark Sidel show, intervention by the state and community norms rather than strict interpretation of the law continue to play an important role in determining the outcome of specific cases even when they do reach the courts. Their chapters discuss two very different kinds of land and property cases. Gillespie finds extensive use of "customary informality," "community norms and practices," and "reason and sentiment in applying the law" (*ly va tinh trong viec chap hanh phap luat*) by local courts in Hanoi in resolving land cases there. As Gillespie suggests, many cases that do come before the courts involve competing rights under a socialist system: rights to property and rights to housing, the urban resident's equivalent of the uplander's access to forest resources.

Although the Vietnamese Constitution and the post-*Doi Moi* policy of building a "law-governed state" require that such cases be decided based on law, Gillespie finds that

> judges quickly exhaust the possibilities of statutory land rights and legal doctrines, and either push cases back to state officials or use "reason and sentiment in applying the law" . . . , a type of situational justice, to resolve cases . . . . [C]ourts continue to rely more on administrative and self-regulatory

norms and practices, than statutory property rights, to resolve housing and land disputes.

Yet even when the judiciary is gradually taking on a greater role in deciding some "ordinary" property and land disputes, it remains subordinated to Party and state decision-making where major, sensitive and politically controversial property and land cases are involved. The courts remain hamstrung in these cases, as Mark Sidel shows in his detailed description of a major recent case of land corruption, by Party and government control, low capacity, narrow definitions of jurisdiction, authority, competence, and corruption. The more politically sensitive the case, it appears, the more it falls to the Party and state to resolve, and the judiciary returns to its almost completely instrumentalized role, while the political authorities instruct the courts on how to resolve such disputes. In these very different kinds of land and property cases – involving ordinary citizens in Gillespie's essay, and land transfers to benefit high-ranking officials in Sidel's chapter – the Party and state continue to play a significant role.

Cases such as the ones studied by Gillespie, Sidel, Nguyen Vu Hoang, and other authors illustrate a theme that runs through many of the essays in this volume: the concept of fuzziness. This is most salient in Ken MacLean's discussion of the transition *into* socialism as opposed to *out of* it as Katherine Verdery applies the latter concept. Fuzziness allowed peasants in Ninh Thanh Loi to be expropriated in 1927. It also characterizes the land tenure system in the upland forests studied by To Xuan Phuc. It could be applied to the legal system in which property rights and housing rights are often pitted against each other; or corruption, Party and state interference, and community pressures that make for unpredictable outcomes in court cases. As Nguyen Vu Hoang's essay shows, fuzziness also characterizes state/society relations. While the presence of the Communist state may seem overwhelming even after the transition to a market economy and the partial withdrawal of the state, its very pervasiveness means that there are many individuals who straddle the fuzzy line between state and society. This makes them effective representatives of the interests of the ordinary Vietnamese among whom they live. Their very embeddedness in the networks of the state bureaucracy enables them to know which doors to knock on, which documents to look for, and, equally importantly, what language to use in order to present their neighbors' case most effectively. This fuzziness also makes a prominent appearance in John Gillespie's chapter, where he discusses the "customary informality" and the "community norms and practices" in which property and land are negotiated in Vietnam and the use of these values by the judiciary in resolving less politically sensitive land and property cases.

Disputes and debates similar to those explored in this volume preoccupy many other societies as well, both those undergoing transition from state management to market regulation (such as China) or within market economies. They find expression in cases pitting eminent domain in the cause of municipal, state, or national projects against the rights of individual property-owners; where lands which were previously open to all suddenly become enclosed; or where community values are invoked in legal decisions or clash with the letter of the law. While the cases examined in this volume are rooted in the specifics of Vietnamese history – imperial, colonial, postcolonial, socialist, postsocialist – they raise issues that transcend national borders and offer a lens through which to explore the importance of property and the changing nature of what constitutes property and how individuals and the state seek to control and use it.

## Notes

1 This volume is the outcome of a workshop on "Property and Property Rights in Vietnam" held in May 2009 at Harvard University with funding from the University's Asia Center. The authors thank Mark Selden for his cogent comments on several drafts of this introduction and the contributors to this volume for their insightful comments on earlier drafts as well.

2 Franz von Benda-Beckmann *et al.* (eds), *Changing Properties of Property*. Oxford: Berghahn, 2006; Thomas Sikor, "Land allocations in Vietnam's uplands: negotiating property and authority," in *Upland Transformations: Opening Boundaries in Vietnam*, T. Sikor, Nghiem P. T., J. Sowerwine, J. Romm (eds), (Singapore: National University of Singapore Press, 2011).

3 Quoted in Nguyen Tai Thu, ed., *Lich Su Phat Giao Viet Nam*, Hanoi: NXB Khoa Hoc Xa Hoi, 1988, 149.

4 *Tho Van Ly-Tran*, v. 1, Hanoi, 1977, p. 545, quoted in Nguyen Tai Thu (ed.), *Lich Su Phat Giao Viet Nam*, p. 149.

5 *Viet Su Luoc*, q. 3, tr.13a-b; quoted in Nguyen Tai Thu (ed.), *Lich Su Phat Giao Viet Nam*, 214.

6 John K. Whitmore, "Property and the State in Fifteenth Century Dai Viet: Public and Private Land," unpublished paper presented at the Harvard property workshop, May 2009.

7 Phan Phuong Thao, *Land Equalization in 1839 in Binh Dinh Seen from the Land Records* (Hanoi: The Gioi Publishers, 2009), p. 159.

8 The most thorough account is by Charles Stuart Callison, *The Land-to-the-Tiller Program and Rural Resource Mobilization in the Mekong Delta of South Vietnam* (Athens, Ohio: Ohio University Center for International Studies, 1974).

9 *Binh Minh*, 17 July 1945 and 2 August 1945.

10 The first recorded use of such settlements, known as *don dien* is associated with the building of the wall at Dong Hoi in 1630; in turn, these settlements were inspired by Tang-era settlements.

11 See for example, Hue-Tam Ho Tai, *Millenarianism and Peasant Politics in Vietnam* (Harvard University Press, 1983), p. 70.

12 In two reports, of 1927 and 1936, the ILO deplored the continued use of *corvée*, which was supposed to have been replaced by higher taxes designed to pay for wage labor.

13 Nancy Peluso, *Rich Forests, Poor People: Resource Control and Resistance in Java* (University of California Press, 1992).

14 Gerald Cannon Hickey, *Village in Vietnam* (Yale University Press, 1965), pp. 195–205.

15 See for example, Le Hong Ly and Hue-Tam Ho Tai, "The Revenge of the Object: Villagers and Ethnographers in Dong Ky Village," *Asian Ethnology*, 67:2 (November 2008), pp. 323–43.

# Part I

# Land, labor and the state

# 1 Property and poverty in southern Vietnam

## Colonial and postcolonial perspectives

*David Biggs*

From the first anti-colonial movements in the 1860s through the Indochina Wars to the present, land rights, landlessness, and poverty have figured centrally in Vietnamese politics. Despite wars, the 1945 revolution, and several instances of sweeping land reform, the present-day contests over land rights retain a distinct historical character. Much has been written by Vietnamese and foreign authors about the economic and political dimensions of rural poverty in southern Vietnam; however, these analyses tend to be situated within the temporal bounds of colonial (1860–1954), postcolonial (1954–), postwar (1975–) or post-*Doi Moi* (1986–) frameworks.[1] Little of this research has considered a broader issue: the ways in which older framings of rural problems have shaped more contemporary views. This essay examines the particular circumstances in which certain discussions of the landless, commonly referred to as *ta dien* (tenant farmers), and what colonial authors called the *malaise agricole* (agricultural slump), were framed for the reading public and decision-makers.

Discussions about tenant farmers and property reform appeared within two different public spheres, one associated with newspapers read by a large cross-section of Vietnamese and colonial society and the other a more restricted, academic sphere shaped by the contributions of a small group of French and Vietnamese social scientists who began studying rural poverty in the late 1920s and into the 1930s.

The media outlets for early writing about rural problems in the south, especially newspapers in the 1920s, played an important role in codifying language about southern poverty and property conflicts. Their depictions were deeply inscribed by differing political and financial concerns; and some views appeared routinely in mainstream media while others were relegated to underground, radical, and overseas venues. As Philippe Peycam, Peter Zinoman, Shawn McHale and others have argued, the newspapers that circulated on the streets of Hanoi and Saigon in the 1930s supported multiple articulations of modern Vietnamese political consciousness.[2] Saigon newspapers played an important role in documenting conditions in the southern countryside and bringing them to national attention. With the fall of the Popular Front in 1938 and the arrival of the Vichy government in 1940, more radical Vietnamese writers in the south went underground; nevertheless, they continued to expound on the "rural malaise" in such works as Phi Van's documentary novel *The Countryside* (*Dong Que*), published in 1942.[3]

Although it, too, played a crucial role in shaping the ways in which state officials understood the causes of rural poverty and sought means to combat it, colonial social science as a field of study has received little scholarly attention. In the mid-1920s, a growing cohort of French and Vietnamese social scientists began paying close attention to the causes of land degradation and the worsening economic situation of tenant farmers. With the worsening state of agriculture in Vietnam after 1930, scholars such as the French geographer Pierre Gourou played a prominent role in shaping the conceptual frameworks for thinking about possible solutions to the problems of landlessness and rural poverty.[4] Gourou, Yves Henry[5] and Nguyen Van Huyen[6] mobilized such tools of statecraft as demographic and economic data, aerial photography, and thick ethnographic description to present a more formalized image of tenant farmers and more systematic views of Vietnamese rural landscapes. Casual discussions with Vietnamese social scientists today reveal that many still look to these works as models for contemporary research and policy.

## Reporting rural poverty and property conflicts

With some notable exceptions, news about extreme rural poverty in Cochinchina did not reach audiences in Vietnamese cities until the mid-1920s. This was largely the result of intense government censorship of native writers and Vietnamese-language newspapers, but it was also due to evolving political arrangements among Vietnam's educated and urban-based elites. One exception in 1907 was Gilbert Tran Chanh Chieu. A retired colonial civil servant and wealthy landowner from Rach Gia, Tran Chanh Chieu took on the editorship of *Nong Co Min Dam* (*Agricultural Forum*), a popular Vietnamese-language newspaper founded in 1901 that addressed agricultural issues from a planter's perspective. As the newspaper's editor in 1907 and 1908, Tran Chanh Chieu took a more critical view of the colonial government's policies in rural areas. One essay, for example, highlighted conflicts occurring on the new network of canals being dredged to open vast areas of farmland to huge industrial estates. "An Interesting Battle" (Une bataille intéressante) criticized the poor planning of canals in his native province for exacerbating floods and causing the inundation of many native-owned farms.[7] Tran Chanh Chieu's critical voice in the press, however, was silenced in 1908 when the colonial government uncovered his key role as one of Cochinchina's leading supporters of a southern variant of the Modernization movement (Duy Tan Hoi) led by the exiled scholar Phan Boi Chau and Prince Cuong De. This southern variant, called Minh Tan (New Light), followed ideas similar to Phan Boi Chau's that were in turn shaped by Meiji reforms in Japan and the Self-Strengthening movement in China.[8] The New Light campaign differed from the northern Modernization movement in that, instead of calling for the adoption of the Romanized script (largely a *fait accompli* in Cochinchina), it advocated economic independence from ethnic-Chinese firms that controlled many everyday transactions in the countryside as well as colonial tax farms (*régies*) in Cho Lon.[9]

It was during a second expansion of Vietnamese newspaper publishing from 1917 to 1928 that several prominent Saigon writers began to highlight severe disparities in landholdings and livelihood in the countryside. This burst of new publishing occurred in the aftermath of World War I when southern Vietnamese who had served the colonial government and helped raise funds to support the French war effort received support to establish new national newspapers such as *La Tribune Indigène* (*Native Tribune*) in 1917 and its Vietnamese-language counterpart *Quoc Dan Dien Dan* in 1918. Bui Quang Chieu, one of the founding editors of *La Tribune Indigène*, came from working in the colonial Services Agricoles, and Le Quang Liem, later a prominent writer for the newspaper, had previously written essays encouraging Vietnamese support for the war bonds.[10] Both were substantial landowners. As Hue-Tam Ho Tai notes, the Saigon elites who managed these moderate papers (compared with conservative, French-owned papers such as *Courrier Saigonnais*) devoted much of their energies to the question of expanding suffrage for the Vietnamese elite and the adoption of an Indochinese constitution (hence *Tribune Indigène*'s moniker as an "organ of the Constitutionalist Party") rather than building a more popular, national coalition.[11]

In the 1920s, Saigon newspapers played an increasingly prominent role in shaping public sentiments about the rural poor, although until the documentary reporting (*phong su*) of the late 1920s, most stories of corrupt land dealings tended to fit within the more urban-centered critiques of corrupt colonial officials. The most radical views of rural injustices were typically relegated to overseas Vietnamese papers such as Nguyen Ai Quoc's *Paria* to which others such as Nguyen An Ninh contributed. The younger generation of Vietnamese radicals such as Nguyen An Ninh, who wrote for *La Cloche Fêlée* (*Cracked Bell*) from 1923 to 1925, began to attract a new generation of urban Vietnamese youth to a more strident anti-colonial position. In the early 1920s, a variety of newspapers such as *Cloche Fêlée* and André Malraux's *Indochine* took special aim at one of the most corrupt of Cochinchina's governors, Maurice Cognacq, and his cronies. The first new articles about property and rural poverty concerned corrupt land seizures led by a Cognacq-backed consortium. The first of a series of articles appeared in *Indochine* on July 11, 1925 and was successful in halting the bizarre land auction of mostly cleared lands in Ca Mau that dispossessed the settlers of an estimated 26,000 hectares.[12]

A more documentary style (*phong su*) of writing on rural conditions commenced with a series of events in late 1925 and early 1926 that spurred a new wave of journalism in Saigon. Indochina's first socialist governor-general, Alexander Varenne, took office in November 1925 and proceeded into his first scandal, the trial of Phan Boi Chau who had been arrested in South China a few months earlier. Varenne's order that Chau be placed under house-arrest was followed by more protests in 1926 after the death of Phan Chu Trinh on March 24. Nguyen An Ninh was arrested on the same day (André Malraux, fearing for his and his wife's safety, had already left Saigon). A new, more radical phase of publishing commenced when Bui Quang Chieu, who had gone to France a few months earlier, returned to Saigon and was elected as vice-chairman of the Colonial Council in October 1926. He used his new role in Saigon politics to build the newspaper to appeal to pro-reform and nationalist Vietnamese readers.[13]

In May 1927, *La Tribune Indochinoise*, the successor to *Tribune Indigène*, began publishing a documentary-style account by Le Quang Liem of the events that led to a violent massacre of villagers in Ninh Thanh Loi (see Figure 1.2) by colonial troops. The governor played down the issue as a "scuffle" although two policemen, a Chinese businessman, and many villagers died in the fighting. The villagers, mostly illiterate, were not Vietnamese but Khmer. For nearly two decades, they had cleared the mangrove forest to establish the village after losing ancestral lands near Soc Trang, but had failed in their efforts to obtain titles to the land they had brought into cultivation. The conflict started when a wealthy Vietnamese official, Canton Chief Ngo, used aliases and connections to acquire over eleven thousand hectares of inhabited land in the region, swallowing up Ninh Thanh Loi. After gaining title to the land, he demanded that the villagers pay him rent. A village leader organized a protest with a local healer who prepared spells and amulets to protect them. The affair ended bloodily; villagers ended up killing an ethnic-Chinese business confidant of the canton chief. After two Vietnamese *gendarmes* died in the ensuing fighting, the colonial militia arrived and set fire to the village communal house *(dinh)* killing over thirty men, women, and children trapped inside. The surrounding village was then abandoned.

In framing this confrontation for the *Tribune Indochinoise's* audience, Liem repeatedly argued that the cause of this violent and tragic encounter was not ethnic conflict but economic injustice and rampant corruption emanating from Saigon.[14] More important was the way in which he described the farmers as tenant farmers. In fact, they had not been tenant farmers, i.e. renters on an estate, but land clearers intent on becoming smallholders.

*La Tribune Indochinoise* conflated other groups into the category of tenant farmers, too. It published a serialized account in August 1927 describing the plight of thousands of "tenants" who were northern migrant workers who had boarded vessels in the north to find work on the colonial estates ranging from rubber in Phu Rieng to rice in the Transbassac. Bui Quang Chieu, now vice-chairman of the Colonial Council, presided over a new committee formed to investigate abuses of these workers, and his newspaper attacked the colonial estates for treating these tenant farmers worse than slaves. One article stated:

> The owner of slaves had interest to spare his livestock, which represented a value; on the other hand, he who buys a Tonkinese for five years sees every year the value of his purchase decreasing by a fifth. He thus may find it beneficial to draw from this purchase in five years all that he can give.[15]

To the end of the decade, exposés in the Saigon papers continued to emphasize rampant corruption with land transfers as well as a growing class of poor people in Cochinchina generally (mis-)labeled as tenant farmers.

The Great Depression triggered more bankruptcy in Cochinchina, especially in rural areas, and it produced an economic crisis that catalyzed protests and spurred the colonial government to respond to the increasing problems of poverty and even land falling out of production. It was especially devastating for farmers in Cochinchina. The price of Saigon No. 1 polished grain fell from a peak price of $13.10 piasters per 100 kg in 1929 to just $3.20 in 1934.[16] All taxes and debts were paid in piasters, which meant rapid foreclosures and even famine for some. Aside from the problems faced by migrant workers and those duped by corrupt land auctions, many farmers who had previously owned their land now joined the landless tenant farmers. One estimate put this floating population at almost two-thirds of Cochinchina's population.[17]

While the Great Depression resulted in accelerated bankruptcies and more concentration of land into large holdings, consolidation into larger, industrialized estates had already been underway since the early 1920s. The devaluation of land after 1930 and the bankruptcy of many middle class landowners – including many French – led to shifts in the demographics of land ownership not only toward powerful French firms such as Gressier & Co. but also from French-born to native-born owners with French citizenship.[18] This seemingly minor shift in estate ownership often had severe implications at the household level for tenants. In the Can Tho area, for example, elderly farmers who were in their teens at the time repeatedly told me about the problems that followed transfer of land from bankrupted Europeans to Vietnamese, Chinese, and Khmer landlords. Native-born landlords, they said, tended not to forgive tenant debts at the New Year and they denied tenants any rights to gather fish or glean unharvested rice.[19] By 1930, some landlords such as Henry de la Chevrotière, a *métis* who inherited a large estate and led a very conservative political faction of landowners in Saigon, hired guards to protect the canals and fields and prevent hungry tenant farmers from "stealing" grain or "illegally" fishing.[20]

* * * *

The thirties have been seen largely as the decade of mass politics in Vietnam. But the emergence of mass political organizations and the expansion of the public sphere do not by themselves explain the more radical form that rural unrest took in that decade. Rather, a brief look at environmental and demographic changes in the late 1920s to early 1930s suggests that they coincided with economic and environmental collapses to create a perfect storm.

The majority of landless, rural poor lived in newly reclaimed floodplains rather than the rich alluvial strips (*miet vuon*) that had been inhabited by Khmers for centuries, followed by Chinese and Vietnamese. The colonial system of land rules that favored French citizens was aimed largely at claiming newly opened lands, and it produced often extreme conditions for tenants who settled in such reclaimed areas as the Plain of Reeds (Dong Thap) or the Transbassac (Hau Giang) (see Figure 1.1). Older, historic villages in the delta's *miet vuon* regions were largely insulated from environmental and economic catastrophes as farmers had greater

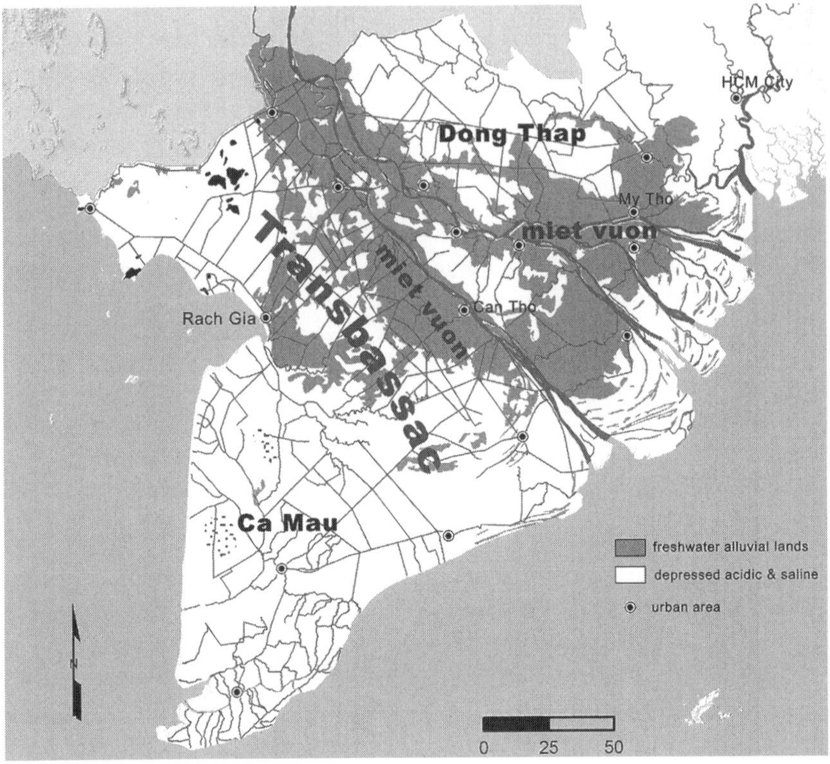


*Figure 1.1* Location of alluvial terraces and depressed floodplains in the Mekong Delta.

Source: Author.

access to historic merchant networks and education while those living in the floodplains lived more nomadic, frontier-style lives. Conceived as legal "empty zones," the Transbassac, Ca Mau Peninsula, and the Plain of Reeds were home to the largest colonial estates owned by French nationals or privately held French companies.

The Indochinese Communist Party's involvement in the 1930–31 Nghe-Tinh Uprising in Annam was timely. It not only established the ICP's credentials as a capable nationalist organization, but it also cemented the reputation of the ICP among many of the rural poor. Given the fluidity and uncertainty of property relations in the Transbassac, it should not be surprising that southern ICP members, typically well-educated youth from Saigon or delta towns, moved first to the Ca Mau Peninsula to establish secret cells in 1931 and 1932. Emerging ICP leaders such as Vo Van Kiet (later Prime Minister of the Socialist Republic of Vietnam) traveled to Bac Lieu and ethnic Vietnamese villages near Ninh Thanh Loi to create what Bernal (1981, 157) describes as "radical 'nodes' or key villages from which the movement spread out." The ICP organized a series of tax protests in key village markets of the region and even granary raids in 1938 after a flood wiped out much of the rice crop.[21]

Trotskyists, who competed with Communists in the South for leadership of the revolutionary movement, did not pay much heed to the plight of the tenant farmers. More committed than the Communists to the idea of a proletarian revolution, they preferred instead to document the lives of workers in cities and towns. Their newspaper, *La Lutte*, featured numerous articles about conditions in the countryside but focused most of its attention on the struggles of village teachers (often members of the Trotskyist underground) and workers involved in industrial occupations such as laborers working for the dredging enterprise. A regular series in the newspaper, "The Life of Workers," featured news snippets from the rural provinces of protests and strikes. In April and May 1938, the series featured accounts of a strike led by over 200 laborers employed in canal-dredging and drainage work by the Société des Dragages in My Tho Province. The strikes involved the enterprise's refusal to raise wages and lasted for fifty-five days before the local director left the colony and returned to France.[22]

In the wake of the Great Depression and amid escalating fear of general insurrections, the colonial government began searching for quick fixes to the problem of dispossessed peasants by relocating them into the relatively barren floodplain of the Long Xuyen Quadrangle (see Figure 1.2). Their motives for removing entire populations to the Quadrangle appear to have stemmed from interconnected political and economic concerns. It was simpler to move dispossessed farmers to new territory than to seize lands from powerful landlords with many allies in Saigon. Ethnic Khmer tenants from Ca Mau thus became the colony's first targeted population for a resettlement scheme. The Office of Colonization that had previously sponsored transport of Tonkinese laborers to colonial estates now coordinated the sale of five-hectare plots of unclaimed land to each applicant family; and it located these plots along three newly completed canals in the western floodplain: Rach Gia–Ha Tien Canal, Tri Ton Canal, and Ba The Canals (see Figure 1.2). The new settlers, eager to gain legal title, quickly set up their houses and fields along the canals. Each household was required to put the land into production and pay taxes with rice (not piasters); there was a flood of applications that included many southern Vietnamese, Tonkinese migrants, and Khmers. By 1932, the provincial chief in Rach Gia worried that he could not control the "type of person" who staked a claim, and others worried that refugees would not possess a suitable "love of the land."[23] Settlement was uneven, and rapid deforestation coincided with intentionally set fires that spread over huge areas of cajeput (tea tree) forest and exposed highly acidic soils.

The Saigon papers, including the *Tribune Indochinoise*, attempted to forge a then-non-existent middle ground in appealing to tenant farmers while distancing themselves from the Communists. In an analysis of the 1938 granary raids, "La Révolte des '*ta-dien*'," the paper described farmers as largely ignorant of ideology and "duped by agitators." It sharply criticized the "Stalinists and Trotskyites" who threatened to induce fratricide among Vietnamese over ideological differences

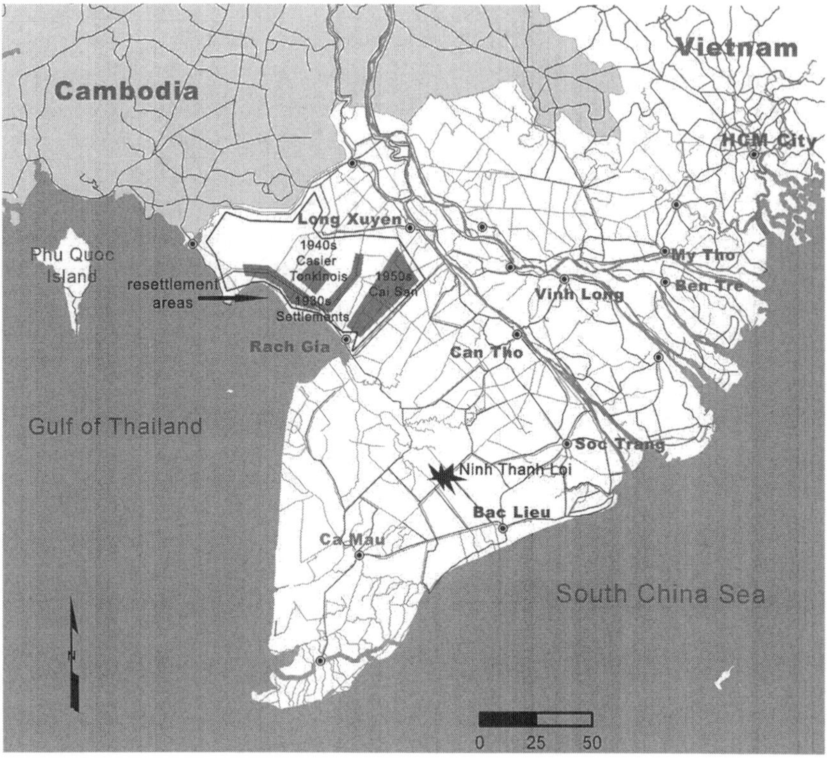


*Figure 1.2* Site of the Ninh Thanh Loi massacre and Long Xuyen resettlement area.

Source: Author.

at a time when collaboration might yield significant improvements in the rural economy. Pleading the moderate case, the article suggested that the peasantry – largely illiterate and susceptible – would only suffer in the crossfire between radicals and government troops.[24] *La Tribune Indochinoise* echoed similar proposals being advanced by the Popular Front government at the time. An investigation into the 1938 granary raids proposed stronger regulation of wage labor contracts and replacement of existing "pseudo-contracts" with a government-standardized salary for seasonal work across the region. By creating an agrarian proletariat (*prolétariat agricole)*, it aimed not to turn tenant farmers into landholders but rather to protect them from usury.[25]

Another legal political party, the Indochinese Democratic Party formed by Dr Nguyen Van Thinh, who later served as the first President of the Provisional Government of Cochinchina from June to November 1946, also contributed to the intellectual debate over landlessness. Like Bui Quang Chieu and other prominent Vietnamese at the time, Dr Thinh spent time in Paris where he completed a doctorate at the Pasteur Institute before returning to Cochinchina in 1926 and entering politics. In letters to newspapers and the governor, Dr Thinh urged further development of resettlement zones (*casiers*) and stronger support for agricultural worker contracts.[26] Vietnamese moderates' emphasis on developing wage contracts and extending reclamation over land redistribution thus represented a fundamentally different approach to landlessness than that espoused by the ICP or the Trotskyists.

However, in attempting to solve the "*ta dien* problem" by turning tenants into farm *workers*, these reformers neglected the more pervasive effects of colonial land policies on the cultural and political life of Vietnamese villages. It was precisely *in* such villages as Vinh Thuạn, An Bien, and Ninh Thanh Loi that ICP leaders built bases and formed secret Party cells. In these villages, they focused their attention on all aspects of village life – economic, political, and cultural. The same villages later became safe havens for youths fleeing the French Sûreté or the Japanese Kempeitai in the 1940s; and ICP cadres used these villages to recruit followers.[27] Contrasted with Saigon-based political parties and the Trotskyists, ICP activists approached property reform and poverty as issues deeply interconnected with problems of illiteracy and social justice.

This more intensive involvement in rural life, especially by urban-educated ICP activists, coincided with some of the most powerful works in the reportage (*phong su*) genre. Southern writers such as Phi Van (1917–77) produced some of the most famous reportage novels and short stories in the 1940s, examining the situation in the countryside from a more integrated economic, political, and cultural approach. A Bac Lieu native, Phi Van, wrote *The Countryside* (1942) as a vivid portrayal of corrupt officials such as Canton Chief Ngo destroying the fabric of rural family life, often denigrating rural women and traditional institutions in the process. Such works incited strong reactions especially among young readers, and they pointed to the moral indignities that often resulted from corrupt land transfers.[28]

## Engineering a solution to rural poverty

Although the Great Depression, the Nghe-Tinh Uprising, and the two-year reign of the Popular Front certainly contributed to widening public debate about the rural malaise and the situation of tenant farmers, it was only under the Vichy government and Japanese military occupation that the government attempted any large-scale land reforms. The state's delay in seeking action was due to several factors. First, rural protests led by the ICP continued until the aborted Southern Uprising in November 1940 that left most of the ICP's rural leadership in Cochinchina either dead, in prison, or hiding in remote areas such as Ca Mau. Second, the Japanese military command did not intervene in the day-to-day operations of the colony until March 1945, but it did place increasing demands on the governor-general to put every hectare of arable land into production to serve the Japanese war effort. Thus, it was feasible during the extreme conditions of wartime to send hundreds of thousands of Tonkinese south to reclaim new land.

Finally, land reform schemes that involved turning landless migrants into *petits colons* who would open up new lands and then reside in them permanently better served a Vichy ideology (*Travail, Famille, Patrie*) than a Communist one built largely around the empowerment of workers. Resettlement instead of redistribution also drew from an older, pre-colonial policy of sending the poor to open up new frontiers through the creation of military-agricultural settlements (*don dien*). The first big polder-style reclamation and resettlement scheme in the Long Xuyen Quadrangle, the *casier tonkinois*, was wholly in keeping with what Eric Jennings describes as the neo-traditional tendencies of Vichy. It embodied Vichy esthetics that blended extreme nationalism with an idealized notion of the national pastoral modeled on almost-mythical national landscapes such as the ancient rice terraces of the Red River Delta. This neo-traditional logic coincided with what James Scott would call the high modernist anchors of the state in such a rural area – school, health clinic, heavy machinery for hydraulic pumping, and at the center a sports stadium to coordinate youth athletics and group activities.[29]

From the 1930s and through World War II, colonial social scientists and technocrats played a powerful role in producing certain views of the delta countryside and its inhabitants that would shape rural policies and post-colonial attitudes for several decades. Not only did hydraulic engineers and others engage in full-scale social and environmental engineering with the first major *casier* schemes, but the growing ranks of geographers, agronomists, and even archeologists, most stranded in Indochina by the Pacific War, engaged in extensive rural-based research projects. For example, Louis Malleret, director of the Musée Blanchard de la Brosse (today the Ho Chi Minh City History Museum), conducted five years of surveys on Funan-Oc Eo Culture in the Long Xuyen Quadrangle.[30] By 1940, a growing corpus of technical literature by geographers, demographers, and agricultural engineers had firmly established the terms that most technocrats used in succeeding decades to debate the causes of rural poverty and to remedy the "*ta dien* problem." Academic studies of rural life extended beyond French academics to growing numbers of Vietnamese scholars. For example, Nguyen Van Huyen graduated with a PhD dissertation on stilt houses in 1933, and twelve years later he took over as director of the Ecole Française d'Extrême-Orient. His published works, including *La Civilisation Annamite* (EFEO, 1944), contributed to postcolonial Vietnamese notions of traditional rural life that still circulate widely today.[31]

Perhaps no other social scientist was as influential in shaping geographers' and policymakers' visions of a neo-traditional delta countryside as Pierre Gourou. His 1936 work, *Les Paysans du Delta Tonkinois*, gained him national and international fame for its detailed study of traditional patterns of soil and water management in the Tonkin delta based on extensive and meticulous field research as well as extensive use of aerial photography. His catalyzing new version of the "view over the village hedge" offered Vichy's social engineers a model of family-based farms and densely parceled landholdings to be surrounded by village- or district-level flood control structures.[32] With economic and environmental conditions worsening in the Mekong Delta's floodplains during the late 1930s, Gourou's followers turned their attention to explaining these failures and proposing solutions based on their research. Geographers and others adapted new technology with older forms such as census data to produce new cartographic tools, especially choropleth maps, that abstracted complex, interrelated social and economic data into easy-to-follow graphics. Gourou's books and articles on rural society in Indochina aimed to present the Mekong Delta to urban and foreign readers in a different light. What had since the colonial conquest been presented in government reports and pamphlets as an industrial and agricultural "new frontier" was by the late 1940s being re-presented as a kind of Indo-Chinese or Vietnamese *terroir*, a landscape built out of the combination of natural resources and indigenous cultural traditions.[33]

Rather than assimilate rural people and the countryside into a modern, urbanizing, and French-centered state, this model argued for more separation between Vietnamese and French landscapes. Those masses formerly uprooted and cast adrift from their traditional culture and agriculture would be re-settled in the neo-traditional zones. With this new formulation of Vietnamese agriculture, Vichy's social engineers went to work in the abandoned floodplains of the western Mekong Delta with the hope of stabilizing the region economically and politically. Gourou's work also reinforced the idea of the polder or *casier* as a landscape form that merged water management with the containment of village life inside the dikes. Given the severe economic privations and costs involved in re-dredging canals, colonial engineers likely saw the fiscal advantage in this self-perpetuating model of flood control.

Considerations for polder schemes had been debated by a small circle of French and Vietnamese public works engineers since 1916, but they did not attract much public interest until the late 1930s when newspapers and reportage stories began to report more frequently on mounting political and economic troubles in the countryside.[34] In order to improve crop yields, the government established in 1942 a rural engineering corps (*génie rural*). Why the Vichy government strove to build *casiers* instead of protecting the old grid of canals and the expansive plantations built along them was most likely due to the extreme dearth of dredging equipment associated with Japanese military occupation and the influence of social scientists such as Gourou. Even to keep old canals clear, the colony was forced to rely upon native contractors directing armies of manual laborers instead of the old public works monopoly that had dominated road, bridge, and canal construction since the 1890s.[35] A 1944 map of the *génie rural*'s operations in Cochinchina shows each proposed research center. These sites continued to function as agricultural research stations after the First Indochina War, and they served as focal points for post-1954 irrigation and resettlement schemes (see Figure 1.3).

While he acted quickly to silence Vietnamese radical movements, Governor-General Decoux encouraged an active debate among his colonial technocrats over land reform. From the *génie rural*'s inception in 1942 to 1945, its members routinely criticized the powerful Department of Public Works for past mistakes, claiming that the dredging operations typically diminished agricultural yields for

*Figure 1.3* 1944 agricultural research projects and proposed *casiers.*

Note: The above map shows the location for planned and active agricultural research stations in the Mekong Delta. The gray areas (added for emphasis) describe the outlines of two agricultural *casiers* that the government began investing in before 1945 at Long Xuyen and Phuoc Long. The choice of Phuoc Long was likely political since the village lies next to Ninh Thanh Loi and Vinh Thuan, both sites of earlier peasant protests. Source: Folio H62/14, TDBCPNV, VNA2.

the sake of navigation.[36] Another report went further, accusing Public Works engineers of corrupt collusion with wealthy landlords:

> In the course of fiery meetings at the Colonial Council a certain number of Vietnamese Councilors asked the Administration to dig channels crossing their grounds, and the Administration for political reasons met their request. It is obvious that they created the system of channels bric-a-brac for sentimental and political reasons.[37]

Public Works engineers responded to these critiques by adopting the cause of *casiers* as a new approach to large-scale water engineering in the delta. They fired back at agricultural engineers for writing "pessimistic reports" that "all of Cochinchina is in danger."[38] They blamed the region's irrigation problems and abandoned lands on uncoordinated local practices in newly opened regions. Unlike farmers in Tonkin, their reports argued that farmers in the Mekong Delta were effectively lazy, refusing to take individual responsibility for local-scale irrigation and instead waiting on the state to intervene.[39]

These dueling interests were more or less reconciled in a 1942–5 program to resettle 750,000 northern Vietnamese into the *terres abandonées* (abandoned lands) of the Long Xuyen Quadrangle (see Figure 1.2). Under a new budget line, "Aid to Rice Farmers," five million piasters would be raised to send Tonkinese peasants down the recently completed Trans-Indochinois Railway to populate the new *casiers*.[40] The same budget category would fund the development of the *génie rural*'s research stations and a new round of studies by public works engineers on building a system of massive sea dikes, moving dams, and giant water pumping stations. As the Japanese war effort weakened, however, the project was scaled back to a budget of half a million piasters over four years.[41] Nevertheless, Public Works engineers commenced building the first *casier tonkinois* for approximately seven thousand people due to arrive in mid-1943.

With the colony's fleet of expensive dredging machines in disrepair owing to a lack of spare parts, the Public Works Department hired labor contractors to manage dredging the main canals by hand, and *Casier tonkinois I* opened in early 1944 when seven hundred fifty families moved there from Thai Binh and Nam Dinh. Upon arrival, the immigrants received new clothes, mosquito netting, raincoats and hats, blankets, and matting. They also received a five-hectare lot upon finishing required manual labor on interior canals, one month's supply of food, cooking supplies, farming tools, and a small boat. Besides these personal amenities, the government built a primary school, a government field post, a market, and a communal house. A sports stadium was to be completed later in the year.[42]

By the end of 1944, however, the farmers had cleared only one third of the land allotted them and many were suffering from severe water shortages. Unfamiliar with the local play of tides and the annual floods, they dug deep canals that drained floodwater outside the protective dikes; but once the rains ended they were unable to keep enough fresh water running in the canals. The government continued to spend 175,000 piasters into 1945 to provide sufficient food for the families.[43] Work continued in 1945 on *Casier tonkinois II* and a new wave of immigrants arrived just as the Vichy government collapsed on March 9 and months before the Japanese left.[44]

While such projects paled in comparison to later US-funded efforts of the Saigon regime to relocate northern refugees after 1954, they represent important models that likely guided planning for the larger refugee resettlement projects produced by Ngo Dinh Diem from 1954 to 1963. Both the neo-traditional, family-centered theme of the program and its location in the western Mekong Delta appeared in later programs such as the massive Cai San settlements (1956–63) in

Long Xuyen that received mostly Catholic refugees from the same northern areas of Thai Binh and Nam Dinh. The *casiers tonkinois* even attracted some American attention in 1945. While US military planners in 1945 were occupied with destroying Indochina's oil depots, coal mines, bridges, and railroads in preparation for possible invasion, a few experts in the Roosevelt Administration were aware of the *casier* project. They translated a French article on the *casiers tonkinois* in October 1945; and this and other country studies on the rural masses were soon turned over to President Truman's Point IV Program.[45] While these Vichy resettlement programs of 1943–5 were short-lived, it is worth noting that the first Vietnamese government formed after the March 1945 Japanese coup acted to continue the policy of sending poor northern farmers to the south. As the famine raged in the north, the official newspaper of the Vietnam Nationalist Party proclaimed that the Minister of Supplies had approved the first group of an estimated one million people to be relocated in the south, presumably in the Long Xuyen Quadrangle.[46]

## Conclusion: Postcolonial to postsocialist solutions to rural poverty

This late colonial discourse over rural poverty and property reform in Vietnam in the last years before 1945 provides an often-neglected historical context that better explains the actions of Ngo Dinh Diem and the Republic of Vietnam in the 1950s and 60s. The mass resettlement of northern refugees into the western Mekong Delta and Central Highlands (1956–63), promulgation of labor contract reform, and even the controversial agroville program (1959–62) had part of their logic firmly planted in this earlier discourse. As Edward Miller's study of Diem indicates, the future leader of the Republic of Vietnam had long been interested in a Third Way alternative to the continuation of colonial land regulations and the ICP-led alternatives.[47] With regard to agriculture, this Third Way involved to some extent a continuation of older, moderate proposals evoked by Dr Thinh and Bui Quang Chieu to establish enforceable contracts governing wage labor in agriculture. Diem's brother and closest advisor, Ngo Dinh Nhu, writing under the pen name Dan Sinh for the newspaper *Xa Hoi* in 1953, articulated for readers a distinctive approach to laws on private property. Contrasting the pro-French Associated State of Vietnam's (1949–55) policies to *both* communism and capitalism, the thrust of Nhu's arguments was that most everyday transactions in the countryside should be protected from government intervention but that the masses would be protected from exploitation. Secondly, Nhu argued that the state had rights similar to eminent domain to require individual participation in developing larger projects such as canals, dikes, and roads.[48]

While it is tempting to think that specific ideas such as cooperatives, agricultural wage contracts, and land redistribution belonged to either the land reform movements of the Democratic Republic of Vietnam led by the Communist Party or the Republic of Vietnam led by Diem and his allies, it is essential to recognize that land reform in both the north and the south involved experimentation with new land or labor contracts and also with cooperatives. Where Viet Minh forces seized former plantation lands in the Mekong Delta, for example, they were careful to establish new tenant contracts that in many cases amounted to a reduction in rent with some added guarantees rather than a transfer of land title to their supporters. For example, one 1951 contract issued by local Viet Minh authorities in a "liberated area" (*dat giai phong*) to a farmer in My Tra Village (Cao Lanh District, Sa Dec Province), notes that the local Resistance Committee in nearby Ba Sao Village consented to rent 1.9 hectares of land confiscated from Mr Tomasi, a French planter, giving a parcel number as described in the old colonial cadastral survey. Besides offering a substantially lower rent (28 *gia* or roughly half a metric ton in rice), the contract also offered many of the basic measures – disaster relief, fixed interest, and limits to publicly required labor – that colonial reformers had pushed since the days of the Popular Front.[49] To the extent that farmers were allowed to add their input into these debates, notably at a public meeting attended by an American land reform advisor in 1956, over and again they emphasized that what they most wanted was not the abolition of private land ownership or even tenant farming but state-enforced limits on the interest rates charged by banks and private lenders.[50]

As other essays in this volume attest, the problem of regulating land rents and farm labor wages attracted much attention in twentieth-century Vietnam and is again attracting attention in the present. In the current era of "market-oriented socialism," the centrist proposals of the Constitutionalists for modifications to agricultural wage labor or even certain of Diem's "Third Way" policies seem more relevant to debates over land and labor than past collectivization schemes or current foreign models of land privatization. Clearly there are continuing tensions between farmers and the state with regard to the extent to which the state can regulate private transactions and the extent to which the state can provide protections for small farmers and the landless. The Mekong Delta countryside today is becoming increasingly urban and increasingly industrialized; thus farming must compete with residential development and new factories for land. Recent scholarship has noted a strong trend toward land consolidation in the hands of private firms with increasing accusations of corruption levied by minority groups and the rural poor.[51] In 2007, farmers affiliated with a movement called "Victims of Injustice" (*dan oan*) captured the attention of the international media and non-governmental organizations such as Human Rights Watch to protest what they claimed were unjust land transactions.[52]

The continuing role of media, especially Internet-based media, and the presence of anthropologists, sociologists, and others studying rural poverty in Vietnam suggests that despite epic political changes in the past century, public discourse over landlessness and proposals for addressing difficulties faced by the rural poor are alive and well. Contemporary conflicts over landlessness, resettlement, and property transfers are colored by past conflicts in the colonial and postcolonial eras; likewise, present-day media reports and social science studies reflect earlier framings of the same issues.

## Notes

1 Several excellent histories examine various dimensions of peasant life during the colonial and postcolonial eras. See Pierre Brocheux, *The Mekong Delta: Ecology, Economy*

*and Revolution, 1860–1960* (Madison WI: University of Wisconsin Press, 1995); Son Nam, *Lich Su Khan Hoang Mien Nam* (Youth Publishers, 2004); Ngo Vinh Long, *Before the Revolution* (Columbia, 1991); James C. Scott, *The Moral Economy of the Peasant: Rebellion and Subsistence in Southeast Asia* (Yale, 1977); and Benedict J. Kerkvliet, *The Power of Everyday Politics: How Vietnamese Peasants Transformed National Policy* (Cornell, 2005).

2 Philippe Peycam, "Intellectuals and Political Commitment in Vietnam: The Emergence of a Public Sphere in Colonial Saigon (1916–1928)," PhD thesis, University of London, School of African and Oriental Studies, 2003; Peter Zinoman, "Introduction to Vu Trong Phung's *Dumb Luck* and the Nature of Vietnamese Modernism," in *Dumb Luck: A Novel by Vu Trong Phung*, Nguyen Nguyet Cam, trans. and Peter Zinoman (ed.) (Michigan, 2002), pp. 1–30; and Shawn McHale, *Print and Power: Confucianism, Communism, and Buddhism in the Making of Modern Vietnam* (Hawaii, 2004).

3 Phi Van, *Dong Que: Phong Su* (Saigon: Dat Nuoc, 1957); see also Ngo Vinh Long, *Before the Revolution*, pp. 145–60.

4 Pierre Gourou, *Les Paysans du delta tonkinois: Etude de géographie humaine* (Paris: Les Editions d'art et d'histoire, 1936).

5 Yves Henry, *Economie agricole de l'Indochine française* (Hanoi: Gouvernement général de l'Indochine, 1932).

6 Nguyen Van Huyen, "Une Source d'étude démographique des communes annamites du Tonkin," *Bulletin de l'Institut Indochinois de l'Etude de l'Homme*, 1938; "Le Problème de la paysannerie au Tonkin," *Collection Tendances*, 1939.

7 Gilbert Chieu, "Une bataille intéressante" *Supplément du Nong Co Min Dam*, 23 October, 1907, p. 1.

8 For a more thorough discussion of the Minh Tan movement see Son Nam, *Mien Nam dau the ky XX – Thien Dia Hoi va cuoc Minh Tan* (Saigon: La Boi, 1971). See also Peycam, "Intellectuals and Political Commitment," p. 64; and Brocheux, *Mekong Delta*, p. 73.

9 Bui Duc Tinh, *Nhung Buoc Dau cua Bao chi Truyen Ngan Tieu Thuyet va Tho Moi, 1865–1932* (HCM City Publishers, 2002), p. 45.

10 Peycam, p. 76.

11 Hue-Tam Ho Tai, "The Politics of Compromise: The Constitutionalist Party and the Electoral Reforms of 1922 in French Cochinchina," *Modern Asian Studies*, Vol. 18, No. 3 (1984), pp. 371–91, 391.

12 Hue-Tam Ho Tai, *Radicalism and the Origins of the Vietnamese Revolution* (Cambridge MA: Harvard University Press, 1992), pp. 134–7.

13 Peycam, p. 111.

14 Le Quang Liem, "La Vérité sur l'echauffourée de Ninh-Thanh-Loi (Rachgia)," *Tribune Indochinoise*, May 20, 1927, 1–2. For extensive coverage of the Ninh Thanh Loi affair as well as others, see Son Nam, *Lich su Khan hoang Mien Nam* (A History of Reclamation in the South) (Ho Chi Minh City: Van Nghe Publishers, 1994), pp. 297–307. See also Pham Cao Duong, *Vietnamese Peasants under French Domination* (Berkeley, CA: Center for South and Southeast Asian Studies, 1985), p. 41.

15 "Commission permanente du 19 Juillet 1927: L'inspection générale du travail," *Tribune Indochinoise*, August 24, 1927, p. 3.

16 Paul Bernard, *Le Problème économique indochinois* (Paris: Nouvelles Éditions Latines, 1934), pp. 123–4.

17 R. Schneyder, L'inspecteur des affaires administratives et du travail à Monsieur Mallet, Directeur du Service local et de l'Information à Saigon, 21 février 1947. File M2/57, TDBCPNV, VNA2. For more comprehensive essays on the problems of landless farmers and land tenure see Yves Henry, *Economie agricole de l'Indochine* (Hanoi: Imprimerie d'Extrême-orient, 1932), p. 224, and Pierre Gourou, *L'utilisation du sol en Indochine française* (Paris: P. Hartmann, 1940), p. 531.

18 The legal bias favoring French nationals (regardless of race) in the 1930s was an artifact of the dual legal system governing land rights that was first established by Admiral de la Grandière in 1863. See Ngo Vinh Long, *Before the Revolution: the Vietnamese Peasants under the French* (New York: Columbia University Press, 1991), p. 12.
19 Ong Muoi, Interview One, April 12, 2002.
20 Ong Hai, Interview Three, April 13, 2002.
21 M. Bagot, "Malaise agraire dans le Transbassac," April 28, 1939, File M.2/63, TDBCDNV, TTLTQG2. For extensive treatment of the ICP bases, see Bui Van Thạnh, "*Bao cao khai quat lich su va phuong huong bao ton, phat huy di tich lich su can cu dia cach mang U Minh Thuong Kien Giang*" (Overview Report on History and Orientation to Conservation for Promoting Historical Sites at U Minh Thuong, Kien Giang) in *Ky yeu hoi thao khoa hoc: Di tich lich su can cu dia Cach mang U Minh Thuong*, pp. 52–5.
22 "La Grève des ouvriers et coolies de la Société des Dragages à Mytho," *La Lutte*, April 7, 1938, p. 4.
23 L'Administrateur des Services Civils, Chef de la province de Rachgia à Monsieur le Gouverneur de la Cochinchine, December 7, 1932, File IB23/096(19), Fonds Goucoch, VNA2.
24 "La Révolte des 'Ta-diên'," *La Tribune Indochinoise*, May 6, 1938, p. 1.
25 M. Bagot, "Malaise agraire dans le Transbassac."
26 Philip Devillers, *Histoire du Viêt-Nam*, 173–4. See also Ralph B. Smith. "The Vietnamese Elite of French Cochinchina, 1943," *Modern Asian Studies*, Vol. 6 No. 4 (1972), pp. 459–82, 469.
27 Bui Van Thanh "Can cu dia cach mang U Minh Thuong," p. 54.
28 Ngo Vinh Long, *Before the Revolution*, p. 146.
29 Eric T. Jennings, *Vichy in the Tropics: Pétain's National Revolution in Madagascar, Guadeloupe, and Indochina, 1940–1944* (Stanford: Stanford University Press, 2001), 170; James C. Scott, *Seeing Like a State*, p. 90.
30 Virginia Thompson and Richard Adloff, "The Cultural Institutions of Indochina Today," in *Journal of Asian Studies*, 6:4 (1947), pp. 414–19.
31 Nguyen Van Huyen. *La Civilisation Annamite* (Hanoi: Ecole d'Extrême-Orient, 1944). Nguyen van Huyen later served as Ho Chi Minh's Minister of Education.
32 David Biggs, "Aerial Photography and Colonial Discourse on the Agricultural Crisis in Late-Colonial Indochina, 1930–1945," in *Cultivating the Colony: Colonial States and their Environmental Legacies*, Oslund *et al.* (eds) (Athens OH: Ohio University Press, forthcoming).
33 Gavin Bowd and Daniel Clayton, "Tropicality, Orientalism and French Colonialism in Indochina: the Work of Pierre Gourou, 1927–1982," in *French Historical Studies*, Vol. 28, No. 2 (2005): 297–327, 298. Unlike other social scientists, however, Gourou did not stay on in Indochina during World War II but instead taught at French universities and served in the French Liberation.
34 C.E. Jammé, "Aménagement de la Plaine des Joncs: Avant-Projet," 20 July 1943, File H.62/7, TDBCPNV, VNA2.
35 Beginning in 1943, the *génie rural* and the Office of Irrigation and Navigation in Southern Indochina (formerly Public Works) commenced with projects farmed out to private, Vietnamese labor contractors. Responsibility for developing and maintaining canals thus was decentralized. See for example "Rach Ca Loc: Décembre 1943" File H61/1, TDBCPNV, VNA2.
36 Hoeffel, "Le Riz," File H6/20, TDBCPNV, VNA2. "Puis il y a toujours le risque de voir, un jour, annihiler les efforts accomplis par une modification du régime hydraulique de toute une région, ou bien encore par l'exécution d'un travail important, non prévu en temps voulu et dont les répercussions n'avaient évidemment pas été envisagées à l'époque des aménagements secondaires."

37 Xacat, "Riziculture et Hydraulique Agricole," August 29, 1944, File H.6/20, TDBCPNV, VNA2. "...qu'au cours des séances de feu le Conseil Colonial un certain nombre de conseillers annamites demandaient à l'Administration de faire creuser des canaux traversant leurs terres, et l'Administration pour des raisons dites politiques, accédait à leur demande. Il est évident qu'un système de canaux crée de bric et de broc pour des raisons sentimentales et politiques.
38 Bigorgne, "L'Hydraulique Agricole en Cochinchine," August 25, 1944, File H.6/20, TDBCPNV, VNA2.
39 Ibid., p. 5.
40 September 30, 1942. Decoux to the Governor of Cochinchina. File H62/10, TDBCPNV, VNA2.
41 Ibid.
42 L'Ingénieur en Chef de la Circonscription d'Hydraulique Agricole et de Navigation de Sud-Indochine (HANSI) à Monsieur le Gouverneur de la Cochinchine, September 1, 1943, File BO/3904, TDBCPNV, VNA2.
43 L'administrateur, chef de la province de Rach Gia à Monsieur le Gouverneur de la Cochinchine, January 22, 1945, File BO/3904, TDBCPNV, VNA2.
44 Budget Général: Aménagement de la Région Rach-Gia – Ha-Tien, January 25, 1945, File BO/3904, TDBCPNV, VNA2.
45 The entire collection of "M Project" reports can be found at the Library of Congress and as part of the Henry Field Papers, Collection Number 72, University of Miami, Otto G. Richter Library Archives and Special Collections Department. See No. T-109. "Studies of Migration and Settlement: Translation Series – Tonkinese Settlement in Cochinchina, October 20, 1945."
46 *Binh Minh*, July 17, 1945.
47 Edward Miller, "Vision, Power and Agency: The Ascent of Ngo Dinh Diem, 1945–54," *Journal of Southeast Asian Studies*, Vol. 35, No. 3 (2004), pp. 433–58.
48 "Kinh te: Quy che so huu cua chung ta," *Xa Hoi,* July 1953, 4. Thanks to Edward Miller for sharing this source.
49 File 21487, PTTĐICH, TTLTQG2.
50 For an account of his meetings with farmers, see Ladejinsky's report for the US advisory organization in Saigon titled "South Vietnam Re-Visited" in Louis J. Walinsky (ed.) *Agrarian Reform as Unfinished Business: The Selected Papers of Wolf Ladejinsky* (New York: Oxford University Press, 1977), p. 261.
51 Nguyen Quang Tuyen. "Land Holding Changes and Kinh and Khmer Farmers' Livelihoods in Thoi Thuan B Hamlet, Thoi Lai Town, Co Do District, Can Tho City, Vietnam," *Asian Social Science*, Vol. 6 No. 1, pp. 132–44.
52 Human Rights Watch, *On the Margins: Rights Abuses of Ethnic Khmer in Vietnam's Mekong Delta* (New York: Human Rights Watch, 2009).

# 2 Bodies in perpetual motion

## Struggles over the meaning, value, and purpose of fuzzy labor on the eve of collectivization

*Ken MacLean*

"We were tired and hungry all the time," said the elderly but still fit woman. Her statement caused the cadres who had been assigned to monitor my interview to suddenly stop what they were doing in the background to listen carefully to what Pham Thi Vach said next. I, too, was surprised by her blunt assessment of rural life, for Vach was nationally known for the contributions she had made toward "building socialism" in the Democratic Republic of Vietnam (DRV) four decades earlier. My efforts to elicit further details from her were unsuccessful; the remainder of our conversation, while pleasant, did not diverge far from the widely available facts that are routinely cited in official depictions of her life.

Pham Thi Vach, who later became a Communist Party member and secretary for the People's Committee in Kim Ty District (Hung Yen Province), first demonstrated her leadership potential in the late 1950s, while still a teenager. Concerned by heavy rains, she mobilized her peers to save the fall harvest one year by carrying out urgently needed repairs to dikes that protect Hung Cuong Commune from catastrophic flood. Leading by example, Vach personally dug, then carried more than 250 cubic meters of muddy soil to help reinforce the earthen embankments holding back the branches of the Red River that completely surround the low-lying commune on all sides. The *ad hoc* campaign, which lasted fifty days, was successful; other noteworthy achievements followed, as did a series of increasingly prestigious awards for the young woman affectionately dubbed the "Red River girl" in the state-controlled press. These awards culminated in the title of "Labor Hero" and a First-Class Medal of Merit, which Ho Chi Minh personally handed to Vach in 1961 in recognition of the role she played in transforming the commune, long known for producing more beggars than rice, into a more prosperous one.

This achievement was later celebrated in verse:

*Hung Cuong has a newly built sluice,*
*A freshly packed dike, a recently planted tree [for]*
*Whoever stops and looks.*
*Nowadays there is a Party, and the banks of the Red River have levees*

(Thanh Duy 1962: 44)

As the poem suggests, the Communist Party played an important role in this transformation. Indeed, a casual review of the policies, books, pamphlets, newspaper articles, and other forms of official discourse published during this period all reach a similar conclusion. But the relationship of the Party to different segments of the state's then rapidly expanding bureaucracy and the rural populations under their administrative purview was far more complicated and fraught with contradictions as well as unanticipated consequences than has generally been recognized. These contradictions do not reflect an inherent conflict between the Party, the state, and local communities. Rather, they arose from a combination of conjunctural factors: competition among different ministries for labor power, mass campaigns that overlapped with one another, and a series of droughts and floods. The competing demands these three sets of factors placed on the time and energy of rural populations continually threatened their ability to feed themselves; as a result, they were "tired and hungry all the time," as Pham Thi Vach recalled.

These contradictions and tensions were perhaps most evident on construction sites where low-level cadres utilized a combination of volunteer, conscripted (*corvée*), and wage labor to (re-)build essential infrastructure in the DRV following independence. Details on the different labor "regimes," drawn primarily from archival documents, highlight why the category of labor was both indispensable and inadequate for understanding official efforts to "lay the foundations" of state socialism in the countryside between late 1956 and late 1959, as its boundaries were neither distinct nor discrete; instead, the category of labor became increasingly "fuzzy," to borrow the term Katherine Verdery has used to describe the property forms found in many parts of postsocialist Europe (1999). The "transition" *out* of state socialism, Verdery noted, did not completely transform the political, economic, and jural systems of these countries or the cultural values and practices that informed them; quite the contrary occurred, as the process transformed some aspects of these systems, but left others intact and reconfigured still others. Consequently, the property forms that emerged there after 1989 typically contained a complex mixture of rights and obligations, which made it difficult to determine where collective claims ended and private ones began (53–5) – hence, Verdery's use of the term "fuzzy" to describe them.

Verdery's observations, although focused on the reorganization of property relations following decollectivization, are not limited to the European context or, for that matter, the "transition" *out* of state socialism. A similar case can also be made about the "transition" *into* socialism, as this process did not wholly eradicate one order and replace it with another. This was especially the case in the DRV between late 1956 and late 1959 when most of the policies, procedures, and organizational models needed to establish a centrally planned economy based on the collective ownership of the means of production were first put in place. The "transition" into state socialism turns out to have been as "indistinct, ambiguous, and partial" (Verdery 1999: 55) as was its unmaking decades later (MacLean 2005). Many factors contributed to this "fuzziness," but few more so than the growing confusion and conflict over the proper meaning, value, and purpose of peasant labor on the eve of collectivization. Labor, it should be recalled, is not an abstract thing, though the category is often quantified as such, but rather an embodied process that generates things that can be used or exchanged. Labor, in other words, is a form of property as well as productive of property. This helps explain why the same action can be seen as a gift in one context, an in-kind contribution in another, and a commodity in still another depending on the bundle of rights and obligations associated with the labor performed (Lampland 1995; Hann 1998). Thus, close attention to disagreements over how and under what conditions low-level cadres could mobilize peasants and temporarily redirect their labor-time toward different Party/state objectives offers insights into a number of interrelated trends, three of which I explore here.[1]

First, low-level cadres utilized a combination of labor regimes to (re-)build essential infrastructure in the DRV; but, since the logic that informed each regime – volunteer, conscripted, and wage, respectively – ran counter to the others, these same cadres frequently found it difficult to mobilize and to manage sufficient numbers of peasants on a consistent basis to achieve all of the Party/state's declared goals. Second, the lack of standardization over the terms and conditions of the different forms of labor used further exacerbated this problem, as the rights and obligations the Party/state extended to volunteer, conscripted, and wage laborers on these (re-)construction projects were neither stable nor widely enforced. Third, the confusion and conflicts that resulted from these disagreements, both "inside" and "outside" the Party/state, were not limited to the construction sites; they had an adverse impact on other domains of life as well, but especially food production as the labor mobilized for large-scale projects could not be released in time for harvesting crops. These patterns, when taken together, complicate the existing historiography on the "transition" *into* state socialism in the DRV, which still depict the events leading to the collectivization of agriculture as being orderly, sequential, and inevitable in nature; in fact none of these terms accurately apply. Instead, quite the opposite was the case, as the labor regimes used at the time contributed to the very forms of inequality and injustice Party/state policies sought to eradicate – namely, exploitation, hunger, poverty, and landlessness. Thus the decision to fully collectivize land in addition to labor, animals, and tools in rural areas in late 1959 did not represent the predetermined outcome of historical processes so much as an official effort to forestall further socio-economic differentiation in the countryside (MacLean 2005: 187–239).

## Labor and its meanings

Postwar efforts to (re-)build the DRV's essential infrastructure did not mark the first time that representatives of the state had sought to take temporary possession of the labor-time of peasants and redirect it toward other ends. Vietnamese had for centuries discharged their obligations to the state through a combination of conscripted labor (*corvée*), taxes, and military service. Indeed, it is impossible to understand state-formation during the precolonial and colonial periods without reference to these demands or popular responses to them, which ranged from passive forms of resistance and flight to armed rebellion and millenarian movements (Scott 2009, 1977; Dutton 2008; Tai 1983). Similar claims can also be made about the crucial role conscripted labor played during the First Indochina War (1946–54), as independence would have been extremely unlikely without it (Pham Luan 1966). However, the relationship of labor to agricultural production, physical property, and personhood began to change profoundly during the final years of the conflict, first in liberated areas and then, following the end of the First Indochina War in 1954, throughout the DRV.

By this point, much of the essential infrastructure in the DRV was in dire need of repair, upgrade, and/or expansion. This was especially the case for its irrigation works, as French officials oversaw the completion of only twelve new systems in Tonkin between 1902 and 1941, many of which failed on a regular basis prior to the First Indochina War. Moreover, all of these systems sustained significant damage during the lengthy conflict, which further increased the likelihood of catastrophic floods, especially in the heavily populated Red River Delta (Ha Ke Tan 1964: 20–1; Phan Khanh 1997: 23–37). To address this problem, low-level cadres used several different methods to mobilize peasant labor at the commune-level and below from 1954 onward.

The first relied upon voluntary labor contributions, such as those carried out by Pham Thi Vach. These "self-supporting" (*tu tuc*) contributions, as they were known during the 1950s, had much in common with the informal labor exchanges peasants routinely organized during the pre-revolutionary era to collectively (re-)build dikes and other related infrastructure on a seasonal basis to prevent natural disasters and to lessen the impact of floods, rot, and drought when they occurred (Tran Duc 1994). Since voluntary contributions were not sufficient to complete mid- and large-scale irrigation works, which frequently required tens of thousands of peasants working in stages over months and sometimes years to complete, relevant ministries also authorized low-level cadres to conscript labor (*dan cong*) and to offer labor contracts (*khoan*) to finish their assigned sections on time. Both methods provided payment in cash and/or paddy; however, the meanings associated with each differed significantly as did the amounts given. Conscript labor was defined as a "duty" (*nghia vu*), which all qualified citizens had a moral if not also legal obligation to provide to the Party/state on an annual basis, so payment was fixed. Contract labor, however, was defined as a commodity, which citizens who had satisfied their annual obligation to the Party/state were able to sell, so payment varied. As a consequence, low-level cadres faced a difficult challenge; they had to mobilize substantial numbers of peasants throughout the year to help (re-)build irrigation works, yet separately track their individual contributions and compensate them differently according to the type of labor (voluntary, conscripted, or wage) performed – even where the task, such as carrying dirt to reinforce a levee, was exactly the same.

Disagreements over the meaning, value, and purpose of different kinds of labor were not limited to irrigation works; rather, they were merely one manifestation of those caused by the Party/state's broader efforts to remake nearly every aspect of life through a seemingly endless series of mass campaigns (MacLean 2005: 133–86). These "emulation campaigns" (*phong trao thi dua*) took different forms, but all were connected to officially authorized "programs of improvement" (Li 2007) which sought to increase the quantity of food produced, the quality of the country's citizens, or, as was often the case, both simultaneously. Since these campaigns followed one another in quick succession and sometimes overlapped with other development initiatives, peasants experienced heavy and frequently conflicting demands on their labor-power, which reduced the amount of time and energy they could devote to other concerns not specifically linked to official objectives. Verdery observed a similar phenomenon in Eastern Europe (1996: 39–57); but whereas, according to her, Eastern European states immobilized the bodies of their citizens in queues, in the DRV (MacLean 2008: 292–4), the Party/state "seized" the time of its citizens by continually mobilizing them to perform labor.

The negative consequences of this loss of time and labor were not limited to the peasants it affected most directly; it also had an adverse impact on policy implementation and Party/state–society relations more generally (Rév 1987: 339–41). These emulation campaigns are best viewed not in isolation, but as zones of contest where the "practice of government" – what Tania Murray Li defines as the calculated attempt to direct conduct in particular ways – continually encountered the everyday "practice of politics" (2007: 12), both "inside" as well as "outside" the formal boundaries of the Party/state (Mitchell 1999). So, although these struggles were certainly not limited to the efforts to (re-)construct the country's irrigation works, the moral legitimacy and economic viability of the nascent Party/state was nonetheless heavily contingent upon the ability of its cadres to engineer a dramatic increase in food production (Szalontai 2005). For this reason, these campaigns are at the center of my discussion. I focus particularly on irrigation works in Hung Yen, which quickly gained national prominence for the labor contributions of its inhabitants. These contributions were significant and warranted official recognition, but they were not without costs of their own.

## Official contradictions

The architects of the new, but not yet socialist, society of North Vietnam faced a number of significant challenges. By early 1955, much of the population, including residents of Hanoi, faced serious food shortages, while nearly one million people urgently needed humanitarian aid to avoid starvation owing to bad weather and the disruptive effects the land reforms had had upon agricultural production.[2] However, the magnitude of the problem did not delay further waves of class struggle connected to the land reforms (1953–6). Indeed, three more followed in rapid succession, even though it quickly became apparent that the redistribution of land, tools, and draft animals to the country's most disadvantaged peasants would not on its own prevent future famines (Yvon 2008).

To help address this problem, the National Assembly, the legislative arm of the Party/state, issued a Three-Year Plan (1955–7) that outlined how the economy of the DRV was to be "restored." The eight policies that constituted its core converged in a number of areas, but diverged in others. Some, in recognition of past promises, provided tax incentives to encourage peasant households to expand the amount of land under private cultivation and to revive small-scale entrepreneurial activities, especially animal husbandry; others, which foreshadowed the future, promoted the partial collectivization of the means of production through inter-households labor exchanges to promote greater harmony in the countryside and to raise agricultural yields simultaneously. The tensions among these policies, which reflected theoretical as well as practical disagreements among political elites over the most suitable path for the development of the DRV, were readily apparent on irrigation works. This was because neither of these desired outcomes – social harmony and increased production – was possible without such infrastructure, yet other emulation campaigns unfolding concurrently also required the labor-time of peasants to complete. Since the amount of available labor-time was finite, the competing agendas of the different ministries involved meant that peasant bodies were in high demand and shortages inevitable.

The Three-Year Plan directly contributed to this competition since efforts to "restore" the economy were not limited to policy interventions in the countryside. The Plan also initiated a period of intense state formation and reorganization, especially in areas that had remained contested territory until the end of the First Indochina War. This was the case of the Left Bank Region (*Khu Ta Ngan*) which included large parts of Hung Yen, Hai Duong, Thai Binh, and Kien An Provinces. Strategically located between the cities of Hanoi and Haiphong, the region's three million inhabitants helped produce much of the north's food supply; yet it had experienced little or no state authority before 1954.

To help fill these administrative gaps, the Prime Minister expanded the geographic reach of the Party/state and created new "organs," such as the Bureau of Irrigation, which he established in April 1955 within the Ministry of Communications and Public Works. This arrangement, like many others at the time, quickly proved to be unwieldy, so the National Assembly approved a large-scale reorganization of bureaucratic responsibilities in September. One product of this reorganization was the formation of the Ministry of Architecture and Irrigation, headed by Tran Dang Khoa.[3] By year's end, Khoa had opened a Department and an Office of Irrigation in each of the country's administrative regions (*lien khu*) and all of the provinces they contained. However, the creation of these new positions exacerbated the severe shortage of personnel who possessed the desired combination of "morality and ability" (*duc, tai*).

This problem was not limited to this particular ministry; it was instead a pervasive one that adversely affected the "practice of government" at all levels of the Party/state for many years. The reasons for this were complex and compounded one another: limited access to formal education stemming from colonial restrictions and nine years of war; ideologically driven purges of politically suspect cadres; class tensions that reinforced divisions between the "old" officials who remained and the "new" ones just appointed; and the sheer pace of bureaucratization more generally (MacLean 2005: 76–186). Between 1955 and 1959, for example, the number of directors and vice-directors at central-level agencies in Hanoi increased by more than 370 percent (Le Duc Tho 1961: 18–19). Nonetheless, the personnel shortages were particularly acute within the Ministry of Architecture and Irrigation, as its cadres needed to have advanced engineering skills in addition to basic administrative ones to be effective.

As Table 2.1 indicates, cadres remained in short supply through 1960. But archival documents reveal something that these figures do not: most of the reported growth was in personnel with administrative rather than technical skills (BTLKT 1957).[4]

Not surprisingly, the shortage of technically qualified personnel had a tremendous impact on initial (re-)construction efforts, as the Ministry of Architecture and Irrigation had little choice but to prioritize tasks that needed only minimal expertise, massive amounts of labor, and simple hand tools to complete. While this delayed the start of some major projects, the approach was nonetheless surprisingly successful. Stunning volumes of dirt and rock were moved and concrete poured to complete eight new irrigation systems and carry out repairs to existing ones throughout the country (Phan Khanh 1997: 46–7; BTLVP 1964: 20). Yet the methods used to achieve these impressive results quickly created problems of their own, as the field reports, conferences, and policies issued during the period covered by the first Three-Year Plan (1955–7) make abundantly clear.

## Inter-ministerial competition (1955–6)

In December 1955, Tran Dang Khoa, the Minister of Architecture and Irrigation, announced an ambitious goal at the conclusion of its annual national conference. He called for a 40 percent increase in the total area of arable land under irrigation by the end of 1956 (BTLKT 1955: 19). The conference minutes did not record the audience's response to this highly ambitious target; nor did the proceedings explicitly acknowledge that the land reforms then being implemented in many parts of the DRV (Moise 1983: 201–2) dramatically limited the ability of the cadres in participating provinces to achieve even modest gains in the amount of arable land under irrigation, as successive waves of class struggle against "landlords" and other categories of ideologically suspect persons consumed much of the labor-time peasants possessed at the time. Other documents produced during this period in addition to those compiled after the fact provide some insights into what happened over the next twelve months.

*Table 2.1* Irrigation cadres and administrative staff (by number and level of education)

| *Cadres* | *1955–1957* | *1958–1960* | *1961–1964* |
|---|---|---|---|
| University | 18 | 99 | 584 |
| Intermediate | 144 | 636 | 3,538 |
| Primary | 1,296 | 1,735 | 1,567 |
| Administrative staff | 707 | 1,610 | 2,590 |
| Totals | 2,165 | 4,080 | 8,279 |

Source: BTLVP 1964: 30.

Rot, caused by waterlogged fields, was a significant problem throughout the Red River Delta in 1955, including Hung Yen, which is only slightly above sea level and receives 80 percent of its annual rainfall between June and September (Le Quy Quynh 1966: 7; BTLKT 1957b: 4). Not surprisingly, the rot raised fears that the 1956 spring harvest would be badly affected and the province's approximately six hundred thousand inhabitants would again face severe food shortages, as they had the previous year when widespread crop failures nearly plunged the DRV into famine.[5] But what made these fears particularly acute was the province's recent history. Since the famine of 1944–5, which claimed over one million lives north of the seventeenth parallel in only six months, severe weather had produced nine droughts and three floods in Hung Yen (Le Quy Quynh 1966: 8).

To avoid disaster, authorities in the Left Bank Region launched a mass campaign that lasted the first half of 1956. During this period, low-level cadres mobilized the equivalent of three million workdays (*cong*) to (re-)build over 43 kilometers of canals and ditches, irrigating approximately 90,000 *mau* of land (SVHTTHH 1995: 61). Even more strikingly, the most difficult and labor-intensive tasks were largely completed during the first three days of the Lunar New Year celebration – an immensely important festival in which all work not related to ritual activities is normally suspended. That year, however, the threat to food security was sufficiently great for the Central Committees for Bac Ninh, Hung Yen, and Thai Binh Provinces to order large numbers of peasants in early February to remove sections of the dikes along the Red River and the Van Giang Canal in order to channel more fresh water into the brackish fields. In Hung Yen, some ten thousand people endured high winds, bitterly cold water, and thick mud to reach the goals officials set for them: "Only when [fresh] water returns to the fields will the conscripted laborers celebrate the New Year." They finished on the fourth day and, according to one local history, thousands of family members arrived at the construction sites to cheer their kin who had "triumphed over nature" (Quoc Phuong 1964: 10; BTLKT 1957a: 10).

The triumph was short-lived. Between December 1955 and April 1956 the DRV received only 30 percent of its normal rainfall, adversely affecting over 145,000 *mau* – 32,000 of which were in the Left Bank Region (BTLKT 1956: 3).[6] The Ministry of Architecture and Irrigation initiated a campaign to "fight [the] drought" in response to this new crisis and its cadres coordinated with their provincial counterparts to outline plans which district- and commune-level officials would later implement. Subsequent inspections noted what had been accomplished under severe conditions and very basic tools. Photos proudly showed teams of men completing hand-dug wells that telescoped downward to reach new sources of fresh water; while others featured women using shoulder poles with baskets attached to gently pour water from the wells onto rice seedlings in parched fields. These and other interventions – such as the innovative use of bicycles equipped with large ceramic cisterns mounted on both sides to deliver water to distant fields – reportedly surpassed the campaign's official targets, saving much of the harvest and more than doubling the total area under irrigation (BTLKT 1957: 11). Again, Hung Yen led all other provinces and the Government Council awarded the province an official pennant in July 1956 for its efforts to "fight drought." However, the methods used in Hung Yen, like those elsewhere, were not sustainable. Nor were they without problems: official statistics give evidence of an overall decline in agricultural yields over the next several years (Nguyen Sinh Cuc 1995: 150).

Several factors other than drought or floods contributed to this decline, but few more so than the land reforms (1953–6) and the "Rectification of Errors" (1956–8) campaign, which immediately followed. Broadly speaking, the former utilized class struggle to redistribute various types of private property in rural areas to millions of peasants who had little or none as a way to destroy existing mechanisms of socio-economic exploitation; the latter sought to return some of the land, tools, animals, and personal belongings from those able to prove that these items had been wrongly seized from them during land reform (Moise 1983: 178–268). Both campaigns were thus highly contentious affairs since any effort to change who owned what pieces of property directly affected the ability of rural families to meet their subsistence needs as well as the size of their financial obligations to the Party/state, which were typically paid in paddy after each harvest. As a consequence, both campaigns encouraged those involved in them to neglect a range of short-term concerns – such as existing initiatives to (re-)build dikes, canals, and other necessary irrigation infrastructure – in order to protect their long-term interests. The overall effect was the same in both instances: greater food insecurity from one harvest to the next. However, each campaign contributed to this outcome in different ways.

The land reforms, which officially began in some liberated areas in early 1953, unfolded unevenly across the countryside in a series of five waves, with many areas also undergoing multiple episodes of "land rent and interest rate reductions" (*giam dia to*) as well as purges of Party members and administrative personnel whose class backgrounds, behavior, or personal relationships made them ideologically suspect in the eyes of others. Since many parts of the Left Bank Region, especially urban centers, had remained under the nominal control of French-led military forces until mid-1954, its residents only participated in the fifth and final wave, which officially began in December of 1955 and continued through July of 1956 (Moise 1983: 201–2).

It is difficult to generalize about what occurred as local circumstances shaped when and how the land reforms were implemented in different parts of the Left Bank Region. The mass campaign to end the drought, for example, delayed the start of the land reforms in many places, such as Hung Yen, which did not begin the process until late February of 1956, several weeks after the three-day effort to divert fresh water to the fields over the Lunar New Year festival. While the delay helped save the harvest, it dramatically reduced the time available to prepare cadres throughout the province, much less ordinary peasants, on the procedures to be used to carry out class struggle, redistribute property, and purge real and imagined "enemies" from local positions of authority (UBCCRDTU 1955: 26–35). The lack of preparation quickly proved to be a problem for the implementation of land reforms as many of the procedures were highly technical in nature and required a working knowledge of concepts drawn from Marxism, Leninism, and Maoism to be fully understood. Moreover, instruction manuals provided to land reform cadres stated that the entire process normally required sixty-five days in each locale to complete. Yet, provincial authorities proudly announced in June that the land reforms had already been successfully carried out in 149 of Hung Yen's communes (SVHTTHH 1995: 60), which suggests that the teams dispatched to the countryside carried out some or all of the "steps" in considerable haste.

An internal review conducted shortly after the June announcement reached the same conclusion. Authors of the report cited a vast array of "errors" (*sai lam*) that had occurred across much of the Left Bank Region and required immediate action to correct, as detailed in Resolution No. 380. Toward that end, regional authorities took steps to address them in August – several months before the Politburo authorized a similar process nationwide (Dang Phong 2005: 258). Resolution No. 380 directed much of the blame toward low-level cadres who reportedly made one of two fundamental errors: either they followed existing guidelines too closely and thus failed to take local particularities into account or they disregarded them entirely and behaved in arbitrary fashion. Both errors, although quite different in nature, produced a similar result: false accusations. According to another internal review, in the Left Bank Region alone, 7,000 out of a total 8,828 Party members had been improperly "disciplined" (*xu tri*) – a vague term that covered a range of different punishments from expulsion to torture and execution – as a consequence of such accusations (Dang Phong 2005: 87). While the full scale of the problem is not publicly known, aspects of them directly affected the mobilization and use of labor on construction sites, especially those related to irrigation.

Heavy rains returned in the fall of 1956, which meant the mass campaigns to end the drought had to abruptly shift their focus to flood prevention. This was again accomplished largely by using woven baskets suspended from tripods to manually scoop water, transferring it from lower-level fields to higher ones. But the above average rainfall meant that hundreds of thousands of peasants nationwide had to be re-mobilized to protect the Winter-Spring Harvest (1956–7) by reinforcing dikes, berms, and other related infrastructure to divert excess water and thus protect the crops ripening in the fields.

Unfortunately, the timing of this particular mass campaign conflicted with another one, the "Rectification of Errors," which officially began in late October of 1956 and continued throughout 1957 and even into 1958 in some locations to address the problems the land reforms had created (Moise 1983: 237–68). During this period, teams of specially trained cadres were sent to the countryside to restore public order. However, this too proved to be a difficult, time-consuming, and contentious process since the Party/state lacked the resources, ability, and political will to properly compensate the tens of thousands of people who lost their freedom, reputations, and property because they had been wrongly accused of a wide range of ideological and/or economic "crimes" (*toi ac*).

The impact of the "Rectification of Errors" campaign on ongoing efforts to (re-)build irrigation works appears indirectly in the progress reports that low-level cadres submitted to their bureaucratic superiors. The details, which were converted into statistical tables, indicate that substantial amounts of labor were in fact devoted to irrigation works in the Left Bank Region during the land reforms, with peasants moving more than 360,000 cubic meters of soil in Hung Yen alone between March and May of 1956. Reports filed afterward, however, reveal that no officially *planned* work was performed at the commune-level after this point, though some ad hoc efforts to protect the next harvest did take place locally (BTLKT 1957).[7]

This pattern was not limited to the Left Bank Region. Progress reports filed with the Ministry of Architecture and Irrigation also indicated a dramatic decline in the amount of conscripted labor provided across the DRV, especially on large-scale projects, during the height of the fifth and final wave of the land reforms. The decline was particularly significant. The labor used to complete these projects – fourteen in total (of which eight were new) – came from three main sources: some 11,000 cadres who had returned from the south after the 1954 Geneva Accords, nearly 6,000 underemployed day-laborers from nearby townships, and substantial numbers of conscripted peasants. In Inter-region III (Son Tay, Ha Nam, Ninh Binh, Ha Dong, and Nam Dinh Provinces) alone, low-level cadres reportedly mobilized 102,999 peasants to provide *corvée* labor on such projects when work on them resumed in March of 1956. Interestingly, the cadres attributed their achievement to the "study sessions" peasants had participated in as part of the land reforms, which they claimed made the latter more aware of their "duty" to the Party/state – though they also admitted that some former landlords and other "class enemies" had been physically forced to work on the sites as punishment (BTLKT 1956: 2).[8]

Despite the number of people initially mobilized, their overall productivity was again much less than planned. Most of the cadres had held political or administrative posts in the south and found both the weather and the working conditions in the north extremely harsh as well as tedious. (According to reports from Hai Duong, a neighboring province, only one in ten could withstand the work for any length of time.) Similar complaints were voiced by the day-laborers, many of whom had performed the same repetitive tasks, transporting soil and rocks, for two or more years and desperately desired employment in state-owned enterprises elsewhere (BTLKT 1956).[9]

Peasants, although more accustomed to such intense labor, had complaints of their own, which they conveyed to inspectors who periodically visited the construction sites. Many claimed not to have been conscripted in accordance with existing guidelines, a topic I examine in the next section. Working conditions, especially food, water, and medical care were also identified as inadequate as were efforts to raise literacy rates, which sought to improve not only peasants' ability to read official discourse, but to publicly perform it for others to learn, using popular forms of oral expression, such as verse, plays, and songs (BTHUBCCRDKTN 1956). But the most widespread complaint concerned the relationship of wages provided to the labor performed. In some cases, the relationship was arbitrary (varying on sites as well as across them); while in others it was reportedly due to the misuse of state funds, specifically embezzlement and profligate spending. Regardless of the cause, these problems were a source of considerable confusion and conflict, which the continued absence of official policies on compensation exacerbated further.

To address these problems, the Ministries of Labor, Finance, and Architecture and Irrigation concluded a joint agreement in March 1956 that established standardized regulations across the DRV regarding the use of wage labor on infrastructure projects. This development, while no doubt welcome, did little to convince peasants to remain on the construction sites as the final wave of the land reforms intensified (*c*. December 1955–July 1956). Not surprisingly, the number of peasants willing to leave their villages to perform their "duty" (i.e. *corvée* labor) at this sensitive time dropped precipitously and remained between 30 and 80 percent below normal levels for the remainder of the year (BTLKT 1957a: 9–18).[10] Ironically, some of those who did go (particularly in Kim Dong, Van Giang, and Khoai Chau Districts of Hung Yen Province), stated that the physical labor was a welcome change, as the ideological study-sessions they had been required to participate in as part of the land reforms were "exhausting" (BTLKT 1956: 3).[11] While it is likely that many peasants held similar views on this issue, comparatively few of them returned to construction sites after the land reforms ended in late 1956. In fact, the number of peasants who provided labor on these sites remained far below what had been planned until early 1958 (BTLKT 1957a: 6).[12] Several factors contributed to this outcome, but paradoxically none more so than the Party/state's own efforts to extend greater protections to volunteer, conscripted, and wage laborers on its construction sites.

## Defending the people's interests (1956–7)

In April 1956, one month after the national guidelines on compensation were announced, the Communist Party issued another set to its members, detailing the kinds of leadership and guidance they were to provide to low-level cadres in addition to conscripted laborers on the construction sites.[13] The document outlined which officials were responsible for ensuring the ideological, economic, and physical well-being of peasants performing *corvée* labor on such sites. Despite these efforts to clarify bureaucratic lines of responsibility, many of the same problems continued through 1957; indeed, they arguably worsened, as evidenced by the three different policies issued in quick succession between July and September of that year.

The first, Decree No. 339, based on suggestions provided by the Ministry of Labor, sought to better protect the "people's interests" through temporary regulations on the "mobilization and use of conscripted labor during peacetime construction."[14] At first glance, the nine-page decree appears unsurprising, as its contents provide expected details on who was eligible for conscription (nearly all able-bodied adults who did not hold official posts) and defined the standard length of service (nine hours per day for thirty days, with one rest day for every nine worked). The decree also set fixed rates of pay for the different types of skilled and unskilled labor performed (between 600 and 1,000 VND/day) and determined what forms of compensation were appropriate for those who fell ill or were injured on site.

But two of the details, in particular, stand out. The first concerned travel subsidies, which specified the amount provided and rest-periods permitted for conscripted laborers who had to travel 11–15, 16–30, and 31–45 kilometers, respectively, to reach a given construction site. Since irrigation projects (unlike road construction in remote areas) were located close to densely populated rural areas, peasants rarely traveled great distances to reach the sites. However, their relative proximity meant that peasants were also expected to walk to and from construction sites on a daily basis, which placed an additional burden on their already limited labor-time. The second clarified internal lines of authority. According to the decree, low-level cadres were no longer authorized to requisition *corvée* without the prior written approval of their superiors; moreover, the text expressly limited their duties to four tasks: the dissemination of policies; the organization of labor on site; its management; and regular progress reports on each. To help reinforce this division of labor, the decree further announced the creation of "command committees" (*ban chi huy*) to help ensure that the temporary guidelines it contained were followed appropriately and implemented in a timely fashion on all construction sites.

Of course, the decree can also be read "against the grain" (Benjamin 1999: 248), which would suggest that the temporary regulations did not reflect existing practice so much as a concerted effort by high-ranking officials to reassert their authority over low-ranking ones by standardizing procedural norms. Two items in the text of the decree lend credence to such an interpretation. The decree exhorted local cadres not to mobilize *corvée* during critical moments in the agricultural cycle, as this could adversely affect the ability of peasants to feed themselves in the future. It also warned these same cadres not to rely upon "commandism" to mobilize others since threats and intimidation would gradually undermine respect for officials and compliance with the policies they sought to implement (see also BLLNDTQ 1956: 7).

Such a counter-reading finds further support in the two circulars the Ministry of Labor promulgated in September, less than two months later. The first, Circular No. 17, provided additional information regarding how the temporary regulations set out in Decree No. 339 should be properly implemented.[15] The details, which covered thirteen pages, are too complex to fully relate here; however, the lengthy explanation of what tasks did and did not qualify as *corvée*, which tools laborers were required to bring to the site and which would be provided for them, and so on, suggests that previous policies had failed to fully resolve disagreements over where the obligations of conscripted laborers *to* the Party/state ended and the responsibilities of its representatives *to* those who performed it began. The content of Circular No. 18, issued shortly afterward, also emphasized this point, albeit indirectly.[16] It detailed what kinds of infrastructure and services low-level cadres had to put in place in order to make conditions at construction sites both safer and more hygienic than they were currently. This included ten pages of guidelines on latrines, on-site medical care, and compensation rates for work-related injuries and deaths, which again suggests that central-level agencies had neglected to establish minimal standards prior to this point.

Efforts to standardize the practices used on construction sites also occurred at the regional and provincial levels. Since these decisions were not always in complete alignment with central-level ones – indeed they often preceded as well as deviated from them – attention to these dynamics can provide insights into actually existing government in particular times and places. Such dynamics were clearly evident in the Left Bank Region where the "Rectification of Errors" campaign badly disrupted nearly every aspect of daily life owing to the immense amount of time and energy it consumed. Indeed, the problems the land reforms had created proved to be so complex that different segments of the Party/state issued at least eleven major policy statements during the first four months of the "Rectification of Errors" campaign in the effort to define and then refine what procedures cadres should use to restore public order, to identify and release victims of false accusations from makeshift prisons, to re-categorize those who had received the wrong "class fraction," to resolve property disputes, and so on (VTTP 1957a).[17] These initial, largely *ad hoc* efforts became better organized and standardized over time (VTTP 1957b; Moise 1983: 237–68); however, they failed to convince rural populations to carry out other essential tasks, such as paying their Winter-Spring Harvest taxes on time, a feat only 211 out of a total of 804 communes in the Left Bank Region managed that year.[18]

Non-compliance was not limited to agricultural taxes. The number of peasants willing to perform their "duty," i.e. conscripted labor, in the Left Bank Region during the height of the "Rectification of Errors" campaign also plummeted from a total of 24,973,250 workdays in 1956 to a mere 6,035,760 in 1957 (BTLKT 1957: 6). Since such work was crucial to the region's food security, Tran Dang Chap, the Director of the Ministry of Labor in the Left Bank Region, issued eight circulars between March and July 1957 that outlined a range of material incentives and organizational reforms he hoped would encourage peasants to once again provide *corvée* labor when needed (UBHCKTN 1957).[19] Tran Dang Chap first raised the wages paid to conscripted peasants in March to correspond to market prices so that *corvée* would no longer make poor peasants poorer. The following month, he also authorized the creation of hierarchically nested public works brigades (*doi*), closely modeled after those used to supply military campaigns during the First Indochina War (Pham Luan 1966), to more effectively and efficiently utilize available manpower (Table 2.2).

This innovation was accompanied by a public awareness campaign that he ordered low-level cadres to carry out in their respective locales. Its purpose was to correct widespread misperceptions regarding *corvée* labor, to disseminate information on current policies, and so on. This required these cadres to accomplish a difficult task: low-level cadres were expected to explain what provisions had been added to protect the "individual rights" of peasants, yet convince them that it was still their "duty" to temporarily abandon their homes and fields to provide *corvée* when requested.[20] To make this task easier, Tran Dang Chap further recommended that the Ministry of Finance coordinate with state-owned rice companies

*Table 2.2* Public works brigades in the Left Bank Region, 1957

| *Brigade* | *Avg. size (persons)* | *Subsumes* | *Command committee* | *Scale of operation* |
|---|---|---|---|---|
| Large | 70–150 | 2–5 medium | 3–5 officials (district-level) | Commune |
| Medium | 20–40 | 2–5 small | 2–5 officials (commune-level) | Village |
| Small | 9–15 | Mutual assistance groups | 1–3 officials (village-level) | Hamlet |

Source: MacLean 2007: 57.

and warehouses to pay conscripted laborers the equivalent of 1.5 kilos of paddy or 500 VND per day, depending on their stated preference.[21]

It is not clear whether the recommendation was ever approved, but other documents indicate that cadres throughout the Left Bank Region did not wait for central-level authorities to offer material incentives. These details emerged as part of a three-month inspection that officials from the Ministry of Labor carried out in the Left Bank Region between mid-July and mid-October of 1957 (UBHCKTN 1957).[22] In the lengthy report that followed, the officials described a wide-range of "short-comings." Some of these were attributed to the "Rectification of Errors" campaign, which they noted had produced "ideological instabilities" across the countryside. The particular forms these "instabilities" took were not identified in this report. However, other documents issued at the time noted widespread fears among peasants that efforts to correct past "errors" would result in new ones. The three most commonly cited were: a change in their current "class fraction" to a politically less desirable one; the loss of some or all of the property acquired during previous waves of the land reforms; and/or personal injury at the hands of those who had been wrongly punished for crimes they did not commit and now sought vengeance (TT 1958).[23]

These fears had a number of immediate effects. First, the immense amount of time and energy devoted to the "Rectification of Errors" campaign contributed to a sharp drop in food production – per capita yields in 1957 were more than 40 kilograms lower than those the year before (Nguyen Sinh Cuc 1995: 150). Second, this decline also prompted the Prime Minister's Office to call on officials in Hanoi and Haiphong to encourage and, where necessary, force people who had sought refuge in the cities during the land reforms to return to the countryside to help raise agricultural yields (TT 1957).[24] Third, local officials in the Left Bank Region also acknowledged a dramatic decline in the number of peasants who had reported to construction sites to perform their "duty." The daily average was a mere 6–7,000 laborers instead of the 14–20,000 actually needed; consequently, the total volume of soil moved, 488,000 cubic meters out of the 671,604 targeted, was approximately one-third less than originally planned (UBHCKTN 1957).

Interestingly, the authors of the report did not attribute the entire problem to the "Rectification of Errors" campaign; instead, they insisted that low-level cadres were primarily to blame, as the majority of them purportedly lacked sufficient "prestige" (*uy tin*) to mobilize others. This problem, the report continued, was made worse by their provincial- and district-level counterparts, who had organized "study-sessions" to disseminate information regarding the eight circulars, but only in a few locations; consequently, general awareness of these policies and the broader political, social, and economic goals to which they were linked remained scattered and uneven. This was particularly the case in two provinces, Hung Yen and Hai Duong. Inspection teams found that at least five different types of labor contracts had emerged, all based upon the volume of earth moved within a set period of time, typically by the day, but sometimes by the hour. Pay rates, however, differed by type. Some contracts set specific targets in advance and paid using official rates. Other contracts also took the quality of work performed into consideration and paid at going commercial rates, which were higher. Still other contracts relied upon a "middleman" to organize a group of laborers in return for a percentage of the money earned. Since many of the contracts appeared to be little more than "wage labor" in disguise, an ideologically unacceptable outcome given its close political associations with "feudal" and "colonial" forms of exploitation, central-level officials ordered their provincial-level counterparts to suppress them (UBHCKTN 1957: 1–2; MacLean 2007: 51–6).

## Rethinking transition (1958–9)

Field reports that low-level cadres submitted to different ministries during the "Rectification of Errors" campaign indicate these and other "short-comings" were not limited to the Left Bank Region. But, as Table 2.3 makes clear, these "short-comings" affected (re-)construction efforts throughout the DRV, most obviously the total volume of earth and rock moved, which declined dramatically despite heavy capital investments in this sector.

Efforts to reverse this overall decline in labor contributions took several forms both during and immediately after the "Rectification of Errors" campaign; they did not, however, reflect a significant change in "government," i.e. the methods used to mobilize and manage voluntary, paid, and conscripted labor on irrigation works.

*Table 2.3* Labor contributions and investment in irrigation works (1955–60)

| *Year* | *Earth (cubic meters)* | *Rock (cubic meters)* | *Concrete (cubic meters)* | *Capital (1,000 VND)* |
|---|---|---|---|---|
| 1955 | 14,224,176 | 256,885 | 3,287 | 9,924 |
| 1956 | 18,222,423 | 220,017 | 7,554 | 15,510 |
| 1957 | 3,889,723 | 162,071 | 10,028 | 10,134 |
| 1958 | 5,538,428 | 234,457 | 5,674 | 12,224 |
| 1959 | 15,164,757 | 168,146 | 1,507 | 10,079 |
| 1960 | 14,381,445 | 128,240 | 2,188 | 9,246 |

Source: Vu Tai chinh Ke toan *et al.* 1994: 184.

Instead, the policies issued, particularly those related to the second Three-Year Plan (1958–60), signaled their intensification.

Rot again destroyed a significant portion of the Winter-Spring harvest (1957–8) across the DRV. This was followed by a drought that lasted much of the year, with Hung Yen Province reportedly among the worst affected areas (Quang Tuynh 1962: 5). In the midst of these natural disasters, the Ministry of Architecture and Irrigation held a large conference in Hung Yen with some 2,500 of its cadres in attendance along with high-ranking Party members and selected "labor heroes." Ho Chi Minh opened the July conference and awarded representatives from Van Lam District with an honorary flag in recognition of their mass campaign to "fight drought," while the province's Youth Union received a certificate of achievement as well. Afterward, Ho Chi Minh inspected construction sites in a nearby commune. Such trips – he made three more to Hung Yen that fall – marked renewed support for a massive irrigation scheme, first proposed in 1956 and then designed with the help of Chinese advisors. "Doing this project," Ho Chi Minh stated during an inspection trip to Hung Yen, "will enable [our] prosperity in perpetuity" (SVHTTHH 1995: 62). The scheme, later known as the Bac-Hung-Hai Project, helped achieve this ambitious goal by providing fresh water to the three provinces it eventually irrigated (Bac Ninh, Hung Yen, and Hai Duong), dramatically improving food security in the process (MacLean 2007).

While it was a notable achievement, the decision to build this project also exemplified the broader turn toward technocratic solutions to development "problems." The emphasis on scientific forms of management quickly became a defining feature of the centrally planned economy then taking shape in the DRV, especially in the agricultural sector where the first cohort of technocrats argued that an increase in scale, made possible through the gradual collectivization of the means of production, would result in a concomitant increase in yields. While this model was eventually abandoned, the assumptions that informed it had two important effects on how labor was mobilized and to what ends it was put on the eve of collectivization.

The first was renewed emphasis on peasant self-reliance, which officials in the Ministry of Irrigation announced at a conference in October of 1958, just as the first stage of construction on the Bac-Hung-Hai Project began. The policy shift, commonly known as the "Three Principles" (*ba chinh*), transferred all of the organizational responsibility as well as much of the cost of construction and maintenance of small-scale irrigation works to peasants themselves. The stated goal of this shift was to force rural populations to assume greater responsibility for their own material well-being and thus rely less upon assistance from the Party/state, which would enable its engineers to concentrate on the completion of large-scale systems (Phan Khanh 1997). This message was reinforced with poems, short stories, and easy-to-follow instruction manuals that used hand-drawn diagrams to illustrate how to reinforce dikes, reinforce the earthen walls of canals with woven bamboo, and so on. It also appeared to work.

The Ministry of Labor reported a tremendous increase in local contributions (see Table 2.3), including in Hung Yen Province where peasants sought to connect their fields to the Cau Canal. Eventually completed in late 1960, the canal and its side channels supplied fresh water to the entire province as well as parts of Hai Duong and Bac Ninh. As part of this effort, conscripted peasants in Hung Yen provided 16,198,000 workdays over a three-year period, during which they reportedly dug and dredged 19,309,000 cubic meters of earth to help (re-)build 6,701 large-, medium-, and small-scale irrigation works. When added together, these stretched 3,219 kilometers. Over this same period, peasants in Hung Yen also voluntarily devoted 1,049,000 more workdays to move 1,668,000 cubic meters of earth as part of seasonal campaigns to reinforce existing dikes, sluices, drainage canals, and so on (Quang Tuynh 1962: 10; Quoc Phuong 1964: 13–20). The statistics, assuming they reflect labor actually performed, are astonishing; they also underscore the extent to which the ability to mobilize huge numbers of peasants remained a crucial component of official efforts to quite literally "build socialism" in the countryside during these years.

The second was renewed support for the "mutual assistance teams" (*to doi cong*) among state planners, who asserted that working collectively would raise agricultural yields more rapidly than working individually. The most basic form was known as an "intermittent work exchange group," which mimicked the informal quid pro quo arrangements rural households commonly used during the pre-revolutionary era. Typically, such exchanges were organized around the most labor-intensive activities associated with the agricultural production cycle: plowing, transplanting, weeding, and harvesting crops. These *ad hoc* arrangements were to be replaced with "regular labor exchange groups" that would, in principle, carry out a much wider array of production-related activities on a routine basis throughout the year, which required the semi-collectivization of draft animals, tools, and so on. "Advanced labor exchange groups," the precursor to low-level agricultural cooperatives, were to take this process one step further by introducing "work points" as a means to quantitatively measure each person's labor contributions in addition to the full collectivization of all property (Tran Duc 1994: 75). In theory, each successive form provided a sufficient number of social and material incentives to households participating in them to voluntarily proceed to the next stage of collectivization where the rewards were portrayed to be even larger. For these reasons official histories typically describe the late 1950s as an important transitional moment in which the tier-like organizational structure of the mutual aid teams provided the "foundation" for the shift from private forms of agricultural production to collective ones (MacLean 2005: 133–86).

Such an interpretation is problematic for several reasons. Among other things, it obscures the fact this process did not occur in an orderly or sequential fashion; quite the contrary, as official statistics reveal that total membership in the mutual assistance teams fluctuated dramatically between late 1956, when the land reforms ended, and late 1959, when collectivization officially began. The reasons for these fluctuations are not yet fully understood; but it now seems clear the "Rectification of Errors" campaign was one of them. In the Left Bank Region, for example, the first teams were not formed until after the campaign ended there in late 1957 and, despite the official support for them, participation rates remained low: a mere

*Table 2.4* Total membership in mutual aid teams (all types)

| *Membership* | *End 1955* | *End 1956* | *Mid 1957* | *End 1957* | *End 1958* | *April 1959* | *End 1959* |
|---|---|---|---|---|---|---|---|
| No. of rural households | 153,000 | 190,200 | 72,000 | 100,900 | 244,400 | 249,025 | 97,600 |
| Avg. no. of households/group | 7.1 | 7.1 | n/a | 5.9 | 7.3 | n/a | 10.6 |
| % of rural households | 40 | 50 | 19 | 22 | 66 | 69 | 38 |

Source: Kerkvliet 1999: 83–4.

27 percent (n.a. 1958: 29).[25] However, average rates elsewhere in the DRV, as Table 2.4 indicates, were even lower.

The coercive tactics low-level cadres often used to pressure peasants to join the teams likely did not help matters. Nor did the problems peasants personally encountered once in them, which led many to conclude that the actual costs of collective forms of production outweighed the promised benefits (Kerkvliet 1999: 58–63).

While these interpersonal dynamics undoubtedly played a crucial role, the statistical patterns suggest why the fluctuations in membership rates on the eve of collectivization cannot be reduced to either mistrust arising from previous waves of class struggle or the forms of domination and resistance reportedly found on the mutual aid teams themselves. The broader context also mattered, as the Party/state dramatically reversed its position on the desirability of private property within the space of only a few years. During the land reforms, the redistribution of private property to those with little or none was officially touted as a way to eradicate a number of problems – most obviously, the interlocking forms of exploitation that contributed to chronic hunger, abject poverty, and landlessness in the countryside. However, the "solution" to these problems failed to end them; instead, their sudden and unexpected re-emergence shortly after the land reforms prompted a new series of policy interventions, the mutual assistance teams among them, which were intended to prevent further socio-economic differentiation through the gradual collectivization of the means of production in rural areas. This began with peasant labor, which I previously noted is a form of property in addition to being productive of it, and later expanded to include all arable land, animals, and tools (MacLean 2005: 190–2). Not surprisingly, this reversal on private property generated significant confusion, anxiety, and disillusionment in the countryside because it asked for and, following collectivization, required rural families to place much of their food security in the hands of others.

These problems were further compounded by the heavy and frequently conflicting demands different segments of the Party/state placed upon peasants whose finite labor-time was continually taken up by a seemingly infinite number of mass campaigns. Indeed, when these factors are taken together, the rapid rise and fall of membership rates in these groups not only becomes much clearer, it also takes on broader significance. The redistribution of property, a key feature of the land reforms, dramatically reduced disparities in the average amount different "class fractions" owned (Moise 1983: 208–9) – but only momentarily.

In the Left Bank Region, the disparities that previously existed across the three poorest fractions – former "landless" peasants (1,442 $m^2$), "land poor" peasants (1,440 $m^2$), and "middle" peasants (1,452 $m^2$), respectively (BCHNHX 1958: 7) – virtually disappeared. However, high population densities in the Left Bank Region meant that these amounts – less than one-fifth of a hectare (10,000 $m^2$) – were rarely sufficient for rural families to meet their subsistence needs even under the best of circumstances, much less reliably accumulate food surpluses year after year. Owing to these material constraints, official efforts to build a new society in the countryside ironically contributed to the re-emergence of the very problem the land reforms were thought to have eradicated: rapid class differentiation.

Usury, tenant-farming, and other forms of socio-economic exploitation reappeared shortly after the land reforms were halted in late 1956. At the time, these practices were commonly portrayed in official publications as "vestiges" of feudalism and capitalism that would disappear over time (Tran Phuong 1960). This assessment, while not altogether inaccurate, nonetheless obscures the role the Party/state played in the proliferation of such exploitative practices. The relevant ministries, for example, did not authorize any large-scale programs to provide agricultural extension services or to improve access to formal credit to peasants following the land reforms; so, most peasants continued to farm as they had beforehand and to borrow money informally at high interest rates whenever circumstances required it. Consequently, the mass emulation campaigns, although directed toward a range of official ends, inadvertently placed a tremendous additional burden on rural families. This was because the constant appropriation of one form of property – their labor – as part of these campaigns increased their economic vulnerability, which made the loss of another – their land – far more likely when confronted with a failed harvest, illness, or other untoward event.

Some of those who had to sell part or all of their land to cover debts appear to have become day-laborers for wealthier peasants and contract-workers on construction sites, whereas others clearly opted to pool their meager resources and enter the growing number of experimental cooperatives (n.a. 1989: 29). However, as the table above indicates, the vast majority of rural households appear to have joined and abandoned the mutual aid teams from one season to the next depending on their actual resources and the perceived risks of continuing to labor either "individually" (*lam an ca the*) or "collectively" (*lam an tap the*). For these reasons, most peasants did not experience a gradual or well-coordinated shift from a system where the relations of production were primarily organized around individual property rights to another that was organized around collective ones; instead, rural populations utilized a range of livelihood strategies – a tactic that the diverse array of private, semi-private/semi-collective, and collective property arrangements then still in existence made possible (MacLean 2005: 133–201) – to survive the continual appropriation of their labor-time by representatives of the Party/state for official ends that may or may not have aligned with their own.

The impacts these dynamics had upon the "transition" into state socialism were significant and multi-faceted. Here, I summarize two of them, as they illustrate why existing accounts of this process need revision. First, close attention to the institutional arrangements that emerged between late 1956 and late 1959 to mobilize and to manage large numbers of peasants involved in mass campaigns to (re-)build essential infrastructure led the bundles of rights and obligations associated with the different labor regimes used on them to become increasingly "fuzzy." In other words, official efforts to make volunteer, conscripted, and wage labor more "legible" and thus amenable to bureaucratic administration tended to have the opposite effect (cf. Scott 1998); they did so because other mass campaigns – most notably the land reforms (1953–6) and the "Rectification of Errors" (1956–8) that followed – radically transformed some aspects of life in rural areas, left others intact, and reconfigured still others. Second, since these campaigns frequently overlapped in time and space, the competition for peasant bodies inevitably generated significant confusion and conflict, both "inside" and "outside" the Party/state, in addition to serious labor shortages.

As a consequence, existing accounts of the "transition" into state socialism also need to be rethought since official efforts to "restore" the DRV's economy through the mass mobilization of peasants clearly contributed to the very socio-economic problems the Party/state had set out to eradicate – namely: increased exploitation, hunger, poverty, and landlessness. When these outcomes, which were neither planned nor desired, are taken into account, the Party/state's decision to fully collectivize agricultural production in late 1959 appears to have less to do with historical inevitability than a range of social, political, and economic contradictions, many of which arose from disagreements over the proper meaning, value, and purpose of peasant labor.

## Notes

1 Neither the "Party" nor the "state" can be accurately understood as coherent entities that think or act like people (MacLean 2005: xv–xviii). Nonetheless, I employ the terms here, including their unorthodox combined form (Party/state), as a strategic essentialism to signal instances where their institutional unity can be *rhetorically* presumed to exist.

2 Bo Lao dong, Bao cao cua Uy ban lanh dao cuu te xa hoi Trung uong ve tinh hinh doi nam 1955 (H.s. 1620).

3 In April 1958, this ministry was again divided into two separate ones – the Ministry of Architecture and the Ministry of Irrigation, respectively. To avoid confusion, I will use the Ministry of Agriculture and Irrigation throughout.

4 Bo Thuy loi Kien truc (Van phong), Tap Bao cao cua BTLKT Tong ket 3 nam cong tac thuy loi (1955–1957) phuc vu ke hoach khoi phuc kinh te (22/10/1957–2/11/1957) (H.s. 87, v/v).

5 Bo Lao dong, Bao cao cua Uy ban lanh dao cuu te xa hoi Trung uong ve tinh hinh doi nam 1955 (H.s. 1620).

6 Bao cao tinh hinh cong tac de dieu va thuy nong da thuc hien trong qui I cua Lien khu III (3/4/1956), in Bo thuy loi va Kien Truc (Van phong). Bien ban Hoi nghi kiem diem viec thuc hien ke hoach thuy loi va kien truc trong 3 thang dau nam 1956 (6/4/1956–10/4/1956) (H.s. 28, v/v).

7 Bo Thuy loi Kien truc, 1957, Bao cao Bo Thuy loi Kien truc Phong quan ly cong trinh va Cuc cong trinh thuy loi ve cong tai thuy nong de dieu nam 1956 (H.s. 61, v/v).

8 Bao cao tinh hinh cong tac de dieu va thuy nong da thuc hien trong qui I cua Lien Khu III (3/4/1956), in Bo Thuy loi Kien truc (Van phong), Bien ban Hoi nghi kiem diem viec thuc hien ke hoach thuy loi va kien truc trong 3 thang dau nam 1956 (6/4/1956–10/4/1956) (H.s. 28, v/v).

9 Ibid.

10 Bao cao tong ket dai thuy nong 1956. In Ibid.

11 Bao cao tong ket cong tac chong lut, chong bao nam mua lut nam 1956 so 36/BC Ban chi huy chong lut Hung Yen, in Bo Thuy loi va Kien truc (Quan ly cong trinh), Bao cao cua Ban chi huy chong lut Hung Yen, Hai Duong ve cong tac de dieu, chong lut, bao nam 1956 (28/5/1956–12/12/1956) (H.s. 74, v/v).

12 Bo Thuy loi va Kien truc (Van phong), Bao cao tong ket 3 nam cong tac thuy loi (1955–1957) phuc vu ke hoach khoi phuc kinh te (H.s. 87, v/v).

13 Qui dinh ve cong tac Dang tai cac cong truong (4/1956).

14 Nghi dinh cua Thu tuong Chinh phu 339-TTg, ngay 27 thang 7 nam 1957 ban hanh ban Dieu le tam thoi ve huy dong va su dung dan cong trong thoi ky kien thiet hoa binh.

15 Thong tu cua Bo Lao dong so 17/TT-DC, ngay 12 thang 9 nam 1957 giai thich viec thi hanh ban Dieu le tam thoi ve huy dong va su dung dan cong trong thoi ky kien thiet hoa binh.

16 Thong tu cua lien Bo Lao dong, Tai chinh, Y te, Thuy loi va Kien truc, Giao thong va Buu dien so 18-TT-LB, ngay 23 thang 9 nam 1957 quy dinh chi thiet cac quyen loi cua dan dong da duoc ghi trong Dieu le so 339-TTG, ngay 27 thang 7 nam 1957.

17 In Marxist-inspired social theory, class categories are typically used to describe the domination of one group by another (e.g. the exploitation of the proletariat by the bourgeoisie), whereas class fractions help distinguish small, but important social, cultural, and economic differences within them (e.g. rich, middle, poor, and landless peasants).

18 Nghi quyet cua Ban Thuong vu khu Ta Ngan so 15-NQ, ngay 2 thang 3 nam 1957 ve van de hoan thanh sua dien san va thu thue nong nghiep cua khu Ta Ngan. This problem was not limited to the Left Bank Region. See Chi thi cua Ban Bi thu so 29-CT-TU, ngay 1 thang 6 nam 1957 ve viec ngan chan va giai quyet cac vu thanh chap tai san.

19 Thong tu cua Uy ban Hanh chinh khu Ta Ngan va tai lieu, cong van cua Khu lao dong Ta Ngan ve to chuc va giao duc ve chinh sach dan cong nam 1957 (30/3/1957–18/7/1957) (H.s. 26/413, v/v).

20 Thong tu so 10/LD-NL ty gop y kien v/v huy dong dan cong va giai quyet mot so mac muu ve chinh sach dan cong (10/4/1957), in Thong tu cua Uy ban Hanh chinh khu Ta Ngan va tai lieu, cong van cua khu lao dong Ta Ngan ve to chuc va giao duc ve chinh sach dan cong nam 1957 (30/3/1957–18/7/1957) (H.s. 26/413, v/v).

21 Thong tu so 11/LD-NL Vu cong ty luong thuc va kho thoc cua Bo Tai chinh su dung nhan luc (24/4/1957). Ibid.

22 Uy ban Hanh chinh khu Ta Ngan (khu lao dong), Bao cao cua khu lao dong Ta Ngan ve cong tac kiem tra va mot so kinh nghiem ve cong tac thanh tra nam 1957 (12/7/1957–13/10/1957) (H.s. 32, v/v).

23 Thong tu cua Thu tuong Chinh phu so 350/TTg, ngay 9 thang 7 nam 1958 quy dinh nhiem vu can dan quan trong cong tac giu gin trat tu an ninh, bao ve kinh te va tai san cong cong cua Nha nuoc o nong thon; Chi thi cua Ban Bi thu so 29-CT-TU, ngay 1 thang 6 nam 1957 ve viec ngan chan va giai quyet cac vu thanh chap tai san.

24 Thong tu cua Thu tuong Chinh phu so 495/TTg, ngay 23 thang 10 nam 1957, ve viec han che dong bao o nong thon ra thanh pho.

25 Duoi su lanh dao cua Dang Lao dong Viet Nam. *Nong dan Ta Ngan quyet tam tien manh tren con duong doi cong hop tac (tai lieu hoc tap cua Ban chap hanh nong hoi xa va cac to truong doi cong, nong hoi*) N.A.: Hop tac xa An loat doan ket, 1958.

# 3 Social demolition

## Creative destruction and the production of value in Vietnamese land clearance

*Erik Harms*

### The road to Tay Ninh

The road from Ho Chi Minh City (formerly Saigon) to the Cambodian border post in Tay Ninh passes through Hoc Mon district, an area formerly known for its areca nut and betel leaf gardens, rice fields, vegetable beds, and more recently, for its rapid urbanization, land speculation, and in-between status as part countryside and part city. Built on the tracks of a former branch of the Mandarin Road connecting Saigon with Phnom Penh, it often figures in the contested histories that have played out along its shoulders. During the modernizing days of the Republic of (South) Vietnam in the 1950s and early 1960s, the road served as a link to the outer-city green-belts, where model tobacco and peanut farms were counted on to spur the transformation of industrial agriculture, and where Catholic parishes were designed to thrive as quaint garden communities organized around the Church – pastoral scenes that might encircle Ngo Dinh Diem's troubled Saigon with green fields of calm. Despite these idealized visions, however, the road was also known for the way it led to spaces fraught with the danger of life outside the city, a place where people, in the words of one Hoc Mon resident, "followed the Republic by day and the VC [Viet Cong, Vietnamese Communists] by night."

In the symbolic landscape of those who supported the deposed southern regime, the road is perhaps best known as one of the key arteries along which the Western Column of advancing North Vietnamese troops made their final push into Saigon in the days leading up to April 30, 1975. In those final days, signposts on the road appeared in the news not only as geographic points on a map but as temporal markers of world-historic significance. For some, even today, these place names trumpet the victorious march of advancing revolution; for others they are toponyms of loss, evoking nothing less than the end of a way of life. Tay Ninh . . . Cu Chi . . . Hoc Mon . . . Tan Son Nhat airport . . . Saigon.

If the road once epitomized the destructive and often violent march of troops into Saigon, it now forms one of the central filaments along which an equally destructive, yet ideologically ambiguous, movement edges its way outward from Ho Chi Minh City through the countryside toward the border with Cambodia. The road is a conduit for urbanization, which has reworked the spatial order of settlement patterns, housing, and social life of Hoc Mon. Houses have been demolished, and the road, quite literally, has carved its way toward Tay Ninh by cutting through the front yards, storefronts, and living rooms of those households that live along its edges. This process has fundamentally altered the social space and morphology of life in communities on the peri-urban fringe (Harms 2011). Yet while the physical transformation of space along this road on the outskirts of the city is arguably just as massive as that experienced during the Vietnam War, the ideological meaning of this new form of demolition is less clear, serving the symbolic work of different agendas (Harvey 2003: 26).

The dramatic images of demolition epitomize ideological contests about social change and transformation because they can mean many things at once, and they can be filled with ideological content like an empty linguistic vessel. Demolition is inherently hyperplastic; it is a process imbued with double meanings and contradictory potentialities that allow observers and on-the-ground social actors of various persuasions to attribute widely divergent meanings to otherwise objective and extraordinarily material acts. Like so many acts of socially situated destruction, demolition is linked to productive regeneration at the same time that it highlights exploitative oppression. For some, "destruction after all is a form of creation."[1] For others, destruction literally destroys lifeways. Accounting for the ways Vietnamese contend with the demolition and reorganization of the spaces in which they live requires accounting for this plasticity of meaning. Demolition is an objective fact; what it means is a social construction.

In 2002–3, while conducting fieldwork exploring issues of social change in Hoc Mon, I spent several months walking along the shoulders of this highway, ultimately conducting in-depth interviews with sixty households about their experiences with this road-widening project that was literally cutting its way through their front yards, living rooms, and businesses. As I saw the effects of this process, which appeared so dramatic, transformative, and visibly destructive, I expected to hear complaints and stories of injustice. To be sure, many residents expressed frustration. They described what amounted to the top-down arrogance of project administrators who solicited no input from the local residents, and revealed precious little information about the project itself. Residents had no idea when the project would actually be completed, and had only vague, often contradictory understandings of what the final road would actually look like. How many square meters would they actually lose from the front of their property? Many could only speculate. Or if they could tell me, it was because they had already lost their living room. By the time I arrived on the scene, the project had sliced through the front of houses on one side of the road, but no one knew for sure if it would do the same to the other. They could only tell me how much land they would be forced to give up *after* they had given it up. Would there be a concrete barrier dividing lanes of traffic? No one knew for sure; that is, until a concrete barrier appeared. What would the final elevation of the road be after grading, paving, and installing the drainage system? Everyone insisted they must wait and see. They would only know for sure when it was finished. And when it was finished, it was about six inches higher than many people had expected, causing terrible water runoff problems for those who had rebuilt their houses lower to the ground than they otherwise might have done had they been well informed of project plans.

As people recounted these stories, I expected them to express anger. Instead, they displayed remarkable patience and acceptance. In many ways, they described the process like the unfolding of fate. Optimistic, they hoped for a good fate, and most of them insisted that they couldn't wait for the road to be finished. For the most part, despite my expectations, I heard stories that articulated hopes and dreams about what the new road might bring. Hoc Mon, they explained, would be closer to the city. There would be less dust. They could use the compensation payments to build two-story houses they could not otherwise afford to build. The area would become more "civilized" (*van minh*). The more we talked, the more I had to conclude that the people I had interviewed seemed to think they were getting a fair return for what they were sacrificing. As one man put it memorably, "How can you have development without suffering?"

At the time, I found this lack of anger – this willingness to suffer for development – difficult to reconcile with critical anthropological perspectives on development. The literature on Vietnamese notions of land, especially within the southern regions, had further led me to expect that any state incursions into what people considered their land would be met with stiff resistance. Comparing the reactions and responses of my friends in Hoc Mon with those documented in other cases throughout Vietnam indicates that the question of land clearance and compensation is not fixed or stable, and that the experiences faced by different residents in different contexts are deeply tied to the specific contours of particular cases. I attempt here to put the lack of anger I encountered in Hoc Mon in comparative perspective by presenting a preliminary sketch of the social relationships produced by the rampant demolition occurring throughout contemporary Vietnam. While these issues are often politically charged, I attempt to step back from them in order to describe some of the nuances and negotiations that emerge in the process of clearing land for development. My aim here is not so much to assign blame or identify a discrete "villain" as to outline the way in which this very process of social reorganization transforms the conditions within which people understand their relationship to land, to other people in society, and to the state that mediates these relationships.

## Land clearance as "social demolition"

Comparison with other cases reveals that demolition, for better or for worse, sets in motion a process through which land must be assigned a literal monetary value. Once these values appear as part of the social context, they eventually become part of the language through which displaced residents can quantify (and, quite literally, evaluate) the kinds of moral relationships demolition itself brings into focus. In a very real sense, demolition contributes to the wholesale transformation of land into what Polanyi has rightly called a "fictitious commodity" (Polanyi 1944: 70). But while Polanyi has shown how economy and society became wholly disembedded from each other with the rise of the market economy in Euro-American contexts, the transformation in Vietnam appears to be less an example of a "Great transformation" than an example of a "revaluation" of how moral claims about justice can be articulated through the mediation of money. While demolition produces a new idiom of monetary value through which residents articulate moral relations to property, these moral relations remain understood in terms of an enduring concept of "fairness" or "reasonableness" (*su hop ly*) which engages people in deeply social relations of mutual obligation.

When state land clearance teams initiate the process of appropriation, demolition, and later compensation, they also initiate the process whereby moral relationships between people become translated into quantifiable idioms of value. When houses are demolished and land is appropriated, the reciprocal exchange of rights and obligations between people becomes translated into a reciprocal exchange of monetized values: a sum of money is exchanged for its equivalent value in land. In this process, demolition converts moral values into money values. In contrast to Western media reports that describe land clearance in Vietnam solely in terms of a communist state violating the proprietary rights of individual citizens, demolition and land compensation practices actually participate in the process through which land is valued as a commodity. Demolishing homes requires assessing them. Tearing them down makes them valuable.[2]

Land-use rights in Vietnam increasingly operate like commodities which can be bought and sold. In Vietnam, this "fictitious commodity" is doubly fictional, because people can buy and sell not actual land, but only the "land-use rights." The material effects of this fiction have not only been documented by a wide literature,[3] but are immediately recognizable throughout the country. Entire sections of newspapers are dedicated to real estate advertisements, glossy real estate magazines are available for sale nearly everywhere, and real estate service centers have appeared throughout Vietnamese cities as well as on the urban periphery and in the countryside. While this is certainly an important change, I argue that instead of wholly transforming the moral relations people ascribe to land, the ascription of monetary value to land initiated by demolition allows various social actors to quantify what are otherwise more nebulous, socially situated moral frameworks for debating and contesting justice and fairness. The demolition of houses continues to be judged primarily in moral terms, but money helps quantify morality in new ways. Even more importantly – and this is what might be considered a unique aspect of late socialist marketization guided by bureaucratic central planning – it is the very process of state-led demolition that produces this monetization of moral relations. Over time, this value, which was itself created from the rubble of destruction, becomes the most effective means of challenging the process of destruction itself. With value as a guiding idiom that helps articulate justice and fairness, it becomes a new quantifiable paradigm through which Vietnamese citizens articulate their demands toward the government that claims to represent them.

Land clearance and the demolition associated with infrastructure development represent a form of "social demolition." I define social demolition in an inclusive anthropological spirit that includes all forms of purposeful, meaningful acts of socially situated destruction, as well as the social response to destructive activity. The meaning of destruction itself is always "socially situated"; meaning does not emerge from the act of destruction alone but from the contested social interpretations of the event. The meaning is larger than the act, and this meaning emerges out of social life. The meaning of destruction, then, is an interpretation situated within fields of power, symbolism, and socio-economic struggle. It does not play out in binary relations but involves negotiation among a wide range of actors with shifting positionalities, sometimes cross-cutting and sometimes interwoven agendas.

In a revealing study of land conflicts in Tu Son district, in the Red River Delta province of Bac Ninh, the anthropologist Nguyen Van Suu notes the need for subtlety and caution in studies concerned with changing patterns of land use in Vietnam. He writes that:

> Inequality in land access among various parties and institutions takes various forms, has varying degrees of impact, and is viewed differently by different parties. Some villagers simply accept it without any protest, especially when the unfairness of it all is of a minor extent. In other cases, it may stir up discontent and lead to heated arguments between the parties or institutions involved.
>
> (Nguyen Van Suu 2004: 291–2)

Suu notes the importance of a subjective interpretation of "unfairness" and positional relations of advantage and disadvantage. Similar conceptions operate in the urban context. For example, David Koh shows that there is much flexibility on the ward level in Hanoi, where ward officials "mediate" between official pronouncements and policies and the everyday urban level. Actual practices are tempered by interpersonal negotiations, social relations, locally articulated moral considerations, and "the socioeconomic situation in general and the housing situation in particular" (Koh 2006: 239). All of these considerations are mobilized by local officials in order to facilitate "fairness." Demolition in these contexts thus corresponds to what I call "social demolition" because the acts quite literally produce new social actions mobilized around socially constructed idioms of "fairness." While wrecking crews may destroy the built environment, the response to this destruction proves fruitful as a site for analyzing how people "socially construct" and "socially produce" their conception of fairness out of the rubble that remains (Low 1996; Lefebvre 1991).

Labeling this "social demolition" does not mean, however, that the production of meaning is always harmonious, or that all social actors agree with the world that demolition produces. Interpretations about what demolition means are never stable. One person's socially acceptable destruction is another person's threat. In what follows, I draw on a range of newspaper accounts in order to draw a preliminary sketch of the dynamic and complex moral claims that emerge in cases where Vietnamese citizens are called upon to release their land to the state for various infrastructure projects, most often roads, new urban zones, and industrial processing zones.

## Site clearance (*giai toa*) in the Vietnamese media

Over the past decade or so, there have been literally thousands of newspaper articles written about the issue of "site clearance," called "*giai toa*" in Vietnamese. Translated directly, *giai toa* means "to reduce" or "to relieve," and it can be used in the course of discussing the resolution of a disagreement, as in "we have reduced some of our disagreements and are ready to sign the contract."[4] In Vietnamese Buddhism, furthermore, the term appears in the concept of releasing the practitioner from unjust suffering (*giai toa oan uc*) (HT. Thich Tri Quang 2008). However, as commonly used in urban development contexts, *giai toa* can also be a cause of suffering. In the case of site clearance, *giai toa* implies destruction, for the object of "reduction" is the built environment itself. In urban development, then, *giai toa* literally means to reduce the amount of built environment blocking the passage of a roadway or other large development or infrastructure project. And the only way to reduce the amount of built environment is to destroy it, demolish it, tear it down, run it over with bulldozers.

Vietnamese newspaper stories about *giai toa*, like the meanings of the term itself, are full of dynamism and differences, at times representing clear cases of suffering and injustice and at other times representing creativity, local level maneuvering, and even occasional forms of support and cooperation for land clearance projects. The lines of conflict are sometimes quite clear and sometimes ambiguous, and they require nuanced conceptions about the relationship between the people and the Party, as well as the relationship between the demands of capital and the socialist state. While the pathways of power may seem clear in some cases, power more often seems to move along complex networks that blur the boundaries among a wide range of actors with seemingly divergent ideological agendas.

While the Vietnamese state-run media is strictly regulated by the Communist Party, it has been surprisingly proactive in detailing examples of popular suffering in the face of *giai toa*. Vietnamese newspaper stories of *giai toa* reveal exploitation and contestation at all levels of society – everywhere from the acts of corrupt cadres and unscrupulous land speculators, to the demands of foreign investors and the machinations of local citizens. As the following examples show, while the contested issues are arguably all connected to issues of private property, the relations expressed are more about "fairness" within social interactions than they are about property rights alone. This "fairness," while always present in the framing of these stories, becomes most visible when draped in the language of value.

In August 2006, for example, *Thanh Nien* newspaper published a story detailing the struggles of close to one thousand households "pushed out into the streets because of *giai toa*" and ineffective resettlement arrangements associated with the building of a National University complex in neighborhood number 6, Linh Trung Ward, Thu Duc district (a rapidly urbanizing suburb of Ho Chi Minh City). According to the article, all of the displaced residents were promised the chance to purchase homes in a housing development. In reality, there was no resettlement space reserved for them at all. To give the article a human face, the piece tells the heart-rending story of an elderly couple who in 2001 had been pushed out of a previous home in district 1. They went on to buy the land for their current house with compensation payments, spent most of their savings rebuilding a new home, and then found themselves about to be displaced again:

> In his crumbling home, 84-year-old uncle [*bac*] Nguyen Thanh Tuy lies curled up in a hammock. With a pair of trembling hands, uncle Tuy's wife is attaching nylon liners inside a rattan basket with painful difficulty. Before 2000, uncle's family lived in Nguyen Thai Binh ward, district 1. In 2001, their home suffered from demolition (*bi giai toa*). With almost 60 million *dong* in compensation payments, uncle's whole family went to find a new place to live . . . uncle bought a $4 \times 14$ m home . . . the house wasn't much of a house, so they also used up all of the back payments for his honorable service to pay for repair work. Now, uncle Tuy and his wife and youngest child all live by the handicraft art of weaving rattan baskets. "If he's healthy then we make about 30 thousand *dong* a day, and when he's sick we only make about 20 thousand. His urinary tract infection and blood pressure continues and will likely defeat him. If we continue suffering from *giai toa* then we'll only have water and will have to beg to eat," uncle Tuy's wife confided. Uncle Tuy is one of close to 1,000 households in neighborhood 6 that lies in the area slated for complete demolition (they are only offered compensation according to agricultural land prices of 150,000 *dong* per $m^2$) because all of neighborhood 6 is part of the planned National University Zone.
>
> (Hoai Nam: 2006)

The article goes on to describe how most of the householders in the area didn't have proper land-use right papers, emphasizing that they were mostly the homes of marginalized laborers. While it was true that many of the houses were built illegally, the article added that the local authorities never prohibited people building there. Indeed, despite the impending demolition, the article noted with alarm that authorities still let people build new homes in the area.

In a similar genre, a 2004 story from *Tuoi Tre* offered a searing and direct critique of the manipulation and exploitation that took place in Trang Bang, as the Linh Trung 3 Industrial Zone was acquiring land near the district seat of Cu Chi (a largely agricultural suburb of Ho Chi Minh City). According to the article, a great number of displaced families received absurdly low compensation payments and were struggling to make ends meet, with little sympathy from local authorities. In addition to detailing the inequities and low levels of compensation, the journalist illustrated the piece with the story of a handicapped man displaced from his property and never compensated, as well as the calamitous story of a 94-year-old man who was displaced twice in one year (Nguyen Huy Cuong 2004).

> The family of great-grandfather [*cu*] Le Van Kich, who is over 90 years old, lives in Suoi Sau hamlet. In the first phase great-grandfather grudgingly

> turned over half a hectare of land to the Industrial Zone, within which there was his ancestral land and a home worth 30 taels of gold, for which he received . . . 160 million *dong* (looks like there was no money for the land). He then moved to another plot of land and built a home in which to live and to . . . die (his wife is also over 85 years old). When he bought the land he sent his son up to the commune in order to inquire, and the commune agreed to the purchase and issued the proper land-use right certificate. On the day celebrating the new home, at 94 years old, great-grandfather held a housewarming party, and while many commune cadres came to share the happiness, only one month later he suffered from *giai toa* again. The compensation price this time was just like the previous time: equal to 50% of the land value and the money the family had invested.
>
> (Ibid.)

In both of these stories, land values and compensation levels quantify, but do not wholly transform, a moral claim about undue suffering; assertions of injustice are expressed in quantifiable sums. Both stories employ kinship terms that establish a familial relationship with vulnerable uncles, aunts, and great-grandparents who, while named, remain otherwise stylized as universal, depoliticized images of "elders." To Vietnamese readers, these elderly victims of insensitive developers and irresponsible cadres could be anyone's uncles and grandparents. The focus on land values enters not as the root claim, but rather as a quantifiable form of evidence that puts a number on the injustice, but only means something when cast against the moral claim of the human story.

In 2005, several articles appeared in multiple papers reporting on discontent among residents affected by the East–West highway project in Ho Chi Minh City. According to *Thanh Nien*, the issue largely boiled down to disagreements about the level of compensation (Hoang Tao 2005). But again, the focus on property value becomes a medium through which to express a broader meaningful framework of social relationships. Importantly, the families in the site clearance area for the project are described as supporting the leadership of the government, and they claim to appreciate efforts to guide infrastructure development and modernize the roadway. However, the residents were unhappy with the actions of the office carrying out the project, which failed to attend to the specifics of their own cases and the hardships they would endure. In the case of this project, residents voiced three major concerns: first, the land was going to be compensated at the value of agricultural land, but the highway project itself was driving up land values, meaning that they would not be able to find new places to live at those levels of compensation. Second, they complained that the amount of money promised in compensation discussions and approved by the People's Committee differed from what they received in actual fact. And third, they claimed that the compensation process ignored the fact that many people had built homes and gardens on their land, and they were not being compensated for the infrastructure costs they had invested in improving the land. Despite these grievances, the authorities knocked down several homes before solving disagreements about compensation. In examples like this, compensation values are of course quite important. But the primary moral claim of injustice turns on the notion that negotiated compromises had been reneged upon, and that, despite the way residents expressed their support for generalized notions of development and modernization, they were asked to make a sacrifice without adequate concern for their fate. The guiding theme is that this situation is unfair, it "is not sensible" (*hop ly*).

The question of sensibility, fairness, and the equitable application of regulations emerges quite clearly as a common theme. In 2007, another article detailed the arbitrary decisions made by the local district 3 authorities regulating compensation and issuing building permits along the Nhieu Loc–Thi Nghe canal in Ho Chi Minh City. While some residents complied with the letter of the law by relinquishing property and moving to other areas of the city, other residents appear to have been granted exceptions. The authorities were not very systematic and they granted building permissions arbitrarily, inconsistently, and unfairly. While some households were arbitrarily denied building permits, others were allowed to build three-story homes, complete with second- and third-floor balconies jutting illegally out over the street. In conclusion, the piece exclaimed: "those who follow the law suffer" (Huy Thinh 2007).

This theme of citizens suffering from the selective application of the law is not isolated. Another article cites the revised land law of 2003 and subsequent decisions that clearly stipulate that there must be some consensus on the land settlement prices before a development project can officially proceed. Despite this, many projects get pushed through even though the locals have not yet agreed to the terms of compensation payments. The article further describes how local officials elide blame by subcontracting the work of site clearance. In District 9, it explains, officials responsible for negotiating compensation terms for a university project "rented" officials from a separate land compensation committee and deflected inquiries and complaints about the process onto their hired hands (Nhom PV Chinh tri – xa hoi 2004). Using rented officials allowed development officials to evade the legal ramifications of the land law and severed the classic moral relationship between the people and their representatives through which articulations of rights and responsibilities should be negotiated.

Many of these examples imply top-down machinations of corrupt officials selectively applying the law to their own benefit. But the media depicts stubbornness at all levels, among both authorities and everyday citizens. At a project intended to build a traffic flyover in Tan Tao (near an important Industrial Zone), for example, both the authorities and the local residents are seen as equally responsible for the long drawn-out and effectively stalled site clearance, which halted the project for more than three years, causing suffering both to local residents left in limbo and to project managers forced to let machinery lay unused. At the root lay complex negotiations about the real value of land. Residents refused to move because they had only been offered compensation at rates based on agricultural land despite the rapid urbanization of the area (Ngoc An 2007). The moral relationship between rights and responsibilities is not only undermined by local residents holding out for higher payments, but can be violated by top-down agents who fail to account for changing circumstances. Unfairness cuts in many directions.

Everyday citizens are not released from blame. Some have been exposed for building unlivable shacks on land in order to claim compensation in advance of land-clearance projects and others have been caught constructing fake additions to their homes in order to increase the square footage of property being valued. In one particularly memorable example, an entire neighborhood of residents in Danang rushed to hire local artists to "decorate" their homes and create impromptu landscaping features and *feng shui* elements before the land compensation teams came to value the land. Enterprising local residents discovered that the official land compensation criteria offered special compensation for architectural flourishes and home improvements, so they rushed to add such elements to their homes in order to receive greater benefits (Kim Em and Dang Nam 2004).

If media reports succeed in showing how creative everyday people can be in their deceptions, they also convincingly show the cadres as quite creative too, especially when spurred on by unscrupulous land developers. In 2007, for example, The People's Committee Chair and a member of the land compensation committee in An Phu ward of Ho Chi Minh City's district 2 were both arrested for facilitating the placement of fake tombstones on land slated for clearance. They sought to illegally gain higher land compensation payments by exploiting a clause that provided special compensation on cemetery land. The officials, working in conjunction with enterprising con-men, signed verification papers on hundreds of dossiers associated with empty "graves." The police confiscated 196 falsified dossiers and 600 million *dong* that had been compensated on false pretenses (*Sai Gon Giai Phong* 2007).

While it may appear that these issues all boil down to a simple question of fights over land valuation, other articles indicate that while money certainly plays a role, other factors are also important. For example, one piece describes a group of families who voluntarily contributed parts of their land to public works projects that would benefit their community. In Ho Chi Minh City's Tan Phu district, 85 families on either side of the Tay Son Road widening project offered up land and "self-demolished" (*tu giai toa*) property worth 11.1 billion *dong* (Ngoc An 2006). Another article celebrates Ho Chi Minh City's Phu Nhuan district as the leader in a movement in which residents voluntarily offer land (*hien dat*) in order to widen roads. From 2003 until 2009 people in the various wards in the district have offered close to 11,300 $m^2$ of land which could be valued at several hundred billion *dong* in order to carry out 50 road-widening projects. By the beginning of 2009, 42 of those projects had been completed and put into use. In describing these types of negotiations, the authors again cite land values as a form of evidence for the sacrifice local residents have made. But ultimately, the descriptions paint a picture of a moral relationship of mutual benefit. In the Phu Nhuan case, residents explained to the journalist that voluntarily offering land was quite difficult to imagine doing in the beginning because people both worried about being exploited and also lacked confidence in the capacity of authorities to successfully complete the projects (Minh Nam 2009). Ultimately, however, a resident explained that making such a sacrifice benefited everyone involved:

> When people "self-giai toa" so that the government can make more spacious roads, they actually benefit more. New roads not only raise land and home values, but lead to the development of service businesses and improving people's living standards; so everyone is in agreement.
>
> (Mai Khanh 2004)

Implicit here is a reconceptualization of land and home value as an index of the just moral exchange of sacrifices and benefits between the people and the government rather than as an end in itself. The question of value is subordinated to the symbiotic relationship in which "everyone is in agreement." Nevertheless citing land values provides quantifiable evidence that a just relationship can be achieved when local residents relinquish land rights and the government lives up to its promises by improving living standards.

As these examples show, the Vietnamese media rearticulates simple economic considerations into a moral framework outlining a vision of rights and responsibilities. While certainly recognizing the emergence of land as a commodity that can be exchanged for money, this construction of what demolition *means* subordinates value to a more broadly conceived framework of understanding an idealized notion of social relations. Critical articles detail violations of this moral relation on all levels of society. Articles have exposed project developers who ignore legal stipulations designed to adequately compensate displaced residents (TNO 2005). They have revealed a general failure of government policies and officials to account for the "psychological effects" of displacement (Quoc Thanh 2004), and have shown the negative effects of delayed or incomplete compensation and the failure to provide displaced residents with alternative housing options (TR 2004; Doan Trang 2005; TNO 2005; Viet Bao 2005). Other pieces have called for policies to improve the "post giai toa" circumstances of residents by developing worker training programs, job placement services, and allowing residents to stay on their land longer (Thanh Nien 2006). And more generally, newspaper articles take great delight in revealing some rather extraordinary and creative acts of deception put on by social actors who seem to come from all levels of society. Demolition, as these articles show through their wide range of examples, is eminently social, irreducible to simplistic binaries of the good people versus the bad government.

## Conclusion: Creative destruction and the social products of demolition

In revealing the complex social processes embedded in acts of demolition, stories of *giai toa* take on a productive quality. They quite literally produce an idealized moral framework for re-conceptualizing the role land disputes play in articulating a fair and just relationship between social agents at all levels of society. This newly conceived relationship transcends binary frameworks by focusing on the intricacies of individual cases and revealing how contests over fairness involve a wide swath of social actors at all levels of social life. The state, we learn, is not always diametrically opposed to the diversity of interests that make up society, and the state itself is a more complex network of actors than we often imagine. This is precisely the point that Gillespie makes in his contribution to this volume, showing that courts involved in Hanoi property disputes employ situational justice, emphasizing "reasonableness" (*hop ly*) in making decisions. Annette Kim (2008) further notes that the Party has demonstrated a willingness to deal with disputes in ways that take account of local contexts, sending legal teams around the country in order to settle controversial claims and to minimize "greediness." This more complex understanding of social relations not only incorporates emergent relations of land as a fictitious commodity with real economic qualities and tangible effects on livelihoods; it also amounts to a model for broadly construed notions of rights and responsibilities that are being refashioned in ways that might accommodate the relationship between market imperatives and collective social goals. Of course, however, just as this moral framework can cast a skeptical light on land-speculators, developers, and corrupt local level cadres, it also poses a challenge to the state to live up to its role as a just sovereign within this moral order. It is in this role that the Vietnamese media finds itself most carefully muzzled, and where the work of foreign journalists and outside commentators plays a key role. As Bill Hayton and Ken MacLean have shown in their important work on the PMU 18 corruption scandal, the Party can quickly pull out the censor's knife when media reports expose its own complicity in unjust practices, high-level corruption, gambling, and land-speculation (Hayton 2010; MacLean 2009).

Nevertheless, while the state has been wary of its own journalists when they challenge its moral legitimacy, the socialist state actually has much to gain from journalistic accounts that draw upon a moral framework such as this. For in doing so, these stories craft a larger argument for the legitimacy of an accountable government that can steward the process of development, transcending the machinations of individuals in order to consider the collective interests of society as a whole. Indeed, while many residents have clearly protested state intervention, there are many others who willingly call on the state to guide the process. Several articles describing the widening of Ho Chi Minh City's Nam Ky Khoi Nghia–Nguyen Van Troi street, for example, have described the conflicts involved, highlighted arguments over compensation, and explored the difficulty faced by many residents who were forced out of their houses, apartments, and businesses (Duc Trung 2004; Thanh Tong 2004; Vo Huong 2005). But again, the conflict is not strictly a binary contest between the state and the people. Some people in the area voiced a desire for *more* state intervention:

> Ms Lan, a building engineer whose home suffered from *giai toa*, said that she understood that the City shouldn't force households to build in a particular way, but, for the collective good, still thinks the City should quickly devise some concrete guidelines about standards and style. That would make the area and the city beautiful. While waiting for the city to study the issue they

> should urge the district authorities, the architect and planning office, and the various ward-level people's committees to come together and issue collective guidelines so the people know how they should build their homes in such a way that doesn't spoil the "face of the city."
>
> (Kien Cuong 2009)

What constitutes fairness can often depend on who you speak to. For someone like Ms Lan in this example, government intervention is a price worth paying if it will contribute to developing a beautiful "face" to the city, and regularizing the architectural style on the street where she lives. Of course, this is a steep price to pay for some of the less fortunate residents who were displaced by the project. The conflict here is not simply one between the people and the party but also between different residents themselves.

Ms Lan, of course, is probably concerned not only with beauty but with property value. In cases of *giai toa*, the conceptualization of land-use rights as a commodity with values dictated by the market plays an increasingly important role in outlining the parameters of what constitutes fairness. While value and price are not the only criteria for assessing fairness or moral rectitude, land values do enter the description of contests over *giai toa* as one of many lines of evidence used to illustrate the moral dilemmas at hand. References to land values support more generalized descriptions of displacement or social upheaval by enumerating otherwise complex social relations and questions of livelihood.

The role land values play in making moral judgments, however, is itself in flux because the process of *giai toa* itself contributes to the production of land value. In important ways, land only acquires monetary value when it is brought into circulation and exchange, and the demolition of the built environment actually initiates the very process that forces land into exchange. It "releases" value otherwise stored in land and housing. When one sits on a piece of land or lives in a house, property value remains only a kind of *potential* value. It is only when one confronts the need to transfer it that the value embedded in a house sitting on land becomes realized. In this way, state-led infrastructure projects themselves contribute to the process in which land becomes construed as a commodity; land commodification is produced by the act of demolition itself. The latent value potentially present in parcels of land, much like the value of "blighted" American neighborhoods slated for renewal, is produced and intensified precisely when it faces destruction. Social demolition releases latent value in things, brings them into circulation and makes them part of an eminently social landscape of moral contest and exchange. Once released, these values become a key factor in moral debates about fairness and social justice.

Let me conclude by returning to the road to Tay Ninh. When I was in Hoc Mon interviewing residents along the side of the highway, this process of attributing value to land was undergoing a transformation that was itself set in motion by the expansion of the road. At the beginning of the project, people primarily conceived of their land in abstract moral terms that subordinated the value of individual plots to a larger goal of developing their area on the margin of the city. They were willing to subordinate their individual interests to the notion that they were making a fair exchange by contributing to a larger infrastructure project that would hopefully benefit everyone in the community. But the process of evaluating the terms of this moral relationship is not fixed, precisely because the highway has itself brought new meanings to land. While it was being built, people willingly subordinated individual questions of value to larger hopes for what the project might bring. And in many ways, this was itself a wise economic decision as much as a moral one. For the value of land in Hoc Mon is now much greater than it was before the road cut through, and the area is now a prime site for real estate speculation and property development. Were they asked to *giai toa* today, however, the story would likely be quite different. Social demolition on the margins of the city produces a whole new landscape of value that has emerged from the rubble of destruction itself. If it is increasingly true that the monetary value of land increasingly figures into how people judge the moral values of fairness, then another thing must be true as well: Demolition, in producing value, has also produced the conditions for its own critique. Perhaps there's a value to that.

## Notes

1 The phrasing is Graham Greene's (1967), but the idea evokes, wittingly or unwittingly, Schumpeter, who most clearly described how the constant reinvention of capitalism "incessantly revolutionizes the economic structure *from within*, incessantly destroying the old one, incessantly creating a new one. This process of Creative Destruction is the essential fact about capitalism" (Schumpeter 1976 [1942]: 81).

2 This process of valuation in the face of demolition parallels the process of determining "replacement value" in the United States. After a natural disaster, for example, insurance companies negotiating with homeowners must bring in an assessor to determine the value of the property.

3 The literature on changes to Vietnamese property rights and the Land Law is extensive. For a useful and accurate summary of key developments, see Quy-Toan Do and Iyer (2008: 534–39).

4 This illustration is actually a direct quote from a newspaper article describing the contract negotiations of the Vietnamese national soccer coach and the national soccer association (Thanh Nien 2001).

# Part II

# Property rights and property disputes

# 4 Legal rights to resources versus forest access in the Vietnamese uplands

*To Xuan Phuc*[1]

Recent decades have witnessed the introduction of devolution[2] projects throughout the world.[3] The premise of devolution policies is resource efficiency, equity, and responsiveness of local bureaucracies to citizens' demands for resources.[4] This paper examines the impacts of forest devolution on forest access and control in Ban Yen village, Da Bac district, in the upland province of Hoa Binh. Through an examination of timber logging and swidden cultivation in this village, the paper shows that the implementation of forest devolution, while it embraces the notion of clearly defined rights, fails to capture the local complexities of forest practices.

## Property relations in postsocialist countries

Considered the primary means to achieve equity, sustainability, and efficiency in resource governance,[5] devolution is premised on the assumption that centralized resource control fails to capture local interests, leading to forest depletion. As a consequence, it is believed, transferring property rights to resources to individuals and securing these private rights on a long-term basis will provide an incentive for local people to protect the resources. De Soto contends that the formalization of property rights to resources and the granting of these rights to the poor ought to be the foundation of efforts to help alleviate poverty.[6] This idea has been widely received, particularly by donor agencies and neoliberal governments.[7] Similarly, the World Bank states that among the most crucial factors in improving the livelihood of the poor is the granting of clearly defined rights and the assurance that such rights will be secured and marketed through a sound land market.[8] Landholders with individual rights to the land are encouraged to invest in their resources, contributing to the stabilization of resources, improvement of incomes and increased land productivity.[9] However, there is evidence that forest devolution, which often embraces the notion of private property, oversimplifies the complexities of resource use and practices on the ground.

Postsocialist property studies have highlighted the fact that the newly established individual rights are embedded in a larger socio-political and cultural context.[10] Exercising such rights in the absence of "routinized rules and crystallized practices" is extremely difficult.[11] Hann observes that in Bulgaria "There are many persons and families . . . for whom the current rhetoric about widening choice and extending property rights must seem a sick joke."[12] Normally, exclusive individual ownership rights are constituted within an environment of complex social relations, policies, and social actors. "These relationships shape what actors are able to do with property, modifying the 'rights' to which they may be entitled and the 'obligation' to which they can be held."[13] Thus, receiving property rights has not done much for people who, owing to many constraints, are unable to transform these into benefits.[14] These constraints include households' access to market and capital,[15] local power structures,[16] and low market resource values.[17] Thus, much more than rights determine the benefit derived from the land; the "cultural system, a set of social relations, and an organization of power" also plays a crucial role.[18] In postsocialist countries, property systems after the reform are often characterized by hybridity, including both public and private forms.[19] The complexities of property systems in postsocialist countries thus suggest that the neoliberal notion of individual ownership of resources is too narrowly defined and fails to capture the complexities of resource practices on the ground.

Benda-Beckmann and Benda-Beckmann (1999) propose an analytical framework to study property that better captures the complexities of property relations.[20] This framework emphasizes different layers of social organization in which property rights are exercised, the multi-functions of property, and the complex of property entities and property objects. Property relationships include property holders, objects, sets of rights and duties associated with the object(s) each holder may hold, and the temporal and spatial dimensions of these rights and duties. These rights and duties are manifested differently at the level of cultural ideas and ideologies and in legal regulations and institutional frameworks, reflecting the different functions (economic, socio-political and cultural) of property. These functions are manifested in different sets of rights, including rights of use (encompassing access and withdrawal rights) and decision-making (management, exclusion, and alienation). In other words, rights are defined differently on the ground than they are in the assumptions underlying the state's policy frameworks. As a result, conflicts over property may emerge within one layer or between different layers of society. Following the framework outlined by Benda-Beckmann and Benda-Beckmann, this paper examines how property relationships are manifested differently at different levels in Ban Yen village and how these discrepancies result in various forms of tension on the ground and how individual rights constituted by forest devolution are embedded in socio-political contexts.

The idea of transferring property rights to land to local populations dates back to 1993 when the government passed a new Land Law. The Land Law mandates that the state allocate agricultural and forest land to individual households for long-term use (twenty years for agricultural land and fifty years for forestland). According to the law, a bundle of rights, including rights to exchange, transfer, lease, inherit, and mortgage, are ascribed to a certain piece of land and given to individual households. When the Land Law was passed, land use certificates (LUCs) were issued by the government and granted to the landholders to guarantee their legal claims to the land. The government envisioned that giving land to individual households and granting them clearly defined rights to the land as well as securing these rights for long-term use would encourage households to invest in resources in a more productive and sustainable manner, thus improving their livelihood while also improving forest conditions. The forestland allocation process was undertaken at a vigorous pace after the government's issuance of Decree 02 in 1994 which guided the allocation of forestland at the local level. By July 2007, more than eight million hectares of forestland were allocated to 1.1 million landholders.[21]

The diverse and sometimes contradictory outcomes of forest devolution, particularly the impact it has had on local livelihoods and forest conditions, have been documented. Some have highlighted the positive impact of devolution on local livelihood, including a reduction in the incidence of poverty and an increase of forest cover.[22] Others have pointed out that improvements in local livelihood and the increase in forest cover are not directly attributable to forest devolution. Instead, they argue that thriving commodity markets in agricultural products, particularly maize in the uplands, are responsible for these changes (Sikor 2001).[23] Other studies have demonstrated the complex outcomes of devolution, highlighting the fact that devolution benefits some while it marginalizes others.[24]

The devolution policy was implemented in a context where different bases for claims governing the same type of resources co-existed. On the ground, forest access and control are determined by a mixture of devolution and customary village rules which are conditioned by larger processes of socio-economic change at the national level. In this context, in Ban Yen, different actors selected the bases that best suited them in justifying their activities, triggering resource competition and conflicts.

## Ban Yen village

The village of Ban Yen was formed in 1963 when two smaller Dao (Yao)[25] villages inhabited primarily by swidden cultivators were merged. In 2004, it had a population of about 250, for a total of 50 households. When the village was established, the district authorities gave its inhabitants 1.8 ha of paddy land as inducement to settle there. This was the time the villagers first learned to cultivate paddy rice. From 1963 to 1988, Ban Yen experienced collectivization and villagers worked on swidden land and paddy land collectively. Collective farming was not productive, however, forcing the villagers to work their own land in addition to the cooperative's land. Villagers constructed their own terraces for wet rice cultivation and worked their own swidden fields in the forest. As the paddy land was very small, villagers relied primarily on swidden cultivation for their livelihood. During this period, forests within the district were controlled by the Tu Ly Forest Enterprise which was subject to the Department of Agriculture and Forestry of Hoa Binh province. In order to practice swidden in the forest cooperative, cadres had to seek permission from the enterprise. However, Tu Ly's management of the forest was very loose, so villagers were free to practice swidden wherever it was convenient. When the cooperative broke up in 1988, the collective swidden land was abandoned and became available to households. However, the villagers did not want to take it up, preferring to expand their own swidden plots to which they had a strong attachment. The collective's paddy land, which was much more productive than the swidden land, was distributed among the households according to each household's labor resources.

In 1991, the government decided to restructure the country's forestry sector; as a result the Tu Ly enterprise shifted from an extractive organization to one focused on forest production. Control over the forest no longer lay with the enterprise; instead it shifted to the district's department of forest protection. In 1995, the district authorities implemented forest devolution; under this policy, a total of 35 households in Ban Yen received 529.7 ha of forestland. In principle, households established after the allocation were excluded from obtaining land. In 1997, the district authorities issued LUCs and granted them to the original 35 households. The LUCs provided the households a bundle of land usage rights and also included rights to transfer, exchange, lease, inherit, and mortgage the land. The landholders were allowed to keep the land for fifty years for production purposes.

The legal framework regulating forest practices in the district changed substantially in 2001 when the provincial authorities decided to reclassify the forest within the district, shifting it from production to protection. They justified the shift by emphasizing the importance of the Hoa Binh watershed, which encompasses Ban Yen where the Hoa Binh hydro-power plant is located.[26] From then on, households in Ban Yen were forbidden to work the land in the forest for production purposes or to extract forest resources such as timber products. Instead, they had to protect the forest in order to ensure the stability of the watershed. The role of the forest shifted from economic development to environmental protection. The individual rights to the land and forest which were granted to the villagers only four years earlier had previously been considered as an impetus for household development; this no longer held validity. No compensation was offered to the villagers. In principle, villagers would obtain forest protection payment from the government in return for which they would give up their production activities in the forest. In fact, such payment was never made, with the exception of payment for a small forest area in the village which was brought into a protection program in 1997–8.

## Timber logging in Ban Yen

In the following section, I explore the changing notions of property rights and access to resources from the time Ban Yen was established in 1963 to the aftermath of the shift from economic production to environmental protection.

From the 1960s, when Ban Yen was established, to the 1980s, the Tu Ly enterprise which managed the forests around the village focused primarily on extracting timber trees. Tu Ly received an annual logging quota from the provincial department of agriculture and forestry. To meet the quota, it hired men from the Ban Yen cooperative to log timber around Ban Yen. Villagers also cut down timber trees for domestic use and housing. Household-based logging for commercial purposes started in the early 1990s after the Tu Ly enterprise left the area. In principle, the district department of forest protection was in charge of forest protection in

1991–5, but its staff never came to Ban Yen to oversee logging practices. Weak legal enforcement on the ground enabled villagers to accelerate illegal logging activities.

Logging in Ban Yen was shaped by a mixture of villagers' customary practices and the increasing market demand for wood, particularly since the second half of the 1990s when the country experienced an economic boom and demand for wood products for housing and construction soared. The logging ban issued in the mid-1990s tightened the domestic supply of wood, accelerating the rise in wood prices throughout the country. This produced numerous benefits for a variety of actors involved in the timber commodity chain.[27] Timber networks expanded beyond the province, involving multiple actors at various levels. Traders from district and provincial centers went to Ban Yen to procure wood and sold it to saw-mills located elsewhere in the district and province. Timber extracted in Ban Yen reached its final destination in Huu Bang commune – a lowland market in Ha Tay province located in the Red River Delta.

Almost all households were involved in logging. Villagers insisted that "the forest belongs to the village." In other words, they did not consider the forest around the village to be the property of the state but of the village. Therefore, they considered the government's policies regarding local forest practices irrelevant to their own situation; they also believed that the government should not restrict their livelihood activities in the forest. Basing their claim on this foundation, villagers continued to cut down trees, though they left untouched those trees located in an area thought to be sacred. To reduce the labor of haulage, logging took place in the most convenient areas, usually near the village and/or stream.

The rise in timber price was highly welcome in Ban Yen, driving its villagers to cut even more trees. Most often, valuable trees such as *sen, tau,* and *doi* were selected. Gradually, as such trees became increasingly scarce, villagers moved deeper into the forest where they cut less valuable ones. In 2004, almost all of the valuable timber trees were gone. By 2008, the timber trees with the highest value had completely disappeared near Ban Yen. Villagers had no choice but to switch to lower market value trees such as *khao* and *sang*. They went even deeper into the forest to procure wood, sometimes crossing into areas belonging to other communes. They even cut trees in the sacred area of the forest. When I asked a young logger in 2008 "Aren't you afraid of the gods when logging here [in the sacred forest]," he replied: "There's no god here." His response reflects the impact of economic incentives on the forest practices and even religious beliefs of the villagers. In general, the absence of private property notions about the forest, intersecting with the increasing market demand for wood products and the enduring dependency of the villagers on the forest, brought about the disappearance of timber trees, particularly high-value timber species previously found near Ban Yen.

Households in Ban Yen derived 60 percent of their total income from timber activities, making timber the most important income source in the village. The households did not benefit from timber trees equally. Their income from timber was contingent on their labor and assets, particularly water buffalo. Only strong male laborers in the 20- to 50-year-old bracket were involved in logging. As a consequence, households with large labor power of this sort were able to derive more income from timber than others. However, having strong labor alone did not necessarily guarantee an income. Households needed to have access to a water buffalo as well to help haul logs from the forest to the village. Those without a buffalo had to hire one if they wanted to benefit from timber.

While the custom-based claim that the "forest belongs to the village" served as the foundation for determining household access to trees, it did not necessarily mean that outsiders would recognize this claim and that they would stop extracting timber in the forest near Ban Yen. In this case, legal rights to the forests as prescribed by the government under the devolution policy have become important for the Ban Yen villagers' efforts to fence off their claims to the trees from outsiders. If outsiders cut a tree from within the village boundaries, the village chairman would collect the households' LUCs and use these to bolster villagers' exclusive and legally recognized claims to the tree. When necessary, villagers sought support from local authorities in the commune to back their claims. Eventually, villagers were able to maneuver legal rights granted by the government so as to prevent outsiders from having access to timber. However, controlling the trees did not guarantee villagers a large share of benefit generated from the timber chain. Market control is more important for the derivation of benefits than is control of the trees themselves. Thus, actors outside of the village; particularly traders and government officials who controlled timber markets, kept about 80 percent of the benefits and timber trades.[28]

The practice of timber logging in Ban Yen highlights issues of (il)legitimacy and (il)legality as perceived by different groups. Practices that are considered by the government as being legal are seen by the villagers as legitimate practice. The government, however, is concerned that local logging leads to the disappearance of certain tree species and thus contributes to environmental degradation and to the endangerment of development processes. It thus considers banning logging as the only solution to these problems. In Ban Yen, the notion that the "forest belongs to the village" is widely held and invoked. Most villagers report that, "We would starve if income from timber was gone." Viewed from this perspective, restrictions on logging practices severely violate their moral claims and endanger their survival. As a result, villagers strongly resist the legal regulations, justifying their flouting the ban against logging by invoking custom, an argument that is embedded in the concept of moral economy.[29]

## Swidden cultivation and the shift to permanent agriculture

Swidden cultivation is another area that reflects the disjunction between legal rights prescribed by the state and actual rights practiced by the villagers. Before they began to engage in logging for commercial purposes in the early 1990s, all of the villagers in Ban Yen subsisted entirely on swidden cultivation. Villagers' claim on swidden land was established through household occupation of the land. Once a specific plot of land was chosen and cleared for cultivation, it automatically belonged to the household that worked it. This claim was maintained not only in the cultivation period but also during the fallow time. Without permission from the owner, other villagers could not work the land. For years, this custom was respected in the village. The exclusionary nature of the household claim to the land embraced a notion of household-based rights. However, this notion was not strictly defined in the neoliberal sense, reflecting the flexibility of the customarily defined rights in terms of time and space.

Within the village boundaries, there were several areas where villagers practiced swidden. Villagers worked their swidden plot for three to four years and then left it fallow before moving on to the next area. In the fallow period, the land became a communal grazing area where households could let their animals roam freely. Until the fallow period ended, no one in the village was allowed to work the land for swiddening. This process rotated year after year and was primarily governed by the village elder and his advisory committee. The elder and his advisors also determined the times during which sowing and harvesting of crops should occur.

Swidden practices reflected the cultural dimension of swidden land and forest resources.[30] Rights to individual swidden plots belonged to individual households, but the exercise of these rights was contingent on the village's customary rules which defined the specific areas where villagers could practice swiddening. The rules also dictated the duration of the rights. For example, if the village elder and his council decided to give up village swidden areas (owing to poor fertility of the soil) households' right to swidden plots would no longer exist. In the area designated for swidden cultivation, villagers could open a new plot for swidden so long as no previous claim existed on the land. Opening up a new plot was labor intensive;[31] consequently, households with more labor power were afforded larger swidden area than households with a smaller labor force. Newly established households which had limited labor power experienced significant difficulties in acquiring swidden land.

In 1963, when the village was settled, the local state demarcated the administrative boundaries of Ban Yen. This territorializing process, to use the language of Vandergeest and Peluso, helps the state hold control over local people and resources within the demarcated boundaries.[32] The boundaries previously designated by the villagers reflected comprehensive notions and practices on different types of forests across space and time. However, the administrative boundaries designated by the state did not match those conceived by the villagers as the latter were much more flexible and inclusive.[33] Usually, the area chosen for swidden cultivation was located near streams because of the importance of access to water. To save time for travel between field and home, members of every household built a hut on their swidden land where they stayed during the planting, weeding, and harvesting seasons. As early as 1990, Ban Yen residents moved their fields deeper into the forest toward their original settlement where the soil was more fertile; however, this area had already been allocated to another village, so Ban Yen villagers' move into it was viewed as encroachment. This triggered a number of conflicts between the two villages as well as between Ban Yen villagers and local authorities.

The 1995 devolution substantially changed the relationship between villagers and the swidden land. Forestland was allocated to the households in Ban Yen for production purposes. In principle, villagers were allowed to use the land to grow crops; however, district officials charged with forest management were confused about the difference between production and protection. As such, they did not allow villagers to use the land for crop productions and all swidden areas in the village were abandoned. Conflicts, both overt and covert, erupted when officials tried to stop villagers' swidden practices. Ban Yen villagers also resisted the new dispensation by working the land to ensure their survival. Strict restriction by the state over swidden practices in the forest near Ban Yen also caused villagers to intensify swiddening in the forest area of the neighboring village. However, devolution took place in that village in 1996–9, putting all of its land under household control. Ban Yen villagers' move into areas of the forest belonging to that village was thus considered a violation of the legal claims of its residents who brought it to the attention of officials from the neighboring district. The officials went to the field, removed crops, measured the swidden areas of each household in Ban Yen and imposed a fine on every household that practiced swidden in the forest. However, none of the households in Ban Yen paid the fine. Nonetheless, the stringent control over swidden land in the neighboring village forced Ban Yen villagers to move back to the forest around Ban Yen. In general, devolution substantially shrank the availability of forestland in which villagers could practice swidden agriculture. This resulted in the expansion of the cultivation period and the reduction of the fallow period, thus reducing crop productivity.

Stringent control over swidden practices in the forest near Ban Yen under forest devolution and the low productivity of swidden crops thus triggered rapid changes in land use practices; they also reinforced the notion of household-based rights to swidden land in the village. At the end of the 1990s, villagers started to fence in their swidden plots. Previously, the plots were defined by fluid boundaries and marked by stones, trees, or bushes. These demarcations were now replaced by concrete and physical boundaries, namely fences made of tree trunks. Behind the fences, households diversified their activities. They used part of their land to plant timber trees such as *xoan* and fruit trees such as jackfruit and plum. They built terraces for wet rice cultivation. Many of them maintained swidden crops on their plots. They also raised pigs and poultry. In the local language, villagers no longer used the term swidden land (*nuong*) to refer to their land; instead they started referring to it as farmland (*trai*).[34] My own host owned a plot of about 4,000 $m^2$, which he acquired in the 1970s. It included 1,200 $m^2$ of terrace on which the household could grow rice twice a year. Another 2,500 $m^2$ was used for growing corn and cassava. The remaining land was planted with fruit trees and softwood trees. The household also raised poultry and pigs. "This is our second home," said my host, emphasizing the importance of the farmland for the household.

This trend is attributable not only to the government's stringent control over swidden practice but to other factors as well. Swidden cultivation with shifting fields has long been perceived in Vietnam as an unproductive form of agricultural activity that is usually associated with backward people and environmental damage.[35] As a result, swidden cultivation was subject to bans, as in Ban Yen. The move from shifting fields (*nuong*) to a more permanent type of cultivation (*trai*) with settled fields helped justify the villagers' occupation of the land and supported their legal claim to it. Households undertook a number of activities inside their farms that strongly emphasized the notion of private property; this in turn reinforced exclusionary household-based claims to the land. In the village, terraces have always been conceived as private property. The construction of terraces on swidden land conveys a clear message to the villagers that the land is privately owned. This message is reinforced by other activities such as poultry and animal farming and the planting of wood trees and fruit trees. All of these make the farm a "second home" for the owners. In other words, the establishment of a farm constitutes a powerful notion of private property in the village: it is recognized locally by the villagers as well as officially by local authorities. In fact, the local government strongly promoted this idea by providing some funding to help villagers construct terraces and by registering the terraced areas and issuing LUCs for terraced land.

The shift from swidden to farm also reflects the growing problem of land scarcity in Ban Yen, challenging the conventional notion of the average Vietnamese and of many government officials that arable land is still abundant in the uplands. In Ban Yen, all of the land in easily accessible areas is fully occupied. This has helped land-owning households monopolize access and fend off land-hungry households. Though access to swidden land is still open for villagers in Ban Yen, new households often find it difficult to acquire enough land for cultivation. Interviews with the heads of young households revealed that they had to borrow land from their parents or rent land from other households. Those without enough land had to move deep into the forest, causing many problems, particularly for young households with limited available labor. The long distance between the village and the fields makes it difficult to carry heavy harvest (mainly cassava) back home.

The gradual shift from swidden fields to a more permanent type of agriculture has redefined the relationship between the villagers and the land, challenging the role of the customary village rules that had previously governed land use practices on the ground. However, outside farms, the notion that "the forest belongs to the village" has continued to play a central role in shaping villagers' access to the land. Where no previous claim exists, villagers can open fields, disregarding the 1995 devolution. My trip to the village in 2007 revealed that six households had just opened new fields in the area call *Suoi Song*. Anh Kim, the vice chairman of Ban Yen, held land allocated with a LUC during the 1995 devolution that was worked by two out of the six households.

The case of timber logging and swidden cultivation in Ban Yen highlights the discrepancy between forestry property as envisioned by the state and actual property relations on the ground. From the government's perspective, forestry regulations are mere mechanisms governing forest practices at the local level. According to this perspective, the granting of clearly defined rights to the forest to individual households is the most optimal way to protect it: this would lead to sustainable uses of the forest by the local people. However, this assumption does not work in areas like Ban Yen. On the ground, forest-use practices are governed by customary village rules and are contingent on various other factors. Table 4.1 below highlights some distinctions between property relations as envisioned by the state and by the villagers.

Using available scientific knowledge, the government often subsumes resources into three categories that define various types of forests in the country: the production forest, the protection forest, and the special-use forest. Classifying the forest in this way reflects the government's emphasis on the economic and environmental functions of the forest. Thus, forests classified as productive are supposed to generate income whereas protected and special-use forests are meant to protect watersheds and biodiversity. The social dimension of the forest is not considered in the government's forest policy. At the local level, however, resources are conceived in a much more complex way, embracing socio-economic and cultural factors. For villagers, forests include different types, each of which reflects different meanings and values. Some are classified as sacred forests where villagers can seek spiritual support. The bamboo forest is a place where villagers can collect various kinds of bamboo products at different times of the year and use them for different purposes. The old forest located far from the village center is an area where they can cut timber trees. Villagers know exactly where they may practice swidden cultivation and release their cattle and where they should not. In general, forests are part of the villagers' socio-economic and cultural life and cannot be

*Table 4.1* Perceptions of property relations

| *Characteristics* | *State-defined property relations* | *Locally defined property relations* |
|---|---|---|
| Property object | Broad categorization of resources (e.g. protection forest, production forest) | Complex understanding of resources with different sub-categories of resources (e.g. bamboo forest, palm forest) |
| Functions | Primarily seen for economic development or environmental protection | More inclusive, encompassing economic, social, and cultural functions |
| Property holder | Single entity; gender insensitivity[36] | Layered holders to singly resources; more flexible regardless of sex and age |
| Property rights | Temporal and spatial static dimension of right; static dimension of rights prevents non-holders from access to property objects | Flexible temporal and spatial dimension of right associated with different kinds of objects; hierarchical nature of right to different kinds of objects; less strictly defined, leaving access to resources open to other villagers |

understood separately from the villagers. This is where the notion that the "forest belongs to the village" comes from.

The state ordinarily views a single person (usually a man) as the legitimate property holder. Under devolution, households were given clearly defined, exclusionary based rights to the land for 50 years. Each household received a plot of land together with a LUC certifying its legally recognized claim to the plot (in most cases, it was the name of the husband that appeared on the LUC, exposing his wife to the risk of losing her land when her husband sold the land for quick cash without consulting her).[37] While the rights enshrined in the LUCs provided landholders with a greater level of control over the land and consequently the trees found on it, they entirely excluded other villagers whose claims were not legally recognized. This went against local concepts of property rights that are far more fluid and flexible than that of the state. Multiple holders with diverse interests communally own property objects. A patch of forest, for example, may be subject to customary rules supervised by the village elder and his advisors. These rules guide how swidden agriculture should be practiced within a particular patch; yet the use of a specific swidden plot within that patch is subject to the desires of the household who owns the plot. When the land is fallowed, the use right to the plot does not remain with the household. The pattern of multiple holders reflects the complexity and multiple uses of the resources at the local level in a way that the state, with its rigid and simplistic "scientific" perspective, fails to capture.

Locally defined rights thus provide the villagers with different levels of access to resources. Households' rights to swidden plots, for example, are contingent on the village's customary rules. Furthermore, right to the trees is distinctive from rights to the land. The flexibility of locally defined rights to resource in terms of its temporal and spatial dimensions keeps access to forestland and forest resources open to all the villagers.

At the local level, legal rights ascribed to resources intersect with locally defined rights in shaping forest practices on the ground. This makes property relations fuzzy for outsiders. This "fuzziness" reflects the common characteristics of property relations in other postsocialist countries.[38] For the villagers, however, property relations are not fuzzy at all. The availability of different foundations for resource claims, or "shopping forum," to use the term coined by Benda-Beckmann, provides villagers with opportunities to "shop around" for the ones that benefit them the most.[39] Villagers use legal rights to the land granted to them to prevent outsiders from extracting resources in the village territory. In the village, forest resources are governed mainly according to customary rules that consider the forest a communal property, reflecting the villagers' claim that the "forest belongs to the village."

In Ban Yen, both legally and locally defined property rights are subject to change, making resource rights unsettled. The change is attributed to the growing scarcity of resources triggered by the increase in the village's population as well as by accelerating market demands for forest products and also to the unreliability of government policy. Under the 1995 devolution, villagers were allowed to use the land granted to them for production purposes. However, the local government's shift from production to protection in 2001 took away the rights it had given to the villagers only a few years earlier. Owing to the scarcity of cultivable land, locally defined rights on swidden land are changing as well, triggered by the villagers' effort to individualize the swidden lands which they now own but were previously governed by customary village rules.

The perception that the "forest belongs to the village," under the context of increasing market demand for timber products[40] and economic difficulties faced by the villagers, has accelerated timber extraction. Timber trees near the village have been vanishing and access to the land has been restricted, particularly for young households with a labor shortage. Conflicts of various types have been observed among the villagers, triggered by differentiated access to resources between the villagers and the local officials. These differences in access are produced by differing notions over forestland and timber trees as well as by different sets of rights over the resources.[41]

While individualization took place on swidden land, it did not occur for trees in the forest near the village. As mentioned earlier, before the Tu Ly enterprise withdrew from the area, logging by individual households for commercial purpose had not occurred, primarily because of the government's suppression of any market beyond its control. At that time, timber trees were of marginal benefit for the villagers and were used mainly for the construction of housing. The abundance of trees in the forest, coupled with the villager's low demand for the trees created no individual, exclusionary type of right to the trees. Additionally, socialist state control over the forest strongly emphasized trees rather than land, with the former being considered particularly important for state revenue obtained through timber export and for the country's demand for construction materials.[42] In Ban Yen, while state control over swidden cultivation was not established until the 1995 devolution, control over trees had always been strong with the Tu Ly enterprise being primarily focused on timber extraction. The notion that the "forest belongs to the village" is associated with different material and symbolic values rather than with specific trees within specific areas. In fact, villagers viewed the trees as the leftovers of the Tu Ly enterprise. After Tu Ly withdrew from the village at the end of the 1980s, the villagers used the term *mot* (glean) to refer to their commercial logging practices.[43] In Ban Yen, the notion that the "forest belongs to the village," intersected with the villagers' notion that the trees were the company's leftovers, providing villagers with open access to the trees. Thus, state law defining property in the face of high market incentives for timber products has driven the extraction of timber trees in the forest and led to the rapid disappearance of timber trees in Ban Yen. In essence, both forestland and forest products in Ban Yen have been governed by a combination of factors both internal and external to the village.

## Conclusion

The case of Ban Yen challenges the conventional assumption that local forest practices are primarily governed by legal forestry frameworks and that giving individual rights to forest resources to individual holders would serve as a strong impetus for the holders to use the resources in a sustainable way, thus improving their long-term livelihood. At the local level, forest access and control is largely shaped by a complex set of factors including both legal regulations and customary rules and is contingent on household assets and market forces. This reflects the embeddedness of property rights in Vietnam and elsewhere in postsocialist countries.[44] Attempts to ascribe individual and exclusionary rights to resources and to allocate these rights to single holders guarantee neither improvement of local livelihoods nor a sustainable use of resources.

At the local level, there exist multiple property holders for single resources. These layered set of rights are distributed differently across spatial and temporal scales. One-size-fits-all types of intervention, such as forest devolution, do not work on the ground unless consideration is given to the complexity of local relationships. Synergizing development and environmental protection would require good forest governance under which accountability, legitimacy, and transparency related to forest access and control must be achieved. Local people should be given an effective legal space in which to exercise their influence over the state on issues related to forest use and management. In addition, legally defined rights to resources should be put on an equal footing with locally defined rights to ensure that different forest governing systems are adequately taken into account. This would require joint efforts by villagers, government, and civil society.

## Notes

1 My thanks to participants in the workshop "Property Rights in Vietnam" held at Harvard University on May 22–24, 2009 for their useful comments. Special thanks to Hue-Tam Ho Tai for insightful comments and editorial assistance.

2 Some scholars distinguish between devolution and decentralization. Resource devolution refers to the transfer of property rights to resources from government bodies to local peoples, whereas decentralization refers to the transfer of management power over resources from the government at the higher levels to lower levels of government.

3 Jesse Ribot, Arun Agrawal and Anne M. Larson, "Recentralizing while Decentralizing How Governments Reappropriate Forest Resources," *World Development* 34.11 (2006), pp. 1864–86; Eve Wollenberg *et al.*, "Between State and Society: Local Governance of Forest in Malinau, Indonesia," *Forest Policy and Economics* 8.4 (2006), pp. 421–33.

4 Jesse Ribot, *et al.*, "Recentralizing while Decentralizing," in Arun Agrawal and Jesse Ribot. *Analyzing Decentralization: A Framework with South Asian and West African Environmental Cases*, Working Paper, 2000.

5 Arun Agrawal and Jesse Ribot, ibid.; Anne M. Larson and Jesse C. Ribot (eds), *Democratic Decentralisation through a Natural Resource Lens*, Special issue of *European Journal of Development Research* 16.1 (2004).

6 Hernando De Soto, *The Mystery of Capital. Why Capitalism Triumphs in the West and Fails Everywhere Else*, (London: Black Swan; New York: Basic Books, 2000).

7 The UK's Department of Foreign Affairs and International Development, and the Asian Development Bank, for example, have taken up the idea by co-financing the project "Making market works better for the poor" in Vietnam, Laos, and Cambodia. The project started in 2003 and is ongoing. More information on the project can be found at http://www.markets4poor.org/about.

8 World Bank, *World Development Report: Building Institutions for the Market*, (Oxford, UK: Oxford University Press, 2002); Gershon Feder and Akihiko Nishio, "The Benefits

of Land Registration and Titling: Economic and Social Perspectives," *Land Use Policy* 15.1 (1999), pp. 25–43.

9 Jean-Philippe Platteau, *Land Reform and Structural Adjustment in Sub-Saharan Africa: Controversies and Guidelines*. FAO Economic and Social Development Paper 107 ed. (Rome: FAO, 1992).

10 Katherine Verdery, *What Was Socialism? And What Comes Next?* (Princeton, NJ: Princeton University Press, 1996); Chris Hann, "Introduction: the Embeddedness of Property," Chapter 1 in *Property Relations: Renewing the Anthropological Tradition*, Christopher Hann (ed.), (Cambridge: Cambridge University Press, 1998), pp. 1–47; Chris Hann, "Postsocialism," Draft prepared for the Handbook on Economic Anthropology, 2003.

11 Katherine Verdery, *What Was Socialism?* Chapter 1.

12 Chris Hann, "Property Relations in the New Eastern Europe: The Case of Specialist Cooperatives in Hungary," in *The Curtain Rises: Rethinking Culture, Ideology, and the State in Eastern Europe*, Hermine G. De Soto and David G. Anderson (eds), (New Jersey: Humanities Press, 1993), p. 113.

13 Katherine Verdery, "Fuzzy Property: Rights, Power, and Identity in Transylvania's Decollectivization," in *Uncertain Transition: Ethnographies of Change in the Postsocialist World*, Michael Burawoy and Katherine Verdery (eds), (Lanham, CO: Rowman & Littlefield Publishers, Inc., 1999), p. 65.

14 Katherine Verdery, *The Vanishing Hectare: Property and Value in Postsocialist Transylvania*, (Ithaca, NY: Cornell University Press, 2003).

15 Slawomira Zbierski-Salameh, "Polish Peasants in the 'Valley of Transition': Responses to Postsocialist Reform," in Michael Burawoy and Katherine Verdery (eds), *Uncertain Transition*, pp. 15–56.

16 Emily Yeh, "Property Relations in Tibet since Decollectivization and the Question of 'Fuzziness'," *Conservation and Society*, 2004, pp. 163–87; Jennifer Sowerwine, "Territorialization and the Politics of Highland Landscapes in Vietnam: Negotiating Property Relations in Policy, Meaning and Practice," *Conservation and Society*, 2004, pp. 97–136; To Xuan Phuc, "Why Did the Forest Conservation Policy Fail in the Vietnamese Uplands? Forest Conflicts in Ba Vi National Park in Northern Region," *International Journal for Environmental Studies* 66.1 (2009), pp. 59–68.

17 Barbara Cellarious, "Property Restitution and Natural Resource Use in the Rhodope Mountains, Bulgaria," in *The Postsocialist Agrarian Question: Property Relations and the Rural Conditions*, Chris Hann (ed.), (Munster: Lit Verlag, 2003).

18 Katherine Verdery, *The Vanishing Hectare*, p. 19.

19 Janet Sturgeon and Thomas Sikor, "Postsocialist Property in Asia and Europe: Variation on 'Fuzziness'," *Conservation and Society*, 2004, pp. 1–18; Katherine Verdery, "Fuzzy Property."

20 Franz von Benda-Beckmann and Keebet von Benda-Beckmann, "A Functional Analysis of Property Rights, with Special Reference to Indonesia," in Toon van Meijl, and Franz von Benda-Beckmann (eds), *Property Rights and Economic Development: Land and Natural Resources in Southeast Asia and Oceania*, (London and New York: Kegan Paul International, 1999), pp. 15–56.

21 In total, about 8.1 million ha of forestland were allocated to 1,109, 451 landholders including organizations, households, and individuals. Dinh Huu Hoang and Dang Kim Son. *Forestland Allocation in Vietnam: From Policy to Reality*. National Workshop on Forestland Consolidation, Ha Long, 2007.

22 Nguyen Van Dang (ed.), *Lam Nghiep Viet Nam (1945–2000)*, (Hanoi: Nong Nghiep, 2001); Dinh Huu Hoang and Dang Kim Son, ibid.

23 Thomas Sikor, "The Allocation of Forestry Land in Vietnam: Did It Cause the Expansion of Forests in the Northwest?" *Forest Policy and Economics* 2 (2001), pp. 1–11.

24 Nguyen Quang Tan, "Forest Devolution in Vietnam: Differentiation in Benefits from Forest among Local Households," *Forest Policy and Economics* 8.4 (2006), pp. 409–20; Thomas Sikor and Nguyen Quang Tan, "Why May Forest Devolution Not Benefit the Rural Poor? Forest Entitlements in Vietnam's Central Highlands," *World Development* 35.11 (2007), pp. 2010–25; To Xuan Phuc, *Forest Property in the Vietnamese Uplands: An Ethnography of Forest Relations in Three Dao Villages*, (Berlin and London: LIT Verlage/Transaction Publishers, 2007).

25 Dao is one of the 53 officially categorized ethnic minority groups in Vietnam. Dao people account for less than 1 percent of the country's total population. Charles F. Keyes, "Presidential Address: The People of Asia – Sciences and Politics in the Classification of Ethnic Group in Thailand, China, and Vietnam," *Journal of Asian Studies* 61.4 (2002), pp. 1163–203.

26 Hoa Binh Hydropower station is the largest hydropower station in the country; it provides about 50 percent of the country's electricity.

27 To Xuan Phuc and Thomas Sikor, *The Politics of Illegal Logging in Vietnam*, Working Paper 5, University of East Anglia, 2008.

28 A fuller account of benefit distribution can be found in ibid.

29 James C. Scott, *The Moral Economy of the Peasant: Rebellion and Subsistence in Southeast Asia*, (New Haven, CT: Yale University Press, 1977).

30 Such practices include various types of worship (for sowing, new harvest, chasing pests and diseases that could harm the crops). They include, for example "village Sunday" referring to the days when no one in the village was allowed to go to visit the field.

31 This involves labor for slashing, burning, and clearing.

32 Peter Vandergeest and Nancy Lee Peluso, "Territorialization and State Power in Thailand," *Theory and Society* 24 (1995), pp. 385–426.

33 These conflicts are described in great detail in To Xuan Phuc *Forest Property in the Vietnamese Uplands*.

34 My interview with villagers in 2004 revealed this point really well. Before interviewing villagers, I went to the forest near Ban Yen and observed large areas of forestland being used for swidden cultivation. But when I asked villagers how large their swidden land (*nuong*) was, they all told me that they did not work the swidden land any longer. Only after I had talked to my host did I come to know that villagers had already dropped the term owing to changes in their land-use practices.

35 Do Dinh Sam, *Shifting Cultivation in Vietnam: Its Social, Economic and Environmental Values Relative to Alternative Land Use*, IIED Forestry and Land Use Series No. 3 ed. (London: International Institute for Environment and Development (IIED), 1994); Le Duy Hung, "Some Issues of Fixed Cultivation and Sedentarization of Ethnic Minority People in Mountainous Areas of Vietnam," in *The Challenges of Highland Development in Vietnam*, Terry Rambo, Robert Reed, Le Trong Cuc, and Michael DiGregorio (eds), (Honolulu: East West Center, 1995).

36 The recently amended Land Law has changed substantially, providing both husband and wife an equal right to the land with both names appearing on the LUCs.

37 To Xuan Phuc, *Forest Property in the Vietnamese Uplands*.

38 Katherine Verdery, *What Was Socialism?*; Janet Sturgeon and Thomas Sikor, "Postsocialist Property in Asia and Europe."

39 Keebet von Benda-Beckmann, "Forum Shopping and Shopping Forums: Dispute Processing in a Minangkabau village," *Journal of Legal Pluralism* 19 (1981), pp. 117–59.

40 To Xuan Phuc and Thomas Sikor, *The Politics of Illegal Logging in Vietnam*.

41 To Xuan Phuc, *Forest Property in the Vietnamese Uplands*.

42 Nguyen Van Dang (ed.), *Lam Nghiep Viet Nam (1945–2000)*.

43 The term *mot* (glean) conveys a clear message that the villagers were taking over the enterprise's leftovers.

44 Katherine Verdery, *What Was Socialism?*; Katherine Verdery, "Fuzzy Property"; Chris Hann, "Introduction: the Embeddedness of Property"; Hann, "Postsocialism"; Janet Sturgeon and Thomas Sikor, "Postsocialist Property in Asia and Europe"; Emily Yeh, "Property Relations in Tibet"; Jennifer Sowerwine, "Territorialization and the Politics of Highland Landscapes in Vietnam".

# 5 Constructing civil society on a demolition site in Hanoi

*Nguyen Vu Hoang*

## Introduction[1]

Hanoi's infrastructure is antiquated and inadequate for the needs of its ever-increasing population. Its road system in particular is in dire need of improvement and expansion. In order for road building to begin, a program of demolition must first take place. Houses in the path of construction sites have to be removed and land cleared.

When their houses are demolished, the dwellers are given some compensation for losing their house and the land on which it is located; they are then forced to resettle in a new place, often far from the area where they earn their living. Examining the clearance of a temporary area (Nha Den hamlet along Nhieu Loc channel), Tran Manh Tien questioned whether the compensation rate was enough for local people to resettle elsewhere and whether this resettlement would also be temporary.[2] More than compensation is at stake, however, or the threat to the livelihood of marginal subjects. Urban development projects also raise issues of state/society relations, rights, legal remedies, and extra-legal means of exerting pressure by a wide variety of actors.

The focus of this essay is a group of residents living in an alley of Thanh Xuan District that I will call "Green Alley" and their struggle to avoid being swallowed up by the project (henceforth called the Project) to construct a third city ring road designed to relieve Hanoi's famed traffic congestion. Those whose residences were situated on the site of the Project were expected to receive monetary compensation and be resettled in a designated area. Like the Hoc Mon villagers studied by Erik Harms in this volume, the residents of Green Alley did not object to the road construction project itself. However, they did not think that the compensation they were slated to receive would be sufficient to ensure the preservation of their already meager standards of living and worried that the high-rise building into which they were asked to move would not be conducive to their modest trading activities. Their growing frustration with the lack of transparency about the Project put them at loggerheads with the local authorities who saw their job as facilitating the implementation of the program of land clearance so that an important intersection of the Third Ring Road could be built. The residents of Green Alley had to confront the manipulations of the local authorities and gaps in the legal structure and administrative procedures. Their sustained, vigorous and inventive campaign against the demolition of their dwellings resulted in a partial but still significant victory.

## Life in Green Alley

There are eleven wards in Thanh Xuan District which was incorporated into metropolitan Hanoi in 1996. In 2007, it covered an area of 913 ha and had a population of 154,600. The population density was about 16,934 persons per square kilometer. Thanh Xuan Trung ward, where Green Alley is located, covers 106.2 ha. In 1996, it had a population of 11,036.[3] Thanh Xuan Trung is further divided into 65 residential groups (*to dan pho*). Twenty years ago, according to residents, Green Alley was the parking lot of a state-owned enterprise. When the enterprise was dissolved and its workforce disbanded, its workers remained in the area and eventually turned it into a residential neighborhood. And now, this neighborhood of three residential groups was to be razed to make way for the ring road and they were to be relocated, apparently into a high-rise building.

In an agricultural country like Vietnam where more than 55 percent of the working age population derive their income from agriculture,[4] economic opportunities in the cities attract massive numbers of migrants from the countryside.[5] A census in Hanoi reports that only 22 percent of the population was born in Hanoi. The remainder is made up of recent migrants. Yet urbanization entails uncertainty and insecurity in terms of housing and livelihood.[6] Threats of unemployment are a major aspect of this economic insecurity. Most migrants from the countryside have limited skills and thus are confronted with the instability of jobs and hazardous working conditions. The livelihood of a large number of the urban (non-)migrants is based on a combination of income from infrequent jobs and household-based activities.[7]

Since most of the migrants do not have their own accommodation, they congregate in squats and temporary dwellings. This creates uncertain social settings for the migrants and difficulties for local authorities. Most houses that accommodate the urban poor in Hanoi were built prior to or in the early 1980s and have degraded over time. As the high price of land and houses prevents them from seeking alternatives, sometimes two or even more households share a small apartment. Living conditions are very poor. In 2007, almost all the households in Thanh Xuan Trung were using charcoal for cooking and were lighting charcoal fires twice a day. The whole area was covered by charcoal smoke every cooking period. Although they knew that charcoal was harmful, it was the only fuel the ward's residents could afford.

Most of the residents of Green Alley had retired from state enterprises when these were reorganized in 1989.[8] Having no other skills suitable for jobs available in new industries, they had to earn a living in the private/household-based sector. In spite of living in an alley, some of the households conducted business from their lodgings. They could open a small teashop, breakfast and lunch snackshop, or rent the street-side for monthly income. Their livelihood was unstable:

they did not know how much money they could earn on a day-to-day basis. It was also barely sufficient for their needs. Some interviewees confessed that they did not dare to visit their relatives during the Tet holidays because they did not have the means to give New Year's presents of lucky money to the children. They also had to *avoid* their friends because their monthly income did not cover the customary gifts of money for weddings and funerals. Although they understood the precariousness of their situation, they were helpless to improve it. However, at least, current conditions provided them enough means for subsistence. The relocation program threatened even their meager livelihood which depended on being able to operate their modest businesses at street level. I asked a woman running a snack-shop in the alley:

> Hoang: You don't think the city ring project is beneficial, do you?
>
> X: No, it is very good. It makes the face of Hanoi better. However, the process of implementation is really bad.
>
> Hoang: Why is it so?
>
> X: Because it compensates us only 30 percent of the market price. It isn't enough money to relocate. Even if we have to, we will have to live in a flat in a high-rise building.
>
> Hoang: What is wrong with that, then?
>
> X: Here we can still sell things to earn money. If we resettle in a high-rise place, who will come up there to eat?! [Angrily]. Should I be an Oshin[9] [servant] for other households? No way!! [Smile]

As this vignette illustrates, Green Alley residents realized that their current situation was better than the life awaiting them in the high-rise building where they were expected to relocate. This belief stemmed from what they had themselves witnessed or overheard from elsewhere. All of my interviewees told me of their fear of falling deep into debt as is common for resettled families. They calculated the compensation that they would receive and compared it with the price of a flat in the high-rise. The result is in a neighborhood head's words: "All the resettlers moving to high-rises are in debt. This project impoverishes people."

## A beautiful symmetry

The Project that ensnared the residents of Thanh Xuan Trung had been under consideration for several years before it was formally enacted by decision 597/QD-TTg/2001 of the prime minister in May 2001.[10] The Project involved constructing the Third City Ring Road of Hanoi that would enlarge Khuat Duy Tien Street and widen Thanh Xuan intersection. The part of the ring road located in Thanh Xuan District was planned to be 2,075 m long and 68 m wide.

At the beginning, the Hanoi People's Committee promulgated a decision, 4664/QD-UB/2001, to execute the decision of the prime minister.[11] According to the document, the People's Committee decided to assign 223,132 $m^2$ in Thanh

Xuan District for the ring road. One month later, the Committee promulgated another decision to include an additional 704.3 $m^2$ in the Project.[12] The land to be taken from Thanh Xuan District was then assigned to the Thang Long State-based Company to carry out the Project. The Hanoi People's Committee also authorized Thanh Xuan District to devise a plan for land clearance.[13] Based on this authorization, Thanh Xuan District promulgated a decision that created a Council for Compensation and Land Clearance (*Hoi dong boi thuong va giai phong mat bang*) to carry out the Project in 2001.[14] All the households located in Green Alley would have to be removed as their site would be turned into a future intersection.

In August 2002, more than one year after the City Ring Road Project had been approved, all the residents in the alley were summoned by the District to a restaurant to receive information about the Project. Each household was given a file that included a plan map and decrees concerning land clearance and compensation. Some participants were taken aback by the map they were shown. It was different from what they had seen in a public exhibit of Hanoi urban planning. While the map included in the exhibit showed a symmetrical intersection (see Figure 5.1), the map they were given was asymmetrical (see Figure 5.2). While the original design spared their neighborhood, the asymmetrical design brought their dwellings into the scope of the Project and thus targeted them for demolition. The residents insisted that, based on the exhibit map, their houses should not be located within the Project area and they should not need to relocate. They refused to accept the legitimacy of the map provided by the District, which, as some of them noticed, lacked the signature of the prime minister. While the planned ring road led to protests throughout Thanh Xuan District over compensation, this paper will focus only on the residents of Green Alley whose prospects for remaining in their own homes were affected by the asymmetrical intersection.

Immediately after the meeting, some local residents sent petitions to various offices at the district and city levels, pointing out the differences between the two maps provided by the authorities of two different levels of government. Their alley

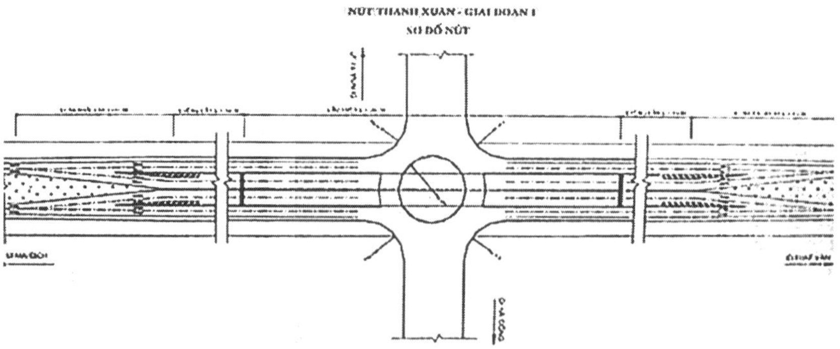


*Figure 5.1* The symmetrically designed intersection in the 2001 Project.[15]

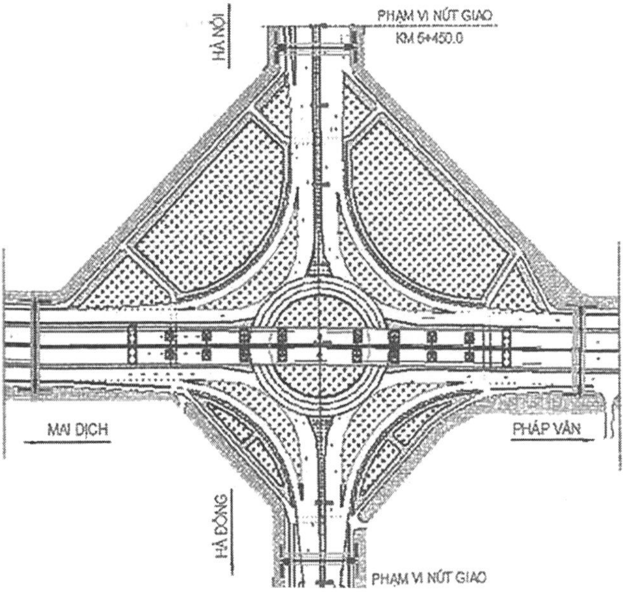


*Figure 5.2* The asymmetrically designed intersection provided by the District.[16]

was indeed very close to the area that would be turned into an intersection of the planned city ring road, yet not exactly on it. Local residents insisted that the "true" map did not incorporate the land of their alley and the four corners of the intersection were in perfect symmetry. Pointing to the asymmetrical shape of the four corners in the map provided by the District, they argued that a mistake must have been made when their neighborhood was included in the planned demolition site for the ring road.

One year later, in August 2003, the Ministry of Communications and Transport and the Hanoi People's Committee promulgated a request to TEDI, the state office responsible for the Project, to redesign the intersection with greater symmetry.[17] As a result of this request, the Project took no action in Green Alley for almost three years (from August 12, 2003 to July 25, 2006), although it continued carrying out clearance in a nearby street at a faster pace. Houses were demolished and people had to resettle with little compensation. Witnessing the difficulties of its residents, those living in Green Alley feared that they would soon be coerced into relocating. They were concerned that they would be impoverished if they received too little compensation from the authorities. They were afraid of losing the modest lodgings that had taken them a whole lifetime to acquire and worried that they would not be able to continue earning money from their ongoing small businesses.

## Organizing opposition

Recognizing the insecurity and strong feelings of the local residents, Thang, a vice-secretary of the Communist Party Cell in Green Alley, and some other Party members proposed a way to solve the problem. The Party Cell organized a meeting in June 2006 to appoint a group of spokespersons. The group included the heads of all three resident groups and some other Party members. The meeting ended with an official decision authorizing nine persons to act on the alley residents' behalf. These spokespersons, who were at the same time members of the Communist Party and heads of the resident groups, were officially recognized by a decision of the Communist Party cell of the alley. This recognition assured the stability of the group and its legitimacy in the eyes of local residents who believed that it was an officially established body and acted under the light of the Communist Party. Most of the spokespersons were professionals, white collar workers or part-time employees of the state such as heads of the three resident groups. They were trusted by the alley residents to lead them because of their knowledge of the way the state system functions. They not only represented the neighborhood in communicating with the authorities but actively led the struggle against the Project. They played a major role in mobilizing and encouraging the residents and in shaping the strategy and methods of the whole protest group. In discussing the organization of wards in Hanoi, David Koh avers that "the government has used these informal bodies to disseminate Party ideology and conduct administration."[18] The case of Green Alley not only shows that the Party is embedded in the local population but also that informal as well as formal organizations can influence what state agencies do.[19]

Mrs Hoa offered her house as a place where the group could hold meetings and where documents collected by its members could be stored. Thang was assigned to head the group of spokespersons. There had been two other possible leaders of the group, but Thang was selected because of his work experience and training. Thang was not only a state cadre of many years' standing but he had also trained as an army scout and was thus experienced in collecting information. He told me that he graduated from Hanoi Polytechnic University and was the first one in the north of Vietnam to create a machine that could make 72 holes simultaneously; it was still in use in heavy industry. Before moving to Hanoi, he had been a foreman in a state enterprise in Haiphong. Although he had moved to the alley only six years earlier in late 2000, his success in running his own business and his kindness to neighbors won him their support. Every year, he was awarded the title of Exemplary Communist Party Member (*Dang vien guong mau*) owing to his contributions to security in the alley.

None of the spokespersons had worked on an urban project before, so at first they did not know where to look for ways to deal with the implementation of the Project. After he assumed the leadership of the group of spokespersons, Thang tried to find a basis for opposing the Project. He recalled: "At first, I did not know where to start, so I bought a book on the 2003 Land Law to study. But I found nothing related to the Project there." Just as he started to feel frustrated, he suddenly remembered that he had friends working in some ministries. Although Thang had been retired for ten years, he had kept in touch with his friends who were current state employees. Although they were not involved in the Project, they were willing to provide documents for him. Thang's success in obtaining the documents can be explained by the notion of social network. Lin and Coleman contend that, through social capital, individuals gain access to and use of resources embedded in social networks.[20] Thang was already part of the same network as the state employees and their relationship had been established and strengthened before he needed them to have access to the "resources embedded in the social network."

Thang was told by his contacts that a project must have its own plan with detailed maps and supporting documents. Equipped with this knowledge, he asked a friend to find a copy of the Thanh Xuan Project for him. Thang said:

> Through my contacts, I obtained a copy of the original plan signed by the Prime Minister in 2001. I kept it secretly at home and scrutinized it alone for one and half months. I then realized that the local authority must have twisted the Project because the intersection as drawn on the original map was symmetrical. If the local authority followed the map correctly, our alley would not be incorporated in the Project.

This discovery not only brought some relief to the alley's residents, it also strengthened their belief in the group of spokespersons. After that, calls for support from the group received enthusiastic responses from the residents.

As officially recognized spokespersons of the residents, leaders were able to send off petition letters on behalf of the whole alley instead of having to painstakingly collect hundreds of signatures; they were also able to assign work for each member of the group. They also used collective action judiciously. Acting as proxy for the residents, they went to several state offices, requesting the staff to provide more relevant official documents and questioning the legitimacy of the Project. When meeting with indifference and non-cooperation, they summoned residents to gather in front of the offices. Thang said:

> We knew the weakness of each cadre and kept attacking those weaknesses. When they did not want to cooperate with us, I only needed to phone a resident in the alley, and hundreds of people would immediately gather in front of the office.

On one memorable occasion, Thang and other spokespersons went to a Ministry in Hanoi. At first, the chief of the administrative office did not allow him to meet the person responsible for the Project. Thang phoned a representative in the alley. Within minutes, hundreds of alley residents gathered in front of the ministry, waving banners. Faced with this crowd, the cadre was compelled to arrange a meeting between Thang and the responsible person. This incident suggests, as Xueguang Zhou argues for China,[21] that, not only is the distinction between the state and society fuzzy, but also that, as Ben Kerkvliet contends, citizens' cumulative activities are influencing policy-making.[22]

## Finding a new leadership style

Oral arguments and public gatherings had helped the spokespersons for the Green Alley residents to obtain the relevant documents, but they did not know how to put these to use. Meanwhile, the Project went on. The local authorities kept coming to the alley with the Project implementers to measure land for clearance. The spokespersons could only argue with the authorities every time they came. But they were at a loss to articulate their reasons for opposing the Project in a way that would not label them as selfish opponents of the public good and to identify the appropriate targets for their claims. Residents also became concerned by threats to their security brought about by both the Project and the strong-arm activities of local authorities. By August 2006, the residents were stymied. They had to find an effective way to publicize their struggle, find support from outside and cohesion from within.

As their struggle was reaching an impasse, Hung, a police officer working for the Hanoi Police Office, realized that his house was going to be cleared by the Project. Knowing that Thang was the chief leader of the alley group, Hung came to him and asked to join in the struggle. Feeling helpless and realizing the need for new allies, Thang warmly welcomed Hung's participation. Despite having no formal proxy and being unfamiliar to the alley residents, Hung quickly gained their trust. As with Thang, Hung's social status and work experience was crucial in winning them over. They believed that his position, experience, and connections would advance their cause. Trained in law in Russia in the late 1980s, Hung had been serving in the police force for almost twenty years. As a police officer, he had professional relations with some news agencies that were useful for the struggle.

Hung immediately took charge. The activities of the group became more organized and intensive. Hung chaired every meeting and always finished the meetings with a long speech about the legitimacy of the struggle. His arguments were so persuasive that after his speech, all the meeting participants applauded loudly. Everybody apparently believed in Hung's leadership and the righteousness of the struggle.

Thang and other leaders had already found the deviation from the original design of the Project that caused their neighborhood to be targeted for demolition and them for relocation. Hung's task now was to make their plight public and force the authorities to follow exactly the "true" Project. Hung realized the potential for action created by the elevation of Nguyen Tan Dung to the office of prime minister in June 2006.[23] Prime Minister Nguyen Tan Dung devoted his inaugural speech to pledging to fight against corruption. In Vietnam, corruption not only means embezzling money or accepting bribes but also, according to the 1999 Criminal Law, abuses of power. As a police officer, Hung was very sensitive to political issues; he quickly caught on to this new direction and adopted the state rhetoric of anti-corruption as the main aim of the struggle. This not only helped re-frame the motives of the Green Alley residents in opposing the Project, it also helped them identify the proper targets of their action and the resources they could bring to bear. From now on, protesters started to see themselves no longer in a purely local context as self-interested individuals but instead as acting within a national framework; that is, driven by their citizenship. They felt empowered to act in the name of justice. Anti-corruption became their new motto and gave their struggle new meaning and legitimacy endorsed by the central state. Their struggle now aimed not only to protect their rights and their property but also to protect the transparency of the government and "national justice."

While Thang, the retired official, had used his contacts with old friends to obtain the relevant documents, Hung's situation was more advantageous because he was a current state employee. He had a much stronger social network than Thang. As a police officer, he could also contact higher-ranking cadres. Hung cultivated his contacts by providing information that they needed. He then gained access to the network containing the resources that were useful to him. And his contacts, in return, provided him with the information he wanted. Hung was thus able not only to access documents that Thang could not obtain, but he also diligently maintained his social network so that information about every meeting or decision of the authorities relating to the Project always reached him early.

Hung and Thang thought that they should make the wider public aware of the problem faced by the denizens of Green Alley and start attacking the authorities through different methods and resources. The group leaders had been sending petition after petition to the central government but these did not seem to reach the proper officials. After waiting for months without receiving a response, Hung decided to use other ways to make their voices heard. He asked other spokespersons to present their concerns to news agencies and to ask them to publicize these concerns. He himself contacted Vietnam Television to make a television program describing the plight of the residents of Green Alley. Suiting state rhetoric to his purpose, Hung quickly convinced the programmers to participate in the anti-corruption campaign launched by the prime minister. In November 2006, an hour-long television program specifically on the problem in Thanh Xuan District was broadcast.

Describing her experience when that first television program aired, Hoa, the owner of the house where meetings were held, recalled,

> We were very happy because it was the first time our problem was publicized. We tape-recorded the clip and played it again and again. Some people who had loudspeakers put their television on the walkway in front of their houses and replayed the video clip for several days. The whole alley was in joy like in a festival!

According to the residents in the alley, since August 2006, about twelve news agencies supported them by publishing articles on their plight. Six television programs demonstrating the illegal deviations from the "true" Project by the implementers and the local authorities were broadcast. Every time newspaper articles or television programs appeared, local people were delighted at the success in expressing their opinions. Hoa recalled her joyful sense of victory every time the media covered their story:

> We were very happy whenever a newspaper or a television program covered the problem of corruption of land in the district. We bought the newspapers, made copies and delivered them to our neighbors and everyone who would be concerned of corruption.

I attended an evening in which a program initiated by Hung and his "comrades" was being broadcast.[24] My journal entry on that day reads:

> The whole alley seemed quiet as everyone was at home watching the program. As soon as the show finished, all residents from both alley and street poured out into their neighborhood, cheering, laughing, and discussing every wise phrase said in the interview and the success of the program. Their fear of being resettled against their will and their hardship were momentarily replaced by joy and excitement. As soon as Hung came out to meet the residents, the whole group clapped to cheer him as if he was their spiritual leader.

The fact that local residents succeeded in making their highly local problem a matter of public interest may shed light on the (re-)emergence of civil society in Vietnam. Scholars such as Kerkvliet and Heng argue that the recently loosened hold of the state in censoring information has led to more freedom of expression through diverse media. Many scholars have pointed out the effect on the emergence of civil society of the creation of a space for citizens to discuss their problems with the authorities. Although the news agencies are state-owned, they were able to question the legitimacy of a state project. Moreover, they created a public sphere in which the authorities addressed the questions that residents had sought to pose through official channels of petition but to which they had not received a response. The point here affirms Heng's argument that although media is a model "of" the state and "for" the state, it is also against the state.[25]

The leaders in Green Alley also pursued their struggle from different angles. Based on the collected documents, they uncovered flaws in the arguments presented by the authorities. Residents continued to question the legitimacy of the plan provided by the district and affirmed that they were not covered by the Project. Armed with Hung's inside knowledge and strategies, their spokespersons at this point knew where to go and whom to meet. Depending on each particular situation, they gathered local residents in front of different offices, such as the ward, district, city council, and various related ministries in order to meet some key persons and request particular documents. Facing the collective action of the residents and legitimate status of the spokespersons, government officials had to provide legal documents to the leaders. The protesters thus collected a number of crucial legal documents signed by specific persons. In an annual meeting of the National Assembly, Hung managed to contact some staff serving the meeting and asked them to distribute three hundred copies of a newspaper article about the problem in the Third City Ring Road to the National Assembly members during the break. Another time, when President Nguyen Minh Triet came to visit the children of the district on the occasion of a mid-autumn festival, some leaders asked a child to give a letter raising the issue of corruption to the president.

## The authorities respond

These more or less peaceful methods in approaching higher officials aside, local residents also planned to have more organized activities and demonstrations. Until 2006, demonstrations were considered unlawful. However, fortuitously for the residents of Green Alley, Vietnam joined the WTO in December 2006. One of the requirements of WTO membership is to allow people to collectively express their opinions through demonstrations. This immediately caught Hung's attention. He soon collected the documents regulating procedures for lawful demonstrations and started planning for one. At several meetings, he affirmed that "a demonstration is now a lawful activity, we will use this method to make our voice heard by the central government, preventing corruption as the Prime Minister has stated." Local people were very excited when it was announced that they would lawfully demonstrate on the street and were eager for that day, planned for sometime in February 2007. However, their planned demonstration was halted before it could be held. A few days before the scheduled date, the area was filled with police who came to each leader's house and grilled them about the demonstration. While Thang was called to the ward office, Hung received a phone call from his superior, requesting him not to lead the demonstration. The key leaders then decided to cancel it.

Intimidation was not the only tool at the disposal of the local authorities who were determined to see the Project to completion. At some point, the front page of an official document was replaced with a different page containing a text that supported the authorities' position on the precise scope of the Project and more specifically the location of the Thanh Xuan intersection.[26] If some of the neighborhood leaders had not been knowledgeable about the special writing style used in official documents, no one would have noticed this deception. Thang got hold of a copy of the proof of this falsified document and quickly spread the word to the media. When he took the tampered document to confront the ward chairman, the latter tore it up in front of local residents. A member of staff then explained to the residents that "that was a photocopying mistake." This was not the only attempt of the authorities to deceive local residents. When the ward office was "besieged" by hundreds of people, the department responsible for the Project agreed to provide copies of official documents to the residents. The authorities apparently underestimated their subjects, especially the neighborhood leaders who had access to official records from alternative sources. Having the "true" plan obtained by Thang in their possession, they quickly pointed out that the "true" map had been replaced in the file by a false one.

According to local people, local authorities at three levels, i.e. city, district, and ward, were in league against them. Meanwhile, the central government was too far for them to reach. The 2005 Law on Complaints and Denunciation does not provide official ways for ordinary people to meet government officials. Moreover, once informed of the possible mistake of the asymmetrical intersection, the city authorities and the Ministry of Communications and Transport decided to legitimize this mistake by sending a document requesting the prime minister to approve the revised plan.[27] Hung, Thang and the local residents were very disappointed to learn of this move because their efforts would be meaningless if the prime minister approved it. Therefore, having experienced the machinations of the local authorities, and having no formal way to approach government officials, local residents could only hope that somehow their grievances would reach the prime minister and the leadership of the Communist Party.

## Partial victory

While the inability of the residents of Green Alley to seek redress by appealing to the highest levels of the Party/state reveals gaps in both the legal system and administrative procedures, their efforts to publicize their plight bore fruit. In December 2007, the Ministry of Communications and Transportation requested that the Project Planning Committee revise the intersection to make it symmetrical.[28] By January 2008, the intersection had been redesigned and in June 2008 the new design was approved by the ministry.

It is perhaps not coincidental that preparations for celebrating the millennium of Thang Long-Hanoi as Vietnam's capital were underway and the Third City Ring Road was incorporated into the preparations. The various government offices involved were eager for the construction site to be cleared by the time of the celebrations in October 2010.[29] It can thus be said that the struggle against the Project was successful insofar as it forced the authorities to restore the "true" symmetrical intersection that had originally been planned and presented in the exhibit on urbanization. Not everyone in Green Alley benefited from the reprieve from demolition and resettlement, however; only those whose dwellings had been included in the asymmetrical plan did. Demolition and resettlement continued apace in other parts of the neighborhood. By the end of July 2009, the People's Committee of Thanh Xuan District had approved the schedule of compensation for displaced households. Over the course of the following month, the People's Committee requested, cajoled, and pressured their owners to accept the compensation and vacate their residences.[30] When requests, cajolery, and pressure did not work, the People's Committee announced that it would resort to coercion, planned for several days at the end of September. Before that happened, most households accepted compensation and agreed to leave their homes. The clearing of the construction site for the Third Ring Road was officially completed by the end of September 2009.

## Conclusion

Through the case study of the two leaders, Hung and Thang, I have presented part of a struggle of residents in Thanh Xuan District against an urban development project. In seeking improved terms, residents confronted political insecurity and lack of transparency. They received information about the Project from the ward authorities who, at first, seemed willing to answer residents' questions about the legitimacy of the Project. However, the lack of substantive information and evasiveness of the answers did not satisfy the residents. In spite of possessing evidence that the original plan for the intersection was not being adhered to, residents had to face the negligence and even hostility of the local authorities. While failing to provide the legal document showing the legitimacy of the Project as it related to the Thanh Xuan intersection, the authorities continued to implement the Project by pressuring local people to move out. Most of the residents were unsettled by the actions of the authorities who kept coming to the alley, measuring the area without interacting with them or with the heads of the resident groups. Residents were not only verbally threatened by local cadres but also through the constant demonstration of executive power. An informant recalled, "The local authorities are corrupt and we can believe nobody in this society. You can ask anyone here if he believes in the cadres from the district and ward. I am sure that they would all say no." The residents lost their faith in the local authorities because their voice was unheeded and their petitions to the ward and the district offices were ignored.

Vietnamese do not have a long tradition of appealing against state officials in court. In imperial times, disputes that could not be resolved at the village level through mediation and conciliation were adjudicated by magistrates, whose main role was to administer in the name of the state. The cost and inconvenience of dealing with the magistrates led ordinary peasants to avoid going to their offices, including in order to lodge complaints. During the early decades of communism, the country did not have administrative courts to judge administrative lawsuits. The recently established administrative court in 1993 has not yet been acknowledged widely. As a result, appeals against administrative cadres to administrative bodies are likely to be unproductive. Yet, as the case of the Thanh Xuan intersection suggests, aggrieved citizens are not wholly without means of redress.

The success of the residents of Green Alley in forcing a redesign of the Thanh Xuan intersection owes much not only to their sustained efforts but also to the personal attributes of two men they chose to lead them and to represent their common interests in dealings with the authorities at both the local and national levels. These two leaders happen to be members of the Communist Party. Their leadership of the opposition to an important state project underscores the need to disaggregate the notion of "the state" and to rethink the ways in which state and society interact in postsocialist Vietnam. Thang and Hung took part in the struggle against a land clearance project endorsed by every higher level of authority because their own interests as residents in the affected neighborhood were involved and they were thus brought to make common cause with the people to whom they ordinarily represented the Party/state. They were able to rise to the leadership of the movement because they were familiar with the state's rhetoric and used it to back their arguments and to make sense of their own endeavors. As members of the Communist Party and employees of the state, they were also able to use their connections within the state bureaucracy to obtain crucial information and advance their cause.

Thang and the leaders of the first phase of protest had not managed to find a fruitful way to make use of the documents they had obtained, which showed their claims to be outside the area slated for demolition to be correct. The timely participation of police officer Hung allowed collective action to resume under new forms. One of the crucial factors in the success of the struggle was the decision to adopt the state rhetoric of anti-corruption. Trained in law and keen on reading politics, Hung quickly embedded the moral legitimacy of the residents' fight to retain their homes in the state rhetoric of public good and national citizenship. The use of state symbols and rhetoric to back their collective action indicates that collective action can succeed when drawing from a rich repertoire of symbols that is shared by both parties involved.

The participation of two members of the Communist Party in the struggle of Green Alley residents against a major state project gives support to Russell Heng's argument that "civil society in Vietnam may emerge or is emerging from within the state itself."[31] Although they were members of the Communist Party, Thang and Hung actively contributed to the struggle against the fraudulent Project, showing that the lower levels of the state apparatus designed to control society can be mobilized against state policy formulated at higher levels. The very embeddedness of the state in society means that its representatives live and work in close proximity to ordinary citizens and often share their interests and perspectives. The leaders nominated by local residents of Green Alley were *the instruments* of state authority at the neighborhood level. However, instead of representing the Party/state in the area in the dispute over the planned ring road intersection, their role shifted to opposing it. The state-established Party cell came to struggle against its "parents." For citizens caught in property disputes stemming from state modernization projects, the fuzziness of the boundaries between state and society may provide a small measure of comfort.

## Notes

1 Research for this essay was conducted in January to April 2007 with funding from VrjieUniversiteit Amsterdam's VU Fellowship, VU Fund, and the Dittmer Fund. My thanks go to the people of Thanh Xuan district and members of the Vietnam Museum of Ethnology for their support, and to Freek Colombijn, Oscar Salemink, and Truong Huyen Chi for their comments on an earlier draft which was presented at the Workshop on New Interfaces: Interdisciplinary Approaches to Histories and Societies Conference, Quang Binh, Vietnam, July 20–22, 2007. Different versions of this paper were published in (2008) "Von xa hoi trong do thi: Mot nghien cuu nhan hoc ve hanh dong tap the o mot du an phat trien do thi tai Ha Noi" (Social Capital in the City: An Anthropological Study of Collective Action in an Urban Improvement Project in Hanoi), *Tap chi Dan toc hoc* (Vietnamese Anthropology Review), 5:155 (2008), pp. 11–26 and in "From Ethnographic Research to Exhibition: A Case Study on Land Compensation Issues in Hanoi" in Vo Quang Trong and Amareswar Galla (eds), *Proceedings of the International Conference on "Museum and Urban Anthropology,"* Hanoi: Vietnam Museum of Ethnology (2009), pp. 336–51.

2 Tran Manh Tien, "Su di dan cua mot lang que mien Trung voi viec do thi hoa o khu xom Nha Den (Tan Dinh, Quan 3)," in *Do thi hoa tai Viet Nam va Dong Nam A* (eds),

(Ho Chi Minh City: Trung tam nghien cuu Dong Nam A–Vien Khoa hoc xa hoi TP Ho Chi Minh, 1996), p. 290.

3 SRV Government, *Quyet dinh 75/CP ve viec thanh lap quan Thanh Xuan va quan Cau Giay*. 1996.

4 SRV General Statistics Office, 2005. *Lao dong dang lam viec tai thoi diem 1/7 hang nam phan theo thanh phan kinh te va phan theo nganh kinh te* (Annual Statistics Data on Labor Working at 1st July Divided by Economic Compositions). Online at: http://www.gso.gov.vn/default.aspx? tabid=387&idmid=3&ItemID=4662 (retrieved October 28, 2006).

5 Dang Nguyen Anh, CecilaTacoli, and Xuan Thanh Hoang, "Migration in Vietnam – A Review of Information on Currents Trends and Patterns, and Their Policy Implications," in *Regional Conference on Migration, Development and Pro-Poor Policy Choices in Asia*, (Dhaka, Bangladesh, 2003).

6 Terry McGee, "The Urban Future of Vietnam," *Third World Planning Review* 3 (1995), p. 255.

7 SRV General Statistics Office, *The 2004 Migration Survey: Major Findings*, (Hanoi: Statistical Publishing House, 2005).

8 Decree 176/HDBT (1989) of the Council of Ministers aiming to rearrange labor in state enterprises. A large number of workers in these enterprises were forced into retirement.

9 Oshin is a word coming from a Japanese television series, indicating the people who have to do housework for other households to earn money.

10 SRV Thu tuong Chinh Phu. *Quyet dinh 597/QD-TTG/2001 ve viec dau tu du an xay dung giai doan 1 doan Mai Dich – Phap Van thuoc duong Vanh dai III – TP Ha Noi*. 2001.

11 SRV UBND TP Ha Noi. *Quyet dinh 4664/QD-UB ve viec thu hoi va tam giao 837,314 m² dat tai cac quan CauGiay, Thanh Xuan, cac huyen Tu Liem va Thanh Tri cho Ban quan ly du an Thang Long de thuc hien du an xay dung giai doan 1 doan Mai Dich – Phap Van thuoc duong Vanh dai III thanh pho Ha Noi*. 2001.

12 SRV UBND TP Ha Noi. *Quyet dinh 5593/QD-UB ve viec thu hoi va tam giao 23.805 m² dat tai quan Cau Giay, huyen Tu Liem, quan Thanh Xuan, huyen Thanh Tri cho ban Quan ly du an Thang Long de dap ta luy hai ben nen duong vanh dai III*. 2001.

13 SRV UBND TP Ha Noi. *Quyet dinh 4187/QD-UB cua UBND TP Ha Noi ve viec to chuc thuc hien cong tac den bu, tai dinh cu khi Nha nuoc thu hoi dat de xay dung duong Vanh dai III giai doan 1 (Doan Phap Van – Mai Dich)*. 2001.

14 SRV UBND quan Thanh Xuan. *Quyet dinh 728/QD-UB ve viec thanh lap Hoi dong giai phong mat bang den bu de giao dat cho Ban quan ly du an Thang Long thuc hien dau tu xay dung duong Vanh dai III giai doan 1 doan Mai Dich – Phap Van*. 2001.

15 Extracted from the Feasible Project in January 2001.

16 http://vietnamnet.vn/xahoi/2008/02/770140/.

17 SRV Bo Giao thong Van tai va UBND TP Ha Noi. *Thong bao 401 Ket luan cuoc hop giua lanh dao Bo GTVT va UBND TP Ha Noi, kiem diem cong tac GPMB va Thi cong cac du an xay dung giao thong tren dia ban thanh pho Ha Noi*. 2003.

18 David W. H. Koh, "Illegal Construction in Hanoi and Hanoi's Wards," *European Journal of East Asian Studies* 3.2 (2004), p. 203.

19 Benedict J.T. Kerkvliet, "An Approach for Analyzing State-Society Relations in Vietnam," *SOJOURN: Journal of Social Issues in Southeast Asia*, 16.2 (2001), pp. 238–78; Irene Norlund, *et al. The Emerging Civil Society – An Initial Assessment of Civil Society in Vietnam*, CIVICUS. Online at: http://www.civicus.org/new/media/CSI_Vietnam_report%20.pdf.

20 Nan Lin, "Social Networks and Status Attainment," *Annual Review of Sociology* 25 (1999), pp. 467–87; James S. Coleman, "Social Capital in the Creation of Human Capital," *American Journal of Sociology* 94 (Supplement: Organizations and Institutions:

Sociological and Economic Approaches to the Analysis of Social Structure) (1988), pp. S95–S120.

21 Zhou Xueguang, "Unorganized Interests and Collective Action in Communist China," *American Sociological Review*, 58.1 (1993), pp. 54–73.

22 Benedict J.T. Kerkvliet, "An Approach for Analyzing State-Society Relations in Vietnam," p. 269.

23 Vietnam News Agency, "Ong Nguyen Tan Dung duoc bau lam Thu tuong Chinh phu," Ministry of Foreign Affair, 2006. Online at: http://www.mofa.gov.vn/vi/nr040807104143/nr040807105039/ns060628085249/.

24 The program named *Tieu diem* was broadcast on March 29, 2007 on VTV1.

25 Russell Hiang-Khng Heng, "Civil Society Effectiveness and the Vietnamese State – Despite or Because of the Lack of Autonomy," in *Civil Society in Southeast Asia*, Lee Hock Guan (ed.) (Singapore: Institute of Southeast Asian Studies, 2004), p. 154.

26 Bao Dau tu, *Co dau hieu "chay" quy hoach o nut giao thong Thanh Xuan*, 2006. Online at: http://dantri.com.vn/c0/s0-137648/co-dau-hieu-chay-quy-hoach-o-nut-giao-thong-thanh-xuan.htm.

27 Nguyen Trang An, "Nut giao Thanh Xuan se lech to ve phia Ha Noi," Vietnamnet, 2007. Online at: http://vietnamnet.vn/xahoi/dothi/2007/01/654651/.

28 Nguyen Trang An, "Nut giao Thanh Xuan (Ha Noi): Meo da thanh can!" Vietnamnet, 2008. Online at: http://vietnamnet.vn/xahoi/2008/02/770140.

29 Chi Hieu, "Chinh phu dong y nut giao Thanh Xuan!" Vietnamnet, 2008. Online at: http://vietnamnet.vn/xahoi/2008/06/787651/.

30 Lan Huong, "Giai phong mat bang, thi cong duong Vanh dai 3, Quan Thanh Xuan: Cuong che dut diem them 15 chu su dung dat." Hanoi Moi. Online at: http://www.hanoimoi.com.vn/newsdetail/quy_hoach/220715/c4327905ng-ch7871-d7913t-273i7-875m-them-15-ch7911-s7917-d7909ng-2737845t.htm.

31 Russell Hiang-Khng Heng, "Civil Society Effectiveness and the Vietnamese State," p. 157.

# 6 The emerging role of property rights in land and housing disputes in Hanoi

*John Gillespie*

## Introduction

An influential group of theorists place their faith in laws and registered property rights to resolve housing and land disputes.[1] Hernando de Soto, a leading exponent of this view, invokes the metaphor of a bell jar to explain the difference between registered and unregistered property rights.[2] Those within the bell jar enjoy state protection of their registered property rights, while those outside the bell jar must fend for themselves. The assumption underlying this metaphor is that state regulators and courts protect property rights more effectively than community-based, self-regulatory systems. Supporters of de Soto urge developing countries such as China and Vietnam to upgrade their land regulation systems by replacing customary informality with Weberian rational laws and legal institutions.[3]

Though acknowledging the stabilizing role played by law, other commentators criticize the metaphor for drawing too sharp a distinction between state-backed property rights and self-regulation.[4] As an alternative, they propose a regulatory continuum, along which are many points representing different degrees of state and self-regulation. For example, at one end registered property owners, such as foreign investors, use land titles as collateral to borrow from banks. This type of activity is regulated in Vietnam by the Land Law 2003, Civil Code 2005 rules governing secured transactions, and other legislation based on imported rights-based regulatory models.

At the other end of the continuum people turn to self-regulatory systems for ideas about what they can and cannot do and only selectively (if at all) follow statutory rights and procedures. Housing and land markets based on community norms and practices are a defining feature of many developing countries and some commentators have observed this practice in urban and rural Vietnam.[5] There is solid empirical evidence for their claim. The Vietnamese Ministry of Natural Resources and Environment estimates that 40 percent of houses in Hanoi lack registered land titles, and even houses with titles are routinely traded outside the state system.[6] An IFC survey puts the level of land transactions taking place outside the state land tenure system at 75 percent.[7] Similarly high levels of unofficial land use are reported in urban China.[8]

In this chapter, I explore how courts in Vietnam navigate and reconcile different regulatory approaches to housing and land disputes in Hanoi. To what extent, and in what circumstances do courts draw on guidance from outside the juridical framework to resolve disputes? What constitutes fair and reasonable access to housing and land? Do courts ultimately have the power to put an end to quarrels and formulate lasting solutions to housing and land disputes? To address these questions, I examine at close range a series of housing and land disputes in Hanoi. The Vietnamese Constitution 1992 requires courts to resolve disputes according to the law. My findings suggest, on the contrary, that judges quickly exhaust the possibilities of statutory land rights and legal doctrines, and either push cases back to state officials or use "reason and sentiment in applying the law" (*ly va tinh trong viec chap hanh phap luat*), a type of situational justice, to resolve cases. Outcomes are negotiated from a syncretic blend of statutory law, state policies, and community norms and practices. Contrary to de Soto's proposition, I find that land titling has not brought legal order to housing and land disputes. Instead, courts continue to rely more on administrative and self-regulatory norms and practices than statutory property rights to resolve housing and land disputes.

To identify the norms and tacit assumptions underlying the different points along the regulatory continuum I draw on a series of interviews with retired state officials and a private land broker. Since most court judgments are not published in Vietnam, and even then only provide a sketchy account of events, I also relied on interviews with judges and lawyers to understand dispute resolution. Altogether I reviewed eighteen land and housing cases, and a further twenty-three cassation appeal cases from 2005–6 that were published on a website hosted by the Supreme People's Court.

Before considering contemporary dispute resolution, it is necessary to understand the regulatory histories underlying housing and land in Hanoi. One of the main themes in this chapter is that people's perceptions and habits are "the end product of repeated action in the past, of prolonged behavior in the past."[9] New regulatory systems appear the way they do because people interpret them from particular sets of beliefs, practices, and goals – the regulatory histories in which they are embedded (Lessig 1995: 949–59).[10] My purpose in mapping the regulatory histories is not to present an authoritative description, but rather to trace the origins of the main narratives that influence contemporary dispute resolution.

## Colonial housing and land regulation (1862–1954)

Although I begin my account with French colonization, it will become clear later in the discussion that precolonial views continue to intermingle with and influence contemporary attitudes to land and housing. From the beginning, the French set out to establish a system of land entitlement based on title by registration.[11] Lands that were of interest to the French, other foreigners, and the tiny francophone Vietnamese élite – primarily urban zones and plantations – were held under a version of the French Civil Code. Title by registration and *hypothèques* (registered mortgages) enabled colonial élites to enlist state power to protect property rights against others, including the state.[12]

The colonial system of land regulation was explicitly dualistic. Formal legal protection did not extend to the vast majority of the population who remained within the orbit of imperial and village rule.[13] By the close of the colonial period in 1954, precolonial patterns of land use coincided with pockets of strong French legal influence in large urban centers such as Hanoi.

## High-socialist period (1954–86) housing and land regulation

To examine the interplay between the different regulatory approaches to housing and land during the high-socialist period that followed the defeat of the French colonial forces by the Democratic Republic of Vietnam in 1954, I draw on the recollections of three key actors. Nguyen Thuc Bao, a former legal adviser to the Minister of Agriculture in the Democratic Republic of Vietnam and a high-ranking party official, played an important role in formulating housing and land policy during this period. Phung Minh, an official in the Hanoi Housing and Land Management, displayed less enthusiasm about socialist policies and lamented the decline of colonial technical and legal standards. In stark contrast to the others, Le Trong lived on the periphery of socialist society, eking out a living as a private land broker in the self-regulating land market.

### *The party ideological perspective*

For decades Nguyen Thuc Bao worked as a policy adviser on housing and land regulation, first with the Hanoi Housing and Land Management Office (*So Quan ly Dien tho Ha Noi*) and later for the Ministry of Agriculture.[14] He recalled that following liberation in 1954 officials in the Cadastral Office (*So Dia chinh*) in Hanoi followed the procedures, if not the spirit, of colonial legality. The 1946 and 1959 Constitutions maintained the fiction of private real estate markets; at the same time party policies encouraged state land management.[15]

Throughout his narrative Nguyen Thuc Bao stressed the important role played by Marxist-Leninist theory in shaping land management practices. He noted that Marxist-Leninist theory treats land as a special commodity (*hang hoa dac biet*), and as such it lacks *gia tri su dung* (consumption value).[16] Since land is not a marketable commodity, it followed that states rather than markets should regulate access to housing and land.

Nguyen Thuc Bao formed a party affairs section (*Ban can su Dang*) in the Hanoi Housing and Land Management Office but recalled that "most of the officials were not re-educated, because these people were loyal to the 'Fatherland'. Cadres nevertheless introduced communist ideology to the French-trained workers."[17] They used a book written by Ha Lan about agrarian reforms in People's Democratic Republics to inculcate revolutionary attitudes about "love between people of the same class" (*tinh yeu giai cap*).[18] Land officials were instructed to understand the class struggle (*dau tranh giai cap*) not only in intellectual terms, but also to get "in touch with the people" (*duong loi quan chung*).[19] Since the people responded more to personal and sentimental relationships than to abstract legal rules, state officials were encouraged to selectively apply the law. In practice this meant balancing legal rules with a broad range of political, economic, and moral norms and practices.

Nguyen Thuc Bao attributed this type of redemptive justice to "situational validity" (*thoa dang*), a practice that emerged in the pre-modern period. It values contextual relevance and enduring solutions more highly than consistently following codified norms and procedures. Eventually this regulatory style evolved into "reason and sentiment in applying the law" – the technique state officials and judges use today to resolve disputes without technically and rigidly applying the law.

Nguyen Thuc Bao also maintained that the state focused primarily on rural rather than urban land reforms. It was not until 1963, almost a decade after the state began nationalizing urban land, that legislation formalized this policy. Circular No 713 TTg on Land Management Authorizing State Management Policies 1963 instructed officials to confiscate (*tich thu*) urban land from party enemies, and requisition (*trung thu*) or acquire (*trung mua*) land from those considered sympathetic to the party.[20] Wealthy, non-exploitative owners were expected to "voluntarily" relinquish occupation, but not ownership rights, in return for a nominal rent. For the first time since the colonial period, legislation explicitly raised political criteria above legal entitlements to urban land.

As Nguyen Thuc Bao recollected, it was not until the early 1970s that Soviet land management practices gained ascendancy over the more chaotic revolutionary regulation. Soviet law emphasized a proprietorial approach to land management.[21] The state allotted land rights to state-owned enterprises, cooperatives, and households, while discouraging horizontal transactions among state and private entities. After years of debate, in 1980 the Party's Political Bureau formally adopted the Soviet model in which land is owned by the people but placed under state management. This principle appeared in the 1980 Constitution and later in the Land Law 1988.

For Nguyen Thuc Bao the main achievement of this period was bringing private land markets under party ideological direction. He acknowledged the regulatory confusion generated by revolutionary land management but on balance believed that socialist outcomes were more important than orderly laws and processes. His story closely resembles the official party narrative he helped shape.

### *The technocratic perspective*

Phung Minh reminisces in his memoirs about the forty years he worked for the Hanoi Housing Land Management Office.[22] Trained under the French as a land surveyor, he worked in the Hanoi Cadastral Department before 1954. Although generally sympathetic to the revolutionary cause, he regretted the erosion of skills and competencies that took place during the high-socialist period. For example, he noted that professional cadastral mapping effectively ceased in the capital after

1959 when the party transferred all the trained cartographers to work on rural projects.[23]

Phung Minh depicts housing and management during this period as arbitrary and haphazard. Officials, for example, subdivided large villas into small apartments using hand-drawn floor plans that only roughly corresponded to boundary dimensions and title documents. But he reserved his main criticism for the callous implementation of nationalization policies. Rather than using professionally trained officials to reallocate housing in Hanoi left vacant by the colonial government officials, foreign nationals, and Vietnamese fleeing to the south,[24] the Housing and Land Management Office recruited soldier cadres (*nhom tiep quan*). Only those with backgrounds in the anti-colonial resistance were considered sufficiently in tune with party policies to handle this sensitive task. As Phung Minh observed, the culture of resistance did not generate respect for the idea that laws and procedures play a role in ordering social relationships; on the contrary, its aim was to subvert state power structures. Reinforcing this antipathy toward legality, many cadres had migrated to Hanoi from rural areas and were unfamiliar with, even contemptuous of, the title by registration system operating in former colonial centers.

A central theme running through Phung Minh's memoirs is that revolutionary policies and incompetent management practices were partially responsible for the explosion of land and housing disputes that followed *Doi Moi* reforms in 1986.[25] He thought that party and state regulatory policies never managed to fill the regulatory vacuum left by the colonial system. To redress revolutionary excesses he argued for technocratic regulation based on due process and professional competencies.

## *A view from the periphery*

Le Trong tells a more heterodox story about land and housing in Hanoi.[26] As the son of a prominent *avocat* in the French colonial system, he was denied a formal education and employment. During the high-socialist period he earned a precarious living as a land broker bringing private buyers and sellers together for a commission.

From the early 1960s until the enactment of the Ordinance on Residential Houses in 1991 only the state was supposed to allocate and transfer land and housing. Le Trong remembered that people were afraid to advertise housing and land sales, as this informed authorities they possessed surplus property. Despite active suppression by state authorities, a covert self-regulating housing market slowly developed to satisfy demand unmet by the cumbersome state land management system. Most sales involved the small residential apartments allocated to families in collective housing (*nha chung*). Following reunification in 1975 the housing demand from returning soldiers generated too many private transactions to suppress and the authorities tacitly accepted self-regulating markets.

Le Trong thought that socialist land laws and policies only marginally influenced the community norms and practices that ordered self-regulating markets. In his view most people believed that colonial land titles conferred full ownership rights, and the state lacked authority to interfere. He believed that colonial notions of property rights conflated in the popular imagination with local normative practices to form distinctive self-regulatory practices. For example, the handwritten documents used to sell land, traced ownership through a chain of transfers back to colonial land titles. Neighbors were encouraged to sign transfer documents to signify there were no outstanding boundary claims. This practice was introduced by the French to record the names of witnesses who could present evidence if the transfer was later legally challenged. It was retained in the self-regulatory system to place community pressure on the parties to honor the transaction.

In many cases transacting parties asked local officials to certify transactions and reinforce the informal monitoring systems available within the community. *Phuong* (ward) level officials certified what were technically illegal self-regulatory transactions to avoid "losing touch with the people" (*xa roi quan chung*). This practice expanded the scope of official regulation well beyond the areas recognized in the juridical framework. Officials justified their support for self-regulation by deploying the utilitarian argument that self-regulating markets partially offset the shortfall in state housing. According to a report prepared by the Hanoi Housing and Land Department in 1971, approximately 12 percent of disputes resolved by state authorities concerned disputes between individuals over private leases, inheritance, and significantly for this discussion, claims about private land transfers.

Le Trong agreed with Nguyen Thuc Bao and Phung Minh that state officials seldom used legal guidelines to resolve disputes and instead appealed to *hop ly* (reasonableness), backed by a mix of political, moral, and sentimental norms to persuade disputants to compromise. He stressed the interconnections binding the state (especially at the local level) and self-regulatory systems. Officials aimed for situational justice and gave little thought to crafting generally applicable principles that could apply to other cases. They negotiated with disputants in a personal and highly contextual language that often (but not always) balanced community interests against central laws and policies. To remain socially relevant officials were expected to show good neighborliness or sentiment among neighbors (*tinh cam lang gieng*) and intervene on behalf of family, friends, and neighbors. Over time this practice has bifurcated central laws and the self-regulatory transactions supported by local government officials.

To summarize, at the close of the high-socialist period several core narratives informed housing and land regulation in Hanoi. Party narratives sought to discredit the colonial idea that land ownership exists as a private individualistic "moment." In its place they advocated class-based regulatory policies, but eventually revolutionary utopianism gave way to the more sober Soviet idea of state proprietorial control. At the same time a technocratic narrative began to gain momentum in party discourse. Instead of political outcomes, it stressed efficiency, professional competencies, predictability, and coherence – in short a proceduralization of state regulation. This narrative reinforced claims by reformers in other social areas that only codification and legality could correct the uncertainty and arbitrariness unleashed by revolutionary regulation.[27] Calls for legal reforms eventually found a powerful ally in Party Secretary Truong Chinh. During the Sixth Party Congress in 1986 he famously argued for "[t]he management of the country to be performed through laws rather than moral concepts."[28] In tandem with legal reforms, self-regulatory markets co-existed with, and increasingly intertwined the state regulatory system. They balanced private ownership rights against broader familial and community obligations. Party narratives had little apparent influence over self-regulatory transactions, even though local government officials were closely involved in private markets. By the close of the high-socialist period self-regulatory markets dominated housing and land sales in Hanoi.

## Legislating for land titles in the post-*Doi Moi* period

The narratives discussed above emphasized different reasons why the state moved closer to a title by registration system in the early 1990s. For example, Le Trong insisted that public agitation for more and better quality housing persuaded the party and state to enact the Ordinance on Residential Housing 1991 and recognize house ownership. Phung Minh attributed reforms to the state attempting to bring order to the chaotic self-regulating market.[29] Reluctant to concede party failings, Nguyen Thuc Bao claimed the idea came from Soviet theory that permitted private ownership over domestic property, and reserved state proprietorial controls for economically productive land.[30] They agreed, however, that the desire to attract foreign capital and technology exerted a powerful influence over reforms. The transitional 1988 Land Law recognized private land use rights, but citizens were not permitted to transfer or deal with housing and land until the 1993 Land Law.[31] This reform opened the way for a series of incremental changes that culminated a decade later in the recognition of real estate markets in the 2003 Land Law. In many respects the new law returned to the colonial title by registration system since it now recognizes comprehensive ownership rights over residential land, while maintaining the socialist rhetoric of people's ownership of land.

Having considered the core regulatory narratives in Hanoi, I now return to the central question whether courts have the power to make effective and lasting decisions over socially important housing and land cases. But first it is worth noting that article 134 of the Land Law 2003 requires complainants to refer disputes in the first instance to ward-level conciliation councils (*ban hoa giai*). State officials and lawyers involved in conciliation unsurprisingly report that legal rights play a marginal role in local level dispute resolution.[32] Parties are encouraged to compromise their legal rights in the interests of securing a compromise. The success rate for resolving disputes is less than 20 percent and most complaints are referred to district level authorities or lodged with the courts.

## Court-based dispute resolution

In this section, I consider evidence that judges understand private housing and land use rights through pre-existing patterns of thought, and resort to administrative measures, as well as community conceptions of just and fair access to housing and land to settle quarrels.

Senior judges report that the number and complexity of housing and land cases is increasing.[33] In 2005, approximately 30 percent of the 50,000 civil law cases concerned housing and land disputes.[34] Increasing litigation rates seem to imply that courts have the capacity and willingness to resolve housing and land disputes.

Yet a growing body of research intimates that litigation rates are a poor measure of judicial effectiveness.[35] Effective courts are supposed to resolve disputes by finding a practical ending and binding outcome so that quarrels in the past no longer burden the present. Evidence considered in this chapter suggests that court hearings (as opposed to pre-trial mediation) rarely perform this function in Vietnam. About 60 percent of housing and land disputes are passed from the courts to the National Assembly and hybrid party state organizations, such as the *Van phong Tiep dan cua Trung uong Dang va Nha nuoc* (Office to Receive Citizen's Complaints of the Central Committee of the Party and the State) for a political resolution.[36]

An alternative way to evaluate judicial effectiveness is to assess the power courts possess to make enduring decisions about socially important housing and land issues (Gillespie 2007: 841–3).[37] According to this approach, courts are ineffective if litigants do not accept judicial findings as final and binding regardless of the number of court actions. There are three generally accepted components of judicial power: jurisdictional power, discretionary power, and the authority to make binding decisions.[38] The following discussion uses this typology of judicial power to assess the effectiveness of Vietnamese courts in resolving housing and land disputes.

## Jurisdiction over housing and land cases

Powerful courts have a broad jurisdiction over matters of controversy. Civil courts in Vietnam are given extensive powers over housing disputes, but their jurisdiction over land cases is limited to "lawful" ownership claims.[39] Since courts lack powers to define their own jurisdiction, what constitutes "lawful" claims remains the exclusive provenance of the government. Where the law does not provide clear guidance, judges are instructed to base their jurisdiction on determinations made by government officials.[40]

Jurisdiction currently extends to registered land-use titles and certain types of long-term occupation. Politically sensitive claims to recover land nationalized by the state, as well as adverse possession claims by squatters are currently excluded from judicial review. In sum, courts have extensive powers over housing disputes, but quite limited powers to consider socially controversial land disputes such as land takings.

## Judicial discretion

Courts also need discretionary power to make meaningful decisions over housing and land matters. There are well-documented political and structural constraints to judicial discretion in Vietnam.[41] Chief among these is the requirement that judges be party members and follow the party line. But direct party interference is generally reserved for high-profile, politically sensitive administrative and criminal cases. The low-profile housing and land cases analyzed in this chapter reveal little evidence of direct party interference, although party policy strongly influences the decision-making environment.

Deference to local government officials is a more significant threat to judicial discretion. Recent reforms have attempted to loosen government control over judges by placing court administration under the central authority of the Supreme Court.[42] However, cases discussed shortly show that local governments still directly guide judicial decisions.

In addition to political and structural factors, epistemological assumptions constrain discretionary power. In civil law jurisdictions like Vietnam, judges are relegated in the official discourse to the secondary function of passively and mechanically applying the law to resolve cases.[43] Judges are not granted explicit rights to interpret law and few decisions are reported, a practice that inhibits the development of explanatory doctrines. Rather, they are expected to assume that legislation is comprehensive, internally consistent, and that for every housing and land issue there is a governing rule. In brief, the law is supposed to have already judged and judges merely mechanically fit facts into the matrix of law.

Judges in every legal system need discretion to bridge the gap between legislative rhetoric and concrete social problems. Even in mature civil law systems, such as in France, statutes alone cannot possibly provide solutions to every problem.[44] This problem is well understood in Vietnam and for decades the Judicial Council of the Supreme Court has issued resolutions to fine-tune the application of statutory law.[45] But as the case studies below reveal, the resolutions contain general and abstract provisions that are themselves difficult to apply in many circumstances. Compounding the problem, most resolutions concern procedural issues and relatively few attempt to guide judicial discretionary power.

Courts adopt various strategies to overcome legislative shortcomings. They use pre-trial mediation to find solutions that are not provided by the law. Alternatively, they refer sensitive issues to local government authorities for resolution, "use reason and sentiment in applying the law" to bring decisions closer to underlying community norms and practices, or refer decisions to judicial committees (*uy ban tham phan*) comprising superior and inferior judges.[46] What is largely missing from their repertoire is the use of legal reasoning to formulate creative solutions to problems that community norms and practices cannot resolve.

### *Compulsory pre-trial mediation*

Some lawyers believe that compulsory pre-trial mediation is the most effective procedure available to judges.[47] Before court proceedings commence, judges are required to conduct mediation sessions to encourage litigants to settle. Court reports do not disclose how many housing and land disputes settle during pre-trial mediation, but judges and lawyers interviewed estimate a 30 percent success rate, much higher than court decisions.

In November 2008, I observed a mediation session in the Hoan Kiem District Court between a petitioner claiming ownership of a villa in the old quarter of Hanoi, and the long-term occupants.[48] The petitioner wanted to regain possession without paying compensation to the occupants. The judge first invited lawyers representing the litigants to summarize their positions and submit corroborating documentation. From that point on he encouraged the litigants to make concessions and compromise. He did this through the elaboration of *ad hoc* criteria of reasonableness and legitimate expectations.

For example, a sticking point in this case was that the occupants wanted the petitioner to subsidize their rent and relocation expenses. Although the Land Law 2003 extinguished a pre-existing legal obligation to pay this kind of compensation, the mediating judge emphasized *gia tri chung* (community values) that recognized a duty of care to find accommodation for long-term occupants. He explained that if the petitioner insisted on his strict legal rights the case might take many years to resolve because the occupants could delay proceedings and appeal decisions.

The judge next presented the litigants with a proposal that appeared to accommodate their claims, but was somewhat different from their original intentions and interests. He suggested that the petitioner should pay relocation expenses and rent for six months, but was not obliged to find alternative accommodation. When the litigants pulled back from the proposal, they did not return to their starting positions but adopted new positions. The petitioner, for example, contemplated paying relocation compensation, while the occupants acknowledged the owner's title over the land. After some weeks of negotiations the case settled without proceeding to a formal trial.

The judge used his considerable discretion to draw on sources that ranged well beyond the juridical framework. But a clear tension existed between applying the law and finding solutions based on community norms and practices. Judges interviewed referred to the well-known proverb "*mot nui cai ly khong bang mot ti cai tinh*" (a mountain of arguments based on reason cannot equal a little argument based on sentiment) to underscore their conviction that land laws play a marginal role in the lives of most litigants.[49] Although judges claimed that they must arrogate discretionary power to find contextually relevant solutions, they conceded that they lacked an unfettered discretion and must avoid the appearance of subverting legal rationality (*duy ly*) with sentiment (*duy tinh*).

### *Resolving disputes with administrative decisions*

In cases involving claims against state interests, civil court judges push the decision back to government officials. Consider Le Van Dinh's action in the Hanoi People's Court to reclaim land from the Hai Ba Trung District People's Committee.[50] Colonial authorities issued a land title to Mr Dinh's parents. The house was destroyed during the evacuation of Hanoi in 1946 and Mr Dinh's parents later sold part of the land shortly before moving to Saigon in 1954. They leased the remaining land to the Tan Viet Cooperative. Over the intervening years a series of cooperatives and state-owned companies leased the land.

In 1992, the director of Cong Ty Dong A, a company owned by the Hanoi People's Committee, invited Mr Dinh to sell the land. Shortly afterward, the director informed Mr Dinh that his family's title was extinguished when the land came under "state management" on June 27, 1963. He produced Official Letter (*cong van*) No. 568 issued by the Hanoi Housing and Land Department on April 15, 1993 confirming that the private interest in the land had been extinguished. The director then sold the land to the Hanoi Housing Renovation and Development Company for 1.33 billion *dong* on behalf of the firm.

Nguyen The Hung, the lawyer acting for Mr Dinh, argued in court that Official Letter No. 568 did not accurately reflect land policy during the 1960s. According to Circular No. 713 TTg Authorizing State Management Policies 1963, only the act of confiscating (*tich thu*) land from party enemies extinguished private property rights. Since Mr Dinh's parents participated in the anti-colonial resistance and were not party enemies their land should have been requisitioned (*trung thu*) – a procedure that placed land under state management without disturbing underlying ownership rights. He also asked the Hanoi People's Committee to explain why the cooperatives and state-owned firms occupying the land paid Mr Dinh's parents rent for thirty years, if ownership rights were extinguished in 1963. He accused state authorities of deliberately misinterpreting land policy to seize valuable real estate.

The presiding judge, Nguyen Kim Khanh, ordered in favor of the Hanoi People's Committee. He did not look beyond Official Letter No. 568 for answers to the questions raised by Nguyen The Hung. During an interview Nguyen The Hung[51] speculated that in deciding claims against the state, judges are expected to "protect revolutionary achievements relating to land" (*thanh qua cach mang ve dat dai*) and give preference to the "state benefit."[52] From the moment the procuracy signaled its interest in protecting the "state benefit" (*loi ich cua nha nuoc*) the judge deferred to the people's committee and subordinated Mr Dinh's property rights to the state. Mr Dinh did not appeal the court's decision.

### *Reason and sentiment in applying the law*

The Vietnamese Supreme Court promotes a decision-making environment in which judges are supposed to passively and mechanically apply legislation to the facts in question. As Mark Sidel's chapter in this volume suggests, in politically sensitive cases judges turn to party and state officials for guidance. But what happens in the overwhelming majority of cases where law provides no clear solution and "state benefit" is not an issue? Judges interviewed say that over decades a tacit practice evolved to deal with this type of "hard" case: superior level judges in public stress strict compliance with statutory law, but in practice allow inferior level judges to smuggle *gia tri chung* (community values) and other non-legal narratives into the courtroom. Judges use "reason and sentiment in applying the law" to soften sharp legal distinctions and make their decisions more socially relevant.

For specifics consider the petition lodged by the Nguyen lineage in the Tu Liem District Court to recover possession of their ancestral lineage hall in Dong Ngac town.[53] The five-room lineage hall was constructed on about 300 $m^2$ of land in 1770. In return for maintaining the building and tending fruit trees, one branch of the lineage lived rent free in the lineage hall. During the early 1990s, lineage leaders began to complain that the occupants were not fulfilling their duties. Finally, the lineage leaders lost patience and in 1995 demanded the return of the building and land.

Rather than contesting lineage ownership over the building and land, the occupants claimed a right to possession based on long-term occupation. Four generations of the same family had lived in the lineage hall since 1907. Both sides agreed that in village practice occupants were entitled to benefit from improvements made to buildings and land. But the lineage leaders insisted that the arrangement did not give rise to rights of possession.

Nguyen Van Thuy, the presiding judge, ordered the lineage leaders to subdivide the land and give one third to the occupants. He argued that the lineage's assertion of ownership was incompatible with a "constitutional right to housing" – a claim that is unsupported by current constitutional law. Article 62 of the 1980 Constitution required the state to provide housing for citizens, but this socialist principle was quietly dropped from the 1992 Constitution. In any event, the duty in article 62 only applied to the state and did not extend to private owners. According to Le Kim Que, a lawyer involved in the appeal decision, the judge invoked the constitutional principle to camouflage his decision to raise a community norm over the statutory right to ownership.[54]

The lineage leaders appealed the decision to the Hanoi People's Court.[55] During the hearing, their lawyer, Le Kim Que, argued that the judge in the first instance erred in law in treating the occupants' claim like an inheritance case. Because the occupants did not own or lease the lineage hall they did not possess property rights to pass from generation to generation. He also claimed that the judge in the first instance allowed community norms and practices, rather than the law, to guide his decision.

The appeal court judges first satisfied themselves that the local district people's committee had not placed the lineage hall under state management during the high-socialist period.[56] Once assured that the "state benefit" was not an issue, the judges proceeded to explain why the District Court judgment was "unsatisfactory to the litigants' demands and aspirations." They attached considerable importance to the years of service provided by the occupants and inferred a moral and social responsibility for the lineage to look after their members. Lineage leaders were ordered to "assist and stabilize the occupants' lives" by providing alternative accommodation.

The judges concluded that the District Court had been unnecessarily generous to the occupants and that a lower level of compensation would satisfy their reasonable (*hop ly*) needs. To compromise, the lineage leaders offered to rehouse the occupants in a smaller area attached to the lineage hall. The judges regarded this arrangement as reasonable in the circumstances, because it provided adequate accommodation without compromising the lineage's right to worship in the lineage hall.

To summarize, the appeal court judges did not attempt to analogize from statutory law or from other cases a general duty for owners to compensate occupiers. Instead they used "reason and sentiment in applying the law" to balance the lineage leaders' legal rights to the land against community expectations that lineage members should provide for one another. The court wound back the generous compensation ordered in the first instance hearing, and instructed the lineage leaders to give the occupants a small parcel of land suitable for a modest house.

Despite legislative changes over the following decade that significantly strengthened the legal presumption of title by registration, recent cases reveal the continuing influence of "reason and sentiment in applying the law." One case is enough to make this point. In 2003, Nguyen Thi Nhu petitioned the Thanh Tri District Court in Hanoi to reclaim approximately 1,000 $m^2$ of land occupied by Nguyen Van Han.[57] Thanh Tri District was originally a rural area that was incorporated into the fabric of Hanoi during the construction boom in the early 1990s. Mrs Nhu's parents, the original owners of the land, died intestate in 1946.[58] As the only surviving child, Mrs Nhu inherited; but soon after her parents' death she left the family home and went to live with her husband. In 1953, Mr Han, a distant and homeless relative of Mrs Nhu, asked for permission to temporarily reside in the house. He had recently been released from Son La jail after serving five years' imprisonment for fighting the French colonial government.

Mr Han and his family lived in the house rent free, but paid local land tax. In 1972, Mrs Nhu repaired the house but did not attempt to reclaim the land until 1981. During one visit, Mr Han allegedly assaulted her by stuffing buffalo dung into her mouth, causing injures that required hospitalization. She then sought the support of the Dong My *phuong* (the ward level government agency) to recover the land. The timing of her petition was unfortunate, because the Constitution 1980 had just nationalized land ownership, and the principle of private ownership of residential houses had not yet been enacted into law. Adding to her problems, as an anti-colonial resistance hero, Mr Han commanded considerable prestige and persuaded local authorities not to intervene.

Decades later, in 2002, when Mrs Nhu detected a shift in government land policy, she reattempted to recover the house and land. Once again the ward People's Committee rejected her claim, and in 2003 she brought the action to the Thanh Tri District Court.

She asked the court to decide between two competing stories. Her claim relied on article 24 of the Ordinance on Inheritance, which gives property in intestacies to the surviving children.[59] In contrast, Mr Han based his claim on community norms and practices. He produced a deed written in *Nom* script purporting to show that the family *chu ho* (lineage head) had assigned him the house and land. Evidence in court confirmed that it was common practice at this time for village scholars to prepare land documents for illiterate farmers. Since the deed of assignment was not notarized under the colonial law, its validity rested on community and family norms and practices. Importantly for our discussion, Mr Han's ownership claim relied on community values that are not recognized in law.

### *Thanh Tri District Court decision*

In the first instance hearing, Judge Do Thi Luyen handed Mrs Nhu a pyrrhic victory. She regained possession of the family house and land, but at the cost of compensating Mr Han. The Land Law 2003 requires owners to compensate occupants for improvements to land, but not to pay relocation costs. The judge based this component of the compensation award on the previously discussed community expectation that relatives should look after one another and the legally unsupported belief that long-term use gave Mr Han a moral claim over the land.

### *Appeal to the Hanoi People's Court*

Mr. Han appealed the decision to the Hanoi People's Court. The Court quashed the decision of the court of first instance on the grounds that there was insufficient evidence to support Mrs Nhu's inheritance claim. This surprising decision disregarded written submissions by the ward People's Committee that confirmed Mrs Nhu's right to inherit the house and land. The Supreme People's Procuracy protested the Hanoi municipal court's decision to the Supreme Court – an intervention that usually signals bribery or some other illegal activity. The Supreme Court canceled the Hanoi People's Court decision on the grounds of error of law and transferred the case back to the Thanh Tri District Court for a rehearing.[60]

### *Retrial, Thanh Tri District Court*

The retrial took place in 2007 before Judge Nguyen Tri Tuyen.[61] On reviewing the evidence the judge confirmed that Mrs Nhu inherited the house and land from her parents. It rejected Mr Han's claim that the lineage head assigned him rights in the house. On close examination, the assignment deed did not clearly identify Mr Han as the beneficiary and it bore the signatures of his nephews, who according to village traditions lacked the seniority to transfer interests in land. Although acknowledging that in some circumstances long-term use, paying taxes, and improving land can generate interests in land, the court preferred Mrs Nhu's account that she lent the house temporarily. It was noted that this type of arrangement is commonplace among relatives. Though finding in her favor, the court once again granted Mr Han compensation amounting to half the value of the land, much more than he was due under the law.

What is instructive about this case is that even the Supreme Court treated Mr Han's claim, which was based on traditional practices, seriously and did not strictly apply the Inheritance Law that accorded Mrs Nhu full legal rights. The compensation awarded to Mr Han reflected the ambiguous status of legal rights since he received more than he was due under the law. Finding enduring solutions to housing and land disputes is widely considered more important than strictly following statutory formulations.

### *Factors that limit the discretionary powers of judges in housing and land cases*

Several countervailing factors influence the discretionary power of courts. Judges perform a filtering function in resolving "easy" cases that exhibit clear legal violations, but push back "hard" cases to local government officials. Judges avoid becoming directly involved and prefer to monitor investigations conducted by local government officials from a distance. Deference of this kind has a long tradition in Vietnam as courts for decades functioned like local government offshoots.[62] Despite reforms aiming to create a more independent judiciary, courts continue to rely on government officials to gather evidence and, in many cases, determine liability.

Another factor limiting discretionary power is the epistemological settings that determine whether judges are receptive to new ideas and approaches. For decades, socialist legal thinking discouraged judges from bringing legal discourse into conversation with community norms and practices. It does not recognize customary rules and practices as sources of law.[63] These epistemic settings prevented knowledge gained by judges from developing into a coherent system of "legal reasoning." Although the epistemological settings have expanded since *Doi Moi* reforms, interviews with Vietnamese judges indicate that superior level judges still discourage inferior level judges from using legal reasoning to find new solutions to otherwise intractable social problems. They worry that, over time, legal reasoning will expand judicial power over new and complex social problems and in the process create an epistemological alternative to the party line.

Vietnamese lawyers also note that discretionary power is further reduced by the practice of "first decide, then try" (*quyet dinh truoc khi xet xu*) in which superior level judges review inferior level decisions before they are announced. In a recent survey,[64] 68 percent of district level judges admitted that they "request case outcomes" (*thinh thi an*) from judicial committees (*uy ban tham phan*) comprising senior judges. Collegial decision-making increases the accountability of inferior court judges at the expense of their capacity to use legal reasoning to expand their discretionary powers.[65]

In contrast with their limited legal discretion, some judges arrogate considerable extra-legal discretionary powers. As the case studies show, judges routinely use "reason and sentiment in applying the law" to expand their discretionary powers over "hard" cases. Solutions based on community norms and practices are first negotiated during pre-trial mediation sessions, and then reappear, sometimes disguised as vague constitutional or legal principles, during formal court proceedings. Judges interviewed claim that norms and practices derived from self-regulatory community systems produce more enduring outcomes than law-based decisions.

## Judicial authority

The final element of judicial power is the capacity of judges to enforce their decisions. There is ample evidence that enforcement is a problem in Vietnam.[66] In a particularly egregious case, a Supreme Court eviction order issued in 1997 remained unenforced in 2006.[67] The plaintiff commenced action to recover her house, which had been acquired (*trung mua*) by the Hanoi City People's Committee during the 1960s. In 2004, the Hai Ba Trung District Justice Department was preparing to enforce the eviction notice when they received a telephone call from Le Quy Don, vice chairman of the Hanoi People's Committee. He ordered a temporary stop on the enforcement "to enable the relevant authorities to reconsider." A newspaper report speculated about possible collusion between the vice chairman and the occupants of the villa, and concluded that the long delay and "darkness" surrounding the case undermined public confidence in law enforcement and the judicial system. Nguyen Van Thuan, vice president of the Law Committee of the National Assembly, epitomized the attitude of state officials to court judgments when he declared

> [i]t would be an honor for the president of a provincial people's court to be invited to work with the chairman of a people's committee at the same level, so how dare an ordinary judge quash the chairman's decision in a land dispute case?[68]

This criticism from one of Vietnam's most senior legal officials reflects the low social status of judges and the reluctance of government officials to accept court decisions. The public's skepticism about the efficacy of litigation amplifies the problem.[69]

To recap, judicial power to enforce decisions is closely tied to the public's perception about judicial integrity. What constitutes integrity is not just a function of honesty and truthfulness. It also corresponds to the validity systems that legitimize judicial decision-making. Findings considered in this chapter suggest that most citizens prefer solutions grounded in community norms and practices to winner-takes-all law-based outcomes. This clash of validity systems is informing public perceptions about judicial integrity and in the process undermining judicial authority over housing and land disputes.

## Conclusion

I began this chapter by suggesting that de Soto's metaphor of a legal bell jar underestimates the interaction and mutuality between state and self-regulatory housing and land systems in Hanoi. After two decades of reform, statutory private rights still struggle to influence judicial and popular views about what constitutes fair and reasonable access to housing and land. My findings show that courts push back "hard" cases – where legislation does not provide clear guidance – to government officials to resolve. Where this tactic is inappropriate, courts turn to the norms and practices embedded in self-regulatory systems to resolve housing and land disputes. All this suggests that judges and litigants do not fully accept the legal proposition that "land use rights" and houses are a private, individualistic "moment".

The main difference between statutory and self-regulatory narratives resides in the contrast between the detailed and concrete stories people tell themselves about living in a particular community, and the abstract and sketchy stories regulators use to unify fragmented and disparate regulatory histories. Most people know more about their ward and district than about their city and nation. They are in a better position to order their world from the thick local descriptions with which they are familiar than to apply thin statutory rules and procedures. To put an end to quarrels about housing and land, judges need outcomes based on thick local descriptions.

This bifurcation between central statutory and local self-regulatory narratives presents a dilemma for court-based dispute resolution. Courts are ill equipped to reconcile different regulatory narratives and resolve disputes to the satisfaction of all concerned. Judicial reasoning is supposed to use laws and legal discourse to determine what constitutes valid and invalid behavior. It resolves problems by manufacturing legal fictions that provide solutions not otherwise found in self-regulatory practices. It is not intended to produce socially grounded decisions that reconcile laws and self-regulatory narratives. The difficulty in Vietnam is that legal doctrines lack the persuasive power to broker lasting solutions to housing and land disputes. In consequence, courts struggle to use law to resolve this kind of dispute.

Working in a weak legal environment, courts understandably turn to the authority of government officials or extra-legal dispute resolution techniques such as "using reason and sentiment in applying the law." Judicial reforms aiming to compel judges to base their decisions on legal narratives may – until land laws command more popular respect – have the unintended consequence of making courts less attractive dispute resolution forums. In the meantime universal laws provide poor signposts for resolving disputes in a fragmented regulatory landscape.

Adding to the problem, courts are ill prepared to synthesize local knowledge into universal legal principles. This task is perhaps better performed by public participation in lawmaking. There is ample scope to bring state regulators into conversation with self-regulatory communities because so far the public has been granted limited opportunities to genuinely influence land policies and laws.

In the end, the legal notion that housing and land rights are universally applicable has not been fully accepted by the courts and the public. As important as these concepts may be to the development of national housing and land markets, they present an extremely thin and only partially correct picture of how property is dealt with on the ground. It is necessary to transcend this individualistic rights-based approach to fully understand the self-regulatory systems that order housing and land in Vietnam.

## Notes

1 Harold Demsetz. "Toward a Theory of Property Rights II." *Journal of Legal Studies* 31.2 (Part 2), (2002): 653–72; Robert Ellickson. "Property in Law." *Yale Law Journal* 102.6 (1993): 1315–400.

2 Hernando De Soto. *The Mystery of Capital. Why Capitalism Triumphs in the West and Fails Everywhere Else*. London: Black Swan; New York: Basic Books, 2000, pp. 47–62.

3 Asian Development Bank. "The Impact of Land Markets on the Poor: Implementing de Soto." Hanoi: Making Markets Work Better for the Poor Discussion Paper 3, 2004.

4 A. Gilbert. "On the Mystery of Capitalism and the Myths of Hernando de Soto: What Difference Does Legal Title Make." *International Planning Review* 24 (2002): 1–19; Jonathon Manders. "Sequencing Property Rights in the Context of Development: A

Critique of the Writings of Hernando de Soto." *Cornell International Law Journal* 37 (2004): 177–98; Jane Glenn Matthews and V. Belanger. "Informal Law in Informal Settlements," in *Law and Geography,* J. Holder and C. Harrison (eds). Current Legal Issues vol 5. Oxford: Oxford University Press, 2003, pp. 281–304.

5 Benedict J.T. Kerkvliet. "Agricultural Land in Vietnam: Markets Tempered by Family, Community and Socialist Practices." *Journal of Agrarian Change* 6.3 (2006): 285–305; Thomas Sikor. "The Politics of Rural Land Registration in Postsocialist Societies: Contested Land Titling in North-Western Vietnam." *Land Use Policy* 23.4 (2006): 617–28; Annette Kim. "A Market without the 'Right' Property Rights." *Economics of Transition* 12:2 (2004): 275–305; Nguyen Quang Vinh and Michael Leaf. "City Life in the Village of Ghosts: A Case Study of Popular Housing in Ho Chi Minh City, Vietnam." *Habitat International* 20.2 (1996): 175–90.

6 Interviews with officials from the Ministry of Natural Resources and Environment, Hanoi, March–May 2006.

7 S. Tenev, A. Carlier, O. Chaudry, and Nguyen Quynh-Trang. *Informality and the Playing Field in Vietnam's Business Sector.* Washington: IFC, World Bank, and MPDF, 2003, p. 68; VNCI, *Land Tenure for the Private Sector.* Hanoi: unpublished report, 2007, p. 21.

8 Samuel Ho and George Lin. "Emerging Land Markets in Rural and Urban China: Policies and Practices." *The China Quarterly* 175 (2003): 696–8.

9 Owen Barfield. *History, Guilt, and Habit.* Middletown, CT: Wesleyan University Press, 1979, p. 74; David Marr. "History and Memory in Vietnam Today: The Journal *Xua & Nay.*" *Journal of Southeast Asian Studies* 31.1 (2000): 1–25.

10 Lawrence Lessig. "The Regulation of Social Meaning." *University of Chicago Law Review* 62.3 (1995): 949–59.

11 Arrêté du Contre-Amiral, Commandant en Chef Bonnard, Saigon, February 20, 1862, cited in (Hooker 1978: 160–1).

12 Martin Murray. *The Development of Capitalism in Colonial Indochina (1870–1940).* Berkeley, CA: University of California Press, 1980, pp. 132–40.

13 Martin Grossheim. "Village Government in Pre-Colonial and Colonial Vietnam," in *Beyond Hanoi: Local Government in Vietnam*, Benedict J. Kerkvliet and David G. Marr (eds). Singapore: Institute of Southeast Asian Studies, 2004, pp. 58–73; Michael Barry Hooker. *A Concise History of South East Asia.* Oxford, UK: Oxford University Press, 1978, pp. 175–80.

14 Interviews, Nguyen Thuc Bao, former legal adviser to Ministry of Agriculture, Hanoi, September 2000. Mai Xuan Yen, Chief Inspector, Land Administration Department expressed similar views during interviews conducted in Hanoi during October 1997 and June 1998.

15 See Constitution 1946 Article 12; Constitution 1959 Articles 14, 19.

16 Tran Quang Huy. *Giao trinh Luat dat dai.* Hanoi: NXB Cong An Nhan Dan, 2001, pp. 12–20.

17 It was state policy to allow Vietnamese officials serving in the colonial government to continue in their positions. *Nhan Dan.* "Tam chinh sach cua nuoc Viet Nam Dan Chu Cong Hoa moi cho cac thanh pho moi duoc giai phong." September 1, 1954, pp. 25–6.

18 Ha Lan. *Cai cach ruong dat o cac nuoc dan chu nhan dan.* No. 5 Liberated Territory: Su That, 1953, pp. 25–9.

19 Hoang Quoc Viet. "Can dam bao cho phap luat duoc ton trong trong cong tac quan ly linh te cua Nha nuoc," in *Nghien cuu Nha Nuoc va phap quyen.* Hanoi: Su That, 1964, pp. 33–6; Thanh Duy. "Co so khoa hoc va van hoa trong tu tuong Ho Chi Minh ve nha nuoc va phap luat." *Tap Chi Cong San* (1997:1): 26–8.

20 Note the similarities to the Law on Agricultural Land Reform 1953 (Luat Cai cach Ruong dat, December 4, 1953), preamble, and article 3. Pham Thi Thu Thanh and Tran Ha. *25 Nam Xay Dung Nen Phap Che Viet Nam.* Hanoi: Lao Dong, 1971.

21 Nguyen Thuc Bao. "Mot so y kien ve quan ly dat dai theo phap luat va trach nhiem doi voi cac hanh vi vi pham phap luat dat dai o nuoc ta." *Nha Nuoc va Phap Luat* (1986.2): 7–15; Nguyen Nhu Phat. "Gop y kien ve van de: Dat dai thuoc so huu toan dan." *Nha Nuoc va Phap Luat* 28.4 (1979): 14–16.
22 Phung Minh. *40 Nam Quan Ly Nha Cua o Ha Noi.* (Hanoi: unpublished paper, October 1998).
23 Ibid. pp. 16–17.
24 Of the 4,866 houses were left vacant in 1956, 1,491 belonged to foreigners, ibid. p. 3.
25 Ibid. pp. 27–30.
26 Interviews, Le Trong, Land Broker, Hanoi, March 2001, November 2008.
27 Nguyen Nien. "Several Legal Problems in the Leadership and Management of Industry under the Conditions of the Present Improvement of Economic Management in Our Country." *Luat Hoc* 14 (1976):33–5, trans. *JPRS*, September 30, 1976, pp. 34–6.
28 Truong Chinh. "Introduction to the Political Report." Vietnam News Agency, December 15, 1988. Part 4, pp. 318–19.
29 Phung Minh. *40 Nam Quan Ly Nha Cua o Ha Noi*, pp. 23–5.
30 Pavan Skomorokhop. "Phap luat Xo Viet bao ve quyen loi dan su." *Tap San Tu Phap* (1961.3): 42–4.
31 Phung Minh. *40 Nam Quan Ly Nha Cua o Ha Noi*, pp. 23–30.
32 Interview, Quang Anh Son, vice chairman, Hanoi People's Committee, Hanoi, December 2008. Interviews, Nguyen Hoang Hai, Hai and Associates, Hanoi, November 2008; Nguyen Quang Tuyen, Land Law Lecture, Law University, December 2008; Nguyen Hung Quang, NH Quang and Associates, Hanoi, March 2008, November and December 2008; Nguyen Bao Huy, Leadco, Hanoi, June 2008 (Interviews with lawyers).
33 Toa an Nhan dan Toi cao. "Bao cao tong ket cong tac nam 2005 va phuong huong nhiem vu cong tac cua nam 2006 cua Nganh Toa An Nhan Dan." Hanoi, 2006, pp. 2–4.
34 Approximately 70 percent of housing and land cases related to compensation claims for site clearance, 10 percent involved administrative abuses by state officials, 8 percent concerned boundary disputes, 7 percent were claims to recover land possession and 4 percent were listed as other issues. VIR. "Firm Foundation Laid to Build Land Laws." *Vietnamnet*, September 10, 2006.
35 Erik Jensen. "The Rule of Law and Judicial Reform: The Political Economy of Diverse Institutional Patterns and Reformers' Responses," in *Beyond Common Knowledge: Empirical Approaches to the Rule of Law,* Erik Jensen and Thomas Heller (eds). Stanford, CA: Stanford University Press, 2003, pp. 345–9.
36 Interview, Nguyen Thi Tuyet Lan, Judge, Hanoi Provincial Court, Hanoi, January 2009; interview, Tran Van Son, Deputy Director, Claims Settlement Department, Office of Government, Hanoi March 2007.
37 Gillespie, John. "Rethinking the Role of Judicial Independence in Socialist-Transforming East Asia." *International Comparative Law Quarterly* 56.3 (2007): 841–3.
38 Solomon, Peter. "Courts in Russia: Independence, Power and Accountability," in *Judicial Integrity,* Andras Sajo (ed.). Leiden: Martinus Nijhoff Publishers, 2004, pp. 226–30.
39 Civil Procedure Code, Article 25; Land Law 2003, Articles 50, 138.
40 Toa an Nhan dan Toi cao. "Bao cao tong ket cong tac nam 2005," p. 12.
41 Pip Nicholson and Nguyen Hung Quang. "The Vietnamese Judiciary: The Politics of Appointment and Promotion." *Pacific Rim Law and Policy Journal* 1.14 (2005): 14–22.
42 Law on the Organization of People's Courts 2002, Articles 45, 46.
43 Khanh Van. "Cai cach tu phap: Nhin tu nhieu goc do." *Tap Chi Nghien Cuu Lap Phap* 4 (2003): 3–8.
44 Merryman, John. *The Civil Law Tradition*, 3rd ed. Stanford: Stanford University Press, 2007, pp. 39–49.

45 JICA. *Nghien cuu chung Viet-Nhat ve viec phat trien an le tai Viet Nam*. Hanoi: Supreme People's Court, 2007, pp. 216–17.
46 Interviews with lawyers.
47 Do Xuan Loi. "Role of Mediation in Judgment Enforcement." *Democracy & Law* (2005): 44–5.
48 The litigants did not want their names disclosed.
49 Interviews, Nguyen Thi Tuyet Lan, Judge Hanoi Provincial Court, Hanoi, January 2009; Nguyen Manh Cuong, Judge Hanoi People's Court, Hanoi, July 2007; Pham Tuan Anh, Judge Hanoi People's Court, Hanoi, July 2007 [interviews with judges].
50 Ban an Hanh chinh So tham So: 1/HSST Toa an Nhan dan Hanoi (Administrative Judgment No. 1/HSST Hanoi People's Court), December 21, 1996.
51 Interview, Nguyen The Hung, Lawyer, Hanoi September 2000.
52 Tran Quan Huy 2001: 231–2.
53 Case No. 52/DSST, October 2, 1995, Tu Liem District People's Court; and Case No. 20/PTDS, January 31, 1996, Hanoi People's Court, January 1, 1996.
54 Interview, Le Kim Que, President of the Hanoi Bar Association, Hanoi, July 1998.
55 Case No. 20/PTDS, Hanoi People's Court, January 31, 1996.
56 The Presiding Judge was Nguyen Khac Vinh and the other judges were Phan Truong and Nguyen Hong Van.
57 Decision No. 19/2004/DSST, Thanh Tri District Court, June 24, 2004.
58 Article 121 in the Land Law 2003 and Article 19 in Decree No. 181/2004/ND-CP, October 29, 2004, permit land transfers through inheritance.
59 A similar provision appears in Article 676 of the Civil Code 2005.
60 Cassation Review Decision No. 62/2007/DS-GDT, Hanoi People's Court, March 7, 2007.
61 Case No. 14/2007/DSST, Thanh Tri People's Court, October 16, 2007.
62 In a recent survey district court judges admitted that they routinely defer to the opinions given by local government bodies (UNDP 2007:298–300).
63 Le Hong Hanh. *Giao trinh ly luan Nha Nuoc va phap luat*. Hanoi: Cong An Nhan Dan, 1998, pp. 291–325.
64 UNDP. *Bao cao khao sat nhu cau cua Toa an nhan dan cap huyen tren toan quoc*. Hanoi: NXB Tu Phap, 2007, pp. 250–2.
65 Bui Ngoc Son. "Su doc lap cua Toa an trong Nha nuoc phap quyen." *Tap chi Nghien cuu Luat phap* (2003.4): 43–50.
66 Nguyen Van Thanh and Dinh Van Minh. *Mot so van de ve doi moi co che giai quyen khieu kien hanh chinh o Viet Nam*. Hanoi: NXB Tu Phap, 2004, pp. 76–147.
67 Duc Hoa. "Ban an ach 10 nam vi mot lanh dao TP Hanoi." *Dan Tri*, July 4, 2006. Online at: http://baotonghop.net/index.php?doc=/c20/s20-127270/ban-an-ach-gan-10-nam-vi-mot-lanh-dao-tp-ha-noi.htm; http://vietbao.vn/Xa-hoi/Ban-an-ach-gan-10-nam-vi-mot-lanh-dao-TP-Ha-Noi/30127270/157/ (accessed June 29, 2010).
68 VNExpress. "Nganh toa an kho kham noi viec xu ly tranh chap dat dai." 2003. http://vnexpress.net/Vietnam/Phap-luat/2003/07/3B9C9DE9/ (accessed June 29, 2010).
69 UNDP. *Access to Justice: Survey from the People's Perspective*. 2004. Online at: http://www.undp.org.vn/detail/publications/publicationdetails/?contentId=1824&language-Id=1.

# 7 Property, state corruption, and the judiciary

## The Do Son land case and its implications

*Mark Sidel*

Property, law and the state interact in many ways in Vietnam, as in China and other societies transitioning from socialism. Conflicts over property reflect different conceptions of rights, and the interplay of state authority and customary rights, as To Xuan Phuc points out in this volume, as well as competing rights between individuals and often within families, as John Gillespie writes, with the state using a combination of customary rights and positive law to enforce its own authority and come to a decision (either through administrative process or through the courts). Property, law, and the state are enmeshed when the state seizes land, either for its own use or in facilitating private, corporate use of property. Sometimes segments of the state and society come together in the land context in ways that actually protect ordinary citizens, as Nguyen Vu Hoang described in his discussion of residents of a Hanoi alley's fight to defend their homes from demolition. In such situations, state power, and society's (here neighborhoods') goals may be focused on a common protective task that is based in officials' self-interest.

These conflicts, and the competing and overlapping ways of resolving them, are reflected in the many Vietnamese corruption cases that involve property. Land is a resource whose value has not been unlocked or fully monetized in some areas of Vietnam – perhaps especially these days in rural areas – and as a result many groups and forces have a stake in property conflicts. Not least among those are government officials, for whom the unsealing of potentially enormous land values in desirable locations for personal benefit, through either the takeover of private land or the conversion of public land to their private use, is a significant temptation. The wealth contained in land is more than a major attraction to government officials; it is also a highly viable target as well.

In Vietnam as in most other countries, state officials are the regulators of land and its disposition as well as the potential beneficiaries of its conversion to their own use. It is thus no wonder that so many Vietnamese corruption cases involve that great under-utilized but available resource of property: Party and government officials may well be carrying out their official tasks while pursuing their own interests at the same time.

In many countries, when individuals' interests in property conflict with state decision-making, the judiciary is one forum for resolving those disputes. In Vietnam, where the courts remain hamstrung by Party and government control, low capacity, narrow definitions of jurisdiction, authority, and corruption, the judiciary has a role in many land and property cases, as John Gillespie's chapter in this volume shows. Officials using and manipulating a weak judiciary to resolve these corruption cases involving land can exacerbate all of these problems, making the application of law arbitrary and further infuriating the public. As Gillespie points out, the state does not always intervene in property cases. But when it does – and when state actors intervene to protect the official corruption that often surrounds land – the results can further weaken public confidence in property rights and the role of state institutions.

Despite the weak and controlled Vietnamese judiciary, rarely have instances of interference with the judiciary and violation of the constitutional norm that "judges ... are independent and shall only obey the law" become a major public and political issue in Vietnam. In 2005 and 2006, however, a significant property case involving judicial interference by high-ranking Party and state officials broke into the mainstream Vietnamese media, illuminating both the scale of the problem and the difficulties in reducing judicial interference in significant land issues in which state officials had corrupt interests.

## The Do Son land case and the emergence of judicial interference onto the public stage

In April 2004, the People's Committee of Haiphong Municipality, one of Vietnam's most important industrial and commercial cities, issued Decision no. 807, signed by the Vice Chairman of the Municipal Party Committee. Among the hundreds of administrative decisions issued by a municipal-level Vietnamese entity in that year or any other, this would not normally have elicited much notice. Under existing Vietnamese law, the Decision allocated plots of land to over 100 local citizens and to others. By law and policy, such land was supposed to go to local residents, with priority given to the poor, disabled, war wounded, veterans, and other vulnerable social groups.[1]

The plots were issued in an area under Haiphong's administration called Do Son – an area of already highly valuable and still growing land values, near the coast, with a casino nearby and numerous other tourism and recreation projects on the drawing boards. One newspaper estimated the land's worth in the thousands of dollars per square meter, with re-sales of land already going for far higher. It was, in the words of a national newspaper, "land with beautiful views, and value in the billions of *dong*."

This Decision drew interest because of who received the land. Among the more than sixty households allocated plots, at least nine of those were members of the Standing Committee of the Do Son Communist Party Committee of the local county seat or other local high-ranking officials, all of whom were not entitled to such land under national regulations for the allocation of land. They received parcels ranging from 60 to more than 300 square meters. Among the recipients were the Secretary of the Do Son Party Committee, in the name of one or more family members, who received 314.2 square meters; the Party Committee's Deputy Secretary, who received 120 square meters; members of the household of the Chairman of the Do Son People's Committee, who received over 700 square meters; and others.

In addition to these allocations, the Decision issued on April 2, 2004 also recommended that Haiphong Municipality approve allocations of 22 parcels of land ranging from 120 to 250 square meters to senior officials working in a number of departments of Haiphong Municipality, including the bureaus of Construction, Finance, Planning and Investment, the Organization Department of the municipal Party Committee, several departments of local Party Committees, and officials working in public security, justice, health, and education in Haiphong – all specifically named.

As local citizens began to talk about this flagrant land grab by officials, a retired local official, Public Security Colonel Dinh Dinh Phu, learned of these corrupt land transfers and began to complain loudly to local and national authorities and media. In the words of the Vietnamese online newspaper *VnExpress*, Colonel Phu engaged in a "firm struggle, holding his ground, leveling accusations of negative actions, including meeting with a number of eminent people." Colonel Phu would become the only real hero in an increasingly complex story of property, corruption, and judicial interference that would, eventually, lead to the highest levels of the Party in one of Vietnam's largest cities.

Colonel Phu's complaints and other reports of the land transfer were picked up by national newspapers and republished around the country. They sparked a wave of public anger and an investigation undertaken by the Government Inspectorate (*Thanh tra Chinh phu*) at the urgent request of the Deputy Prime Minister responsible for anti-corruption matters. The Inspectorate concluded that the procedures used for deciding on the allocation of the land were completely lacking in integrity, official reporting had been untruthful, and investigators had been interfered with. Responsibility both for the corrupt allocation of the land and for interference in the investigation process was laid directly at the feet of the local Party Committee and important local Party and State officials.[2]

The Government Inspectorate asked the central Party Secretariat in Hanoi and the Deputy Prime Minister to force the Haiphong Party Committee to make amends and to punish local officials. But with respect to the untruthful reports, provision of falsified files, and other issues, the Inspectorate also noted that those actions likely constituted violations of land law and other laws and regulations, and suggested to the Deputy Prime Minister that he send these matters to the Ministry of Public Security for investigation and possible charges.

In response, the Haiphong Party Committee formed a group of senior officials to handle the matter and to determine, along with the Standing Committee of the Do Son Party Committee, collective and individual responsibilities in the allocation of the land. Nine members of the Standing Committee of the Do Son Party Committee wrote self-criticisms and accepted personal responsibility for the violations.

The individuals concerned were issued internal disciplinary penalties under the Party Constitution and rules, raising questions about the dual applicability of overlapping constitutional and legal documents. Similar self-criticisms were made and similar internal discipline was issued to officials in the Haiphong Bureau of Natural Resources and Environment who had engaged in corrupt behavior, "causing the municipal People's Committee to allocate land in error."

The Deputy Party Secretary of Haiphong in charge of the group handling the problem – a process that was being watched carefully by Hanoi – noted that "some of the individual leaders' understanding of their errors is still childish, and does not reflect understanding of the seriousness of their errors." And he announced that the disciplinary process would end within a month, by May 13, 2005. The Haiphong Party Committee issued a collective warning to the Standing Committee of the Do Son Party Committee, and issued warnings to and removed five key local Party and state officials from office.

Most or all of this was posturing to end the investigations and to protect higher officials – backed up by penalties, but the relatively mild penalty of disciplinary warnings within the Party – against officials at the local Do Son Party Committee and local Party and state agencies. The Deputy Prime Minister in charge of the investigation at the central level, Truong Vinh Trong, who had become known as a sort of anti-corruption fighter, was not assuaged by these local moves to end the scandal. He responded to the Government Inspectorate report by accepting the recommendation of the transfer of information to the Ministry of Public Security for investigation of potential crimes, instructing the Ministry to carry out an investigation and to "issue charges in the case in accordance with law where there is clear evidence of a crime."

The Ministry of Public Security carried out its investigations in May and June of 2005 and announced in early July that it had lodged charges of abusing of functions and power in the Do Son case with a notice of those charges to local authorities and defendants.[3] Attempts to forestall more serious charges continued, for example through the removal of more local officials.

But none of this could forestall criminal charges: on August 11, the investigative police under the Ministry of Public Security in Hanoi filed charges against three senior Do Son Party and state officials for "using their position and powers to carry out an incorrect decision to allocate land in the Do Son township (Haiphong), causing widespread anger among the people." A month later charges were filed against a fourth public leader, the former Director of the Haiphong Bureau of Natural Resources and Environment, for his involvement in the affair.[4]

There the matter lay, at least in terms of press coverage, until early 2006. Under Vietnamese criminal procedure, the charges leveled by the Ministry of Public Security went next to the state prosecutors' office (the procuracy) with the recommendation of an indictment. The procuracy brought formal indictments against the officials in 2006. In August 2006, three of the four charged defendants went on trial at the Haiphong People's Court on charges of using their powers to allocate land to 33 individuals or families not authorized to receive the land. On August 28, their trial ended with the issuance of a warning (*canh cao*) and a fine of 50,000 *dong* each (then about US$3.25). The fourth defendant, the former head of the Haiphong environment bureau, had not been brought to trial; he was only punished internally and administratively.

Public and media fury now reached a new crescendo in the wake of this shambles of a trial over land. One newspaper noted that "the views of the people of Haiphong were expressed strongly against the overly light treatment meted out by the court against these defendants." Another newspaper noted sarcastically, "they've let them 'eat the land'!" And a third national newspaper issued a blistering attack on the proceedings, pointedly asking whether the trial had been conducted in a "strict and clear" manner.[5]

Two days later, as protests among the public and in the media continued to grow rapidly and loudly, Prime Minister Nguyen Tan Dung suggested in a formal official letter (*cong van*) to the Procurator-General of the Supreme People's Procuracy and the President of the Supreme People's Court that they lead an investigation to clarify collective and individual responsibility for the public prosecution and the trial in the Do Son case. And he announced that the government would investigate whether the Haiphong Party and state authorities had "interfered excessively (*can thiep qua sau*) in the case."

The Prime Minister said that "at a time when the Party, state, and people are resolutely implementing" laws and policies against corruption, "if this case has not been handled strictly and clearly it will reflect poorly on the struggle against corruption." He suggested that the Procurator-General and Chief Justice provide guidance for a formal review of the proceedings carried out by the Haiphong People's Court, with a view toward formally protesting against and opposing the results of that trial. Once again Deputy Prime Minister Truong Vinh Trong was assigned to re-investigate the case, now along with the local court's process and verdict, and to report back in a month.[6]

The intervention from Hanoi further emboldened local activists who were protesting the warning and fine issued by the Haiphong court. Colonel Dinh Dinh Phu, who had led the original protests against the land grab and demanded indictments of the key officials, told the press that "if a citizen of Do Son takes a couple of plants from the house of Party Secretary Vu Duc Van he'll be sentenced to six months imprisonment. But if some of us give ourselves more than 100 pieces of land with a value of billions of *dong* he is given a warning." Local residents told the press that the court in Haiphong had been "influenced" to reduce the punishments against the defendants by Haiphong Party authorities.

Almost immediately central investigators and national reporters learned that the local Haiphong Party leaders, working through the Haiphong People's Committee, had on two occasions "suggested" that the Supreme People's Procuracy "waive prosecution" of some of the officials implicated in the Do Son land scandal. Those two requests came in October 2005 and March 2006, also in the form of official letters (*cong van*). The reasons given were variously that they had accomplished much in their work, that their health was precarious, that waiving prosecution would not cause economic damage, and that that the officials in question had already been punished administratively in a timely manner. The requests were signed by one of Haiphong's most powerful officials, the Vice Chair of the city's People's Committee.

But the involvement of high officials went even beyond that level. Newspapers revealed that these requests for exemption from prosecution had been sent to and approved by the Haiphong Communist Party Committee, the most powerful body in the city. And the Party Secretary of Haiphong, the powerful Nguyen Van Thuan, who was also a member of the Central Committee of the Communist Party, admitted that he had "proposed waiving prosecution under the jurisdiction of the municipal People's Committee."

The press further reported that in early May 2006 the Supreme People's Procuracy in Hanoi had agreed to Haiphong's request to waive prosecution against one of the accused officials. They did so because the Haiphong People's Committee had canceled the land allocations and "corrected all of the consequences of this matter," because the evidence was not fully clear, and because he had contributed greatly to the local area. The Supreme People's Procuracy sent out a mid-level official supposedly responsible for the decision on the prosecution to tell the press that he had been influenced by the official letters (*cong van*) sent by the Haiphong authorities in his decision to waive prosecution and end the case against this official. At the time his prosecution was waived, he was the only municipal-level Haiphong official formally charged in the case; the others were officials in Do Son township, not in the central Haiphong administration.[7]

For its part, the Supreme People's Court came to the media placing blame solely on the local court for the mere warning and small fine issued to the other three accused officials. The presiding judge of the Supreme People's Court's criminal tribunal told the press that the original charges that could have been brought against the original three local officials – misusing official powers in the exercise of public duties under Article 281(1) of the Criminal Code – would have carried a punishment range of reform through labor of up to three years or imprisonment of one to five years. This was considered a "serious crime," he told the press, and "a warning could not be applied in these circumstances even where the circumstances were relatively light."

By now, a local though important property and corruption case was emerging as a significant national issue. In the midst of this chaos the central political and legal institutions acted quickly, convening a meeting four days after the Prime Minister's official letter (*cong van*) to announce that they had completed a full-scale review of the Haiphong case and had decided to overrule the original judgment issued by the Haiphong local court and to re-investigate and re-prosecute the officials whose prosecution had been waived. The meeting explicitly decided that the sentences given to the three charged defendants were too lenient, and that the court had incorrectly defined the substance of the crimes of which they were accused. At least one newspaper reported that some of the officials might now be tried under the more serious provisions of Article 281 of the Criminal Code Article, which called for five to years' imprisonment upon conviction.

For the first time, central officials formally announced that the Haiphong Party and state authorities had sent official documents to the municipal people's court "in order to interfere in the trial; they did not act in accordance with regulations." As central legal institutions scrambled to protect themselves, Procurator-General Ha Manh Tri said that the documents issued by the Haiphong People's Committee to the local court to "interfere with the court proceedings were not in accordance with regulations, and violated the principle that in administering justice the courts act independently and obey only the law." Another official attending the joint meeting of central-level legal institutions told *VnExpress* that "the participants in the meeting stated that the institutions responsible for defending the law must work independently, and must not be subservient to local authorities."

The President of Vietnam (who had significant responsibility for supervision of the judiciary and judicial reform in his role as a member of the Party's Political Bureau) stepped into this increasingly complex affair in early September 2006, calling the Haiphong court's verdict an "incorrect and unjust case," a strong term in Vietnamese. Once again, a senior official called for extra-judicial order to be used to force the judiciary to handle the matter correctly; the President told the Supreme People's Court that "the leaders of the judiciary must directly issue guidance on this matter, not shielding this case." The leaders of the Supreme Court chimed in to lambaste the Haiphong court's verdict, decrying the damage caused to the Party and state.[8]

## Sidestepping a constitutional guarantee through policy and official letters (*cong van*)

In short order, the issue of interference with the judiciary in a property case – or "over-interference" (*can thiep qua sau*), an assumption that some interference was justified – was regarded as a major problem not because judicial autonomy was trampled but because the Party and state were suffering political losses in the process. And the entire process was carried out extra-judicially, with the courts as mere pawns of dueling official letters issued by national and local Party and state officials.

Because the courts were compromised and subservient, officials both seeking to escape from justice and those wanting justice to be done could not rely on the courts: they worked through official letters and verbal instructions, all seeking to force the courts to do their bidding. Official letters were the mechanism both for illegality, and for extra-judicial attempts to order the courts to set that illegality right. Central Party officials demanded that the Supreme Court and Procuracy reopen the case through official letters. Haiphong authorities sought to escape their own prosecution by forcing the local courts and the national procuracy to waive prosecution of local officials, also through *cong van*. One of the defendants had written several official letters to the Haiphong authorities attesting to the legality of the land allocations.

The political stakes continued to be raised in September when the national press revealed a report by the Haiphong local court to the Supreme Court in Hanoi, documenting direct communications by the powerful Party Secretary of Haiphong, Nguyen Van Thuan, urging the local prosecutors and judges to respect the decision of the Supreme People's Procuracy to exempt the Director of his Environment Bureau from prosecution, or to issue a light punishment if that was needed. After the fact – having complied earlier – the local court directly termed this "interference" with the court.

But they also revealed the fundamental difficulty in naming and overcoming judicial interference in Vietnam: under local Party regulations, since the officials charged were cadres under the Haiphong Party Committee, the local people's court and procuracy had reported as required to the Standing Committee of the Haiphong Party Committee on the case. Because the courts were required to seek guidance from local Party authorities in cases in which Party officials were charged, interference with the judiciary was actually institutionalized – at the same time as it was officially barred by the Constitution. In the case of charged Party members, in effect, interference is built into the system. The Haiphong Party Secretary even directly cited precedents of other cases in which local courts sought guidance from Party authorities in dealing with cases in which Party officials were implicated – a cynical resort to extra-judicial precedential authority in a country where elements of the common law are still being resisted. The courts are not allowed to use precedent in their daily work, but Party secretaries have a form of *carte blanche* to cite it in defense of corruption and judicial interference.

The Party Secretary's instructions to the local court were direct and specific: "If there are ameliorating factors," he noted that the defendants could be punished under a specific section of Article 281 of the Criminal Code that brought far lighter punishment – namely a warning and a small fine. Having interfered with the national procuracy to obtain exemption from prosecution for one Haiphong Party official, the Party Secretary then told the local court that it must obey the national procuracy's decision not to prosecute him. All proceeded as the Party Secretary instructed. *VnExpress* noted dryly that on August 28 the Haiphong court issued a verdict that "coincided relatively closely" with the "views" of the Haiphong Party Committee, including both the light sentence (the warning and the 50,000 *dong* fine), and letting that official escape prosecution.

Under these circumstances, the Deputy Prime Minister criticized the "over-interference" in the trial process in Haiphong and called for a full investigation and report to the Prime Minister – despite the fact that the interference that occurred was actually built directly into the system of trying Party officials. In turn, the Supreme People's Court announced that it would supervise a retrial of the case in Haiphong.

Beginning in early December 2006, the powerful Party Secretary of Haiphong mounted a strong defense of his actions. He argued that he and the Standing Committee of the Haiphong Party Committee

> must provide their views [on cases] to implement regulations when trial bodies ask for their views.... Although the municipal Party Committee has views, this never means detailed guidance, but falls within the realm of a general line and resolving [issues]. And the conclusions put forward are

collective, certainly not the personal views of the Secretary of the municipal Party Committee.

And he cited a Decision issued by the Political Bureau of the Party (Decision no. 52), requiring Party committees such as his own to reply to questions asked by courts about Party cadres, in effect wrapping himself in the mantle of institutionalized judicial interference under Party regulations.[9] In turn, the central legal institutions, also struggling to protect themselves in a property case that had gone severely awry, proposed more serious charges against at least one of the defendants.

As various forces splintered to protect themselves, the local Haiphong court tried to speak up in contradiction of the Party Secretary's defenses, providing a frank description of the mechanism of judicial interference in Vietnam. "I felt quite lonely in trying this case," said Duong Van Thanh, Deputy Chief Judge of the Haiphong People's Court and the chief judge at the first Do Son trial, in a newspaper interview.

> Of course no one told me that I had to try this case this way or that way. But there were 'hints' (*goi y*) and 'directions' (*dinh huong*) for the trial, and I had to consult those. If the upper levels have proposals, then it's difficult for me to do things differently.... If the upper levels set a direction for trial, I must follow.

All of those investigated were "cadres under the administration of the Haiphong municipal Party Committee," making the situation very difficult, according to a report that Judge Thanh wrote to the Supreme People's Court in Hanoi.[10]

By the fall of 2006, the discussion of judicial interference in the Do Son land case began to fade from the newspapers. In the end, there appears to have been no significant sanction, either judicial or Party-based, for the actions taken by the Haiphong Party and state officials to interfere with and mold the judgment of the local court. The Deputy Prime Minister forced Haiphong Party Secretary Nguyen Van Thuan to attend a meeting to describe and explain the Haiphong authorities' interference in the case, but there appears to have been little other punishment. Eventually an expanded pool of defendants was put on trial for the criminal aspects of their corrupt misallocation of land in Do Son; they were convicted this time around, and sentenced to jail terms. By 2007, the case had faded from the headlines, but public anger in Do Son and Haiphong and demands for accountability by higher officials forced the authorities to revisit the possibilities of charges against more senior officials.

## Property, corruption, and judicial independence in Vietnam

The Do Son land case was one of the few occasions in recent times in Vietnam where the press, Party, government, and judiciary have openly raised the failure by Party and state officials to comply with constitutional guarantees of judicial independence. So in one sense public discussion of some judicial independence issues was itself a step forward.

But while Haiphong Party and government officials were criticized for interfering with the judiciary, the critique of that interference was ambivalent, and the Party and government's methods for resolving that interference relied entirely on their *own* interference with and direct instructions to the courts and prosecutors (seeking to trump the original Haiphong interference with the local courts). The Vietnamese courts themselves have virtually no means of ensuring their own autonomy without political direction, and the consequences of Do Son show little promise for enhanced protection of judicial independence and the constitutional guarantee that embodies it, whether in important land cases or in other cases. As a matter of practice and policy, direct external Party interference may be waning in less charged and smaller land and property cases, but that cannot be said for important and sensitive cases involving, for example, official corruption. These conflicts are particularly serious in land cases, where the sensitivity of property issues, official corruption, and weak courts coalesce in an uneasy mix that brews steadily rising public indignation over the disposition of land.

## Demanding results from the courts in high profile land cases, not seeking their autonomy

This kind of high profile land case illustrates the continuing dilemmas for a system in which officials pursue private gain in property while also ruling the system that adjudicates land issues. How can the judiciary secure substantive implementation of the 1992 Constitution's guarantee that "[i]n administering justice, judges and assessors are independent and shall only obey the law" when it is surrounded by political authorities giving them contradictory orders – all of which need to be obeyed? The Do Son land case shows that the courts have no means to exercise autonomy in high profile cases that attract political direction without recourse to political support from a higher level than the political officials interfering in judicial processes.

That support from above – in this case the Party Central Committee and the government in Hanoi, acting through the Prime Minister and Deputy Prime Minister – does not, in fact, take steps to ensure judicial autonomy. Rather, they merely represent a higher level of interference and intervention in judicial decision-making, a results-oriented attempt to assuage public anger by interfering once again in judicial processes to get the "right" result.

The language used indicates the Party's own understanding of judicial interference in such major land cases – and the need for it. On a number of occasions, Party and state officials refer to Haiphong's "over-interference in the judiciary" (*can thiep qua sau*). The term indicates that a certain amount of "interference" (*can thiep*) is acceptable, but that when it goes too far (*qua sau*), that is unacceptable. Never in this process did Party and government authorities in Hanoi state the principle that *no* interference with the judiciary is acceptable.

In addition, the harms done by judicial interference are almost never stated in terms of the effects on fairness in property rights, judicial performance, harm to the process of doing justice, violations of fairness, or other rationales for fair handling of significant land cases and judicial independence. Rather, the Haiphong authorities are criticized for their interference because of the political damage done to the Party, government, and to their policies. So, for example, the President of Vietnam tells the Supreme Court that "the prestige of the Party and state has been damaged" by the local court's handling of the case under instructions from Haiphong Party authorities. The Prime Minister also focused on the political fall-out, not the implications for the courts or the setback to fair and transparent property regimes: "[A]t a time when the Party, state, and people are resolutely implementing" laws and policies against corruption, he said, "if this case has not been handled strictly and clearly that reflects poorly on the struggle against corruption."

In the specific context of this case and the weaknesses of judicial independence in Vietnam, political authorities stepping in to criticize local Party and government officials' domination of lower courts is, in one sense, a positive development. But the means used leave much to be desired – in effect, a re-interference with the judiciary, treating the judiciary as an object for instructions rather than a deciding institution in its own right. Higher-level interference with the judiciary has substituted for lower-level interference, as a result of popular dissatisfaction, the failures of local political leaders and the local court, and the weakness of that court.

It may be that this instrumentalization of the judiciary in the longer-term interest of strengthening judicial independence is the only step forward possible in the Vietnamese polity at this time, but it is primarily a means to guarantee that the courts follow Hanoi's will, rather than bow to local interests, and it does not substantially strengthen judicial independence. It did little, at least in this case, to strengthen public trust in a property rights regime.

## Party regulation and interference versus the constitutional guarantee of judicial autonomy: Land cases and beyond

Hidden in the corners of the Vietnamese coverage of the Do Son case are tantalizing references to specific Party rules and policies that appear to require local prosecutors and courts to seek guidance from local Party organizations when Party officials within their jurisdiction are investigated or charged with crimes, and that give Party organizations the prerogative to give "guidance" to the local courts, in land cases as well as other matters. These features of legal and administrative life are well known in Vietnam, but they are rarely referred to in the public press or in Party or judicial documents.

It is, however, reasonably clear that Party documents and practice seem to require local prosecutors and courts to seek guidance from local Party organizations when their officials are investigated, charged, or tried, and give Party organizations the right to provide "guidance" to the courts in other cases as well. In one sense, this is in direct contradiction with the constitutional principle that "In administering justice, judges and assessors are independent and shall only obey the law." In another sense, however, more conservative Party officials and legal scholars argue that the role of the Party in cases can be made consistent with Article 130 of the Constitution. They say that judicial autonomy in Vietnam is largely limited to the trial stage, that the courts are obligated to come to their own conclusions and "only obey the law" at trial, but that pre-trial guidance in the form of official letters, oral communications, and other "guidance" does not eviscerate that constitutional guarantee of autonomy at trial. Other Vietnamese scholars and judges scoff at that attempt to bridge clear Party interference with the constitutional guarantee of autonomy, noting that judicial autonomy at trial is a formalism signifying nothing when Party and state officials have, in effect, determined the result through guidance to the court before a proceeding begins.

## Land, corruption and the courts: The results of Do Son

Despite the strong reaction in the media and in Haiphong to the Party's interference in the trial of the local Do Son officials, there was little punishment for the officials involved in that interference. The tie between land and senior local officials proved too strong, it appears, for justice to be done. The central Party apparatus in Hanoi and the Haiphong Party Committee treated the judicial interference as an internal Party matter. The Haiphong Party Committee wrote a self-criticism that was given some publicity in the newspapers. But no public disciplinary action, either within the Party or outside, was taken, or at least none can be found.

Nor were new rules announced – either within the Party or outside – to control and channel such interference in judicial affairs in major property cases. Any such new rules or guidelines would have been difficult to draft in any case, for the Party's leadership role over the courts falls within the role for the Party defined in Article 4 of the 1992 Constitution, and a Party role in judicial affairs is a fact of life at central, provincial, and local levels throughout Vietnam. The Party's role is well known. It occurs in many contexts, but among the most common is for Party or state officials to provide "guidance" (*chi dao*) to local courts in handling sensitive matters, a process that is allowed by the Party but is conceptually indistinguishable from judicial interference.

The only potentially hard question for the Party was when interference went too far in land cases – the "excessive interference" in the Do Son case, as Hanoi Party and state officials called it. The Party was not prepared to address that difficult problem in 2006 and 2007, because the Party's right to give "guidance" as the constitutionally appointed dominant political authority in Vietnam clearly conflicted with any prohibition on judicial interference – a contradiction that could not be resolved on a clear and long-term basis, without rethinking the Party's relationship to the courts. And so the Party officials' interference in the Do Son land case faded from view even as a reinvigorated police and prosecutorial net retried the original defendants and then gradually, over the next several years, charged other officials – including a high-ranking Deputy Party Secretary of Haiphong – in connection with the Do Son land grab.

But echoes of the judicial interference in such major land cases lasted. At the National Assembly session in November 2005, deputies severely criticized the Do Son judicial interference incident in terms that implicitly recognized the contradiction of Party rule and an independent judiciary. One senior deputy told the Assembly

> We do not have the separation of powers [in Vietnam], but the courts must be independent, obeying only the law in judicial work. Now we have situations in which phone calls and letters are sent to chief judges before trials. That is not appropriate, and it provides external influences which are a source of incorrect verdicts.

In late 2006, the Secretary of the Ho Chi Minh City Party Committee, Le Thanh Hai, told the popular Saigon daily *Tuoi Tre* that

> in Ho Chi Minh City, we affirm that the Party Committee never interferes in the process of investigating and trying cases, especially cases involving corruption because those generally relate to officials, and it is very easy to be understood as shielding one's own. The viewpoint of the Party Committee requires that investigation and trial must proceed in accordance with law.... The Party Committee affirms one point, that it does not shield anyone.

But officials' private interests in land and their public responsibilities continued to clash in high profile corruption cases and the domination of the state institutions that were supposed to resolve them. Gradually, additional cases of official interference in judicial and prosecutorial decision-making began to appear in the Vietnamese media, sparking additional controversy and discussion. In March 2007, for example, the Secretary of the Party Committee of the large city of Vinh in central Vietnam was criticized in the national media and in the Party for interfering in the investigation and disposition of several cases in which lower-level officials had taken land for their use or arranged for its assignment to others. In the absence of effective Party action to limit interference in land cases, it was inevitable that other cases would occur.

If the Do Son land case has lessons for us on issues of land and property in Vietnam, it may be to indicate that while regular disputes over land and property are being increasingly resolved by the courts or by mediation processes without over-interference, as John Gillespie argues, large and sensitive property and land cases still command the attention and direction of Party officials, putting their public duties in direct conflict with their private interests. This is some distance from the case described by Nguyen Vu Hoang, in which ordinary citizens were able to organize to defend their homes from demolition because the community's leaders were Party members. That common protective task is absent from land corruption cases, where officials have a direct stake in property transfers and conflicts and where they are regulators of land and its disposition as well as the potential beneficiaries of its conversion to their own use, carrying out their official tasks while pursuing their own interests at the same time.

Officials using and manipulating a weak judiciary to resolve these corruption cases involving land can exacerbate all of these problems, making the application of law arbitrary and further infuriating the public. As Gillespie points out, the state does not always intervene in property cases, and perhaps less frequently over time in more ordinary land disputes. But when it does – and when state actors intervene to protect the official corruption that often surrounds land – the results can further weaken public confidence in property rights and the role of state institutions. In such cases, state officials have behaved corruptly to take land, then sought to manipulate a weak judiciary through pressure to countenance their property grab.

Even where, as in the Do Son land case, the public, the press, and the Party decided that the local courts had been cowed by local Party officials and issued incorrect decisions, the remedy was more political and administrative interference to reverse the result. Thus, in sensitive and significant property and land cases, ironically, the weakness of the judiciary before political authority may be so profound that only further political interference has significant hope, at least at this stage in Vietnamese legal history, of strengthening the role of the courts in adjudicating these cases in the interests of justice and against corrupt behavior by officials. Such is the power and value of property, both to corrupt officials seeking to unlock the value of Vietnamese land for private gain, and to hollow out state institutions that are intended to resolve such cases.

## Notes

1 This account of the Do Son case is drawn from multiple articles in Vietnamese newspapers and web news services during this period, including *Thanh Nien*, *Lao Dong*, *VnExpress*, *Tuoi Tre*, *Vietnamnet*, and other outlets. On the background of the case and the officials' initial decisions, see, for example, *VnExpress*, 26 October 2004, 8 April 2005,17 April 2005, 22 April 2005, and 28 April 2005, in most cases republishing reports from national newspapers such as *Thanh Nien*, *Tien Phong*, *Tuoi Tre*, and others.
2 On the initial local and national government investigation, see, for example, *VnExpress*, 7 July 2005, 8 July 2005, 11 July 2005, 27 September 2005, 21 February 2006, 29 August 2006.
3 See, for example, *VnExpress*, 7 July 2005; *Saigon Giai Phong*, 7 July 2005.
4 See *VnExpress*, 11 August 2005, 27 September 2005, 21 February 2006; *Saigon Giai Phong*, 12 August 2005.
5 On the trial, sentence, and public reactions, see, for example, *VnExpress*, 29 August 2006; *Tuoi Tre*, 29 August 2006, 30 August 2006.
6 See, for example, *VnExpress*, 1 September 2006; *Tuoi Tre*, 1 September 2006, 2 September 2006; *Saigon Giai Phong*, 2 September 2006.
7 Among the many newspaper articles discussing these developments, see, for example, *VnExpress*, 5 September 2006, 6 September 2006, 7 September 2006; *Tuoi Tre*, 6 September 2006; *Saigon Giai Phong*, 6 September 2006.
8 See *VnExpress*, 7 September 2006, 8 September 2006; *Tuoi Tre*, 7 September 2006, 8 September 2006, 9 September 2006; *Saigon Giai Phong*, 8 September 2006.

9 On developments in the case during these months, see *VnExpress*, 12 September 2006, 15 September 2006, 21 September 2006, 26 September 2006, 3 October 2006, 9 October 2006, 11 October 2006, 18 October 2006, 29 October 2006, 3 November 2006, 22 December 2006; *Tuoi Tre*, 12 September 2006, 15 September 2006, 21 September 2006, 25 September 2006, 3 October 2006, 9 October 2006, 10 October 2006, 18 October 2006, 29 October 2006, 8 November 2006, 24 November 2006; *Saigon Giai Phong*, 12 September 2006, 16 September 2006, 18 September 2006, 21 September 2006, 27 September 2006, 3 October 2006.

10 See *VnExpress*, 8 September 2006, republishing a report from *Tien Phong*; *Tuoi Tre*, 8 September 2006.

# Part III

# Intangible property

# 8 The commodification of village songs and dances in seventeenth- and eighteenth-century Vietnam

*Nhung Tuyet Tran*

## Introduction: *ca tru* as intangible cultural heritage

In its application to UNESCO on behalf of the musical performance genre known as *ca tru*, the Vietnamese Ministry of Culture argued that the form needed to be recognized as an "intangible cultural heritage," because of its "importance in safeguarding and promoting national cultur[al] identity."[1] UNESCO's acceptance of this argument and the granting of the coveted certification as intangible cultural heritage not only cemented *ca tru*'s status as a reflection of authentic Vietnamese culture, timeless in the face of modernization, it also elided the history of the evolution of this musical genre and its audiences over several centuries.

While most ethnomusicologists agree that the contemporary form of *ca tru* likely emerged from its nineteenth-century incarnation, there is little agreement on the relationship between earlier forms of this genre and the nineteenth-century version. Tran Thi Kim Anh, in an essay on the village performances in the Le period, surmises that *ca tru* ceased to figure in the records as a communal activity in the nineteenth century for two reasons. First, the Nguyen government failed to set up a musical board to oversee and establish rules and regulations regarding local performances. Second, the Nguyen dynasty's expansion and settlement in the Southern realm, away from the country's traditional center of culture in the Red River Delta, led to a dilution of such traditional practices at the village level.[2] Such an argument is Thang-Long (Hanoi) centric and conveniently places the responsibility for the seeming disappearance of *ca tru* as village performance and marker of authenticity on the reviled Nguyen Dynasty, which also bears the onus of losing the country to French imperialists. It also fits well into the contemporary Vietnamese state's claim that it is the sole arbiter, master, and protector of authentic tradition.[3]

The following essay suggests instead that modern *ca tru* evolved from a gradual process of transformation from communal activity to private pastime that was shaped by market forces and contemporary notions of property rights in the seventeenth and eighteenth centuries. It thus presents *ca tru* as an example of early Vietnamese concepts of intellectual and artistic property rights before the advent of Western influence.

## *Ca tru* as communal performance

The phrase *ca tru* is comprised of two Sino-Vietnamese characters: the first, *ca*, for song, or a piece of music, and the second, *tru*, for a bamboo tablet. In the nineteenth century, each tablet would be inscribed with a specific amount of money. Upon entering the inn/performance space, men would pick up the tablets and beat the praise drum or hand the female singer(s) as many tablets as they saw fit;[4] these could later be exchanged for copper coins. Presently, the performance of *ca tru* is comprised of a male playing a three-string lute (*dan day*), a female singer (*a dao*) who also plays a bamboo percussion instrument (*phach*), and a male playing a praise drum (*trong chau*).[5] Historically, the category was broader and encompassed songs and dances performed by local troupes at the doors of the villages' communal houses during ritual feasts to the villages' guardian spirits (*hat dinh*); formal performances for official audiences (*hat quan*); private performances for wealthy individual scholars (*hat choi*); and local singing competitions (*hat thi*).[6] This essay examines the performances by local troupes in front of communal houses as a form of cultural property in seventeenth- and eighteenth-century northern Vietnam.

In the seventeenth century, the Avignonese Jesuit Alexandre de Rhodes defined the communal house, *dinh*, as the "house where the village joins to discuss their affairs," (*casa em que se ajunta a aldea pera seus negoisius*) and defines the "communal song house," (*dinh hat*) as "the house where they sing to the devil" (*caza em que cantao ao diabo*).[7] De Rhodes' inclusion of the word "communal song house" in his dictionary suggests that by the first quarter of the seventeenth century, such practices were ubiquitous enough to define for future missionaries.[8] That the dictionary lacks an entry for the term *tru* or *ca tru* indicates that De Rhodes did not find them prevalent enough to define and describe. In the sources examined for this paper, the terms *dinh ca*, *dinh mon*, and *tru* are all used to refer to communal performances, suggesting that ordinary villagers and elites enjoyed these alongside one another until these performances retreated behind the walls of elite residences. Several inscriptions use the term *xuong tru* to refer to the same performance, but the combination of terms, *ca tru*, appears not to have been prevalent in the seventeenth and eighteenth centuries.[9] For simplicity's sake, I use *ca tru*, as it is popularly known, to refer to the communal performances that appear in the sources.[10]

Although there exist many records referring to the village songs as a communal activity, none describes what these performances might have looked like in the seventeenth and eighteenth centuries. Drawing on tidbits of information from documents dating to the Le period (1428–1788), Vietnamese scholars suggest that these performances were intended to please the tutelary spirits of the village and were performed during major festivals.[11] There is general consensus that during annual festivals, each community might send a troupe to perform songs and dances to please the village's tutelary spirits.[12] In each village, a performance troupe (*giao phuong*) representing a lineage held proprietary claims over the song and the customary right to perform it in front of the village's communal house (*dinh mon*).

The troupe's performance rights came with ancilliary benefits: its members were entitled to collect a fee from the village *and* any tips that the audience might reward them with. Bui Trong Hien has suggested that government officials would carry bamboo tablets and praise drums to the performances and they would drum or throw the bamboo pieces toward the beautiful female singers if they found their performances worthy of praise.[13] These tablets (*tru*) had numeric characters carved onto them, with each representing a monetary value.

Hien's description of these songs and dances allows *ca tru* to co-exist as both communal activity and exclusive entertainment for elite consumption, linking an earlier form of the performance to its contemporary incarnation through the use of the bamboo tablets (*tru*). However, Hien does not explain how the transformation came about. This ommission may not actually matter for his argument, since the linking of a "traditional village activity" to a contemporary performance enables the formation of a broader national identity, as Lauren Meeker has argued for another musical form known as *quan ho*.[14] Thus, tracing the evolution of musical performances in village communities in the seventeenth and eighteenth centuries into their most recent form is less important than what they represent: both a uniquely Vietnamese tradition that is bounded by the "bamboo hedge" of the village, long an important signifier of Vietnamese tradition and authenticity, and a form of artistic performance that is worthy of international recognition for its antiquity, symbolism as national treasure, and esthetic value.

The state's official narrative of the authenticity of the *ca tru* musical form was based in part on Nguyen Xuan Dien's study of its history and development, which the government included as reference material in its application for UNESCO certification.[15] Dien's study begins with the obligatory claim that "*ca tru* is a unique cultural vestige of Vietnam" (*ca tru la mot di san van hoa dac sac cua Viet Nam*) as he meticulously locates moments where the performance appears in ancient texts or in village iconography.[16] For Dien, these moments demonstrate that *ca tru* is indeed an ancient Vietnamese practice rooted in the Red River Delta, bolstering its importance as a signifier of Vietnamese culture and national identity. While it is true that the performance has long historical roots, its evolution does not necessarily fit neatly into the state's narrative of cultural authenticity and timelessness.[17] The transformation of *ca tru* in fact demonstrates that culture is continually changing and adapting to the material and social worlds. In its evolution from village entertainment to national treasure and internationally recognized "intangible cultural heritage," *ca tru* went through another stage: commodification and privatization as a strategy of survival for hard-pressed artists' troupes and their village communities.

## The setting: socio-economic turmoil in the seventeenth and eighteenth centuries

The seventeenth and eighteenth centuries were years of particular socio-economic tumult in northern Vietnamese society; to raise cash, some local performance troupes sold their customary claims to perform in front of a particular communal house to that village or groups of wealthy individuals. These transactions became more prevalent as the economic dislocations of the civil wars continued into the eighteenth century. This essay argues that by the seventeenth century, the performance rights of village songs and dances known as *dinh mon/dinh hat* and later as *ca tru* were transferred between performance troupes and local communities, and as the economic dislocations worsened, from performance troupes to groups of elite men. This shift in the customer base of the performance rights, in turn, led to a transformation of the artistic form itself. As the troupes moved their performances from communal spaces where all villagers could watch to spaces sheltered behind the walls of elite residences for the enjoyment of (male) audiences, the status of the female performers in the troupes also seems to have shifted. Women who previously seemed not to be negatively marked by their artistry became marked as "servants" who provided special services to their elite male masters. Thus, studying these transactions allows us a glimpse into how the socio-economic dislocations of the Trinh-Nguyen wars affected local life in early modern Vietnam.

During the seventeenth and eighteenth centuries, four families – the Le (1428–1788), Mac (1527–92), Trinh (1533–1783), and Nguyen (1558–1778) all claimed sovereign authority in different parts of the country we now call Vietnam. Although the Mac were officially ousted at the end of the sixteenth century, they maintained a base at Cao Bang near the Chinese border from which they could launch military expeditions well into the second half of the seventeenth century. As civil warfare gripped the Vietnamese landscape, each of these polities – the Le and the Trinh in Hanoi and surrounding areas, the Mac initially in Thang-Long (Hanoi) and later in Cao Bang, and the Nguyen in the newly settled southern region near the contemporary city of Hoi An – tried to maximize their extraction of resources from the populace under their control. In the north, the Trinh family could not provide basic infrastructural support for areas within their domain. Strapped for cash, local communities in the Red River Delta found creative ways to raise money to make ends meet. Among these strategies, one of the most popular was to proffer that a community would assume the duty to maintain a donor's ancestral rites in exchange for a donation of cash and land. Community leaders then elected these donors' souls to honored positions within the village's pantheon of spirits, promising to make offerings to them immediately following those made to the village's tutelary spirits (*bau hau*).[18] Commercialization in the early modern period brought about a more general transfer of communal land into private hands; the commodification of other forms of property was another step in this process.

Local artist troupes employed similar survival strategies by selling their long-held performance rights to sing in front of a particular village communal house (*mai dinh mon/mai tru*) to raise much-needed funds. The parties to the transaction appropriated the legal terminology of codified law with respect to landed property and used this legal language in contracts that transferred customary claims over artistic practices. The stele inscriptions that recorded the transfer of performance rights to village songs and dances demonstrate that, by the seventeenth century, local custom recognized the tangibility of cultural performance.

My argument is threefold. First, local troupes sold their claims to perform in front of particular villages as one among a number of survival strategies. They did so to make up for economic shortfalls in times of need.[19] Second, these transactions demonstrate that local communities recognized that the traditional claims to performance had a tangible value and that these claims could be transferred. The erection of stele inscriptions that drew upon legal discourse to legitimate the sales reflects cultural patterns that explicitly and implicitly viewed the village songs and dances as "cultural property."[20] While the parties to the contracts explicitly used legal language to legitimate them, they were careful to limit the state's role in interferring with the contracts. By using accepted legal discourse but also limiting the purview of the state, the parties to the transactions established an alternative mechanism of enforcement, an issue I will return to at the end of the essay. Finally, the details provided in the inscriptions – from the shifting parties to the contracts to the terms of the sale themselves – provide clues to the transformation of village dances into a mode of artistic performance for elite consumption. They demonstrate that the socio-economic dislocations of the Trinh-Nguyen civil wars lie at center of the transactions and were key to the transformation of the musical form and the shift in status of the female performers.[21] On a comparative note, the existence of these contracts demonstrates that the idea of cultural property was not merely an import associated with Westernization and that the concept of intellectual property did not originate solely in the European Enlightenment.[22] The transactions reveal the irony of the UNESCO designation of the form as "intangible cultural heritage," for in the seventeenth and eighteenth centuries, those who took part in *ca tru*, as performers or audience members, viewed it as wholly tangible.

## The commodification of *ca tru* performance

My argument rests on a close reading of twenty-three contracts of sale negotiated between troupes and local communties or groups of elite men. Of these, eight of the stele inscriptions date from the seventeenth century and fifteen date from the eighteenth century. By examining the changes in the transactions between buyers and sellers, the terms of those transactions and the parties who entered into these contracts, we can trace the transformation of the performance from a communal celebration to an elite pastime. The transfer of performance rights to village songs reveal the strategies that individuals and communities employed in the face of socio-economic hardship. These strategies provide a window for understanding the history of Vietnamese property rights in early modern times.

As descriptive and frank as they are about the economic conditions that led to sale of these performance rights, the inscriptions can be vague about what exactly is being sold. That is, what exactly do the terms *dinh* (lit. communal house) and *dinh mon* (lit. doors of the communal house) mean when used in contracts for the sale of performance rights? The inscriptions suggest that what is being sold is not the songs or performances themselves, but rather, the customary right to perform those songs at the communal houses *and* the ancilliary monetary rights attached to those performances. Because the right to perform in front of an important communal space on festival days is intricately linked to the spiritual and cultural practices of a village, the sales also commodifed local influence.

Perhaps because the product that was being sold was flexible, the contracting parties took great pains to borrow from the official language of property law to legitimate the transactions. Recorded as "contracts," (*van khe*) these transactions often specified the "quality" of the commodity being sold. For example, performance rights could be sold as "newly acquired" (*tan mai*); sold "conditionally" (*dien*), or as a "final sale" (*mai tuyet*), all terms that were well established in early modern Vietnamese law. Many of the contracts also repeated a refrain often seen in the legal codes, magistrates' manuals, and testimentary records, that "the country has its regular laws, and contracts are established to demonstrate its application" (*quoc huu thuong phap co lap van khe vi chieu dung gia*).[23] The contracting parties also borrowed the form as well as language of contract law, with the eligible members of the community witnessing the validity of the sale with their signature (*ky*) or mark (*chi*), usually by finger joints.[24] To see how the communities drew upon the language of landed property law to legitimize the sale of performance rights, we now look to the contracts.

### *Example I*[25]

In the first year of the Canh Tri reign (1663), the members of the performance troupes (*giao phuong nhan thuong ha*) in the prefecture of Yen Son, both old and young, could not meet their communal obligations (*dich quan*) and agreed to sell their "newly acquired" right to perform and the right to collect tips for those performances at the doors of the communal house (*tan mai dinh mon tru tien*) in Hoa Ban Village. The document stipulates that henceforth, when the village of Hoa Ban held festivals or inducted new members into its community, the troupe from Yen Son Prefecture would have no claim to interfere in the village's affairs. Two years later, the village of Hoa Ban erected a stele commemorating the election of Mr Nguyen Doan Lang as village headman (*trum truong*) for Mr Lang had provided the village with sixty-five strings of cash to purchase the performance rights in the previous transaction.

In addition to recording the sale of the right to perform, the inscription reveals several interesting aspects of village life. Although the term "*giao phuong*" has typically been understood in modern Vietnamese as a "performance troupe," which I follow in this chapter, the details of the transaction suggest that it means much more. The stipulation that the troupe relinquish claims to interfere in that village community's decisions as a result of the sale suggests that the right to perform in front of the communal house included political influence in a territorially bounded space.[26] When the troupe sold its right to perform, it acknowledged that henceforth, it would not interfere with the admission of new members into the village community. The benefactor who assisted the village in purchasing the right from the troupe, moreover, was officially elected as the top village headman. These stipulations suggest, then, that the customary claim to perform in a village included other forms of authority over village life, and that authority was somehow territorially bound. Finally, the designation of the performance right as "newly acquired" suggests that the particular performance troupe in Yen Son prefecture had only recently received this right. Though the stele inscription does not provide evidence for it, it is possible that the village of Hoa Ban previously sold that right to the performance troupe, only to repurchase it with the assistance of a benefactor.

### *Example II*[27]

In the first year of the Canh Tri reign (1663), the hamlets with performance troupes in the villages of Lap Thuong, Cu, and Tien Lu in Quoc Oai District sold their customary rights to perform and the right to collect fees in front of the communal house in the village of Tu Tram to that village for twenty strings of cash. The document is signed by the (named) village headmen, with "all levels, old and young" (*thuong ha lao tieu dang*) serving as witness to the finality of the sale.

### *Example III*[28]

In the first year of Duong Duc (1672), the performances troupes from Lap Thuong and Tien Lu hamlets in the province of Ha Tay claimed rights to perform the local songs on festival days in front of the communal house in Son Lo Village, stating that these rights had been passed down to them as a trade for generations (*to nghiep dinh*). Economic circumstances were forcing the troupes to sell their performance rights to the officials of Son Lo Village for a little more than 174 strings of cash. As a contract (*van khe*) between these communities, the stele would stand as reminder of the sale. The leaders of the various hamlets, who apparently held some form of influence over the performance troupes and authority to enter into the contract, explicitly stated that the reason they decided to sell their proprietary claim (*chu*) was to raise funds for communal purposes (*vi quan dich – dong tien*).[29] The stele recorded the names of each hamlet head as agreeing to the sale and also stipulated that, following the transfer, none of the troupes who were parties to the agreement could demand authority over the performance rights. The final phrase in the inscription demonstrates the parties' efforts to legitimize the transaction by using the formal language of landed property law:

> The country has regular laws [thus we] enter into this contract [and agree] that it will be clear that the purchaser of this communal house [performance/song] shall be the one who has use over it (*quoc huu thuong phap co lap van khe hoan dinh mai chu vi chieu dung gia*).

Paradoxically, while the parties do draw upon the language of formal law to legitimize these transactions, they are also careful to insulate themselves from the reaches of state power and the throne's universal claim over property. Thus, in many of these contracts, when referring to the transaction and the laws that govern these transactions, the text refers to the state's "private laws or private regulations," (*tu uoc*) laying claim to an organic enforcement of "the law," an issue that I will return to at the end of this essay.

### *Example IV*[30]

In the third year of the Chinh Hoa reign (1682), the performance troupe in the upper hamlet in the village of Thuong Mo, Tu Liem District, sold its rights to perform in front of the communal house in Huu Cuoc Village to the village itself for forty strings of cash. The stele stipulates that following the closing of the deal, the performance troupe would not bear any responsibility for "fraud" (*gian*) in the sale. Thus, in future years, should the village of Huu Cuoc invite other troupes to perform in front of its communal house, the selling troupe should have no authority to protest.

The contracts described above reveal five important features about the communal performance now known as *ca tru* and their role in Vietnamese village life in the seventeenth century. First, each of the contracts explicitly highlights the economic hardships of the period: the troupes would not have sold their ancestral claims were they able to meet the communal needs of the day. Second, while the contract might represent the sale as one that all members of the troupe agreed upon, only the hamlet leaders "signed" the sales agreements. This distinction is important in light of the apparent change in status for the women who performed in these troupes but who were not named as parties to the agreement. Third, the sale of the performance rights or the ancilliary rights to collect rents or tips suggests a general consensus on the tangibility and monetary value of these claims. Fourth, the erection of the stone stele to mark the sale suggests that there was some kind of local recognition that the performance right could be transferred and that the performance troupe owned something akin to the "intellectual copyright" over that performance. Moreover, that right was protected by local custom. Finally, because these contracts were transactions between troupes in one hamlet or village involving their claims to perform in front of communal houses in other villages, these processes suggest far more interaction between villages than the current historiography, in which the model of village insularity continues to prevail, suggests.[31] These themes are echoed in other examples from the same century.[32]

## From communal celebration to elite pastime

While there is evidence from the seventeenth century that some performance troupes did sell their rights to private individuals, a dramatic shift occurs in the eigtheenth century. Within a hundred years, the economic turmoil appears to have left few villages able to purchase these rights/claims; it then enabled groups of private individuals to purchase these rights. More troupes were also selling their rights. The increase in sales and the shift of buyers from village communities to groups of private individuals took performances from just outside the gates of the communal houses into private halls and led to the devaluation of the performance rights and of the performers themselves. Specifically, female performers appear to have shifted in status. In the later inscriptions, when the performance rights were sold to groups of elites, these women appear in the sources as semi-professional performers who owed services to the elite men. Finally, the change in buyers also signaled a shift in the commodity being sold. While the seventeenth-century sources suggest that the product sold were the performance rights at the doors of the communal houses, it appears that in the eighteenth century, when the troupes sold their rights, still termed *tru* or *dinh mon* in the sources, the terms refer to the performances and services that the troupes owed the elite men.

## *Example I*[33]

In the twenty-first year of the Canh Hung reign (1760) the Dong Lineage performance troupe could not meet its communal obligations and looked to raise cash for this purpose. For generations, the Dong Lineage held the rights to sing and dance in front of the communal house gates of Phu My Village. Because of the dire financial situation, the leaders of the lineage troupe entered into a "private contract" (*tu uoc*) with officials and gentlemen (*quan vien quan tu*) of the village of Phu My. In exchange for seventy strings of cash, the troupe sold conditionally (*dien*) its claim to perform the songs in front of the communal house. That the contract was one of a conditional sale rather than a final one suggested that the troupe hoped that it could retrieve the performance rights at some later date.

In the regulations adjudicating the sale of the performance right, the contract sets out particular conditions for the Dong Lineage performance troupe. First, it refers to the contract between the hamlet and the officials as a "private contract," suggesting that those who entered into the agreement mutually agreed that this was beyond the powers of the state, even though the buyers were government officials. Marking the contract as "private" was important because the officials who purchased the rights likely had to distinguish their "private" act from their public roles as representatives of the state. Despite claiming that the transaction was beyond the limits of state interference, the contract, as those before it, drew upon landed property law legitimated by the state. Second, in what we might call the "fine print" of the contract, the first regulation required that on the seventh day of the first month of each year, the Dong Lineage troupe "should place in care of the hamlet officials two beautiful women to serve them early in the morning" (*tuan nien chinh nguyet qu yxa pho quan giap dao nuong nhi no tao thoi*). In requiring the troupe to present the officials with these two "beautiful women," the contract places an important new clause in the sale of performance rights. The right to perform in front of the communal house was not simply halted but taken from a communal space into a private space – that of the officials. As the female performers moved inside the walls of elite men's structures, what was once a performance for "all in the community above and below" to enjoy was transformed into an elite male indulgence. Inside these private spaces, the services that the women rendered were also kept beyond the knowledge of the community. In describing what the beautiful women were to do behind the walls as "service" to the officials, this inscription suggests that the performers' status had changed. The label also suggests the social rules that would govern these relationships: the elite men would be masters and the female performers, servants; and as we know in early modern Vietnamese contexts, masters enjoyed sexual access to their female servants.[34]

### *Example II*[35]

The requirement that the performance troupe provide the elite buyers with women to serve them extended beyond this particular incident to other transactions. In 1763, in a different district in the same prefecture, the Xuan lineage troupe from Huong Canh village likewise sold permanently their share of the right to perform in front of the communal house to the leaders (*trum dang*) of the village. The first article to the agreement stipulated that on the eighth day of the second month, the hamlet agreed to have beautiful women greet and host visiting officials, suggesting, again, a transition in roles for the female performers in the troupe (*ban giap ung cuong su dao nuong phu gia nghenh*). Like the other transactions, the parties to this agreement drew upon the language used in the transactions relating to landed property (*giao uoc; giao khe*). The existing scholarship refers to the women who perform in the elite settings as *dao nuong*, which we might translate as "beautiful women," but the specification that they were to serve these elite men suggests that they might have held a debased status, as courtesans would have possessed in the same period. By the nineteenth century, most *ca tru* performances were held in the private residences of wealthy men or in performance houses that young (male) students frequented, and these female performers were rewarded for their singing with the bamboo tablets – money.

### *Example III*[36]

In the first year of the Canh Thinh reign (1793) in the Tay Son dynasty (1788–1802), a village performance troupe sold the rights to perform to the mandarins and elders of the village for a total of eighty strings of old cash.

> The officials accepted the conditions and wrote up [this] contract (*co tien bat thap quan vien lap khe viet giao thuan*), and accepted that they would purchase ownership of the songs that had been transferred [in the village] for generations (*mai chu nhiem xuong ca truyen van dai*).

Language again is important. The parties attempted to legitimize the transaction by referring to the official status of the buyers, the officials, as the ones who drew up the contract, yet it was designated as a "private sale." This stele, as the others before it, ends with the phrase that the country has its regular laws, and thus the officials (who must know the law) drafted the contract to comply with it. The inscription also includes a number of regulations with respect to the performances, much of which is unreadable except for one line stating that all members of the village would respect the terms of the contract.

The preceding examples provide in greater detail a general trend in the twenty-three inscriptions examined for this paper – that as the economic turmoil wore on, the rate of sales increases and transfers toward groups of elite individuals. Table 8.1 outlines the details of seller and buyer, but also highlights an important feature.

Table 8.1 provides a rough timeline of several important transitions in the transfer of performance rights to the musical form collectively known as *ca tru*. First, although up to half of the stele inscriptions recording the sale of performance rights from the seventeenth century were sold to groups of officials, the rate of sale to private individuals changes significantly for the eighteenth century. It is important to note that when officials purchased the performance rights in the seventeenth century, the contracts represented these sales as purchases for the benefit of the village, and there were no stipulations on the services of the female performers. In the eighteenth century-inscriptions examined here, 85 percent of the sales went to officials from villages or districts. As the table outlines, the face value of the performance right decreased in the eighteenth century, with its high at about 120 strings of cash in 1704 and low of twelve strings in 1797, which suggest two possibilities. First, the economic situation was so dire and there were so few buyers that performance troupes had to lower the asking price in the eighteenth century. Second, the smaller face value also enabled more groups of individuals to come up with enough funds to purchase these performance rights. Because there are no figures to gauge inflation, the actual value and change in value is unknown, but the face value gives us some sense of the depreciation of these performance rights.

## Conclusion

The preceding discussion drew upon contracts for the sale to the performance rights of a musical form collectively known as *ca tru* in seventeenth- and eighteenth-century Vietnam. It examined how early modern Vietnamese commodified and sold their ancestral claims to perform in front of communal houses on particular festival days. In selling their performance rights, these local troupes also relinquished a certain amount of local authority. The transactions also provide clues to why the nineteenth-century (and re-imagined) contemporary form of *ca tru* manifests itself as a performance for the enjoyment of elite audiences, whether they are comprised of official scholars of the Nguyen Dynasty or Vietnamese officials and academics (not mutually exclusive categories), Western academics, or international consumers of "authentic Vietnamese culture." The contracts demonstrate that, as economic conditions worsened, the value of the performance rights decreased and the troupes sold the new commodity, now transformed and understood as services, to groups of elite men. This transformation triggered a likely transformation in the status of the female performers, too. While there is little indication of the status of the female performers when they danced for community enjoyment, which suggests that they belonged to commoner status, once their services were directed toward the enjoyment of elite men, they came to

*Table 8.1* Data from *Corpus of Vietnamese Inscriptions*, Vols 1–6

| *Title* | *Record #* | *Year* | *Seller* | *Purchaser* | *Price in string* |
|---|---|---|---|---|---|
| New Stele Contract | 1979–80 | 1657 | Hoang Hamlet Performance Troupe | Officials of Tra Lam Village | 30 |
| New Stele Recording the sale of the Temple Performance Rights | 1945 | 1663 | Singers from Ca Cong Village | Officials of Tu Tram Village | 20 |
| New Stele Recording the Sale of Temple Performance Rights | 1933–34 | 1663 | Yen Son District Performance Troupe | Hoa Ban Village | 60 |
| Sale of our Ancestors' District | 2278–81 | 1672 | Dan Phuong District Performance Troupe | Officials of Village | 100 |
| Final Sale of the Temple Performance Rights and Regulations thereof | 6897–98 | 1681 | Dan Phuong District Performance Department | Thien Mạc Prefecture | 60 |
| Stele Recording a Contract for the Sale of the Right to Collect Tips | 3280 | 1682 | Upper Hamlet Performance Troupe | – | 40 |
| Stele Recording Performance Song | 3487 | 1682 | Thuong Mo Village Performance Troupe | Officials from Ba Duong Village | 45 |
| Contract recording the sale of the Tru | 2689 | 1684 | Second Hamlet Troupe | – | 40 |
| Stele on the Tru Performances | 4199–4200 | 1704 | Dai De Hamlet Troupe | Hamlet Officials | 120 |
| Stele Recording Tru Songs | 1069–70 | 1735 | Dong Family Troupe | Hamlet Officials | 43 |
| Performance Troupe engraves this Stele [as] Record | 6889–90 | 1743 | The District Performance Troup | Huong Cao Village | 25 |

*Table 8.1* Continued

| *Title* | *Record #* | *Year* | *Seller* | *Purchaser* | *Price in string* |
|---|---|---|---|---|---|
| Thien Mac Prefecture sells its District | 6895 | 1755 | The "Office" of the performance Troupe in PhuTho District | Officials in Thien Mac Village | 16 |
| Stele of the Performance Troupe | 1587 | 1759 | Office of the Performance Troupe | Officials in Hoe Thi Hamlet | 12 |
| Regulations for the Village Temple Doors | 1634–35 | 1760 | Dong Lineage Troupe | Officials of Phu My Village | 70 |
| Establishing the Troupe Stele | 6400–01 | 1760 | Leaders of the Thung Troupe | Officials in Kim Da | 12 |
| Stele at the Temple Doors | 1585–1586 | 1765 | Xuan Lineage Troupe | Village Officials | 20 |
| No name | 6998 | 1769 | Thinh Lineage Troupe | Inner Hamlet, Dong Mai Village | 30 |
| Regulations [for the sale] of the Temple Gates | 1628–29 | 1770 | Dong Family Performance Troupe | Village Officials | 18 |
| Performance Troupe Stele | 1041 | 1778 | Ho Dong Hamlet Troupe | Village officials | 30 |
| Six Hamlets establish Contract Stipulations l | 6557–6558 | 1783 | Performance troupes from 6 hamlets | 6 hamlets | 38 |
| Stele established [to mark] the Dinh Sale | 1977–78 | 1793 | Kieu Family Troupe | Village Officials | 80 |
| Regulations for the Temple Doors | 6888 | 1796 | Performance Troupe office | Village Officials | – |
| Contract for the Temple Monies | 2701–02 | 1797 | Performance Troupe | Hamlet of Doai Khe | 12 |

acquire a debased status, and are identified in the sources with the servant or slave radical. While providing some insight into the transformation of *ca tru*, the transactions raise a number of issues about property rights, village society, and legal enforcement.

Whether I am right about the transformation of village musical performances into an elite pastime, the inscriptions themselves highlight important issues about the notion of property rights in Vietnam and in comparative perspective. The transactions suggest that local communities agreed on the tangibility of performance rights and ancillary benefits that came with these performance rights. By using the language of landed property law, the parties to the contract tried to use official language to lend credence to their contracts. In claiming that the state had regular laws that enabled them to create a contract, parties drew upon state authority. However, they were careful to designate their contracts as "private agreements," probably to limit the state's authority over the transactions.

If the parties were specifically limiting the state's influence in the transactions, by labeling them as "private," then how would these sales be enforced? Here, I can only offer a few tentative suggestions. Again, the use of language and form is important. By repeatedly using the phrase, "all those above and below" assent to the contract, a term borrowed from village regulations common at the time, the parties represent the transaction as a collective agreement. We know from the text itself, however, that only senior men from the troupes and/or the villages were authorized to sign the contracts. Not simply recorded on rice paper but carved onto a stone stele and erected at important communal sites, the form that the contract took likely served as an enforcement tool. After all, if everyone in the community agreed to the sale and allowed for the erection of a large monument to record that sale, who would dare contradict its validity? Thus, while the texts do not really tell us how the contracts would be enforced, their language and form suggest that the community relied upon shared understandings of communal agreement (indeed, the communal house was where these agreements were fashioned) and the physical marker of that agreement to enforce the contract.

Finally, the parties' use of the language of property law to legitimize the transaction while putting it outside the purview of the state is important to understanding property rights in Vietnamese history. Although political power itself was divided between three (and subsequently two) rival families, the states still adhered to an official governing philosophy of the supremacy of the emperor. In theory, the emperor owned "all under heaven" and if we take this political philosophy literally, then there would be no such thing as property rights in pre-modern Vietnam. In everyday life, as the inscriptions demonstrate, ordinary Vietnamese enjoyed landed property rights and began to commodify cultural property in line with the established practices of landed property rights. The transfer of proprietary claims to musical performance thus challenges not only presumptions of the lack of property rights in Asia but also the notion that intellectual or cultural property was simply an import of Western modernization. The commodification and sale of these performance rights by artist groups tied to a specific community to other communities challenge the assumption that the notion of *intangible properties* is linked to the emergence of individualism.[37] The inscriptions demonstrate, instead, cultural patterns that explicitly recognized musical performance as tangible property that could be transferred. I am not arguing that these patterns were uniquely Vietnamese, but rather reflective of survival tactics that were created by the socio-economic circumstances of the period. The transfer of *ca tru* performance rights in the seventeenth and eighteenth centuries demonstrate that, rather than an unchanging marker of Vietnamese culture that emerged from the Red River Delta cradle, the form itself has had its own life or lives.

## Notes

1 Socialist Republic of Vietnam, *Nomination File: Intangible Cultural Heritage for Inscription on the Urgent Safeguarding List: Ca Tru Singing*, http://www.unesco.org/culture/ich/doc/src/00309-Community%20consent-EN.pdf, (February 2009, accessed May 2009).
2 Tran Thi Kim Anh, "Ca tru qua mot so khe uoc va dieu luat," in *Dac khao ca tru Viet Nam*, pp. 36–58: 38.
3 Oscar Salemink, "Contestations over Cultural Heritage," in this volume.
4 Do Bang Doan and Do Trong Hue, *Viet Nam ca tru bien khao* (Saigon: 1962), p. 52.
5 For more on contemporary forms of *ca tru*, see the ethnomusicologist Barley Norton's website Ca tru: Vocal music from Northern Viet Nam, http://www.goldsmiths.ac.uk/music/catru/, accessed May 8, 2009.
6 Nguyen Xuan Dien, *Lich su va nghe thuat Ca Tru: Khao sat nguon tu lieu tai Vien Nghien Cuu Han-Nom*, (Hanoi: NXB The Gioi, 2007), p. 18. Do Bang Doan and Do Trong Hue provide a slightly different schema, suggesting that *ca tru* could be broken into three types of performances: the communal performances to honor tutelary spirits (*hat dinh*), the leisure performances for officials and wealthy scholars (*hat choi*), and the local contests to assess talent (*hat thi*). Do Bang Doan and Do Trong Hue, *Viet Nam ca tru bien khao* (1962): pp. 57–8.
7 Alexandre de Rhodes, *Dictionarium Annamiticum, Lusitanum y Latinum*, (Rome: Propaganda Fide, 1651), p. 321.
8 De Rhodes spent the better part of the first quarter of the seventeenth century in Vietnam and was permanently banished in 1640. After his banishment, he lobbied Rome for the ordination of native priests, and composed a catechism modeled after the *Spiritual Exercises* and a Vietnamese-Latin-Portuguese dictionary as tools for future missionaries.
9 *Xuong tru bi ky*, Ms. 1069–70; *Xuong tru bi ky*, Ms. 3487; *Xuong tru bi ky*, Ms. 4199–4200.
10 The manuscript numbers refer to the code used by the Institute of Han-Nom Studies, Hanoi, Vietnam. Digital images of the inscriptions can be found in *Tong tap thac ban van khac Han Nom*, published by the Institute for Han-Nom Studies, the Ecole Française d'Extrême Orient, and the Ecole Practique des Hautes Etudes. Hanoi: 2005, vols 1–6.
11 Tran Thi Kim Anh, p. 45.
12 Phan Ke Binh, *Viet Nam phong tuc* (NXB TP Ho Chi Minh: 1996), p. 283.
13 Bui Trong Hien, "Khong gian van hoa—cac chuc nang van hoa xa hoi va nhung hinh thuc bieu hien cua nghe thuat," in *Dac khao ca tru Viet Nam*, pp. 59–107:87.
14 Lauren Meeker, Musical Transmissions: Folk Music, Meditation, and Modernity in Northern Vietnam. PhD dissertation, Columbia University, 2007.
15 Dien's doctoral dissertation, upon which this monograph was based, was the only reference matter submitted with the application for "Intangible Cultural Heritage" Status. Conversation with Nguyen Xuan Dien, July 16, 2009. The nomination form lists

three books used as additional documentation evidence, but does not list the names of the books submitted by the Ministry of Sports and Culture. http://www.unesco.org/culture/ich/index.php?USL=00309.

16 That the oldest sources come from the Red River Delta bolsters the Hanoi-based state's claim to authentic culture.

17 Prasenjit Duara argues that to demonstrate the nation's march toward modernity, nation states often identify particular cultural features and imbue them with a timeless past, authenticating the nation's role in the modern world. Prasenjit Duara, "The Regime of Authenticity: Timelessness, Gender and National History in Modern China," *History and Theory* 37:3 (1998): 287–308.

18 Nhung Tuyet Tran, "Gender, Property & the Autonomy Thesis in Southeast Asia: the Endowment of Local Succession in Early Modern Vietnam," *Journal of Asian Studies* 67:1 (2008): 43–72. See also Nhung Tuyet Tran, *Familial Properties: Gender, State and Society in Early Modern Vietnam* (University of Hawaii Press, forthcoming).

19 Nhung Tuyet Tran, *Familial Properties*, op. cit.

20 I do not use the term "culture" or its variants to refer to some reified notion of authenticity, but rather to patterns of behavior that are historically derived and live within the mind and the material artefacts that form a particular world.

21 When I first came across these inscriptions during my dissertation research in 2001–2, the thousands of ink rubbings collected at the Han-Nom Institute had not yet been cataloged, and I only had a few examples of this phenomenon. In 2005, the Han-Nom Institute, Ecole Française d'Extrême Orient, and the Ecole Pratique des Hautes Etudes collaborated to digitize these rubbings. The inscriptions used for this paper come from the digital images provided by this project, each of which is simply numbered from one on. See *Tong tap thac ban van khac Han Nom*, published by the Institute for Han-Nom Studies, the Ecole Française d'Extrême Orient, & the Ecole Pratique des Hautes Etudes (Hanoi: 2005, vols 1–6.), hereinafter, *Corpus of Vietnamese Inscriptions.*

22 The notion of nontangible property – which includes copyright, intellectual property, and cultural property, legal scholars suggest – had its origins in the European enlightenment and was rearticulated in the common-law courts of the Anglophone countries and in the charter of the United Nations Convention. See John H. Merryman, "Two Ways of Thinking about Cultural Property," *The American Journal of International Law* 80:4 (Oct. 1986), pp. 831–53; Carla Hess, "Enlightenment Epistemology and the Laws of Authorship in Revolutionary France, 1777–1793," *Representations* 30 (1990), pp. 109–37 and "The Rise of Intellectual Property, 700 B.C.–A.D. 2000: An Idea in the Balance," *Daedalus* 131:2 (Spring 2002), pp. 26–45.

23 *Mai dinh mon bi ky*, Ms. 569 and 576, *Corpus of Vietnamese Inscriptions.*

24 For a discussion of the joint mark in contracts and testamentary records, see Nhung Tuyet Tran, "Beyond the Myth of Equality: Women's Inheritance Rights in the Le Code," in Nhung Tuyet Tran and Anthony Reid, *Viet Nam: Borderless Histories* (Madison: University of Wisconsin Press, 2006). Of course, it is impossible to mark one's finger joints on stone inscriptions, and as far as I can tell from the rubbings, no one used his joints to mark his approval of the sale (as in the case of contracts signed on paper). However, the use of the same format is telling of how the parties went to great lengths to legitimize the transactions.

25 *Tan tao mai dinh van khe bi ky* and *Tan tao trum truong tu dinh bi ky*, Ms. 1933–34, *Corpus of Vietnamese Inscriptions.*

26 In my discussions with Vietnamese scholars of *ca tru* on the meaning of "*giao phuong*," despite the frequent use of the land character denoting space, most have categorically rejected my suggestion that the term suggests territorial meaning. Indeed, the second character for the term *giao phuong* denotes an administrative unit, similar to a hamlet or a suburb in other usage. In classical Chinese usage during the Ming and Qing period,

the performance troupe was also linked to brothels. Email correspondence with Michael Szonyi, May 16, 2010.

27 *Tan tao mai dinh bi ky*, Ms. 1945, *Corpus of Vietnamese Inscriptions.*

28 *Lap khoan xuong nhi ky*, Ms. 1962, in *Corpus of Vietnamese Inscriptions.*

29 The two middle characters in the phrase are undecipherable.

30 *Mai tru van khe chi bi*, Ms. 3280, in *Corpus of Vietnamese Inscriptions.*

31 For an overview on the scholarship, see Phan Huy Le, "Research on the Vietnamese Village: Assessment and Perspectives" in Tran and Reid, *Viet Nam: Borderless Histories* (Madison: University of Wisconsin Press, 2006), pp. 23–41.

32 See, for example, *Mai tru van khe chi bi*, Ms. 3280; *Thien Mac chau mai ban huyen giao phuong ty*, Ms. 6897–98; *Mai tru van khe chi bi*, Ms. 2689; *Thuy tong mai ban huyen phuong ty doan mai dinh tru tien van bi ky*, Ms. 2278–81.

33 *Dinh mon su le* and *Thach bi thuyen tao*, Ms. 1634–35, in *Corpus of Vietnamese Inscriptions.*

34 Tran, "Gender, State & Society in Early Modern Vietnam."

35 *Dinh mon bi ky*, Ms. 1585–86.

36 *Thach bi mai dinh* and *Luu truyen van dai*, Ms. 1977–78, *Corpus of Vietnamese Inscriptions.*

37 Michel Foucault, "What is an Author?" in *Textual Strategies: Perspectives in Post-Structuralist Criticism*, Josue Harari (ed.), (Ithaca: Cornell University Press, 1979), pp. 141–60.

# 9 Appropriating culture

## The politics of intangible cultural heritage in Vietnam

*Oscar Salemink*

On June 14, 2008, Professor Nguyen Chi Ben, the director of the Vietnam Institute of Culture and Information (formerly known as Vietnam Institute of Culture and Arts Studies or VICAS), stopped by Amsterdam to discuss matters of common interest with me. Accompanying him were his assistant; the governor of Bac Ninh province; and the director of the provincial Department of Culture and Tourism. The delegation was on its way to Paris, headquarters of UNESCO, to plead for official UNESCO recognition of the Bac Ninh *quan ho* musical tradition as intangible cultural heritage (ICH).[1]

The term ICH was introduced in Vietnam by UNESCO, which in 1994 sponsored two back-to-back "expert meetings" in Vietnam on the intangible cultural heritage of ethnic minorities and of the culture of the imperial city of Hue. It only caught on, however, after the official UNESCO recognition of five sites – the three historical sites of Hue, Hoi An, and the My Son temple complex, and the two natural sites of Ha Long Bay and Phong Nha cave – resulted in a phenomenal boost in tourist visits and in national pride. In 2003 and 2005 respectively, *nha nhac* court music from Hue and the "Space of Gong Culture" (*khong gian van hoa cong chieng*) of ethnic minorities of Vietnam's Central Highlands were proclaimed "Masterpieces of the Oral and Intangible Heritage of Humanity;" in 2008, both were transferred to the new ICH List of "Intangible Cultural Heritage in Need of Urgent Safeguarding." In 2007, the year before Nguyen Chi Ben visited me in Amsterdam, Vietnam had nominated *quan ho* as well as *ca tru* singing for UNESCO recognition;[2] in May 2009, both forms of musical heritage were officially recognized by UNESCO.[3]

This anecdote illustrates the extent to which the nomination is a political process at various overlapping and interacting "levels," involving local political ambitions within a national context as well as national, political, and cultural interests in an international arena, and invoking the artistic and academic authority of national and transnational "experts."[4] In this paper, I analyze the appropriation and the uses of "intangible cultural heritage" in the Vietnamese context with reference to local, national-level, regional, and international political discourses. Locally, heritage claims can be interpreted as a way to counter certain political demands or – alternatively – to seek the promotion of a region. Nationally, the politics of heritage help establish political legitimacy for Vietnam's postsocialist Communist regime; internationally, UNESCO recognition puts Vietnam on the global radar screen as an old civilization and venerable culture.

The 2003 UNESCO Convention for the Safeguarding of Intangible Cultural Heritage defines the intangible cultural heritage as "the practices, representations, expressions, knowledge, skills – as well as the instruments, objects, artifacts and cultural spaces associated therewith – that communities, groups and, in some cases, individuals recognize as part of their cultural heritage."[5] Conceptually, my analysis is inspired by Laurajane Smith's comprehensive book *Uses of Heritage* (2006) which is predicated on

> the idea of heritage not so much as a "thing," but as a cultural and social process, which engages with acts of remembering that work to create ways to understand and engage with the present.... Indeed, the work starts from the premise that all heritage is intangible. In stressing the intangibility of heritage, however, I am not dismissing the tangible or pre-discursive, but simply deprivileging and denaturalizing it as the self-evident form and essence of heritage. While places, sites, objects and localities may exist as identifiable sites of heritage... these places are not inherently valuable, nor do they carry a freight of innate meaning.[6]

In her book, she identifies an "authorized heritage discourse" "that privileges expert values and knowledge about the past and its material manifestations, and dominates and regulates professional heritage practices" vis-à-vis popular and community heritage discourses and practices.[7]

Smith does not speak of heritage in terms of property but in terms of control, especially with reference to indigenous discourses on heritage. In Article 2, the Convention itself speaks of "world heritage properties" and refers to intellectual property rights with reference to heritage. In a special issue of *Museum International* devoted to intangible cultural heritage, Richard Kurin discusses "the ownership of cultural property" as a "technical, legal issue" that might be resolved with reference to intellectual property rights.[8] Noriko Aikawa and Wend Wendland bring out the extent to which debates and discourses of protection and safeguarding of (intangible) cultural heritage are wound up with notions of protection of intellectual property rights.[9] The conceptual move that necessarily precedes discourses and practices of protecting heritage as cultural property is, however, hardly touched upon by these authors. The idea that certain "intangible" cultural practices can be property, can be owned, inevitably reduces heritage to a definable "thing," an object that can be claimed and disputed.

With respect to heritage policies the Vietnamese state is not a monolithic entity but rather an arena of contestation in which conflicting interests are played out and resolved; still the outcome of these contestations inevitably integrates perceived national interests into one discursive frame. With reference to the discourse of ICH, the state and its experts appropriate the practices labeled heritage; practices, practitioners and, indeed, the "cultural space" in which they take place, become the object of state interventions. To the extent that heritage is presented as overriding the local or parochial, the state authenticates, reifies and instrumentalizes local processes under the umbrella of the nation, effectively as property of the state. In the process, the people who embody these cultural practices are necessarily marginalized from their heritage, rendering its preservation and revitalization more difficult.

In this paper, I develop a critical view of heritage *qua* property with reference to the process of appropriation, i.e. assuming decisive control over the definition, management, and use of the heritage as cultural property. I shall first explore what I call "monumental politics" in Vietnam, in which localized interest groups seek recognition from the political center for their site of remembrance, worship or of ritual practice as historical or cultural monument. A next section compares this process of competition for localized heritage status within a domestic Vietnamese context with the international competition for world heritage under UNESCO aegis, thus metaphorically globalizing village politics. In the subsequent section, I take a closer look at the politics of ICH in Vietnam's Central Highlands in terms of cultural appropriation, in the midst of long-standing political contestations surrounding that region.

## Monumental politics of heritage claims

While attending a temple ritual in a village festival near Chau Doc in the Mekong Delta in June 2005, I observed the sacred objects being taken out of the beautifully carved wooden boxes in order to be shown to the spirits of the village founders and other "exceptional dead" (Malarney 2007). These consisted of two documents: one was a royal certificate of investiture (*sac phong*) with the seal of emperor Minh Mang (reigned 1820–40), issued in the nineteenth century; the other document was much more recent and bore the stamp of the Ministry of Culture and Information, recognizing the village temple as a historical and cultural monument (*di tich lich su van hoa*). Indeed, a visitor to a temple, pagoda, shrine, or communal hall in contemporary Vietnam will often see a couple of public announcements outside or inside the main hall, including a plaque briefly indicating the history and meaning of the site; a list of "meritorious contributions" (*cong duc*), with names and amounts contributed; and a public announcement that the site was recognized by the Ministry as a cultural or historical monument since a particular date – usually during the *Doi Moi* period.

In our introduction to a symposium on "Living with the Dead: The Politics of Ritual and Remembrance in Contemporary Vietnam," Michael DiGregorio and I draw attention to this historical parallel between state certification of local ritual practice and heritage claims by the Board of Rites of imperial times and the Ministry of Culture of postsocialist Vietnam.[10] DiGregorio in particular describes the fierce competition between local patrilineages for recognition as the founding patrilineage and hence for the social and political seniority associated with that recognition. This contestation translates into struggle over sacred sites and over the identity of mythical heroes, in particular the founder of the village.[11] Usually, such a struggle is resolved in favor of one or the other party when the site – temple, shrine, pagoda – receives a certificate of recognition as historical/cultural monument (*giay cong nhan di tich lich su van hoa*) from the Ministry of Culture. As the ritual in the village near Chau Doc shows, the significance of this recognition goes beyond the historical or cultural value of the site (monument) as heritage. It is seen as an implicit official endorsement of the identity of the spirit worshipped at the site; of the ritual manner in which the worship is conducted; and of the political and moral credentials of the people – the village, commune, or its authorities – who submitted the claim in the first place.

The political context of this competitive local bidding for (central) state recognition lies in Resolution No. V of the Central Committee of the Communist Party, which was adopted in 1998, rather than in the 2001 Law on Cultural Heritage. Resolution No. V proclaims to "build a progressive culture, imbued with national identity." It offers alternative historical and cultural narratives of the Vietnamese nation and thus provided an umbrella for the religious upsurge which took place during the *Doi Moi* era. Since the initiation of *Doi Moi* in 1986, Vietnam's rapid economic development has been wound up with capitalist market reforms and integration into the global market – a process that culminated in Vietnam's admission into the WTO. The neoliberal reforms that Vietnam enacted in "partnership" with the World Bank, International Monetary Fund, United Nations Development Program, and foreign donors not only affected the market but also the state, which partially retreated from various domains (health care, education, welfare) in a process euphemistically called *xa hoi hoa* (socialization) – meaning that people themselves have to pay for the services they need.

In the mid-1990s, the Communist Party decided to piggy-back on the religious resurgence in order to shore up its legitimacy which had suffered from the unpopularity of the failed Socialist experiment and from the credibility gap created by its embrace of a capitalist road to development. After Resolution No. V was adopted in 1998, the religious upsurge began to be translated into the official imaginary of the nation. On the one hand, this Resolution formed an umbrella for all sorts of local, bottom-up efforts to re-invent traditions and invest these with new forms and meanings. On the other hand, it created a handle for the state to claim a greater role in the organization of rituals and festivals, or alternatively to create new rituals, in an attempt to channel the discourse over Vietnam's identity in new directions after the withdrawal from a Socialist modernity.[12]

The Ministry of Culture and Information, for instance, selected ten local festivals that were supposed to assume a "national character" and that were to play an important role in politico-cultural propaganda and in the promotion of tourism.[13] One example is the Hung King Festival in Phu Tho,[14] which, until the mid-1990s, had largely been a local event, providing occasion to young men and women to court each other. In the mid-1990s, the festival was elevated to the status of a national festival celebrating the birth of the nation. From 2000 onward, the organization of the festival became more and more politicized, with attendance by national political leaders and nationwide media coverage; since 2009, it is the only national holiday in Vietnam celebrated according to the lunar calendar (the tenth of the third month). The symbolism of the festival itself changed considerably as well, with drum and dance performances that purportedly took their cue from the imagery of the Dong Son culture of the times of the Hung kings (roughly from the sixth to the third century BCE). During the conflict-ridden 1970s and 1980s the interpretation of the Dong Son drums – which were found all over Southeast Asia as well as in southern China – was the object of an "archaeological war" between China and Vietnam.[15] For Vietnam, the Dong Son culture symbolized not only an early period of cultural bloom but also the assertion of an original Vietnamese culture before the strong Sinicizing influences of the subsequent centuries. From the 1970s, the iconography of the drums began to be used as political symbols, on stamps, in war cemeteries, in public architecture, temples, museums, logos. Moreover, the Dong Son imagery was compared with the material culture of present-day ethnic minorities in the Central Highlands who – assumed to have been uninfluenced by Chinese civilization – came to be seen as "contemporary ancestors" of the *Kinh* (lowland Vietnamese), metaphoricially denying them "coevalness."[16] The "drum dance" performed during the Hung King Festival resembles the opening ceremony which was performed during the 2009 International Gong Festival in Pleiku, celebrating the intangible cultural heritage of the "Gong cultural space of Vietnam's Central Highlands."

I have drawn attention elsewhere to the way that the paternalist Party-State celebrates cultural diversity among both Viet majority and ethnic minorities by emphasizing aesthetic and expressive aspects of culture, at the expense of other cultural dimensions like religion, lifestyle, and livelihood. This process of folklorization of culture goes hand in hand with strong disciplinary control exerted by state agencies over local cultural practices.[17] This has also been noted by scholars such as Professor To Ngoc Thanh, President of the Vietnam Folk Art Association, who, in an interview with *Lao Dong* newspaper about the preservation of intangible cultural heritage, critiqued the tendency by "state bodies" to control "grassroots cultural activities" for propaganda and education purposes. In the same interview, however, he sees these practices as expressions of "national culture."[18] In other words, both local cultural practices, rituals and festivals, and local historical and cultural monuments are validated through formal investigation and recognition by the Ministry of Culture. As experts of the Ministry assume the authority to validate cultural practices as heritage, they appropriate these practices, which become the cultural property of the state.

It is important, however, to note the two-way, multiple-level validation movement at work with regard to heritage authentication. One direction is "top-down," arrogating authority to state agencies to select, edit, change, and script form and meaning of certain cultural practices at specific sites as heritage, thus controlling the practices and disciplining the people involved. In a way, this is a continuation of the pre-*Doi Moi* policy of "selective preservation" which sought to select which "progressive" and "patriotic" cultural elements were worthy of preservation.[19] The other direction is "bottom-up," in the sense that local communities – often after or even during some local contestation between groups over cultural and political primacy – seek recognition from the central government (the Ministry of Culture) for their site or practice, and hence substantive validation for both their "grassroots cultural practices" and for the groups involved. By labeling certain practices and sites "heritage," these communities reify and objectify these sites and practices in an effort to appropriate them as their cultural property, authenticated and validated by the state.

However, the picture is more complicated than this metaphor of a two-way street suggests. Just as the *Doi Moi* reforms constitute the outcome of a (fragmented) movement of peasant discontent over poverty,[20] the adoption in 1998 of a policy more congenial to local cultural practices – often using religious idiom – through Resolution No. V basically gave official political blessing to a groundswell of cultural as well as ritual and religious practices that had begun in the early 1990s.[21] This strongly suggests that collectively, local initiatives did have considerable political influence, even in the absence of liberal democratic procedure (through free elections) or of a vibrant civil society.[22] Moreover, as argued above, a Party-State led by a Communist Party which enacts (neo)liberal reforms is in need of political legitimacy beyond socialism, which was abandoned as practical economic policy and largely discredited as ideology in the 1980s.[23] If the slogan of "industrialization and modernization" (*cong nghiep hoa, hien dai hoa dat nuoc*) which is the official policy aim by the year 2020 is commonly understood to mean "Westernization," then Resolution No. V offers an alternative vision of modernity, namely a uniquely Vietnamese modernity brought out in the phrase "progressive culture imbued with national identity." This nationalist vision of modernity not only abandons the socialist internationalism that became redundant with the collapse of the Soviet Union, but necessarily embraces local cultural practices as expressive of the – simultaneously "traditional" and "modern" – nation and hence legitimizing the Party-State.

Consequently, the (central) Party-State is as much in need of the cultural validation offered by local cultural practices as the local communities are in need of the official recognition and political validation offered by the Ministry of Culture. The keyword linking cultural practices at the local and central levels and characterizing both the "bottom-up" and "top-down" flows of cultural and political validation is *dan toc*, with its multiple meanings and connotations of nation/al and/or ethnic/ity. *Dan toc* consists of the particles *dan*, meaning "people" (as in *nhan dan* – the people or the masses in Marxist terms; or in *nguoi dan* – "common people"), and *toc*, meaning clan or patrilineage, as in *gia toc*.[24] At both levels, cultural and political practices are legitimated through a process of mutual validation with reference to the discourse of the (ethnic rather than political) nation (*dan toc*) for domestic purposes. In the process of heritage claims validation, certain cultural practices and sites become property, claimed by various parties. Local communities – or factions therein – claim ownership over certain sites and cultural practices in competition with other communities or factions. The state claims the authority to assess and validate, and in so doing appropriates the heritage on behalf of the nation. The cultural practices and sites claimed as heritage thus effectively become the property of certain parties.

## Globalizing village politics: UNESCO as global "Ministry of Culture"

There is a vast body of literature on the politics of culture[25] and on culture and tourism.[26] Studies of the politics of heritage may be more recent, but similar debates occur, with the addition of the international competitive element provided by the UNESCO World Heritage list. Much of the heritage literature can be characterized as "expert literature;" it is produced by those who are involved in the research, assessment, valuation, and management, either on behalf of UNESCO or of a national institution or agency. They are insiders and "expert professionals," both authors of and participants in what Laurajane Smith calls the "authorized heritage discourse."[27] This is evident from the contributions to the 2004 special issue on intangible cultural heritage of the journal *Museum International*, but also from the 2002 debate on "Masterpieces of Oral and Intangible Culture: Reflections on the UNESCO World Heritage List" in *Current Anthropology*. In both volumes, for instance, Richard Kurin offers a "critical appraisal" of the 2003 Convention and of the process from his position as Director of the Smithsonian Institution Center for Folklife and Cultural Heritage and from his vantage point as insider to UNESCO decision-making processes.[28] But insiders and experts are not really willing or able to step outside the "authorized heritage discourse" and take seriously the "unauthorized" views and interests that Laurajane Smith focuses on in her *Uses of Heritage*.

In *The Politics of World Heritage*, edited by David Harrison and Michael Hitchcock (2005), the contributors pay much attention to the roles of UNESCO and of national states, but also to the expectation of economic valorization of conservation through tourism – hence the subtitle *Negotiating Tourism and Conservation*.[29] The essay by Tim Winter on memory and remembrance during New Year celebrations at the Angkor Wat heritage site in Cambodia focuses on the meaning the site has for Cambodian tourists who flock there during these days to meet others, enjoy themselves but also to bask in the past glory of the Khmer people.[30] Their behavior seems to confirm Charles Keyes' reformulation of Max Weber's notion of ethnicity as a group which sustains its belief in common descent by narratives of past glory and suffering.[31] In a paper on culture and tourism in Vietnam, Tomke Lask and Stefan Herold offer a vastly different perspective by pleading for institutionalized mechanisms for greater community inclusion and participation in heritage protection and "management." They hold that "World Heritage" is increasingly approached in an international context and it seems therefore appropriate to advocate for the protection of World Heritage sites in our globalized world," thus placing much responsibility with UNESCO and other multilateral organizations.[32] In "Mundo Maya," Graeme Evans goes one step further and offers a trenchant critique of the international tourist exploitation of heritage sites which, he argues, are claimed and should be owned by the indigenous Maya groups that once created the monuments.[33] What these papers in their diverse orientations show are the manifold interests at play in the conservation and management of (world) heritage sites: economic, political, historical, cultural.

Similar elements are also at play for Vietnam. The first Vietnamese site inscribed in the World Heritage list in 1993 was the "complex of monuments" in the former imperial capital of Hue, which had been damaged badly during the Indochina Wars; its "feudal" heritage was viewed with suspicion by Communist leaders during the period of high socialism – and for a time after unification, leading to further decay.[34] Within Vietnam, the inscription of the Hue site on the list was pushed by the dynamic and well-connected former director of the Hue Monuments Conservations Center, Mr Thai Cong Nguyen, by the foreign policy community interested in promoting Vietnam's policy of "making friends with every nation" through integration into multilateral organizations; as well as by other political leaders and scholars originating from or sympathetic to Hue – combining to overcome domestic opposition to such nomination. Internationally, Vietnam found supporters in France and Japan as well as in the person of Dr Richard Englehardt, UNESCO regional advisor for culture in Asia and the Pacific.

After Hue was inscribed and became the focus of international attention, sympathy, and support, various other candidate sites – represented by the People's Committees of the provinces where these sites were located – were proposed to Vietnam's central authorities, leading to further bids to UNESCO for Ha Long Bay (inscribed in 1994);[35] the town of Hoi An and the nearby ancient Cham sanctuary of My Son (1999); and the Phong Nha-Ke Bang national park (2003). Thus, in the short period of ten years, three cultural and two natural heritage sites in Vietnam were admitted to the World Heritage List. The Vietnamese government was responsive to local efforts to propose particular sites for nomination to UNESCO as World Heritage sites. It was also proactive in lobbying with UNESCO and with other potential partners. Nguyen Kim Dung of the Ministry of Culture writes that "[t]he Government of Viet Nam views the identification, protection and promotion of intangible cultural heritage as vital in the present period of rapid socio-economic transformation" in the context of globalization.[36] From an avalanche of professional and popular publications and from frequent reference to the sites in cultural and tourist-oriented websites it seems clear that many Vietnamese take great pride in such official international recognition, while many tourist companies and organizations see great economic potential in the development, management, and exploitation of heritage sites, objects, and stories in tourist contexts.[37]

The Law on Cultural Heritage, which was passed on June 29, 2001, formalized Vietnam's commitment to implement the 1972 UNESCO World Heritage Convention and elaborated the roles of the state and its agencies as well as of other partners. Article 23 of the 2001 Law concerns the safeguarding of the "works of literature, art, science, oral tradition, and folklore of the multi-ethnic Vietnamese community" through collection, compilation, classification, etc., focusing mainly on ethnic minorities.[38] In a subsequent government decree of November 11, 2002, specifying the Law on Cultural Heritage in policy practice, explicit mention is made of intangible cultural heritage as cultural practice that is embodied in people and the protection of which should primarily target "cultural carriers." Interestingly, this mention of "intangible cultural heritage" *preceded* the adoption of the

UNESCO Convention for the safeguarding of the Intangible Cultural Heritage of October 17, 2003, which was ratified by Vietnam two years later, in October 2005. By that time, UNESCO had already recognized Vietnamese court music from Hue (2003), and the "Space of Gong Culture" from Tay Nguyen (Central Highlands) as two Vietnamese "Masterpieces of the oral and intangible cultural heritage of humanity."

The UNESCO "stamp of approval" is important to the Vietnamese leadership, both in terms of foreign policy and domestically. Internationally, the prestigious recognition by UNESCO on behalf of the entire world renders specimens of Vietnam's cultural heritage both unique – as specifically Vietnamese – and universal – of cultural value for all of humanity – at once. In a world characterized by competition between countries, the UNESCO recognition validates Vietnam's cultural prominence in accord with its professed foreign policy of friendship with all nations and of multilateralism.[39] Moreover, UNESCO recognition may bring economic benefits, not just in terms of international financial contributions to conservation, preservation, and safeguarding projects,[40] but also in the guise of booming international tourism to the sites.[41] Domestically, the official UNESCO recognition symbolizes international respect for Vietnam's cultural heritage, thus validating Vietnam's cultural prominence as well as its cultural policies, like the 1998 Resolution No. V. In a postsocialist state where "national identity" (*ban sac dan toc*) has come to replace socialism as the regime's political legitimation, UNESCO recognition becomes a powerful cultural policy instrument, comparable to the tributary relations that precolonial Vietnam rulers entertained with the Emperor of the Middle Kingdom, who embodied universalizing authority as well.

Clear parallels can be drawn between the domestic competitive process whereby local ritual or religious practices and their sites of worship or commemoration receive the blessing from Vietnam's central authorities either in the form of the imperial seal of recognition or the modern certificate of recognition as historical/cultural monument on the one hand, and the international competitive process by which particular places or practices are recognized as World Heritage by UNESCO, purportedly acting on behalf of the world, or of all humanity. At both levels, the nominations for recognition themselves bring closure to competition and contestations at lower levels still, whereas the act of recognition reaffirms the position and prestige of the supreme authority in question – be it Emperor, Communist government, or UNESCO. Internationally, then, UNESCO performs a similar function to the one that the Chinese Board of Rites once fulfilled in offering validation for the cultural policies of precolonial Vietnam's Ministry of Rites (*Bo Le*).[42]

It is important to keep in mind that although in its heritage conventions UNESCO formally allows NGOs to nominate sites, objects, or practices, it remains an inter-governmental organization which will only accept a nomination if it is supported by the government of the country where this heritage is located. That state must assume special responsibilities regarding the management, the conservation or preservation, and the protection or safeguarding of the heritage.

In order to do that, the state must make the heritage "its" property, to be investigated, managed, and showcased by its experts and its officials, thus turning the heritage and the communities living close to ("buffer zone") or embodying that heritage ("culture carriers") into sites of intervention and discipline by the state. At the same time, the heritage becomes a source of national pride and an icon of the nation in the international arena, hence becomes exclusive "national property."

## Intangible cultural heritage and highland controversies

I began this paper by relating how Dr Nguyen Chi Ben came to Amsterdam in order to discuss issues of common concern – the publication of a monograph of mine in Vietnamese, and my participation in a workshop in Tay Nguyen that he was organizing as part of the "Space of Gong Culture" Intangible Cultural Heritage (ICH). In fact, my involvement with intangible cultural heritage policy in the Central Highlands of Vietnam had begun some fifteen years earlier, in March 1994, when I was invited to participate in an "International Expert Meeting for the Safeguarding and Promotion of the Intangible Cultural Heritage of Minority Groups in Viet Nam." ICH was then a new concept within UNESCO, and was very much in line with the Lévi-Straussian concept of culture long dominant within UNESCO.[43] A new subdivision for intangible cultural heritage was established in Paris, largely funded by Japan and staffed by Japanese officials (Ms Noriko Aikawa was the Director of the Intangible Cultural Heritage section of UNESCO during those years).[44] At the time, the (linguistic/anthropological) notion of intangible cultural heritage constituted an experimental departure from the established (historical/archaeological) practice of heritage conservation focusing on material objects.[45]

The 1994 "International Expert Meetings" in Vietnam – one in Hanoi dealing with ethnic minorities, and one in Hue focusing on the intangible cultural heritage of the old imperial capital – were the first major initiatives of that subdivision.[46] At the time, Vietnam was still largely isolated and the *Doi Moi* reforms were only beginning to take effect. The surprising choice on the part of UNESCO of Vietnam as a field for intangible cultural heritage experimentation is a simple function of intersecting interests on the part of the two main national-intellectual influences on the emerging intangible heritage discourse. On the one hand there was and continues to be a keen Japanese interest in Vietnam as a field of study, as was evident from the influence on and participation in the expert meeting by Professor Yamaguti Osamu and Professor Yosihiko Tokumaru (both from Osaka) and by Professor Kazushige Kaneko (Tokyo) who developed the notion of "ethno-forms." On the other hand, the influence within UNESCO of Claude Lévi-Strauss's notion of culture was embodied by the prominent French anthropologist Georges Condominas whose scholarly career began with fieldwork in Vietnam's Central Highlands. Condominas wrote the introduction to the edited volume that resulted from the Expert Meeting and continued to advocate for the research and safeguarding of intangible cultural heritage until his death in 2011.[47] Finally, within UNESCO there was also the strong presence of the

Paris-based French-Vietnamese ethnomusicologist Professor Tran Van Khe who played a notable role in the Expert Meetings on the intangible cultural heritage both of Vietnam's ethnic minorities and of Hue.

While this may explain the somewhat surprising UNESCO interest in Vietnam, it does not explain why Vietnam would be interested in safeguarding and promoting the intangible cultural heritage (ICH) of ethnic minorities whose cultures were often branded "backward" and "primitive" – as is clear from a contribution on cultural policy by Vietnam's former vice-minister of culture, Nong Quoc Chan[48] – or, respectively, the "feudal heritage" of the imperial *ancien régime*.[49] I shall not go further into the issue of the Hue heritage whose built monuments had just been inscribed on the World Heritage List one year before. Regarding the ICH of ethnic minorities, a number of scholars who were firmly grounded in Vietnam's political institutions nonetheless deplored the onslaught of Vietnam's development programs – like "sedentarization" and "selective preservation" – on cultural diversity and vibrancy among ethnic minorities.[50] These included the aforementioned late Nong Quoc Chan – an ethnic Tay poet – but also prominent ethnologists and folklorists like Dang Nghiem Van, To Ngoc Thanh, and Phan Dang Nhat.

For them, the concept of "intangible heritage" performs two discursive tricks that make it stick in the context of Vietnamese culture politics. First, the UNESCO notion of heritage is clearly associated with a notion of culture as a bounded entity linked to a clearly delineated ethnic group.[51] This renders it compatible with Vietnam's project of official ethnic classification which is predicated on the assumption of distinct cultural entities operating outside of history rather than historically constituted through processes of tribalization and ethnicization.[52] Second, despite all UNESCO assurances that intangible cultural heritage is "living" and directly dependent on "culture carriers," the notion of heritage allows for reification of cultural practices and their separation from the flow of everyday life with which they are – or better, were – connected. I have previously called the effects of this cultural policy "folklorization," meaning that particular cultural practices are decontextualized from the cultural setting in which they acquire locally specific (social, economic, ritual, religious) meanings, and re-contextualized for a different public for whom aesthetic meanings are paramount criteria.[53] The result of policies predicated on such notions is the ossification of these cultural practices, studied, preserved, safeguarded, and promoted out of context.[54]

It is not only certain cultural policies that promote processes of folklorization. John Urry (1990) and many others have pointed at the influence of the market forces through the "tourist gaze" which transforms cultural practices and even lifeworlds of some communities to spectacles to be watched by others.[55] This external gaze and the concepts used to describe and evaluate certain cultural practices are often internalized by those whose culture is under external scrutiny as picturesque, exotic, or simply attractively "traditional" – usually seen in opposition with the everyday routine of modern life.[56] This market-driven folklorization and exoticization takes place in Vietnam – and in Vietnam's Central Highlands – as well, as may be clear from any tourist brochure or website about that region. And while we may make an analytical distinction between the folklorizing effects of state-driven cultural policies and the exoticizing effects of a market-driven tourist gaze, in actual practice these effects are very much mixed up as political and economic interests tend to be hand-in-glove. The combined effect of such processes is what I would like to call the *appropriation* of culture, or better, of specific cultural practices that tend to be wound up with the lives of particular categories of people, in this case ethnic minorities. Their cultural practices are studied, recorded, interpreted, authenticated by cultural experts, and appropriated as part of a wider, national cultural heritage, that is celebrated for its diversity (*tinh da dang*) and richness (*phong phu*). In other words, through this process of cultural appropriation, particular cultural practices are taken out of context, re-interpreted and re-packaged by cultural "outsiders," and presented to an outside audience as "authentic heritage" which should be preserved and revitalized. Complex and multifarious cultural processes are reduced to spectacles to watch, organized by those who claim political and cultural authority over this process of authentication. Through this appropriation culture becomes property – no longer of the "culture carriers" (UNESCO's unfortunate term which implicitly reduces "culture" to a thing, or even a burden to carry) but of state- and market-mandated cultural experts.

One anecdote may serve to illustrate this. When I was invited to participate as a junior scholar in the 1994 Expert Meeting on minorities, I was asked to be the *rapporteur* of the meeting as I was one of the few participants fluent in the three official languages of the Meeting (English, French, and Vietnamese). I later accepted to edit the proceedings of the meeting which should become the first flagship UNESCO publication focusing on the ICH of one country, to be published in French, English, and Vietnamese.[57] Up until 1996 when I began working in Hanoi for the Ford Foundation, communication with the Vietnamese contributors – which in the pre-Internet age had to go through diplomatic UNESCO channels – turned out to be impossible, but from 1996 onward I could more easily get into direct contact with my Vietnamese colleagues. Nevertheless, in 1997 a Vietnamese translation of the papers presented at the meeting – unedited, and without permission from the foreign authors – appeared as *Giu gin va bao ve ban sac van hoa cac dan toc thieu so Viet Nam* (Preserving and Protecting the Cultural Identity of Vietnamese Ethnic Minorities), published by the Ethnic Culture Publishing House (Nha Xuat Ban Van hoa Dan toc), the publishing vehicle for Nong Quoc Chan's Ethnic Minorities Arts and Culture Association (*Hoi Van hoa Van Nghe cac Dan toc*).[58] Interestingly, my paper was missing from that 1997 Vietnamese-language publication; and the NCSSH (now the Vietnam Academy of Social Sciences) also wanted me to "edit" my contribution for its 2002 Vietnamese-language publication. The apparent problem with my paper, entitled "Who Decides Who Preserves What? Cultural Preservation and Representation," was that it asked the simple question: what would be the role of the people, whose cultural practices are deemed worthy of preservation by outsiders, and what would be their own priorities, based on a more comprehensive notion of culture as an embodied process of material and symbolic practice from which it is useless to take out specific cultural elements at will for preservation?[59] This is, of course, a political question which calls into question the political practice of intangible cultural heritage in Vietnam and elsewhere.

The politics and the political uses of intangible cultural heritage was brought out even more clearly in the cultural policy responses to the conflicts and contestations over land and Protestant conversion in Vietnam's Central Highlands.[60] One of the contributors to the UNESCO volume, Professor Phan Dang Nhat, pleaded for research and preservation of what he called "the timeless epics of the ethnic minorities of Viet Nam."[61] Phan Dang Nhat's successor as director of the Institute of Folk Culture Studies (now Institute of Cultural Studies) of the National Center for Social Sciences and Humanities, Professor Ngo Duc Thinh, began to work on compiling the (oral) customary legal practices and chants among Vietnam's minorities in the mid-1990s,[62] and in the late 1990s laid the groundwork for a big project on the recording, transcription, translation, contextual interpretation, and publication of the very rich and diverse oral traditions – especially epics (*su thi*) – of Vietnam's Central Highlanders. In the spring of 2001, the Vietnamese government unexpectedly decided to spend close to one million US dollars on the latter project, by far the biggest amount spent by the Vietnamese government on a single research project in the social sciences and humanities.[63] Although the project had been prepared well in advance, the timing of the government's decision, which came shortly after the February 2001 protests and riots in the Central Highlands with the ensuing repression, refugee streams into Cambodia, and international fall-out, inevitably wedded cultural policy to the local and transnational political contestations at hand. The (far-fetched) claims for political autonomy of Ksor Kok's Montagnard Foundation notwithstanding, the massive conversion to evangelical Protestantism among Central Highlanders was the major bone of contention.[64] In various reports mention was made of attempts by local cadres to "undo" conversion by forcing Highlander converts to engage in non-Christian rituals that cadres imagined to be part of the "traditional religion,"[65] the irony being that these same traditional religious and ritual practices had been branded "superstitious," "unhygienic," and "wasteful" by the very same regime.[66] An official public celebration of Highlander culture – in the form of epics – constituted a significant political statement in that context, because both the mythical contents and the ritual context is *directly* antithetical to the brand of evangelical Protestantism currently dominant in the Central Highlands. Moreover, the sixty-three bi-lingual (Vietnamese and vernacular) volumes resulting from the project form a formidable monument stating clearly that these epics do not just constitute the oral heritage of these ethnic groups, but indeed are part of the national heritage of Vietnam, and hence the cultural property of the Vietnamese nation.

The 2003 nomination by Vietnam (and 2005 UNESCO recognition) of the "Space of Gong Culture" in the Central Highlands as one of the world's masterpieces of intangible cultural heritage has a similar political context, apart from the cultural motivation which combines aesthetic criteria with a discourse of "vanishing culture."[67] The performance of Tay Nguyen gong music at the 2006 Hue Festival, as well as the putative "*Dong Son* culture" drum dances during the Hung King Festival which are made to resemble a Central Highlands gong performance, can both be interpreted as embodiments of an imaginary past of the Viet nation. This idea, that the "traditional culture" of present-day ethnic minority people in the Central Highlands is a direct outcome of and very similar to the *Dong Son* culture, was very much alive at the conference on "Economic and Social Changes and Preservation of the Gong Culture in Vietnam and the Southeast Asian Region" which was organized in the context of the International Gong Festival in Pleiku, November 2009.[68] In this manner, culturally distinct ethnic groups are incorporated into a vision of the nation as multi-ethnic. In the first paragraph of his policy paper on Vietnam's intangible cultural heritage, Nguyen Kim Dung of the Ministry of Culture and Information writes that "[t]he Government aims to ensure that the country's diverse culture with 54 ethnic groups play a role in promoting social and economic development."[69] Similarly, the Law on Cultural Heritage passed on June 29, 2001, stipulates that: "The State's policies shall encourage work to collect, compile, translate, inventory, classify and preserve works of literature, art science, oral tradition and folklore of the multi-ethnic Vietnamese community" (Law on Cultural Heritage, Chapter 3, Article 23).

Thus, the preservation and promotion of intangible cultural heritage in Vietnam is explicitly associated with the multi-ethnic nation, making these diverse cultural practices the responsibility of the state as guardian of the "multi-ethnic Vietnamese community." In other words, the work of preserving and promoting the diverse "intangible cultural heritage" of Vietnam's ethnic groups becomes tantamount to celebrating the nation, both for domestic (Hung King Festival) and international (Hue Festival) audiences.

In the specific context of the "unruly" Central Highlands, other factors come into play as well. As elsewhere in Southeast Asia, Central Highlanders used to play gong music during ritual occasions, such as life cycle rituals (especially burials), seasonal rituals, and other ritualized celebrations.[70] It is such rituals which are singled out by evangelical Protestants as pagan, thus rendering a revival of such ritual contexts in the name of preservation of intangible cultural heritage a frontal assault on the cultural politics of Protestantism in highland Vietnam. Paradoxically, such rituals were – and to some extent still are – singled out by Communist (and before that, South Vietnamese) cadres as superstitious, unhygienic, wasteful, or at best uncivilized. As I have argued elsewhere, the policies of sedentarization, the massive migration and the conversion of forest to coffee plantations, and the policy of selective cultural preservation have made the highly localized animist religions and the resource-intensive rituals incompatible with the rapidly changing environment of the Central Highlands.[71] With the loss of ancestral land, rituals and gongs lose their meaning, except as valuable currency in the international trade in ethnic art.[72] This is precisely the unwelcome critical observation about social, economic, and political contextualization of cultural heritage that I offered in my contribution to the UNESCO volume on intangible cultural heritage of ethnic minorities in Vietnam.[73]

To a large extent this observation about cultural context is shared by Vietnamese researchers and officials, as is brought out by the notion of the *Space* of Gong Culture which was nominated for UNESCO recognition, rather than a narrow focus on the performance itself. Dr Nguyen Chi Ben of VICAS was charged by the Ministry of Culture, Sports and Tourism with a project to research how the "Space of Gong Culture" heritage can be preserved and revitalized sustainably in the context of rapid social, economic, ecological, and demographic change in this hotspot of globalization called Tay Nguyen.[74] In a twist of irony, he invited me to be part of that endeavor, which culminated in a conference on "Economic and Social Changes and Preservation of the Gong Culture in Vietnam and the Southeast Asian Region" (Pleiku City, November 13–15, 2009), in the context of an International Gong Festival. The International Gong Festival brought together gong music troupes from various Vietnamese provinces and from various countries in the East and Southeast Asian subcontinents to Pleiku, to perform their village- or court-based ritual music for Vietnamese audiences and for each other. The scientific workshop brought together around seventy researchers, mostly Vietnamese. Many researchers from various provinces (and even from neighboring Laos and Cambodia) pleaded for inclusion of the minority gong tradition from their province – outside the five provinces making up the Tay Nguyen region – into the ICH fold of "Space of Gong Culture." They sought recognition for "their heritage" from the Vietnamese state and from UNESCO. This form of cultural appropriation was commented upon by the only ethnic minority person present at the Conference; she noted the absence from the discussion of people from the ethnic minority communities which are – in UNESCO parlance – the "culture carriers" of the ritual gong music.

The irony of cultural appropriation can be seen very clearly here, as it is directly connected with forms of economic, ecological, and cultural dispossession that I have analyzed elsewhere by analogy with Marx' notion of "enclosures of the commons."[75] On the one hand, the official (state, UNESCO) recognition of specific cultural practices as national or world heritage can be interpreted in terms of cultural redemption of certain local cultural values, and hence as (partial and insufficient) compensation for losses incurred through the appropriation of the living environment of Central Highlanders. On the other hand, heritage authentication and recognition is by itself a form of cultural appropriation in which cultural practices are reduced to property which is decided on and disposed of by cultural outsiders. In other words, the cultural "proprietors" are not the same people as the "culture carriers," risking the effect that cultural appropriation through heritage becomes one more instance of (cultural) dispossession. This was brought out clearly by the spectacular opening ceremony of the International Gong Festival on November 12, 2009. In this mass performance, choreographed by the vice-minister of culture, *tuong* opera singer Le Tien Tho, the number of performers on stage outstripped the number of spectators at the "VIP grandstand," but the audience was national rather than local as the ceremony was broadcast nationwide. Massive groups of dancers, mostly ethnic Vietnamese schoolchildren from around Pleiku clothed in fantasy minority clothes, took the stage in alternation with troupes of gong players whose music was lost in a cacophony of loud music fragments and sounds, including a romanticized narrative of peaceful traditional life on the Central Highlands. This hallucinating whirlwind of sounds and sights concluded with a dancing parade of domesticated elephants, ridden by local ethnic minority mahouts, and with a grand finale of fireworks. Even while celebrating the "gong culture" of the Central Highlands, this massive show had little to do with the subtle music of the Highlanders, played during life cycle rituals and other festive occasions. Highlander gong music became the occasion, pretext, and footnote in this show, put up for a national Vietnamese audience and an occasional foreigner.

In this section, I have argued that UNESCO privileged Vietnam as an experimental site for intangible cultural heritage work, because Vietnam is where the cultural interests of UNESCO's two main influences – France and Japan – intersect with one another, and with the interests of a group of scholars and officials in Vietnam. Moreover, the UNESCO notion of culture resonates with official Vietnamese notions of cultural diversity linked to discrete ethnic groups, while the notion of intangible cultural heritage is in line with Vietnam's cultural policies of separating out particular cultural practices from the flow of everyday life. The specific example of the recognition of the "Space of Gong Culture" in the Central Highlands as masterpiece of intangible cultural heritage can be analyzed from the above perspective. But it can also be seen as a cultural policy to counter religious and political "subversion" in the Highlands, while simultaneously incorporating these cultural practices – and hence the people who embody these – into the multi-ethnic Vietnamese nation. Their cultural practices are appropriated by outside cultural experts who claim (state) authority over authentication, and are reduced to cultural property decided on and disposed of by outsiders. As property (rather than as lived and embodied practice), culture can be appropriated by outsiders in a process that might be interpreted as a form of cultural dispossession from the so-called "culture carriers" in UNESCO parlance. In this sense, the intangible cultural heritage of the Central Highlanders is objectified and instrumentalized for ulterior political purposes, which implies that the people embodying cultural practices branded "heritage" – the "culture carriers" – are instrumentalized as well.

## Conclusion

This paper is predicated on the assumption that – with respect to heritage policies, among other things – the Vietnamese state is not a monolithic entity with a singular agency, but rather an arena of contestation in which conflicting interests are played out and resolved. The outcome inevitably integrates perceived national interests into one frame, in this case of an "authorized discourse" of intangible cultural heritage. To the extent that it is presented as overriding the local or parochial, it reifies and instrumentalizes local processes under the umbrella of the nation. Partly because of these contextualized political contestations, the preservation and revitalization of intangible cultural heritage is rendered difficult, as the people who embody these cultural practices are instrumentalized along with their heritage. The recognition of cultural heritage can be interpreted as a form of cultural redemption compensating for other forms of dispossession, but it simultaneously entails further cultural dispossession as culture is reduced to property and appropriated by outside cultural experts.

What can we learn from this essay about the process of cultural appropriation in connection with heritage politics in postsocialist and postsecular Vietnam? First, I observed that the cultural celebration of the nation as laid down in Resolution No. V of 1998 has become a necessary and routine legitimization of the political regime, holding up an umbrella reconciling tensions between "socialism" and the market, between majority and minority ethnic groups, between cultural chauvinism and cosmopolitanism. Second, the cultural policies and cultural politics of intangible heritage in Vietnam are based on coalitions between diverse actors inside and outside the country who manage to reconcile diverse interests. More importantly, the competitive process validating and authenticating local sites or practices gives local players a role while bestowing the role of arbiter to the central authorities, thus facilitating the interaction between lower and higher levels of government. Third, in a similar vein Vietnam competes with other countries on a competitive playing field over UNESCO recognition of its cultural practices as world heritage or masterpiece of intangible cultural heritage. Fourth, the politics of cultural heritage suits a variety of political purposes at once, but in the process requires and facilitates the appropriation of particular practices as cultural heritage by authoritative outsiders, and instrumentalizes both the intangible cultural heritage and the people embodying this heritage.

This is not to say that such processes are masterminded by a monolithic state. Rather, the Vietnamese state can be seen as a competitive arena of diverging interests, played out at various levels – both domestically and internationally – and held together by a unifying cultural discourse of the (multi-ethnic) nation. While it is inevitable that cultural heritage and the people involved in these cultural practices are instrumentalized to suit ulterior political purposes, it is not a one-way street. Many communities and localities willingly participate in the process of seeking cultural validation from up above in pursuit of their own agendas.

## Notes

1 According to the 2003 Convention for the Safeguarding of the Intangible Cultural Heritage, the intangible cultural heritage (ICH) – or living heritage – is the mainspring of our cultural diversity and its maintenance a guarantee for continuing creativity. The Convention states that the ICH is manifested, among others, in the following domains: Oral traditions and expressions including language as a vehicle of the intangible cultural heritage; Performing arts (such as traditional music, dance, and theatre); Social practices, rituals, and festive events; Knowledge and practices concerning nature and the universe; Traditional craftsmanship. The 2003 Convention defines ICH as the practices, representations, expressions, as well as the knowledge and skills, that communities, groups and, in some cases, individuals recognise as part of their cultural heritage (cf. http://www.unesco.org/culture/ich/index.php?pg=00002, accessed 11 August 2008).

2 For *quan ho* singing, see Le Ngoc Chan (2002) *Quan Ho Singing in North Vietnam: A Yearning for Resolution*, University of California, Berkeley, unpublished PhD thesis; Le Ngoc Chan (n.d.), Quan Ho Singing in Ritual-festivals in Bac Ninh Region (Vietnam). See http://home.vicnet.net.au/~aaf/quanho.htm, accessed 11 August 2008; and Meeker, Lauren (2010), "How Much for a Song? Local and National Representations of Quan Ho Folksong," *Journal of Vietnamese Studies* 5(1), 125–61. For *ca tru*, see the work

by Barley Norton (1996; 2005; http://www.gold.ac.uk/music/catru/). See also Nhung Tuyet Tran, this volume.

3 See http://www.unesco.org/culture/ich/index.php?RL=00183 and http://www.unesco.org/culture/ich/index.php?USL=00309, accessed 4 January 2010.

4 Thaveeporn Vasavakul (2003), "From Fence-Breaking to Networking: Interests, Popular Organizations and Policy Influences in Post-Socialist Vietnam," in Benedict Kerkvliet, Russell Heng, David Koh (eds), *Getting Organized in Vietnam: Moving In and Around the Socialist State*, Singapore: ISEAS, pp. 25–61; Smith, Laurajane (2006), *Uses of Heritage*, London and New York: Routledge; Salemink, Oscar (2007), "The Emperor's New Clothes: Re-fashioning Ritual in the Hue Festival," *Journal of Southeast Asian Studies* 38(3): 559–82.

5 Article 2 of the Convention begins as follows: "1. The 'intangible cultural heritage' means the practices, representations, expressions, knowledge, skills – as well as the instruments, objects, artefacts and cultural spaces associated therewith – that communities, groups and, in some cases, individuals recognize as part of their cultural heritage. This intangible cultural heritage, transmitted from generation to generation, is constantly recreated by communities and groups in response to their environment, their interaction with nature and their history, and provides them with a sense of identity and continuity, thus promoting respect for cultural diversity and human creativity. For the purposes of this Convention, consideration will be given solely to such intangible cultural heritage as is compatible with existing international human rights instruments, as well as with the requirements of mutual respect among communities, groups and individuals, and of sustainable development. 2. The 'intangible cultural heritage', as defined in paragraph 1 above, is manifested inter alia in the following domains: (a) oral traditions and expressions, including language as a vehicle of the intangible cultural heritage; (b) performing arts; (c) social practices, rituals and festive events; (d) knowledge and practices concerning nature and the universe; (e) traditional craftsmanship." See http://www.unesco.org/culture/ich/index.php? pg=00006 (accessed 6 January 2010).

6 Smith, Laurajane (2006), *Uses of Heritage*. London and New York: Routledge, p. 2–3.

7 Smith, *Uses of Heritage*, p. 5.

8 Kurin, Richard (2004), "Safeguarding Intangible Cultural Heritage in the 2003 UNESCO Convention: A Critical Appraisal," *Museum International* 56(1–2): p. 67.

9 Aikawa, Noriko (2004), "An Historical Overview of the Preparation of the UNESCO International Convention for the Safeguarding of the Intangible Cultural Heritage," *Museum International* 56(1–2): 137–49; Wendland, Wend (2004), "Intangible Heritage and Intellectual Property: Challenges and Future Prospects," *Museum International* 56(1–2): 97–107.

10 DiGregorio, Michael and Oscar Salemink (2007), "Living with the Dead: The Politics of Ritual and Remembrance in Contemporary Vietnam," *Journal of Southeast Asian Studies* 38(3): 436.

11 DiGregorio, Michael (2007), "Things Held in Common: Memory, Space and the Reconstitution of Community Life," *Journal of Southeast Asian Studies* 38(3): 441–65.

12 Taylor, Philip (2001), *Fragments of the Present: Searching for Modernity in Vietnam's South*. (Honolulu: University of Hawai'i Press); Malarney, Shaun K. (2007), "Festivals and the Politics of the Exceptional Dead in Vietnam," *Journal of Southeast Asian Studies* 38(3): 515–40; Salemink (2007), "The Emperor's New Clothes."

13 Personal communication by Dr Nguyen Chi Ben.

14 Malarney (2007), "Festivals and the Politics of the Exceptional Dead;" Salemink, Oscar (2006a), *Nieuwe rituelen en de natie: Nederland in de spiegel van Vietnam* (New rituals and the nation: The Netherlands in the mirror of Vietnam). VU University Amsterdam: Inaugural lecture, 9 June 2006.

15 Han, Xiaorong (1998), "The Present Echoes of the Ancient Bronze Drum: Nationalism and Archeology in Modern Vietnam and China," *Explorations in Southeast Asian*

*Studies* 2(2); Han, Xiaorong (2004), "Who Invented the Bronze Drum? Nationalism, Politics, and a Sino-Vietnamese Archaeological Debate of the 1970s and 1980s," *Asian Perspectives* 43(3): 7–33.

16 Fabian, Johannes (1983), *Time and the Other: How Anthropology Makes its Object*, New York: Columbia University Press.

17 Salemink, Oscar (2003a), *The Ethnography of Vietnam's Central Highlanders: A Historical Contextualization, 1850–1990*, London: RoutledgeCurzon; Honolulu: University of Hawai'i Press (Anthropology of Asia Series).

18 "Folk Art Faces Challenges from Modern and Foreign Cultures," *Viet Nam News*, August 13, 2001.

19 Cf. Salemink (2003a), *The Ethnography.*

20 Kerkvliet, Benedict (1997), *Land Struggles and Land Regimes in the Philippines and Vietnam during the Twentieth Century*, Amsterdam: Centre for Asian Studies Amsterdam, Wertheim Lecture; Kerkvliet, Benedict (2005), *The Power of Everyday Politics: How Vietnamese Peasants Transformed National Policy*, Ithaca, NY: Cornell University Press and Singapore: ISEAS.

21 In *Ghosts of War in Vietnam*, Cambridge: Cambridge University Press, Heonik Kwon (2008) drew attention to the emerging issue of war dead in the former South Vietnam, but that is certainly not the only consideration. There is abundant literature suggesting that the ritual and religious revival involves concerns about health, wealth, and well-being in situations of uncertainty; is predicated on growing wealth; and is not just facilitated by more liberal state policies, but actually encouraged by the Party-State's attempts at creating politico-religious legitimacy for its rule. Rather than providing precise references, I refer the reader to the work by – among many others – Hy Van Luong, John Kleinen, Shaun Malarney, Kirsten Endres, Philip Taylor, as well as myself.

22 Gray, Michael (1999), "Creating Civil Society? The Emergence of NGOs in Vietnam," *Development and Change* 30: 693–713; Salemink, Oscar (2006c), "Translating, Interpreting and Practicing Civil Society in Vietnam: A Tale of Calculated Misunderstandings," in David Lewis and David Mosse (eds), *Development Brokers and Translators: The Ethnography of Aid and Agencies*, Bloomfield: Kumarian Press, pp. 101–26.

23 The extraordinarily well-attended museum exhibition "Hanoi Life under the Subsidy Economy (1975–1986)" (*Ha Noi thoi bao cap*) in the Vietnam Museum of Ethnology (2006–7) and the popular reactions to it speak volumes in this regard.

24 Pelley, Patricia (1998), "'Barbarians' and 'Younger Brothers': The Remaking of Race in Postcolonial Vietnam," *Journal of Southeast Asian Studies* 29(2): 374–91; Pelley, Patricia (2002), *Postcolonial Vietnam: New Histories of the National Past*, (Durham: Duke University Press, 2002); Koh, Priscilla (2004), "Persistent Ambiguities: Vietnamese Ethnology in the Doi Moi Period (1986–2001)," *Explorations in Southeast Asian Studies* 2(2), http://www.hawaii.edu/cseas/pubs/explore/vol5no2.html; Salemink, Oscar (2008b), "Embodying the Nation: Mediumship, Ritual, and the National Imagination," *Journal of Vietnamese Studies* 3(3): 257–90.

25 Hobsbawm, Eric and Terence O. Ranger (eds) (1983), *The Invention of Tradition*, Cambridge: Cambridge University Press; Comaroff, Jean and John Comaroff (1991), *Of Revelation and Revolution: Christianity, Colonialism and Consciousness in South Africa*, Volume 1, Chicago and London: University of Chicago Press.

26 Volkman, Toby (1990), "Visions and Revisions: Toraja Culture and the Tourist Gaze," *American Ethnologist* 17(1): 91–110; Dahles, Heidi (2001), *Tourism, Heritage and National Culture in Java: Dilemmas of a Local Community*, Richmond: Curzon Press; Hitchcock, Michael (2005), "Afterword." In Harrison, David and Michael Hitchcock (eds), *The Politics of World Heritage: Negotiating Tourism and Conservation*, Clevedon: Channel View Publications, pp. 181–6.

27 Smith (2006), *Uses of Heritage.*

28 Aikawa, Noriko (2004), "An Historical Overview of the Preparation of the UNESCO International Convention for the Safeguarding of the Intangible Cultural Heritage," *Museum International* 56(1–2): 137–49; Condominas, Georges (2004), "Researching and Safeguarding the Intangible Heritage," *Museum International* 56(1–2): 21–31; Kurin, Richard (2004), "Safeguarding Intangible Cultural Heritage in the 2003 UNESCO Convention: a Critical Appraisal," *Museum International* 56(1–2): 66–77; Munjeri, Dawson (2004), "Tangible and Intangible Heritage: from Difference to Convergence," *Museum International* 56(1–2): 12–20; Nas, Peter J. M. *et al.* (2002), "Masterpieces of Oral and Intangible Culture: Reflections on the UNESCO World Heritage List (with comments by HRH Princess Basma Bint Talal, Henri Claessen, Richard Handler; Richard Kurin; Karen Fog Olwig; Laurie Sears; and reply by Peter J.M. Nas)," *Current Anthropology* 43(1): 139–48.

29 Harrison, David and Michael Hitchcock (eds) (2005), *The Politics of World Heritage: Negotiating Tourism and Conservation.* Clevedon: Channel View Publications. This collection was also published as a thematic issue of the journal *Current Issues in Tourism* 7(4–5), 2004.

30 Winter, Tim (2005), "Landscape, Memory and Heritage: New Year Celebrations at Angkor, Cambodia," in Harrison, David and Michael Hitchcock (eds), *The Politics of World Heritage: Negotiating Tourism and Conservation*, Clevedon: Channel View Publications, pp. 50–65.

31 Keyes, Charles F. (1997), "Ethnicity, Ethnic Group," in *The Dictionary of Anthropology*, Thomas J. Barfield (ed.), Oxford: Blackwell, pp. 152–4.

32 Lask, Tomke. and Stefan Herold (2005), "An Observation Station for Culture and Tourism in Vietnam: A Forum for World Heritage and Public Participation," in Harrison, David and Michael Hitchcock (eds), *The Politics of World Heritage*, p. 119.

33 Evans, Graeme (2005), "Mundo Maya: From Cancun to City of Culture: World Heritage in Post-colonial Meso-America," in Harrison, David and Michael Hitchcock (eds), *The Politics of World Heritage*, pp. 35–49.

34 Lockhart, Bruce (2001), "Re-assessing the Nguyen Dynasty," *Crossroads* 15(1): 9–53; Long, Colin (2004), "Feudalism in the Service of the Revolution: Reclaiming Heritage in Hue," *Critical Asian Studies* 35(4): 535–58.

35 Galla, Amareswar (2002), "Museum and Heritage in Development: Ha Long Ecomuseum, a Case Study from Vietnam," *Humanities Research* IX(1): 63–76.

36 Nguyen Kim Dung (n.d.), "Intangible Cultural Heritage Safeguarding System in Vietnam," Hanoi: Ministry of Culture and Information, http://www.unesco.org/culture/ich/doc/src/00174-EN.pdf, accessed 12 August 2008.

37 See, for instance, Huynh Yen Tram My, Truong Vu Quynh, Nguyen Dong Hieu (eds) (2007), *Nhung di san the gioi o Viet Nam.* Danang: NXB Da Nang. In my "The Emperor's New Clothes" (2007) I describe how the Festival Hue became a source of great pride for residents of Hue and for many other Vietnamese, and how the Festival space became a forum for cultural competition with representative arts and artists from other countries.

38 Nguyen Kim Dung (n.d.), "Intangible Cultural Heritage Safeguarding System," p. 1.

39 As further evidence of "competitive multilateralism," the election of Vietnam to the UN Security Council on October 17, 2007, was discussed a lot and celebrated widely in Vietnam.

40 Most of the Intangible Cultural Heritage projects on the UNESCO list receive funding from funds-in-trust from a particular donor country – in the vast majority of cases Japan (see http://www.unesco.org/culture/ich/index.php?pg=00107, accessed 12 August 2008).

41 This is clear from the prominent attention paid to World Heritage sites in public relations and advertisements (see, for instance, the official website of the Vietnam Authority of Tourism http://www.vietnamtourism.com) as well as from rising figures of tourist

visits to such places as Ha Long Bay, Hue, Hoi An, My Son, with Phong Nha lagging behind because of its "remoteness" from the tourist track.

42 Precolonial (especially nineteenth-century) Vietnam was not only culturally and politically oriented toward China, as brought out in Alexander Woodside's (1988) *Vietnam and the Chinese Model: A Comparative Study of Vietnamese and Chinese Government in the First Half of the Nineteenth Century*, Cambridge: Harvard University Press. It also recognized China's suzerainty over Vietnam, even while preserving its political independence. In that sense, Vietnam's internal claims were validated with reference to a supposedly superior, international authority, much like UNESCO these days.

43 Eriksen, Thomas Hylland (2001), "Between Universalism and Relativism: A Critique of the UNESCO Concepts of Culture," in Jane K. Cowan, Marie-Bénédicte Dembour, and Richard A. Wilson (eds), *Culture and Rights: Anthropological Perspectives*, Cambridge and New York: Cambridge University Press, pp. 133–47. Claude Lévi-Strauss (1908–2009) was a very influential French anthropologist whose work on cultural diversity formed the philosophical basis for much subsequent "urgent" or "salvage" anthropology which aimed to record and if possible, save "cultures" before these would become "extinct" (= change), a practice for which the concept of intangible cultural heritage was intended to give legitimacy.

44 Currently, it is called the Division of Cultural Objects and Intangible Heritage.

45 Aikawa, Noriko (2004), "An Historical Overview of the Preparation of the UNESCO International Convention for the Safeguarding of the Intangible Cultural Heritage," *Museum International* 56(1–2): 137–49; Munjeri, Dawson (2004), "Tangible and Intangible Heritage: from difference to convergence," *Museum International* 56(1–2): 12–20.

46 The eventual result of the expert meeting in Hue would be the recognition of *nha nhac* imperial court music as masterpiece of intangible cultural heritage, and a revival of court dance and local folk music (*ca Hue*). At the time of the expert meeting, much attention went to Hue cuisine as intangible heritage, although I personally prefer tangible food.

47 Condominas, Georges (1957), *Nous avons mangé la forêt de la Pierre-Génie Goo (Hii saa Brii Mau-Yaang Goo). Chronique de Sar Luk, village mnong gar (tribu proto-indochinoise, des Hauts-Plateaux du Vietnam central)*, Paris: Mercure de France; Condominas, Georges (1965), *L'Exotique est quotidien*, Paris: Plon; Condominas, Georges (2001), "Introduction," In Oscar Salemink (ed.), *Viet Nam's Cultural Diversity: Approaches to Preservation*, Paris: UNESCO Publishing (Memory of Peoples), pp. 15–32; Condominas, Georges (2004), "Researching and Safeguarding the Intangible Heritage," *Museum International* 56(1–2): 21–31.

48 Nong Quoc Chan (2001), "Cultures of the Ethnic Minorities of Viet Nam: Some Problems and Realities," in Oscar Salemink (ed.), *Viet Nam's Cultural Diversity: Approaches to Preservation*, Paris: UNESCO Publishing (Memory of Peoples), pp. 111–20.

49 Long (2004), "Feudalism in the Service of the Revolution."

50 Salemink (2003a), *The Ethnography*.

51 Eriksen, Thomas Hylland (1993), "In which Sense Do Cultural Islands Exist?" *Social Anthropology* 1(1): 133–47; Eriksen (2001), "Between Universalism and Relativism."

52 Condominas (1965), *L'Exotique est quotidien*; Salemink (2003a), *The Ethnography*. See also Pelley (1998), "'Barbarians' and 'Younger Brothers;'" Pelley (2002), *Postcolonial Vietnam*; Koh (2004), "Persistent Ambiguities."

53 Salemink (2003a), *The Ethnography*.

54 Salemink, Oscar (2001b), "Who Decides Who Preserves What? Cultural Preservation and Representation," in Salemink, Oscar (ed.), *Viet Nam's Cultural Diversity: Approaches to Preservation*, Paris: UNESCO Publishing (Memory of Peoples), pp. 205–12; Salemink, Oscar (2009), "Where Is the Space for Vietnam's Gong Culture? Economic and Social Challenges for the Space of Gong Culture and Opportunities for Protection." Paper for the international conference Economic and Social Changes and

Preservation of the Gong Culture in Vietnam and the Southeast Asian Region. Pleiku City, Vietnam, November 12–15, 2009.

55 John Urry (1990), *The Tourist Gaze: Leisure and Travel in Contemporary Societies*, London: Sage.

56 But look at Condominas' masterful play with the notion of "exotic" in his *L'Exotique est quotidien* (The exotic is everyday practice) (1966).

57 The French and English editions were published simultaneously in 2001 as *Diversité culturelle au Viet Nam: enjeux multiples, approches plurielles*, Paris: Editions UNESCO (Mémoire des peuples); and *Viet Nam's Cultural Diversity: Approaches to Preservation*, Paris: UNESCO Publishing (Memory of Peoples). The Vietnamese version was published in 2002 as *Tinh da dang cua van hoa Viet Nam: Nhung tiep can ve su bao ton*, Hanoi: UNESCO/Trung tam Khoa hoc Xa hoi va Nhan van Quoc gia, but with a different editor (!), namely the former President of the National Center for Social Sciences and Humanities, Professor Nguyen Duy Quy.

58 Nhieu tac gia (1997), *Giu gin va bao ve ban sac van hoa cac dan toc thieu so Viet Nam*, Hanoi: NXB Van hoa Dan toc.

59 Salemink (2001b), "Who Decides Who Preserves What?"

60 Writenet (2002), "Vietnam: Indigenous Minority Groups in the Central Highlands," *Writenet Report* 5/2001, Geneva, United Nations High Commissioner for Refugees, Centre for Documentation and Research, January 2002 (http://www.unhcr.org/refworld/pdfid/3c6a48474.pdf); Writenet (2006), "Vietnam: Situation of Indigenous Minority Groups in the Central Highlands," *Writenet Report*, Geneva, United Nations High Commissioner for Refugees, Centre for Documentation and Research, June 2006 (http://www.unhcr.org/refworld/docid/44c0f55a4.html); Salemink, Oscar (2006b), "Changing Rights and Wrongs: The Transnational Construction of Indigenous and Human Rights Among Vietnam's Central Highlanders," *Focaal, European Journal of Anthropology* 47 (2006): 32–47.

61 Phan Dang Nhat (2001), "The Timeless Epics of the Ethnic Minorities of Viet Nam," in Oscar Salemink (ed.), *Viet Nam's Cultural Diversity: Approaches to Preservation*, Paris: UNESCO Publishing (Memory of Peoples), pp. 85–104.

62 Ngo Duc Thinh and Phan Dang Nhat (eds) (1999), *Luat tuc va Phat trien Nong thon Hien nay o Viet Nam (Ky Yeu hoi thao khoa hoc)* (Customary Law and Rural Development in Present-day Vietnam: Conference Proceedings), Hanoi: NXB Chinh tri Quoc gia (National Political Publishing House).

63 At the time I was involved in both the customary law and the epics projects led by Ngo Duc Thinh, both as a fellow anthropologist (contributing for instance to Thinh's 1999 volume on customary law), and as a program officer for a private donor organization (The Ford Foundation), funding the training of local ethnic minority researchers to ensure local cultural sustainability of the project. The "epics" project has resulted in sixty-three (63!) publications.

64 Land was an important issue as well, but did not make passions flare as high as the conversion issue did. Information – often notoriously unreliable – on or from the Montagnard Foundation can be found at their website http://www.montagnard-foundation.org.

65 Human Rights Watch (2002), *Repression of Montagnards: Conflicts over land and religion in Vietnam's Central Highlands*, New York etc.: Human Rights Watch; Writenet (2002), "Vietnam: Indigenous Minority Groups."

66 Nong Quoc Chan (2001), "Cultures of the Ethnic Minorities;" Salemink (2003a), *The Ethnography*. Protestantism was introduced to Vietnam's Central Highlands primarily by the Christian and Missionary Alliance (http://www.cmalliance.org) and by the Summer Institute of Linguistics/Wycliffe Bible Translators (http://www.sil.org and http://www.wycliffe.org). Before 1975, these organizations were not very successful numerically, but after the American departure the phenomenal growth of Protestantism

among various ethnic groups was largely home-grown, according to Salemink (2006), "Changing Rights and Wrongs."

67 "Disabled man preserves Vietnam's epics in the mountains" http://www.thanhniennews.com/features/?catid=10&newsid=27768; "Highlands Oral Epics in Danger of Being Lost," http://vietnamnews.vnagency.com.vn/showarticle.php?num=02CUL-200308 (accessed 7 January 2010); Ivy, Marilyn (1995), *Discourses of the Vanishing: Modernity, Phantasms, Japan*, Chicago: University of Chicago Press.

68 See, for instance, PGS.TS. Nguyen Khac Su, Phan Thanh Toan, *Co tang van minh dau tien cua van hoa cong chieng Tay Nguyen* (Original civilizational basis of Tay Nguyen culture). Paper presented at the conference "Economic and Social Changes and Preservation of the Gong Culture in Vietnam and the Southeast Asian Region," Pleiku, November 13–15, 2009.

69 Nguyen Kim Dung (n.d.), "Intangible Cultural Heritage Safeguarding System," p. 1.

70 Salemink, Oscar (2008a), "Trading Goods, Prestige, and Power: A Revisionist History of Lowlander-Highlander Relations in Vietnam," in Peter Boomgaard, Dick Kooiman, and Henk Schulte Nordholt (eds), *Linking Destinies: Trade, Towns and Kin in Asian History*, Leiden: KITLV Press, pp. 51–69.

71 Salemink (2003a), *The Ethnography*; Salemink, Oscar (2003b), "Enclosing the Highlands: Socialist, Capitalist and Protestant Conversions of Vietnam's Central Highlanders," RCSD Conference "The Politics of the Commons" (co-hosted by IASCP), Chiang Mai University, July 11–14, 2003, http://dlc.dlib.indiana.edu/dlc/handle/10535/1787.

72 Salemink, Oscar (2009), "Where Is the Space for Vietnam's Gong Culture?" During field research I found that poor Highlanders sell off their cultural assets such as gong sets, but also their antique Chinese jars. Sadly, they also find their graves robbed of the famous funerary statues.

73 Salemink, Oscar (2001b), "Who Decides Who Preserves What?"

74 Elsewhere, *contra* notions of the Central Highlands as remote and backward as captured in the phrase *vung sau vung xa*, I have called this region a hotspot of globalization in terms of cash crops, becoming almost overnight the world's No. 2 coffee producing region, No. 1 pepper and cashew producing region, and big rubber, tea and cocoa producer, as I argue in my "Enclosing the Highlands" (2003b). More recently, there has been growing controversy over the leasing out of enormous tracts of land in the Central Highlands to a Chinese company over open air bauxite mining, risking to destroy, pollute, and poison most of the region characterized as a "gong cultural space," cf. Salemink 2009, "Where Is the Space."

75 Salemink (2003b), "Enclosing the Highlands."

# 10 Would a *saola* by any other name still be a *saola*?

## Appropriating rare animals, expropriating minority peoples

*C. Michele Thompson*[1]

*"What's the use of their having names," the Gnat said, "if they won't answer to them?" "No use to them," said Alice, "but it's useful to the people that name them, I suppose. If not, why do they have names at all?"*[2]

## Introduction

In March 1993, the late Professor Tran Quoc Vuong (1934–2005) showed me, at his home in Hanoi, the intact skull of an animal. It was long and narrow, with two horns considerably longer than the skull itself. Vuong asked if I had ever heard of *Pseudoryx nghetinhensis*; I had not. Had I ever heard of a *saola?* Again, I had not. Vuong then said: "This is a *saola*. I have had this skull for nearly ten years. However, last May scientists *discovered* the existence of the *saola* and they have given it the scientific name *Pseudoryx nghetinhensis*."[3] Vuong went on to say that minority groups living in the mountains of Vietnam had long known of the *saola* but that scientists, the implication being Western and Western-trained scientists, had not believed them. "Now that they have named it," he continued, "they will claim it and it may not long survive its *discovery*!"[4]

Tran Quoc Vuong was prescient. In September 2009, the International Union for Conservation of Nature (IUCN) warned: "Last chance to save the *Saola* from extinction." On the website of the World Wide Fund for Nature (WWF) is a release concerning the *saola* with the title "Recently discovered, already threatened." The number of *saola* given was "70–1,000 in the wild, but likely to be less than 500."[5]

Probably 99 percent of the people in the world have never heard of the *saola*; among those few who have heard of it, however, it has received a lot of attention since its discovery. This is at least partly because the "discovery" of a "new" large mammal is so very rare that such an event causes a stir among naturalists, biologists, conservationists, and others in academic communities connected to those fields or with interests in the area where such a "new" animal exists.[6] It is also true, however, that, for the members of such communities, the *saola* did not exist until it had been properly discovered and, perhaps even more importantly, given a proper scientific name, *Pseudoryx nghetinhensis*.[7]

This essay will argue that, with regard to biota, to name is to claim. In historic perspective, various items of the rich and varied biota of Vietnam have been claimed by different parties at different levels. Recognition of rights to the biota of Vietnam is intimately connected to the various types and systems of nomenclature applied to said biota. I will propose a multi-faceted paradigm within which different groups commonly lay claim to control of and rights to biota. Each facet requires recognition of a name, or names, as part of that control. The interface between these facets is where the struggle for rights over biota takes place. As an example of very rare biota, the *saola* illuminates the different stages of this process of recognition and control, as well as the actors and the stakes involved in it.

## Discovery

The "discovery" of the *saola* in 1992 came from "hunting trophies of an unidentified large mammal hanging from the rafters in local houses"[8] seen by Vietnamese and foreign biologists who were members of a survey team working in the Vu Quang Nature Reserve (now Vu Quang National Park).[9] According to Pam McElwee, the team "had been expecting to find the forest missing a number of valuable timber species" about which they would write a report to the Ministry of Forestry.[10] The team included: Mr Vu Van Dzung from the Forest Inventory and Planning Institute (FIPI) who was the head of the team; Mr Do Tuoc and Mr Le Van Cham, both also of the FIPI; Dr Nguyen Van Sang of the Institute of Ecological and Biological Resources; Dr Nguyen Thai Tu of Vinh University; and Dr John MacKinnon of the World Wildlife Fund (WWF).[11] On site in Vu Quang they were joined by Mr Binh and Mr Ngon from the Ha Tinh provincial Forest Protection Department, and the staff of the Vu Quang Nature Reserve respectively.[12] The team was thus made up of ethnic (*kinh*) Vietnamese plus one Westerner.

The team worked without major discovery or incident from May 9 to May 21, 1992. From May 18 to the afternoon of May 21, the team resided "at the Vu Quang Border Defense Unit (Border Defense Unit No. 567) in Kim Quang commune" surveying the biota of that part of the reserve.[13] On the afternoon of May 21, the survey team divided itself into two groups and it was the task of one of those two groups, composed of Dzung, Sang, Tu, and Tuoc, to interview "hunters living in the villages around the border-defending [*sic*] unit."[14] In the home of one of these hunters the members of the team saw horns of wild goats called serows and also "a pair of very strange horns, which were long and pointed."[15] The team members asked the hunter about the unusual horns; he told them that the horns came from an animal similar to a serow but larger, darker, and with longer horns. The scientists present took photos of the horns to show to the rest of the survey team.[16] Unsure of just what they had found, the survey team continued to follow its schedule and moved the next day to the northeast section of the nature reserve. There, they found two more sets of the strange horns.

At that time, the only physical evidence the scientists had of the existence of the *saola* was three sets of horns. However, they believed the hunters who had killed these specimens when the latter said that the animal, although uncommon, certainly still existed. The scientists' conviction that this still unknown animal was not an extinct species was buttressed by the physical state of the sets of horns. "One specimen was so fresh that it still had maggots on it."[17]

Apparently, at that point, the team had not recorded any name used by the local hunters. Instead, one of their first acts was to give it a name that made sense in Vietnamese. Then and there, "the team decided that this was a new species in the *Bovidae* family" and they gave the species the name *de sung dai* for which a straightforward translation would be "goat with long horns," the implication being that the horns are longer than on a regular goat.[18] The name was invented "to avoid [the *saola*] being mistaken with the serow"[19] but also largely because the ethnic Vietnamese in the area had no name specifically identifying the animal that had just been discovered.

The Vietnamese scientists eventually recorded two "local" names. As reported in *Oryx*, these were *Sao La*, said at that time to mean spindle horn or spindled horn, used in Nghe An Province, and *Son Duong*, meaning "mountain goat," used in neighboring Ha Tinh Province.[20] These "local" names were thus connected to administrative units rather than to specific human communities, although the two provinces are home to several different minority groups.[21] When the *saola*'s existence in Laos was proven, another "local" name, Yang (with no translation given), was recorded there.[22]

## What's in a name?

The natural way for a scientist to protect his or her rights to the prestige of a significant discovery within the scientific community is to name the new species, and to not only name it but to give it a name that will not be challenged as inappropriate or incorrect[23] with regard to the conventions on scientific nomenclature.[24] After all, as evolutionary biologist Carol Kaesuk Yoon notes, "The field of taxonomy is infamous among biologists for its intractable arguments."[25]

The bestowal of an internationally recognized scientific name is a ritual that is, in some sense, akin to a baptism; and as in the baptism ritual, the scientists/godparents are considered to have certain rights to and responsibilities for the animal/child. The scientists involved in the original "discovery" of the *saola* acted as quickly as possible to assert their rights to the new "discovery" and they began the process of choosing a scientific name for the beast they had come to believe in well before they had seen a live specimen. As part of this process, and before they could possibly publish in a venue that would establish their right to be scientifically enshrined as the discoverers of the *saola*, they announced their discovery in a more popular, but still respected, publication devoted to science with a capital S. In this publication, and as part of the naming and claiming process, they also gave the animal another, English-language, common name. This is not unusual in the naming-as-claiming process.[26] Since English is the principal language of international science, creating an English-language common name for the newly discovered and about-to-be scientifically classified animal is a means for most zoologists worldwide to remember it; and if the English name makes sense in relation to the scientific name when it is presented, this will offer additional scientific/academic cachet to the scientist(s) who proposed it.

A number of scientific arguments concerning the *saola* in the years immediately following its discovery centered on its proper position within the taxonomic structure codified in the eighteenth century by Carl Linnaeus.[27] If members of the team had continued to refer to the new mammal as some variety of goat, they would have implied that they considered, based on the evidence they had, that this mammal belonged not only to the family Bovidae but to the subfamily Caprinae. Interestingly enough, however, the team did not simply translate the Vietnamese name, long-horned goat (*de sung dai*), that they had bestowed on the mysterious animal none of them had yet seen. Nor did they continue to call it a goat in English. Instead, they chose a name that would tie international recognition of the animal itself to the area within Vietnam – Nghe An and Ha Tinh provinces – where its horns had first been found by Western-trained scientists. Further, the name they chose hinted that the team members considered that the new mammal belonged in the subfamily Bovinae. The first name presented to the world in 1992 by the scientists who had "discovered" the *saola* was the Vu Quang Ox.[28] By also publicizing the English translation of what they referred to as its Vietnamese name, long-horned goat, these zoologists were effectively stating that the folk taxonomy of the Vietnamese common name placed the new animal within the family Bovidae and the subfamily Caprinae (which includes most, if not all, creatures referred to in English as goats). Yet, the English name they announced placed it within Bovidae BUT in the subfamily Bovinae and specifically the tribe Bovini. Given that this is just where the *saola* ended up in taxonomic placement and given that the *saola*, in several respects, looks more like a goat than an ox, this was brilliant naming on the part of these scientists.[29] Whether or not their choices of names were as deliberate as they appear in hindsight, the zoologists involved in the first discovery of the animal now known internationally as the *saola* had claimed at least two of the most likely taxonomic positions for their discovery by their choice of common names with which to christen it.

When the team decided, while still in the field in May 1992, that the animal whose remains they had seen belonged, in taxonomic terms, within the family Bovidae they had too little physical evidence to determine the exact taxonomic position of the *saola* within one or another of the subfamilies of Bovidae. More evidence for a number of purposes, including the question of taxonomic placement, was clearly required. Less than a year after the initial discovery of the *saola*, the WWF agreed to fund a second survey which was carried out from November 12 to November 25, 1992. The second survey team had only three members: "Mr. Vu Van Dzung and Mr. Hoang Trong Tri from FIPI and Mr. Pham Mong Giao from the FPD."[30] In the course of this second survey, the team collected a "total of 20 specimens" most of them just "horns and part of the skull."[31] The team also "collected a complete skin" which "was brought to Hanoi for stuffing, and a small piece of head skin was separated and sent overseas for DNA testing."[32] This piece of skin went to Danish scientist Peter Arctander who specializes in DNA analysis. With the necessary addition of DNA analysis, the search for the proper taxonomic placement of the *saola* became a truly international effort and also a truly international discussion.[33]

By May 3, 1994, this DNA had been used to establish that "the Vu Quang Ox represents a new genus as well as a new species."[34] The DNA sample would eventually show just how rare, in terms of genetics, the *saola* is, and an entire new tribe, Pseudorygini, within the subfamily Bovinae would be established because of the *saola*. The current consensus is that the *saola* is so rare and so solitary in terms of genetic relatives that it should be placed not only in its own separate genus (*Pseudoryx*) but also in its own tribe (Pseudorygini) within the subfamily Bovinae[35] (Table 10.1).

*Table 10.1* Taxonomic placement of the *saola*

| *Kingdom* | *Animalia* |
|---|---|
| Phylum | Chordata |
| Class | Mammalia |
| Order | Cetartiodactyla |
| Sub-order | Ruminantia |
| Family | Bovidae |
| Sub-Family | Bovinae |
| Tribe | New tribe created after "discovery" of the *saola. Pseudorygini* |
| Genus | New genus created after "discovery" of the *saola. Pseudoryx* |
| Species | *Pseudoryx nghetinhensis* |

While the team of field biologists waited for Arctander to complete his analysis of the *saola* DNA, further discoveries were made. In "early 1993, biologists doing surveys in areas outside the Vu Quang Nature Reserve found specimens from *saola*."[36] By late 1993, scientists had collected more than twenty partial specimens from which estimates were made regarding such topics as the *saola*'s average size, average diet and dietary preferences, all aspects of its appearance, unusual maxillary glands, behavior in various situations, urinary habits, breeding habits, fecal droppings, social habits, sexual dimorphism, and other issues important to zoologists, particularly those specializing in ungulates.[37] Information came from local inhabitants on both sides of the Lao/Vietnamese border about the habits of the *saola* and was tentatively accepted by scientists[38] and "several photos taken by remotely operated cameras" of the *saola* in the wild were procured.[39]

Just one year after the discovery of the *saola*, on June 3, 1993, came the publication in *Nature* which announced not only the "discovery" of the *saola* but also the scientific name chosen for it by the scientists who had discovered it, *Pseudoryx nghetinhensis*.[40] During all of this time and even with all the commotion over the discovery of the *saola*, scientists had yet to see a live specimen. Soon, however, came the capture of the first *saola* to be made available to scientists.[41] Apparently, at least two other *saola* were captured during "the two years of searching in Vietnam" which "led to the capture of a Vu Quang ox" in the late spring or early summer of 1994.[42]

The discovery of *saola* outside the Vu Quang Nature Reserve expanded the number of local authorities with jurisdiction of one sort or another over Vietnamese territory in which *saola* were known to exist and over the people living in that territory. At approximately the same time, the first evidence for the existence of *saola* "in Laos was found by Robert Dobias."[43] This meant that claims to the *saola* now involved two neighboring countries, the ethnic minorities on both sides of the border between them, and the international organizations and international academics working in both.

The WWF, the international organization that had funded both the first and the second official survey of Vu Quang, quite reasonably felt that it should have a voice in deciding how best to conserve the animal it had helped to discover. Indeed, it is not surprising that the WWF felt that it had certain "rights" to the *saola*. As for the Vietnamese government, it was rightly proud of the discovery of several new species within its borders and of the rediscovery of others thought to have already become extinct.[44] In 1992, when the *saola* was first discovered, Vietnam was one of the poorest countries on Earth; it had been under an embargo imposed by the United States for over fifteen years, and its government could see very clearly the public relations value of these biological discoveries. Further, the Vietnamese government had a need for technical and financial assistance to resolve environmental problems, many of which were not of its own making. Even as late as 1998, it was "hard to imagine a land beset with more environmental problems than the Socialist Republic of Vietnam.... Thirty years of violent and protracted warfare left Vietnam with every problem imaginable."[45]

Laos was even poorer than Vietnam but it was also less densely populated and clearly had as much potential for fantastic discoveries of wildlife as Vietnam. The Vietnamese government, and to a lesser extent the Lao government, made almost immediate attempts to wrest control of the *saola*, or at least the territory in its known range, from the minority peoples who had had contact with, and almost exclusive rights to, the *saola* for millennia. In doing so, they asserted a national right to the *saola* which superseded the right to it traditionally held by those same minority peoples. They were encouraged, and more importantly funded, by international organizations such as the WWF and by Western governments strongly interested in international conservation efforts. Indeed, since 1995, more than 200 million dollars in aid specifically for conservation efforts has been pledged to Vietnam by foreign governments and international conservation organizations.[46]

At the time, late May 1992, of the Vietnamese government's first actions prompted by the discovery of the *saola* one can say that the ministries involved were reacting as much to the *idea* of the *saola* as to the *saola* itself.[47] After all, at that point they had no live *saola*, they had no scientific observation of its full intact anatomy, nor did they have any scientifically conducted studies of its behavior. If it is possible for a living being to be intangible property, then at that point the *saola* was about as intangible as a living being can get. However, the interest of international donors in the *saola* and in the potential of its known range to offer even more new species and species long thought lost was very real indeed. It was in the context of this national and international interface that the name *saola* was appropriated and applied to the animal that had first been christened with the common names *de sung dai* (long-horned goat) and Vu Quang Ox. It was also in this context that the term *saola* was forcibly introduced into the Vietnamese language in a manner that has resulted in the term itself being presented in international forums as "a native Vietnamese name."[48]

In April 1994, the anthropologist Frank Proschan made "inquiries with members of several different ethnic groups in six villages concerning the name of the animal *Pseudoryx nghetinhensis.*"[49] Proschan undertook this research because some "Hanoi scientists were trying to give the animal a good proper Vietnamese name."[50] According to Proschan, at that time certain Vietnamese scientists were being opposed by other Vietnamese and Western scientists and conservationists of the WWF who argued "that if you want to do a conservation campaign, you should use the name by which the local people call the animal, rather than some exonym that nobody would recognize."[51] Proschan argued that: "To understand most fully why /saavlaa/ is the most appropriate name for this animal, it is important to know about the ethnodemography of the region and the ethnohistory of the groups within the animal's geographic range."[52]

In his unpublished paper, Proschan argues that the point to be determined is which name, in case there is more than one, is most commonly known if a conservation campaign is to be successful. He notes that the animal's range, as it was known at that time (April 1994), was comprised of "mountainous districts with predominantly minority populations" and that "virtually no Kinh [ethnic Vietnamese] reside in the forested mountain areas of those districts where the /saavlaa/ can be found."[53] Proschan goes on to demonstrate that even those Vietnamese who had recently moved into the fringes of this area had no name for the *saola*. His research among five different ethnic groups living in *saola* territory showed that there was one and only one name commonly known in that area "regardless of the group's language or dialect – i.e., /saavlaa/."[54] Based on this research, Proschan was able to provide important evidence that Vietnamese and international experts could deploy in support of the decision at the national and international levels to use the term "/saavlaa/ (in phonetic transcription)." Proschan's recommended Vietnamese spelling was "xao la" and his recommended Romanization of the term was "*saola*."[55] Following the circulation of Proschan's paper in Hanoi starting in the summer of 1994, the term *saola* was adopted by Western scientists and by most international conservation organizations and interest forums on mammals such as the Ultimate Ungulates group. Further, "the temporary name 'long horned goat' has been replaced by the name '*saola*' in all Vietnamese publications."[56]

By 2004, a few more "local" names for the *saola* from minority languages had been recorded. The *saola* is noted as "bearing the name in Ta Oi language of 'Censor.'"[57] However, the Ta Oi who live in a slightly different area of Thua Thien-Hue Province are said to refer to the *saola* as "A Ngao" while the Ka Tu who also live in Thua Thien-Hue Province are said to call them "Xoong Xor" a name which appears to be simply a different transcription of "Censor."[58] But the name *saola* is the one that has gained worldwide currency.

## Death by discovery

The IUCN Red List of Threatened Species notes that today hunting is one of the major threats to the continued existence of the *saola*. This is noted numerous times in the documents from the workshop "Rediscovering the *Saola*," and a recent press release from the Saola Working Group "identified snaring and hunting with dogs (to which the *saola* is especially vulnerable) as the main direct threats to the species."[59] However, it is also noted that the *saola* itself is not usually the principal target of either subsistence hunting or hunting for the medicine or bushmeat trade.[60] Indeed, as Robichaud notes, the *saola* "has no value in traditional medicine and is not an important source of bushmeat."[61] This is due in part to the extremely low population density of the *saola* and in part to the fact that it has managed, so far, to escape being drawn into the faux Chinese medicine trade.[62] However, even though it is not a specific target, the *saola* population is heavily affected by the sheer level of hunting for profit to supply the bushmeat and medicinal trade.[63] It is particularly unfortunate for the *saola* that much of this hunting is done with snares which grab any animal within a certain size range that comes along.[64] Hunting also adversely affects the *saola* population in Laos.[65] Indeed, in Laos "snare lines – fences of brush with snares at intervals in openings – may extend for hundreds of meters over slopes and ridges and catch small to medium-sized ungulates unselectively."[66]

Scientific enthusiasm over the discovery of a new animal has also contributed to the decline in *saola* numbers. The "searching" which resulted in the capture of a "Vu Quang Ox" in 1994 was prompted by national and international interest in the *saola* which also, upon occasion, resulted in financial compensation for specimens, or partial specimens such as horns, of *saola*.[67] The "Records of *saola* obtained through survey" indicate that a pregnant female was captured in December of 1992, and a small juvenile was captured in July of 1992;[68] neither survived long enough to be delivered to scientists. A four-to-five-month-old female juvenile captured in the late spring of 1994 and kept in captivity at the Forestry Inventory and Planning Institute survived about three months after its capture before dying.[69] Another captured young *saola* survived long enough to be delivered to Hanoi where it also died. None of the *saola* kept captive survived longer than five months and most did not last nearly that long.[70] Thirteen of the rare beasts were captured, in part so that scientists could study them.[71] At least two, not included in the official thirteen previously noted, were also captured with the intent of bringing them to government officials, but they did not survive the journey.[72] All of these enigmatic, mysterious *saola* exhibited what William Robichaud describes as "a tragic frailty in captivity."[73] These included a pregnant female that was observed extensively by Robichaud for nine days after she was captured.[74] After eighteen days of captivity this female, nicknamed Martha, died of an undetermined cause or causes. Since the male fetus she carried died with her in January of 1996, we can count fourteen *saola* that have died specifically in the service of science since the "discovery" of the *saola* in 1992.[75]

A national and international tendency to place most of the blame for low, and declining, numbers of *saola* on the shoulders of those minority peoples who had co-existed with *saola* for eons before its discovery quickly became apparent. The international team of scientists which published the first article to come out in a top academic journal stated that: "It is important to inform local villagers of the precious nature of this species and put a firm ban on further hunting. The rush to acquire specimens of the new species must be stemmed and firm penalties demonstrated for poaching."[76] However, it would appear that this "rush" started when the *saola* was "discovered." For example, the pregnant female examined by Robichaud had been captured in response to a reward of $1,000 offered by "the head of Lao parastatal development company."[77] In Laos, after two *saola* died in General Cheng's private zoo "Cheng, to his credit, then put out a notice canceling the reward payment and instructing villagers not to capture any more."[78]

## Scientific and local knowledge

If indigenous minority peoples in Laos and Vietnam have more than one name for *Pseudoryx nghetinhensis*, it would seem that they should know the *saola* best. Indeed, this is true. According to the IUCN's most recent "Red List of Threatened Species," documented sightings of *saola* by villagers in recent years number only "in the tens [per year]."[79] This is still ten times more sightings than any scientist has had and the IUCN's list only includes "documented" sightings.[80] In fact, local minority people still have more actual contact with the *saola* than other residents of Vietnam or Laos, more than scientists or officials from either country, and more than the international scientists whose careers revolve around the *saola* and around national and international efforts to try to protect it. Further, the IUCN itself, and the projects it funds, relies on data collected from villagers and hunters to estimate population numbers for the *saola*. Information about the *saola*'s habits indeed comes only from the inhabitants of the Truong Son mountain range between Vietnam and Laos who have actually seen *saola* in the wild, who have perhaps eaten *saola*, and who know enough about the movements and habits of the *saola* to be able to capture it.

From a local perspective, the notion that the *saola* was discovered in 1992 is misleading. According to scientific evidence and reasoning, the *saola*'s current distribution "suggests that these forests [on the Vietnam/Laos border] are old and have been climatically stable" perhaps from as long ago as the last ice age and that the *saola* "appears to be a conservative ancestral forest form."[81] Inhabitants of the geographic space that is now Vietnam and Laos have had a very long relationship with the *saola*. Indeed, scholars speculate that images on "jade earrings dating from 2,000 years ago, attributed to the Sa Huynh culture [which flourished between 1,000 BCE and 200 CE in modern central and southern Vietnam], depict what may be *saola* (*Pseudoryx nghetinhensis*) heads."[82] Andreas Reinecke discusses these earrings, and the animal represented on them, in detail and concludes that *Pseudoryx nghetinhensis* "perhaps was elevated to a cult animal for the Sa Huynh people."[83] Reinecke further argues that formerly unidentified animals depicted "on some of the bronze drums of the prehistoric Dongson culture [1,000 BCE to first century CE]" are *saola*.[84] From a later time period it appears that the "goat antelopes" noted by the Chinese overlords of what is today northern Vietnam during the Tang Dynasty (618–907 CE) could have been *saola*. In his classic analysis of Tang Dynasty reference to the biota of what is today southern China and northern Vietnam, Edward H. Schaffer linked "goat antelopes" with forested highlands, such as those the *saola* now inhabits, and with serows, an animal also found in the same general area as the *saola*.[85]

At least a few Frenchmen during the French colonial period knew of the *saola*; as Frank Proschan notes, "the first scientific documentation of the animal's existence (long before zoologists recorded its existence) came in the 1912 *Dictionnaire Laotien-Français* of the missionary Théodore Guignard."[86] Further, since "Guignard served for many years in Cua Rao, in western Nghe An, that is in the area of Vietnam bordering Laos; his dictionary may thus include words of the local Tai language as well as standard Lao."[87]

Yet information about the people who live in close proximity to the *saola* is remarkably sparse in the literature on the *saola* and much of it is downright incorrect. The initial impression given in the most accessible literature is that the local houses in "local communities" in Vietnam where hunting trophies of the *saola* were first observed belong to ethnic (*kinh*) Vietnamese.[88] The geography and ethnodemographic distribution of the area make this claim extremely unlikely. The description of *saola* as "a native Vietnamese name" comes from a website for aficionados of ungulates so it is perhaps not surprising that the webmasters of this site do not pay much attention to the specifics of ethnodemography in Vietnam. It is true that the people who helped scientists discover the shy *saola* are citizens of Vietnam; in that sense, they are indeed Vietnamese. But since most, if not all, of these individuals are members of minority groups, it is surprising that more attention has not been paid to ethnicity in the scholarly literature.

It takes considerable delving into the readily available Western-language literature to find the name of an ethnic group associated with the *saola*. The earliest published mention in an academic context of the name of a specific ethnic group in fact comes from research done in Laos, not Vietnam.[89] As for the informal literature, mainly websites, even Vietnamese-language sites such as the Vietnamese Wikipedia gloss over the role of minority peoples in the discovery of the *saola*.[90] One must rely on personal contacts with anthropologists who have worked with the scientists who "discovered" the *saola* and with those who are trying to save it to find out much at all about the peoples who *know* the *saola* best.[91] Even when their role is noted, the minority peoples who cooperated with scientists to help them discover the *saola* are not named. Instead, particularly in the early literature, they are generally referred to as "local hunters" or "tribal hunters."[92] Even in documents produced twelve years after the "discovery" of the *saola*, for an international workshop on the *saola* and "conservation planning" for it held in 2004, one has to read closely through the more than one hundred pages of the proceedings to find mention of any of the specific ethnic groups whose members have provided scientists with most of their past and current information on the *saola*.[93] The workshop "was attended by Vietnamese and Lao scientists, international specialists, representatives of conservation and protection agencies and *representatives from upland communities*" and it included a remarkable exercise.[94] Tony Whitten, senior biodiversity specialist at the World Bank, asked everyone to stand and he spoke to them as follows:

> Those people who have never seen a *saola* or any part of a *saola*, please sit. Next, those people who have never seen a living *saola*, please sit. Only those who have seen a living *saola* remain standing. Now there are 12 people in this room who have seen a living *saola* (out of our workshop of almost seventy participants). Finally, those people who have not seen a living *saola* in the forest, please sit. Now there are three people standing. These are the only people in this room of experts to have seen a living *saola* in the forest. These are the people we need to seek information from.[95]

The three people left standing are not named, nor is their ethnic group mentioned; it would appear that these are the "representatives of upland communities" noted in the overview.

So far, only one zoologist, William Robichaud, has paid close attention, in print, not only to the term *Sao La* but also to the peoples and languages associated with this term:

> In the Lao and Lao related languages in the animal's range on both sides of the Laos-Vietnam border, *saola* is the word for a pair of parallel wooden posts that support part of a local apparatus that is similar to a spinning wheel (*sao* = post(s); *la* is the apparatus). Indigenous people gave this name to the animal because the tapering posts resemble a pair of *saola* horns. An approximate translation of the species' common name, then, is "spinning wheel posts."[96]

His information came from Proschan who suggested that, when the Tai arrived in the area some 1,000 years ago, they did not have a name for *Pseudoryx nghetinhensis* "within the ancient Tai lexicon of biota," so they bestowed on it a name "borrowed from another domain of human experience – textile technology."[97] Robichaud also noted the meaning of another local name, apparently common among the inhabitants of Bolikhamxay Province of Laos, without transcribing it phonetically. Robichaud calls these people Hmong and reports that *saola* "are known locally as the 'polite animal' because 'they always step slowly and quietly through the forest' and are not obstinate or excitable."[98] A recent addition to the English-language Wikipedia gives the Hmong term meaning polite animal as *saht-supahp*. Proschan notes this is actually a Lao term; this further indicates that the Hmong, too, "had no indigenous term for the animal."[99]

## Naming and expropriating

The lack of interest on the part of the national and international scientific communities in the people who are most closely associated with the *saola* on a day-to-day basis raises the question: does knowledge of the *saola* confer *control* over it and rights to it? Can the *saola* in general, at the present time, be considered the property of the minority communities that know the *saola* best and have recently been sharing their knowledge with the outside world? What about rights to the *saola*'s habitat which they have shared for centuries?

Before the recognized "discovery" of the *saola*, those local peoples who hunted the forests of the Truong Son range and who killed or captured a *saola* were free to do as they pleased with any and all parts of it. This was true for the mountain-dwelling minority peoples who formed the majority of the human population in the *saola's* natural range and for those few ethnic Vietnamese and Lao who either lived in the mountains also or who came there to hunt.[100] This is how Professor Tran Quoc Vuong came to have the *saola* skull in his apartment: the people in an ethnic minority village gave it to him when he visited them.[101]

Both the *saola* and the minority peoples who first "named" it face threats from all of the issues facing the "Vietnamese Uplands" which are discussed in detail in the essay by To Xuan Phuc in this volume. Further, the rights of the minority peoples of both Vietnam and Laos who happen to live in or very near the present-known range of the *saola* to the *saola* itself and to the other biota of the area have been strongly challenged[102] to the extent that one can say that the only *certain* power they have regarding the *saola* is negative. They can contribute to its demise. They can also contribute to its survival but only by cooperating with prohibitions, laws, and programs that have been, and will continue to be, designed at the national and international levels of the contested space in which the *saola*, the idea of the *saola*, and even the *ideal* of the *saola* exist. However, I would argue that even the potential of these upland peoples to contribute to the survival of the *saola* has been marginalized through national and international factors within a "process in which people are marginalized as their perspectives are cast to the side or excluded."[103]

As Hue-Tam Ho Tai has pointed out, "To an extent, the 'discovery' of the *saola* is a consequence of the expansion of the state into hitherto isolated areas, making it possible for scientists, both domestic and foreign, to follow."[104] It is also true that the discovery of the *saola* has given the government of Vietnam unprecedented international support for expansion of its control into these isolated areas and for measures aimed at controlling, at the most basic level, the day-to-day existence of those highland peoples who had long known and named the *saola*. Those at the lowest and most local level of the controversy surrounding the *saola* have been almost completely disenfranchised with regard to "rights" to the *saola*. As demonstrated above, these groups are so glossed over in the literature concerning the *saola* and the national and international efforts to preserve it that they are not even perceived as being connected to the *saola* even though they live close to its habitat. Their own livelihood has been threatened as well.

The Vu Quang Nature Reserve where the *saola* was discovered was not originally established to protect rare species of flora or fauna. In Vietnam's rather complicated system of national parks and reserves of various sorts[105] it originally became a nature reserve "because it had been the highland headquarters of

Phan Dinh Phung, a tenacious resistance fighter of the 1890's, who launched anti-French raids on the coast from his mountain lair."[106] For some thirty years before it was made a reserve, Vu Quang had been the site of a sizeable timber harvesting operation and this continued even after its designation as a reserve in 1986. After the "discovery" of the *saola*, the international press described the area as a "lost world"[107] following the lead of the Vietnamese scientists who conducted the original survey and who described Vu Quang as "the only remaining area of pristine forest in northern Vietnam."[108]

However, because of this "large timber operation employing several hundred people" that "extracted valuable hardwoods from the forest," Vu Quang fell under the purview of the Vietnamese Ministry of Forestry.[109] Vu Quang may not have been truly "pristine" but in 1992 it was certainly remote and difficult to reach. Indeed, as late as 1998 for five months every year "floodwaters keep the oxbow river on the northern boundary impassable, and workers at Vu Quang must stockpile fuel wood and food before the rainy season sets in."[110] The sheer difficulty of getting to Vu Quang is one of the reasons why scientists had not surveyed it before 1992 when the Vietnamese Ministry of Forestry received funds from the WWF to "evaluate the biodiversity value, and to prepare factual economic and technical foundations (now called a feasibility study) of this newly nominated protected area."[111]

Local authorities responded to the discovery of a second "new" large mammal in the Vu Quang Nature Reserve by more than tripling the reserve's size and banning logging."[112] With aid from the government of the Netherlands and from WWF the expanded Vu Quang Nature Reserve was set up in 1995. The increase in size of the reserve meant that it "now included eight communities of several thousand people each."[113] The first official assessment of the ethnic minority villagers "was finally completed in April of 1997. But the two-year delay between the closing of the reserve and the social survey meant that the Vu Quang conservation project had been rapidly progressing *without any local advice*."[114] This advice would have been from the very people of whom Tony Whitten said "These are the people we need to seek information from."[115] Yet, "for a long time, no research of any sort was done to understand the lives of villagers,"[116] their relationship to the *saola* and to the other flora and fauna of the Vu Quang Nature Reserve, and to each other. Instead, a tremendous number of restrictions on their activities were imposed.

Occasional hunting of the *saola* by the minority peoples was redefined as poaching. "Following the death of the two juvenile *saola* in Hanoi, Viet Nam's Ministry of Forestry issued a ban on further capture, trade, or holding of *saola* and ordered that no financial compensation be paid to anyone in possession of a *saola*."[117] Because of the discovery of the *saola* and the other "new" species in its range, those minority peoples in the immediate area where the *saola* was first discovered have lost the right to legally hunt species that are not endangered and to collect honey, bamboo, rattan, fruit, medicinal plants, and other forest products in the territory newly encompassed by the expanded park created to protect the *saola* and other rare species.[118] Even hunting to protect the food sources these peoples are still allowed from "common non-endangered animals like wild pigs that often destroy minorities' swidden crops if not kept in check" is strongly discouraged.[119] Further, according to anthropologist Pam McElwee, it has even been suggested that these peoples should give up cultivating rice, their main source of food.[120]

It would appear that there is a very deep-seated human need to find order in the universe and among the diverse biological entities that inhabit the earth.[121] The art/science of taxonomy has a long history in the West; for example, while Aristotle is most often presented as a philosopher and as the tutor of Alexander the Great, he is also sometimes referred to as the Father of Biology because of his writings on the natural world, its flora and fauna, and their relationships.[122] As for the non-Western world, ethnobiologists such as Brent Berlin have argued for quite some time that *all* systems of taxonomic classification that are based on the evidence presented by ordinary human sensory perceptions "are constrained in essentially the same ways – by nature's basic plan – in their conceptual recognition of the biological diversity of their natural environments."[123] However, what does not come through even in academic discussions of the human tendency to sort, organize, categorize, and repeatedly *name* individual examples of the biota of Earth is that to name something is to assert a right to it. Humans have at least as much of a tendency to claim that biological entities are the property of one group or another as they have to categorize such entities and naming them and defining the relationships between them appears to be an integral part of that process.

At this point the story of the *saola* as a living being is a sad one. A recent issue of *Science* reports on "an eleventh-hour effort to prevent the *saola*, a rare ungulate, from slipping into oblivion."[124] William Robichaud notes that the *Saola* Working Group is "starting to ramp up a major push to conserve *saola*."[125] The complex and intertwined relationships between the various factions laying claim to the *saola* form

> a story about people who decide the fate of species and ones who don't... a story about quarrels and edicts, ceaseless mud and torrential rains, men with guns and men with pens, all of which conspire against protecting natural areas.[126]

Since the earliest human legends and creation myths natural resources have been considered to be property available to individuals, to groups of individuals, and to polities once mankind developed them. Flora and fauna of all sorts fall into this category of natural resource/property and conflicts over who should control them are as old as history.

The elusive, enigmatic, mysterious, and above all rare *saola* has, since its discovery, had as much value as an idea and an ideal as it has had as an actual live animal. Because of an animal that no Western scientist has ever seen in the wild, news bulletins were released, articles were written by scientists for both the popular and academic press, academic groups were formed, articles were written by journalists for a variety of publications, scientific careers were enhanced, parks were created and expanded, stamps were issued,[127] and international conservation campaigns were launched. At Vu Quang itself, the boom centered on the *saola* has resulted in the construction of buildings with meeting rooms and guest quarters for visiting scientists and "a new park headquarters and mess hall."[128] Indeed, one can say that because of the discovery of the *saola*, Vu Quang is not as remote and isolated as it was before this famous discovery. The fate of the actual living members of the species *Pseudoryx nghetinhensis* is uncertain and will probably remain so for some time. Indeed, it is possible that no one will ever be able to claim ownership of or relationship to an individual *saola* again. But local minority peoples in Vietnam and Laos lost their rights to the *saola* when those occupying the next level of potential control came to believe in its existence, then when they named it, named it more than once, and finally when they collaborated with national and international organizations to appropriate the name *saola* and the idea and the ideal of the *saola*. Minority peoples lost more than the rights to the *saola*: they also became interlopers in areas where they had lived for centuries, their livelihood as threatened as the survival of an elusive animal that is at once very old and totally new.

## Notes

1 This essay benefited greatly from the assistance of Nguyen Lan Dung, Nick Enfield, Nguyen Van Hue, Pam McElwee, Frank Proschan, Vo Quy, and Bill Robichaud, and from the comments of Mark Sidel, Hue-Tam Ho Tai, and the participants at the Workshop on Property and Property Rights in Vietnam.

2 Lewis Carroll, *Through the Looking Glass*, as quoted in Brent Berlin, *Ethnobiological Classification: Principles of Categorization of Plants and Animals in Traditional Societies.* (Princeton: Princeton University Press, 1992), dedication page.

3 Personal communication, Tran Quoc Vuong, March 1993. Vuong must have known of the proposed scientific name for the *saola* from his contacts in the academic community in Hanoi, as the name *Pseudoryx nghetinhensis* was not officially used until later – June 3 of the same year.

4 Ibid.

5 http://www.iucn.org/knowledge/news/?3851/Last-chance-to-save-*Saola*-from and http://www.worldwildlife.org/species/finder/*saola*/*saola*.html. This organization was called the World Wildlife Fund until 1986 when the umbrella international organization became the World Wide Fund for Nature. The US branch is still legally called the World Wildlife Fund. A recently published article in *Science* also contends that the *saola* may not long survive its "discovery." Richard Stone, "The Saola's Last Stand" *Science* NS vol. 314 no. 5804 (1 December 2006), pp. 1380–1, 1383.

6 The *saola* is one of only five large mammals "discovered" between 1892 and 1992. Indeed, the last time a large mammal was "discovered" prior to the "discovery" of the *saola* was 1937. That was a type of wild cow called the kouprey and it was also found in Indochina. Since the *saola*'s "discovery" four (or, depending on whose taxonomic argument you believe, three) other large mammals have been discovered in the same border area shared by Vietnam and Laos.

7 See, for example, Tony Whitten, "The Saola – Brief History," in *Rediscovering the Saola* for mention of the *saola* and other "new" species "discovered" in Vietnam as though these species truly did not exist until they had been *scientifically* discovered. The other articles in this volume are written from the same viewpoint.

8 Eleanor Jane Sterling, Martha Maud Hurley, and Le Duc Minh, *Vietnam: A Natural History*, (New Haven: Yale University Press, 2006), p. 14.
9 Vu Van Dung and Do Tuoc, "The Discovery of the Saola (*Pseudoryx Nghetinhensis*) in Vietnam," in James Hardcastle (ed.), *Rediscovering the Saola: Proceedings of the workshop "Rediscovering the Saola: A status review and conservation planning workshop,"* (Hanoi: WWF Indochina Programme, 2004), pp. 11–14. http://assets.panda.org/downloads/*saola*proceedingenglish.pdf.
10 Pam McElwee, "The Nature of a Beast: Endangered Species Protection and Environmental Conservation in Vietnam," (Unpublished paper, 1st Place, Atlantic Monthly Student Writers Awards, 1998), p. 3.
11 Vu Van Dung and Do Tuoc, "Discovery of the Saola," p. 11. I have found some variation in the spelling of the names of members of this team.
12 Ibid. I have not been able ascertain full names for either of these men.
13 Vu Van Dung and Do Tuoc, "Discovery of the Saola," p. 11.
14 Ibid.
15 Ibid.
16 Ibid.
17 Vu Van Dung *et al.*, "Discovery and Conservation of the Vu Quang Ox in Vietnam," *Oryx: the Journal of the Fauna Conservation Society* vol. 28 no. 1 (January 1994), pp. 16–21, p. 16.
18 Vu Van Dung and Do Tuoc, "Discovery of the Saola," p. 11.
19 Ibid., p. 12.
20 Vu Van Dung *et al.*, "Discovery and Conservation," p. 19.
21 Frank Proschan, "The /saavlaa/ or *Saola* (*Pseudoryx nghetinhensis*)," unpublished paper circulated among scientists in Hanoi in the late spring and summer of 1994 when they were making a decision as to what to use for what one could call the public relations name of *Pseudoryx nghetinhensis*, p. 1. See Proschan's discussion of the ethnodemography of the area, pp. 1–2. Proschan further notes that "the lingua franca in large parts of Nghe An is the local Tai language rather than Vietnamese." Personal communication, 7 December 2009.
22 G. Schaller and A. Rabinowitz, "The *saola* or spindlehorn bovid *Pseudoryx nghetinhensis* in Laos," *Oryx: the Journal of the Fauna Preservation Society* vol. 29 no. 2 (April 1995), pp. 107–114.
23 A fair number of names are turned down. See, for example, International Commission on Zoological Nomenclature, *Opinions and declarations rendered by the International Commission on Zoological Nomenclature* 20 volumes 1943–59 (London: International Trust for Zoological Nomenclature). These opinions and declarations can now be found in electronic databases rather than as physical volumes.
24 http://www.iczn.org/iczn/index.jsp. The ICZN (International Commission on Zoological Nomenclature) Code. 4th ed., (January 2000). The ICZN is a subgroup of the International Union of Biological Sciences. The literature on this subject is vast, dry, and detailed. There is also a body of literature intended to guide scientists through the process. See, for example, Wilbur Irving Follett, *An Unofficial Interpretation of the International Rules of Zoological Nomenclature: as Amended by the XIII International Congress of Zoology, Paris 1948 and by the XIV International Congress of Zoology, Copenhagen 1953*. Unpublished paper distributed by the Society of Systematic Zoology.
25 Carol Kaesuk Yoon, *Naming Nature: the Clash between Instinct and Science.* (New York: W.W. Norton, 2009), p. 6.
26 The English language common name can even honor the scientist who "discovered" the animal in question. See the case of the Thai biologist Kitti Thonglongya and Kitti's Hog-Nosed Bat as discussed in Jeffrey A McNeely and Paul Spencer Wachtel, *Soul*

*of the Tiger: Searching for Nature's Answers in Exotic Southeast Asia* (New York: Doubleday, 1988), pp. 256–9.

27 See for example, Alexandre Hassanin and Emmanuel J. P. Douzery, "Evolutionary Affinities of the Enigmatic saola (*Pseudoryx nghetinhensis*) in the context of the molecular phylogeny of Bovidae," The Royal Society, *Proceedings: Biological Sciences*, vol. 266 no. 1422 (7 May 1999), pp. 893–900. See also John Gatesy and Peter Arctander, "Hidden Morphological Support for the Phylogenetic Placement of *Pseudoryx nghetinhensis* with Bovine Bovids: A combined Analysis of Gross Anatomical Evidence and DNA Sequences from Five Genes," *Systematic Biology*, vol. 49 Issue 3 (Sep. 2000), pp. 515–38.

28 WWF News Bulletin, Gland Switzerland July 17, 1992 as noted by Vu Van Dung and Do Tuoc in "Discovery."

29 Quite a number of articles were written concluding that "the *saola* is most closely related not to Bovinae but to Caprinae." Editor's note in G. Schaller and A. Rabinowitz, p. 110.

30 Vu Van Dung and Do Tuoc, "Discovery," p. 16.

31 Vu Van Dung, *et al.*, "Discovery and Conservation," p. 16.

32 Vu Van Dung and Do Tuoc, "Discovery," 16.

33 For an overview of Arctander's work with *saola* DNA, see Gatesy and Arctander, "Hidden Morphological Support."

34 Malcolm W. Browne, "Scientists Hope More New Species Will Be Discovered in Vietnam," *New York Times*, 3 May 1994.

35 M. Hernandez-Fernandez and E. S. Vrba, "A Complete Estimate of the Phylogenetic Relationships in Ruminantia: A Dated Species-level Supertree of the Extant Ruminants," *Biological Review* 80 (2005), pp. 269–302.

36 Vu Van Dung and Do Tuoc, "Discovery," p. 16.

37 William Robichaud and Robert Timmins, "The Natural History of Saola (*Pseudoryx Nghetinhensis*) and the Species' Distribution in Laos Based on the Workshop Presentation '*saola* ecology-the bare basics (i.e., all we know)'," in *Rediscovering the Saola*, pp. 14–23. See also the overview of scientific and popular publications on the *saola* in its entry on the Ultimate Ungulates website http://ultimateungulate.com.

38 See Robichaud and Timmins' discussion of use of information from "local people" p. 2. See also G. Schaller and A. Rabinowitz, "The saola or spindlehorn bovid *Pseudoryx nghetinhensis* in Laos," *Oryx: The Journal of the Fauna Preservation Society* vol. 29 no. 2 (April 1995), pp. 107–14 and Dung *et al.*, "Discovery and Conservation."

39 Eleanor Jane Sterling, Martha Maud Hurley, and Le Duc Minh, pp. 14 and 19–20. While one is not quite certain of the effect of these cameras on the *saola*, as Ken MacLean notes, some of the resulting photos feature "saola looking surprised." Personal communication 24 May 2009.

40 Vu Van Dung *et al.*, "A New Species of Living Bovid from Vietnam," *Nature* (1993) 363, pp. 443–5.

41 There is considerable disagreement about the date of the capture of this particular *saola*. Vu Van Dung and Do Tuoc, "Discovery," p. 17, state that this "live young *saola*" was captured "in late May 1993"; however, all of the other available sources state that it was captured in 1994. I believe that the 1993 date must be a typographic error.

42 Malcom W. Browne, "Vietnam Finds First Live Example of Rare Ox," *New York Times*, 23 June 1994.

43 G. Schaller and A. Rabinowitz, p. 107.

44 Pam McElwee, "Nature of a Beast," p. 1.

45 Ibid., p. 2.

46 Pam McElwee, "Does Vietnam have 'Indigenous Knowledge'?" Paper presented at the conference on Modernities and Dynamics of Tradition in Vietnam: Anthropological Approaches, Binh Chau Vietnam, December 2007.
47 Vu Van Dung and Do Tuoc, "Discovery," p. 16.
48 See http://www.ultimateungulate.com/Artiodactyla/Pseudoryx_nghetinhensis.html.
49 Proschan, 1. Robichaud credits Proschan in Robichaud and Timmins, p. 1.
50 Proschan, personal communication 22 May 2009.
51 Ibid.
52 Ibid.
53 Ibid., pp. 1–2.
54 Proschan, p. 3.
55 Proschan, p. 1.
56 Vu Van Dung and Do Tuoc, "Discovery," p. 18.
57 Hoang Ngoc Khanh, "Saola Conservation in Thua-Thien Hue Province," in *Rediscovering the Saola*, p. 41.
58 Tham Ngoc Diep, Dang Thang Long and Do Thuc comps, "A Luoi district, Thua Thien Hue province," in "Annex 3 Report of Survey of Saola *Pseudoryx Nghetinhensis*" in *Rediscovering the Saola*, p. 85.
59 http://www.iucnredlist.org section on the *saola*, see also Hardcastle (ed.), *Rediscovering the Saola* and Saola Working Group, press release 3 September 2009 "Last Chance to Save the Saola from Extinction? Meeting in Laos Urges Prompt Action," p. 2. My thanks to William Robichaud for sending me this document.
60 IUCN Red List, p. 6.
61 Robichaud, interview, as quoted by Richard Stone in "Last Chance to Save the 'Panda of Indochina'," in *Science*, Vol. 325 (Sep. 4, 2009), p. 1193.
62 I refer to the "faux Chinese medicine trade" because classic Chinese medicine and medical theory makes no call for the wholesale consumption of rare species that occurs in response to fads for consumption of a variety of rare and endangered fauna. The *saola* itself is unknown to the classic Chinese (and Vietnamese) pharmacopoeia. Parts of it may, however, be used as medicine by minority peoples, see speculation concerning this in Vu Van Dung *et al.*, "Discovery and Conservation," p. 18.
63 See "Case Study Three: Tiger *Panthera tigris*," pp. 44–6 and Appendix 5 "Complete list of the wild animal species confiscated by the Da Nang forest Protection Department from 2000–2006," p. 87, both in Nguyen Dao Ngoc Van and Nguyen Tap, comp. *An Overview of plants and animals used in traditional medicine systems in Vietnam*, A TRAFFIC Southeast Asia Report (Ha Noi: TRAFFIC Southeast Asia, Greater Mekong Programme, 2008).
64 See the discussion of snares in *Rediscovering the Saola*, pp. 83, 87 and *passim*.
65 William Robichaud, "Summary of saola, herpetological, and wildlife trade studies in Nakai-Nam Theun NBCA and the proposed Nam Theun extension" (Vientiane: Wildlife Conservation Society for IUCN, 1999).
66 G. Schaller and A. Rabinowitz, p. 113.
67 This monetary incentive to hunt down and try and capture *saola* appears to have been primarily private.
68 Appendix 3 in James Hardcastle (ed.), *Rediscovering the Saola*," pp. 90–1.
69 Vu Van Dung and Do Tuoc, "Discovery," p. 17. The official reason given for the death of this *saola* was liver flukes. However, Professor Do Tuoc contends that the real cause of death was the fact that this *saola* was fed, by unauthorized persons, fruit that would be indigestible for any ungulate with their complicated digestive system and that this caused a blockage. Do Tuoc personal communication January 13, 2011.
70 One was released and hopefully survived. Robichaud, "Captive *Saola*" p. 394.
71 http://ultimateungulate.com.

72 W.G. Robichaud, "Physical and behavioral description of a captive *saola, Pseudoryx nghetinhensis*." *Journal of Mammalogy* vol. 79 no. 2 (1998), p. 401. It is an unhappy probability that more of these rare animals died after being captured for scientific purposes and that this has not been widely reported.
73 Robichaud, "Captive *Saola*," p. 405.
74 Ibid., pp. 395–6. Robichaud is the founder of the Saola Working Group and the editor of its newsletter.
75 After the death of all of these *saola* the Vietnamese Ministry of Forestry imposed a ban on their capture and on any financial compensation for captured *saola.*
76 Vu Van Dung *et al.*, "Discovery and Conservation," p. 21.
77 Robichaud, personal communication, 3 November 2009.
78 Robichaud, personal communication, 6 October 2009.
79 http://www.iucnredlist.org, page 5 of the section on *Saola.*
80 Ibid. Since only documented sightings are listed, there may be many more undocumented sightings per year.
81 William Robichaud and Robert Timmins, p. 14.
82 Eleanor Jane Sterling, Martha Maud Hurley, and Le Duc Minh, p. 27.
83 Andreas Reinecke, "Bi-Cephalous Animal Shaped Ear Pendants in Vietnam" *Bead Study Group Newsletter* 28 (Winter, 1996), 7.
84 Ibid.
85 Edward H. Schafer, *The Vermilion Bird: T'ang Images of the South.* (Berkeley: University of California Press, 1967), pp. 25, 206, 222.
86 Proschan, "The /saavlaa/ or *Saola* (*Pseudoryx nghetinhensis*)," p. 1.
87 Proschan, personal communication 7 December 2009. Proschan also notes that the French language version of Wikipedia "provides a citation to Guignard, although this is not found in either the Vietnamese or the English versions." http://fr.wikipedia.org/wiki/Saola#ethnology.
88 Eleanor Jane Sterling, Martha Maud Hurley, and Le Duc Minh, p. 14.
89 Robichaud, "Captive *Saola*," *passim.* The meticulous reporter Malcolm W. Browne did mention "local T'ai tribal hunters" in "Scientists Hope More New Species Will Be Discovered in Vietnam" *New York Times*, 3 May 1994, but his careful rendering of credit where credit was due does not seem to have been followed by other authors.
90 http://vi.wikipedia.org/wiki/Sao_la.
91 My thanks to Nick Enfield, Nguyen Van Hue, Pam McElwee, and Frank Proschan.
92 See Vu Van Dung *et al.*, "Discovery and Conservation," *passim* and also the news report by Malcom W. Browne in the *New York Times* of 23 June 1994. "Vietnam Finds First Live Example of Rare Ox." As noted previously, Browne does mention the "T'ai" in his 3 May 1994 *New York Times* article.
93 See articles in James Hardcastle (ed.), *Rediscovering the Saola: Proceedings of the workshop "Rediscovering the Saola: A status review and conservation planning workshop*," (Hanoi: WWF Indochina Programme, 2004). The Van Kieu, Ta Oi, and Ka Tu (once spelled Ca Tu) are mentioned approximately eight times on pp. 41, 76, 83, 85, 87, and 103.
94 "Workshop Overview" in *Rediscovering the Saola,* p. viii. Emphasis added.
95 Tony Whitten, 3.
96 Robichaud, "Captive *Saola*," p. 397. Robichaud credits Proschan for this information.
97 Proschan, personal communication, 7 December 2009.
98 Robichaud, "Captive *Saola*," p. 401.
99 Proschan, personal communication, 7 December 2009.
100 Proschan's paper makes it clear that at the time of the discovery of the *saola* and for at least two years after that point "virtually no Kinh reside [resided] in the forested mountain areas of those districts where the /saavlaa/ can be found," p. 2.

101 Personal communication, Tran Quoc Vuong, March 1993. Unfortunately, I do not remember which group Vuong told me gave this skull to him nor where he was when he acquired it.

102 For overviews of a variety of laws, regulations, and programs attempting to restrict the hunting and capture of *saola* and to protect its habitat, see Malcom W. Browne "First Live Example." See also information on the work of the WWF on http://www.worldwildlife.org/what/wherewework/mekong/results.html; the IUCN Redlist section "Conservation Actions" at http://www.iucnredlist.org; and William Robichaud, *Saola Conservation Action Plan for Lao PDR* (Vientiane: IUCN Lao PDR Programme, 1999). For the effects of these regulations on the minority peoples of Vietnam see McElwee, "The Nature of a Beast" and "Does Vietnam have "Indigenous Knowledge?"

103 Anna Lowenhaupt Tsing, *In the Realm of the Diamond Queen: Marginality in an Out-of the Way Place*, (Princeton: Princeton University Press, 1993), p. 5.

104 Hue-Tam Ho Tai, personal communication, 19 May 2009.

105 See Eleanor Jane Sterling, Martha Maud Hurley, and Le Duc Minh, Chapter 10 "Conservation: The Future of Vietnam's Living World."

106 McElwee, "Nature of a Beast," p. 3.

107 See McElwee's discussion of the fascination of the international press with the term "lost world." McElwee, "Nature of a Beast," pp. 2–3.

108 Vu Van Dung *et al.*, "Discovery and Conservation," p. 16.

109 McElwee, "Nature of a Beast," p. 3.

110 Ibid., p. 6.

111 Vu Van Dung and Do Tuoc, "Discovery of the *Saola*," p. 11.

112 Eleanor Jane Sterling, Martha Maud Hurley, and Le Duc Minh, p. 354.

113 McElwee, "Nature of a Beast," p. 6.

114 Ibid. Italics added.

115 Tony Whitten, p. 3.

116 McElwee, "Nature of a Beast," p. 8.

117 Robichaud, "Captive *Saola*," p. 405.

118 McElwee, "Nature of a Beast," p. 7.

119 McElwee, "Indigenous Knowledge" p. 17 *of unpublished manuscript.*

120 McElwee, "Nature of a Beast," p. 8.

121 See Carol Kaesuk Yoon, "The Case of the Fish that Wasn't," Chapter 1 of *Naming Nature.*

122 Stephen J. Vicchio, "From Aristotle to Descartes," in R. J. Hoage (ed.), *Animal Intelligence: Insights into the Animal Mind* (Washington: Smithsonian Institution Press, 1986) and Allan Gotthelf (ed.), *Aristotle on Nature and Living Things; Philosophical and Historical Studies: Presented to David M. Balme on his Seventieth Birthday* (Pittsburgh: Mathesis Publications, 1985).

123 Brent Berlin, p. 8.

124 Richard Stone, "Last Chance to Save the 'Panda of Indochina'," *Science*, Vol. 325 (4 September 2009), pp. 1192–3.

125 Robichaud, personal communication, 6 October 2009.

126 McElwee, "Nature of a Beast," p. 1.

127 Both Laos, 1997, and Vietnam, 2000, have issued stamps celebrating the *saola.*

128 McElwee, "Nature of a Beast," p. 7.

# Property and state in Vietnam and beyond

*Thomas Sikor*[1]

The contributions to this book generate important conceptual and comparative insights on property. Conceptually, they demonstrate how negotiations over property are deeply enmeshed with dynamics of state formation. In Vietnam, property has been a central preoccupation of rulers, their agents and ordinary people during critical periods of state-making, whether in the fifteenth century under the new Le dynasty, in the nineteenth and early twentieth centuries under French rule, in the 1950s and 1960s in the Democratic Republic of Vietnam, or since the 1990s with the *Doi Moi* reforms. The broad temporal coverage represented in this volume illuminates certain features of the relationship between property and state that transcends specific political regimes and socio-cultural contexts and thus can be fruitfully explored in different temporal and geographic environments.

As shown in the individual chapters, on the one hand, governments commonly employ property laws and reforms when they seek to establish, augment, or consolidate state control over resources and people. On the other hand, the state figures centrally in people's claims to resources time and again. Urban residents and rural villagers commonly call upon "the state," state law, or state officials in their everyday dealings about land and other resources. Even though they may not always do so, the state is a primary politico-legal institution they invoke to authorize their claims as property rights. People become involved in processes of state-making when they assert ideas about how "the state" sanctions their claims, how certain laws do or do not apply, and what kinds of actions particular state agents should or should not undertake in relation to their concerns. The latter, the agents of the state, are active participants in these dynamics of state formation. They can go about their business of enforcing property rights, arbitrating in property disputes, or implementing property reforms in different ways. People's and state agents' property practices thus feed into everyday processes of state formation.

In this epilogue, I seek to develop these conceptual insights on the linkages between property and state on the basis of an admittedly partial reading of the contributions to this volume. My account draws on recent theorizing on how property and authority constitute each other recursively.[2] In a nutshell, Lund and I argue that property is intimately bound up with authority, authority understood as power considered legitimate.[3] Property is one of the fields in which people attribute legitimacy to various kinds of politico-legal institutions and thereby contribute to the constitution of authority relations. As these institutions get to "authorize" claims on resources as property, people solidify their authority in comparison with other institutions. At the same time, authorization by politico-legal institutions grants or denies legitimacy to claims on resources. Claims are only recognized as property if people can legitimize them in reference to the sanctioning authority of politico-legal institutions. These dynamics of property and authority contribute to processes of state formation because the state, its constituent parts, and its agents are key elements in them. State here refers simultaneously to a politico-legal institution, in the sense of an idea or ideal set of practices, and a forum in which various kinds of social actors struggle for control over people and resources. The recursive constitution of property and state is particularly visible in postsocialist societies[4] but also occurs in other institutionally pluralist societies.[5]

Furthermore, I employ the conceptual framing to derive comparative insights about key dynamics of state formation in contemporary Vietnam. The negotiations over property documented in this book, I suggest, indicate critical features of ongoing state formation: the centrality of property in the exercise of state power; struggles over control between the central party-state and local cadres; and, the permeability of the Vietnamese state to customary arrangements and community norms. Property emerges as a critical field in which the central party-state seeks to consolidate its authority through legislative action and discursive means. Property legislation and discourse serve the top echelons of the Communist Party and central government to discipline local cadres and to accommodate the influence of customary arrangements and community norms. Property law and discourse also connect with an increasingly pervasive anti-corruption campaign that works to insulate the central party-state from criticisms of state practices on the ground.

## State property projects

Identifying property legislation and reforms as projects commonly undertaken by states in their efforts to control people and resources would be nothing new. Governments have long used land reforms, the nationalization of land and other assets, collectivization of agriculture, privatization, etc. for economic and political aims. In fact, Vietnam may be a prime example for how governments have employed property legislation and reforms, even if one looks at the country's most recent history only. When Vietnam was divided after World War II, the regimes in the north and south undertook land reforms in an effort to secure political support from the peasantry. The Democratic Republic of Vietnam followed land reform with the collectivization of agricultural land and nationalization of forestland to mobilize people and resources for the war and industrialization. From the mid-1980s onward, the government of unified Vietnam promoted the decollectivization of agriculture and privatization (or equitization) of industry and trade to enable economic growth and ensure its political survival.[6]

An original insight generated by this book is, however, the large repertoire of property interventions available to governments. These interventions include classic state property projects, such as the land colonization schemes used by governments in historical and contemporary times to raise taxes and ameliorate political pressures. David Biggs looks at an experimental colonization scheme in colonial Vietnam, historical precedent to the large US-funded refugee resettlement projects and the massive New Economic Zone program implemented by the Communist party-state. He shows how the experimental scheme was prompted by the growing number of landless people and the deplorable plight of tenant farmers in the 1930s, which provided fertile grounds for the organization of tax protests and granary raids by the Indochinese Communist Party and caused fears of insurrection on the French side. This experimental colonization scheme in turn harked back to the military-agricultural settlements of precolonial Vietnam, which themselves were inspired by Chinese models dating back to the Tang dynasty.

Governments have often targeted land for their property interventions in more recent times, but historically people's labor has been equally attractive to them. Ken MacLean demonstrates how the recruitment of labor for public works is a critical means for ruling regimes to assert property claims to labor. MacLean puts the spotlight on the rules guiding the recruitment of workers for large infrastructure projects in the newly independent Democratic Republic of Vietnam. The rules specified the procedures under which local government officials could conscript labor, recruit volunteers, and contract wage labor at construction sites. The critical question looming in the background was how the emerging socialist state should use its claims to a part of people's labor in a way that would maximize its ability to extract economic surplus from the countryside. There was a clear trade-off between the need to provide long-term protection against floods and droughts and the short-term need to boost food production to avoid famine.

State delineations of property may also take more indirect forms. The property laws written under the incoming Le dynasty in the fifteenth century gradually changed from a gender-neutral treatment of inheritance rights to one that supported different rights for sons and daughters. Early jurisprudence did not state any difference between the rights of male and female heirs, emphasizing the significance and enforcement of the testament instead. It is impossible to determine, from available evidence, whether sons and daughters actually inherited equally. Starting in the 1460s, the legal code granted sons preferential rights to a portion of inherited private property. Erik Harms' analysis of a land clearance project outside Ho Chi Minh City indicates how state delineations of property, in law and discourse, influence the kinds of objects considered available for property claims. Harms reports his bewilderment that people affected by the land clearance did not resist the demolition of their houses. Their acceptance of the project came from their view of the project as legitimate; legitimate in the sense of what futures they envisioned for their country and city. This view reflected not only the applicable regulations on land clearance and government discourse of modernization, but also implicit delineations of the object at stake: it was the urban development project and not people's individual houses. Once people had accepted the delineation as legitimate, they had little grounds to resist the demolition of their houses.

This book thus indicates that governments have at their disposal a large repertoire of property interventions not limited to direct interventions into the use of resources, such as land reforms, colonization schemes, or the conscription of labor. Other state interventions seek to influence the use of resources in more indirect ways through the exercise of control over the use of valuable resources, control in the sense of exercising capacities to check and direct property practices.[7] This control gets enacted in many ways, such as through legislative action, discursive means, law enforcement, and dispute resolution. It has profound effects on property practices, as it influences the very kinds of actors, objects, and relationships recognized to constitute property relationships.

## Conflicts over property, struggles within the state

Governments' tendency to initiate property laws and reforms does not imply that the state is actually acting as a unitary organization. This volume shows that the very agents of the state themselves react to state property projects in many ways, actively negotiating how they set out to act upon them in practice. These agents include the top echelons of the central government, members of parliament, high court judges, line ministry staff, and various kinds of local officials. As these actors are all involved in the creation, enforcement, and implementation of property legislation, it does not come as a surprise that their practices and interpretations are often at odds. Moreover, the making, implementation, or arbitration of property may open up forums in which different state entities compete against each other. Property thus may end up at the core of struggles within the state about control over people and resources.

The courts may find themselves in an ambivalent position toward other arms of the state. On the one hand, they are expected to enforce the laws and regulations made by the legislative and executive branches of the state. On the other, their mandate requires them to prosecute legal violations and to resolve property disputes independent from the other branches, even if the violations or disputes involve state officials. In Vietnam, Mark Sidel finds courts experience serious restrictions on their independence (see also Gillespie, this volume). In a widely publicized dispute over land in Haiphong, conflict arose when a local People's Committee allocated highly attractive land to a number of district and provincial leaders in an apparent case of favoritism. Media reports about the allocation led to criminal charges against four local officials and a trial at the Haiphong People's Court. Yet the entire case was handled extra-judicially, the courts turning into mere pawns of dueling state and Party officials reaching all the way up to the Prime Minister and President. The ambivalent position of the courts in Vietnam became particularly evident from the fact that central officials never criticized

Haiphong officials for *intervening* in the court case: the offense was that they *over-intervened*. Some interference into court proceedings was thus deemed acceptable and even desirable, but only to a point.

Property claims and their recognition may pit local cadres against central government officials, as illustrated by the politics of recognition of intangible cultural heritage examined by Oscar Salemink. Local groups seek recognition from the central government for their sites of remembrance, worship, or ritual practice as historical or cultural monument. If successful, the Ministry of Culture issues them a certificate of recognition as historical/cultural monument. The central government thus acts as arbiter in a competitive process of validating and authenticating local sites or practices, a process that possesses striking historical parallels with state certification of local ritual practice and heritage claims by the Board of Rites of imperial times. The central government is in the position to recognize – or reject recognition to – the intangible cultural heritage claims endorsed by local officials. Seen from this angle, central and local governments offer competing forums for the recognition of cultural heritage.

Negotiations over property thus may create, deepen, or just reflect cleavages in the state. At the same time, they may also give rise to unexpected coalitions, as Nguyen Vu Hoang reveals. Nguyen Vu Hoang examines the efforts of a group of Hanoi residents to defend their land rights against a public infrastructure project. The residents were able to enlist support from state officials, in particular two local officials and Communist Party members, who knew how to mobilize support from the neighborhood Party Cell and from within national state entities. Forming an ephemeral albeit effective coalition with central state agents they were able to overcome stiff opposition from the district and ward People's Committees, which long appeared determined to remove them from their land as set out in the construction plan made by the People's Committee of Hanoi. They succeeded when they presented their opposition in the terms of the national anti-corruption campaign, causing the Ministry of Communication and Transportation to step in and request alterations to the plan.

Accusations of power abuse and corruption appear to be an integral element of negotiations over property within the state, as illustrated by Nguyen Vu Hoang's account. Local officials, in particular, may find themselves exposed to accusations of power abuse by local people and the target of anti-corruption campaigns enacted by central governments. In this book, accusations of improper behavior and self-enrichment appear in a wide variety of settings in the past and present, extending from the fifteenth century and the land reform campaigns in the mid-twentieth century to land allocations and land clearance projects in contemporary Vietnam. Corruption charges thus look like a frequent legal and discursive means employed by people and state officials alike in struggles over property.

The contributions to this book thus indicate how property negotiations are deeply implicated with contestations about control over people and resources within the state. Various kinds of state actors seek to establish, affirm, or strengthen their power by asserting control over property. Vice versa, as various kinds of state actors struggle over control, they offer support to multiple claims on resources. Conflicts over property consequently may be as much due to competing claims to use rights as to conflicting assertions of control embedded in wider struggles within the state, as illustrated by Sidel. Property conflicts thus are linked to cleavages within the state, cleavages that may run along different fault lines.

## Contestations over property and the state

Yet negotiations about control over property are not confined to struggles among state actors, this book shows. Negotiations over property extend beyond the state, challenging the state's primacy as definer and enforcer of property rights in relation to other politico-legal institutions. There are a variety of other politico-legal institutions which also offer to endorse the property claims made by people.[8] People have a choice when they make property claims on land or other assets. For example, a family can reference its claim to a particular residential plot to the laws and agents making up the state. Yet the family may also be able to justify its claim by asserting that family members have lived on the land for a long time, other people in the neighborhood consider the family's claim legitimate, or transnational human rights conventions protect its right to safe residence. Thus, in more abstract terms, the family may refer to the state, custom, community norms, or transnational law when it seeks to demonstrate the legitimacy of its claim and thereby get the claim recognized as a property right. The state does not hold a monopoly over the exercise of control about property, but people routinely make and unmake the authority attributed to the state as an institution sanctioning property in practice.

Custom, in its many incarnations, emerges as an alternative politico-legal institution to which people reference their property claims. Custom, understood as a more or less congruent set of norms and regularized practices, may compete with the state for the endorsement of property rights. Competition between state and custom comes out in a particularly stark manner in To Xuan Phuc's discussion of property rights to forest and forestland in a northern mountain village. Statutory rights and customary rights are radically different from each other with regards to the use of forest for the extraction of timber and use of forestland for swidden cultivation. State and custom not only accord forest use rights to different actors, but they are also based on very different notions of use rights in terms of their temporal duration and spatial extent, their exclusivity, and the way the bundle or disentangle rights to multiple resources. Moreover, the different conceptions of use rights connect with different ideas about the exercise of control rights, and ultimately about the politico-legal institution deemed legitimate to govern property over forest.

State and custom may not necessarily be at loggerheads, but be related in a mutually accommodating manner, as indicated by John Gillespie. Gillespie explores how Hanoi judges use "reason and sentiment in applying the law" to resolve land and housing disputes. They employ customary understandings of property rights despite the explicit mandate written down in the Constitution that courts have to resolve all disputes according to statutory law. Yet judges tend to quickly encounter the limitations of statutory land rights and legal doctrines and therefore draw on customary norms and practices. What results from judges' flexible and pragmatic interpretations of the exercise of control rights over property is a relatively symbiotic relationship between state and customary norms. Judges' actions also make the boundary between state and custom highly permeable in practice.

Transnational norms are another set of institutions validating property claims, as highlighted by Michele Thompson's discussion of the *saola* (see also Oscar Salemink, this volume). Although local people and Vietnamese scientists had long known about the existence of the *saola*, its status changed fundamentally after international scientists "discovered" it, gave it the scientific name *Pseudoryx nghetinhensis*, and declared the animal an endangered species. From then on, life was never the same again for either the few remaining *saola* or the local people living around their habitat. Vietnam's central government enlarged Vu Quang Nature Reserve and declared all local hunting as illegal with backing by international conservation organizations and donors. The validation provided by transnational conservation agreements thus bolstered the application of existing Vietnamese laws and regulations, affording the government's claims on forests and wildlife additional legitimacy and thereby fortifying state control over a remote area.

At the same time, these observations do not imply that people always seek ways to reference their property claims to politico-legal institutions other than the state. Many assert claims to critical resources on the basis of state laws, regulations, and practices even where other options are available. They may even invoke the state as an idea in times of political turmoil and civil warfare, where the state does not step up in the form of a single and clear political organization. This is the rather surprising finding by Nhung Tuyet Tran, as she discovers that local performance groups referred to statutory law when they sold their customary rights to village songs and dances in the seventeenth and eighteenth century. When performance groups sold their rights to perform in front of a particular communal house, villagers not only erected stelae to document the sale in the customary way; they also included references to statutory land law in the stele inscriptions to bolster the legitimacy of treating their customary rights as "cultural property" and transferring them to third parties. The contracting parties hoped for validation through the laws of the state to bolster the credence of the contracts, as weak and fragmented as the state was at that time.

Negotiations about property, therefore, are simultaneously contestations over the state, understood as a politico-legal institution. When people assert claims on resources, they may justify these claims on the basis of state laws, regulations, and practices, or they may call upon customary or transnational norms to legitimize the claims. The relationship between the state and other politico-legal institutions is not necessarily a competitive one, as Gillespie and Thompson show. The state may accommodate validations of property claims originating from other institutions (Gillespie), or may even employ them usefully to bolster state validations (Thompson). The boundary between the state and other institutions thus may be permeable in practice, as clear as it is conceptually. Yet the property claims endorsed by the state may in other instances be at loggerheads with the claims sanctioned by other institutions, as highlighted by To Xuan Phuc. State control over property, therefore, is not automatic but needs to be established, consolidated, adjusted, or strengthened in a never-ending process, as people continuously weaken, undermine, or unravel state control by asserting claims and invoking validations in contradiction with state laws, regulations, and practices.

## Negotiating property and state in Vietnam

Not only does this book provide fascinating conceptual insights about the linkages between property and state, but it also offers a novel perspective on critical dynamics of state formation in Vietnam. Vietnam's rulers have generally displayed keen interest in property. Various precolonial, colonial, and postcolonial regimes have asserted use rights to critical resources, such as through the nationalization of land and the conscription of labor. In addition, Vietnam's rulers have time and again demonstrated a major preoccupation with the exercise of control over the use of resources by their subjects by codifying statutory rights, registering actual rights, and many other tactics. Most prominently, land rights have remained a primary target for the exercise of state control from the fifteenth century onward. This historical emphasis on control over land, or more broadly territorial control, sets Vietnam apart from its neighbors, where territorialization occurred as part of modernizing projects in the late nineteenth and twentieth century only.[9] The centuries-long tradition of territorializing efforts also highlights the economic *and political* antecedents of the land allocation program enacted as part of the *Doi Moi* reforms in the 1990s. Land allocation has been as much about creating the necessary conditions for economic growth as about re-establishing state control over people and resources on new foundations.

Struggles over the exercise of control over property reveal significant cleavages within the contemporary state. A central axis in these struggles is discrepancies and conflicts between the laws and regulations designed by the central party-state and local officials' property dealings. Local cadres often find themselves at odds with central officials, as has been observed more broadly in Vietnam[10] and other postsocialist countries.[11] In comparison, the relations between the executive party-state and the judiciary appear much less strained, as courts lack the autonomy granted to them in other postsocialist countries.[12] Vietnam does not experience the struggles between law-governed and executive exercise of state control characterizing state formation in other postsocialist societies, such as Romania.[13]

The negotiations over property documented in this book also reveal a Vietnamese state that is surprisingly permeable to and accommodating of the influence of other politico-legal institutions.[14] Statutory law often lacks "persuasive power," as Gillespie observes. In reaction, people invoke customary arrangements and social norms to justify property claims on resources, not only in remote rural areas but in the very centers of Hanoi and Ho Chi Minh City. Local cadres and judges use the decision-making spaces available to them to accommodate claims based on community norms and custom. This permeability has allowed the state in Vietnam to avoid the kind of direct challenges to its very existence encountered in other postsocialist (and postcolonial) societies. In the Albania of the 1990s, for example, people's turn to customary regulations for the distribution of land and resolution of property disputes mounted a massive challenge to the state's ambition to be the primary definer and enforcer of property rights.[15] At the same time, the permeability implies that state control over people and resources in Vietnam looks much less complete and uniform than contained in accounts of a strong party state insulated from societal influences.[16]

These insights support interpretations of state formation in Vietnam which put the spotlight on struggles about "rule by law."[17] A key dynamic in contestations over the Vietnamese state arises from broader efforts by the central political leadership to establish and justify "rule by law" as a way to re-establish state control over people and resources on new foundations. "Rule by law" accords the executive party-state primacy over the legislative and judiciary branches, as it exempts the top echelons of party and executive state from accountability to the law (ibid.). In addition, it is an integral component of ongoing efforts by the central party-state to control the actions of local cadres. Law has thus emerged as an instrument by which the central party-state seeks to strengthen its hold over citizens and the other parts of the state alike, in an effort to avoid the "parcellization of sovereignty" observed in other postsocialist settings.[18]

Property legislation and discourse assume center stage in contestations over "rule by law" in Vietnam. On the one hand, the party-state seeks to use property legislation to assert its authority against potentially competing politico-legal institutions, such as community norms and customary arrangements. Control over land is just the most prominent field, as indicated by the land allocations, land registrations, and resolution of land disputes which have kept many government officials busy over the past two decades. Yet property laws and enforcement extend to other assets, such as houses and apartments, and intangible resources, such as endangered wildlife and cultural heritage. Even the recognition of local cultural practices, as inauspicious as it may appear, may work to provide "cultural validation" to the party-state, as Salemink notes, as the process of recognition also serves to augment the authority of the recognizing party state.

On the other hand, the central party-state employs property legislation to discipline local cadres, as illustrated by central party and government officials' passion for writing legal texts which specify what the agents of the state should or should not do in their dealings with land. The resolutions, laws, decrees, decisions, and technical guidelines are often written at a level of detail that does not allow any space for discretionary decisions, and leaves cadres with the task of reconciling contradictory demands. Moreover, it is the very discretionary decisions made by local officials and judges which allow the Vietnamese state to accommodate the influence of other, potentially competing politico-legal institutions such as community norms. Local cadres and judges thus find themselves in a vulnerable position, as they are required to comply with the laws and regulations enacted by the central party-state yet also face people's expectations to act in reasonable ways – reasonable according to social norms and customs.[19] In many instances, their practices may not catch the attention of central officials, yet at times the cleavages may break out in the open. If they do, the ensuing conflicts are often couched in terms of power abuses, arbitrary behavior by cadres, and corruption.[20] Accusations of self-enrichment and power abuse seem to have particular traction at the beginning of the twenty-first century after the central government has embarked on an anti-corruption campaign, as indicated by Harms' survey of media reports.

These observations, finally, support a provocative interpretation of these corruption charges: they may be as much about the assertion of central party-state control and state authority as due to unlawful actions by local cadres.[21] Just like the never-ending flow of property laws and regulations, anti-corruption laws and discourse may serve the central party-state to discipline local officials (Sidel's chapter discusses corruption in the context of a major land case). The discourse of local power abuses, arbitrary cadre behavior, and corruption has long served Vietnam's rulers to discipline local cadres as part of a broader struggle over authority within the Vietnamese state.[22] The recent anti-corruption campaign may just be another means by which central party and government officials seek to make sure that local cadres comply with their orders. In addition, talk of corruption may simultaneously help the party-state to divorce the state, understood as a politico-legal institution, from the actions of state officials considered undesirable or improper by the wider population. The talk may operate to separate the concrete practices of state agents from the very idea of the state, thereby defending, sustaining and embellishing the authority people attribute to the state as an institution. Or in other words, the property discourse and anti-corruption campaign may allow the party-state to construct the image of a "good state" – and claim its own – against the template of dispossession and power abuse.

## Notes

1 I thank Hue-Tam Ho Tai, Eric Harms, Ken MacLean, and Oscar Salemink for very useful comments.

2 C. Lund, *Local Politics and the Dynamics of Property in Africa*, (Cambridge and New York: Cambridge University Press, 2008); T. Sikor, and C. Lund, "Access and Property: A Question of Power and Authority," *Development and Change* 40, (2009), pp. 1–22.

3 Weber, Max, *Wirtschaft und Gesellschaft*, (Tübingen: Mohr, J.C.B., 1976).

4 D. Stark, and L. Bruszt, *Postsocialist Pathways: Transforming Politics and Property in East Central Europe*, (Cambridge: Cambridge University Press, 1998); Janet Sturgeon, *Border Landscapes: The Politics of Akha Land Use in China and Thailand*, (Seattle and London: University of Washington Press, 2005); J. Allina-Pisano, *The Post-Soviet Potemkin village: Politics and Property Rights in the Black Earth*, (New York: Cambridge University Press, 2008).

5 M. Nuijten, *Power, Community and the State: The Political Anthropology of Organisation in Mexico*, (London: Pluto Press, 2003); C. Lund, *Local Politics and the Dynamics of Property in Africa*.

6 A. Fforde and S. de Vylder, *From Plan to Market: Economic Transition in Vietnam 1979–1994*, (Boulder: Westview Press, 1996); Benedict J.T. Kerkvliet, *The Power of Everyday Politics: How Vietnamese Peasants Transformed National Policy*, (Ithaca: Cornell University Press; Singapore: ISEAS, 2005).

7 T. Sikor, "Land allocations in Vietnam's uplands: Negotiating property and authority." *Upland Transformations in Vietnam*, T. Sikor, P.T. Nghiem, J. Sowerwine, J. Romm (eds), (Singapore: National University of Singapore Press, 2011).
8 T. Sikor and C. Lund, "Access and Property."
9 Peter Vandergeest and Nancy Lee Peluso, "Territorialization and State Power in Thailand," *Theory and Society* 24 (1995), pp. 385–426.
10 Kerkvliet, Benedict J.T. and David Marr (eds), *Beyond Hanoi: Local Government in Vietnam*, (Singapore: Institute for Southeast Asian Studies, 2004); Benedict J.T. Kerkvliet, *The Power of Everyday Politics*.
11 Katherine Verdery, *What Was Socialism? And What Comes Next?* (Princeton, NJ: Princeton University Press, 1996); Janet Sturgeon, *Border Landscapes*; J. Allina-Pisano, *The Post-Soviet Potemkin Village*.
12 Stephanie Balme and Mark Sidel (eds), *Vietnam's New Order: International Perspectives on the State and Reform in Vietnam*, (New York: Palgrave Macmillan, 2007).
13 T. Sikor, J. Stahl. and S. Dorondel, "Negotiating Post-Socialist Property and State: Struggles over Forests in Albania and Romania," *Development and Change* 40 (2009), pp. 171–94.
14 T. Sikor, "Land allocations in Vietnam's uplands."
15 C. de Waal, "Post-socialist Property Rights and Wrongs in Albania. An Ethnography of Agrarian Change," *Conservation and Society* 2, (2004), pp. 19–50; T. Sikor, J. Stahl., and S. Dorondel, "Negotiating Post-Socialist Property and State."
16 Benedict J.T. Kerkvliet, *The Power of Everyday Politics*; Andrew Wells-Dang, "Political space in Vietnam: a view from the 'rice-roots'," *The Pacific Review* 23, (2010), pp. 93–112.
17 Stephanie Balme and Mark Sidel (eds), *Vietnam's New Order*.
18 Katherine Verdery, *What Was Socialism?*
19 Thomas Sikor, "Local Government in the Exercise of State Power: The Politics of Land Allocation in Black Thai villages," in *Beyond Hanoi: Local Government in Vietnam*, B. Kerkvliet and D. Marr (eds), (Singapore: Institute for Southeast Asian Studies, 2004), pp. 171–200.
20 M. Gainsborough, "Corruption and the Politics of Economic Decentralization in Vietnam," *Journal of Contemporary Asia* 33, (2003), pp. 69–84.
21 T. Sikor and To Xuan Phuc, "Illegal Logging in Vietnam: *Lam Tac* (Forest Hijackers) in Practice and Talk," *Society & Natural Resources* 24 (7): 688–701 (2011).
22 M. Gainsborough, "Corruption and the Politics of Economic Decentralization in Vietnam."

# Glossary[1]

ả đào
An Biên
An Quảng
An Phú
ba chính
Ba Sao
Ba Thê
Bá Dương
bác
ban cán sự Đảng
ban chỉ huy
ban hòa giải
bản giáp ứng cương sứ đào nương phù giá nghênh
bản sắc dân tộc
Bản Yên
Bắc – Hưng – Hải
Bắc Ninh
bị giải tỏa
bia hậu
Bình
Bộ Lễ
Bùi Hoài Sơn
Bùi Quang Chiêu
ca
Ca Công
ca trù
ca trù là một di sản văn hóa đặc sắc của Việt Nam
Cà Mau
can thiệp
can thiệp quá sâu
cảnh cáo
Cảnh Hưng
Cảnh Thịnh

Cảnh Trị
Cao Bằng
Cao Lãnh
Cần Thơ
Châu
Châu Đốc
chỉ
Chính Hòa
chịu trách nhiệm và báo cáo công tác
Chợ Lớn
Chu Minh Tuấn
chủ
chủ nợ
chúc thư
cổ tiền bát thập quan viên lập khế viết giao thuận
công
công đức
công nghiệp hóa, hiện đại hóa đất nước
công thần
Công ty Đông Á
công văn
Cù Sơn
Củ Chi
cụ
Cửa Rao Vàng
Cường Để
Dao
dân
dân công
dân oan
dân tộc
dê sừng dài
di tích lịch sử văn hóa
dịch quan
Diệm
duy lý
Duy Tân hội
duy tình
*Dư địa chí*
Dương Đức
Dương Văn Thành
Dzũng
Đà Bắc
Đại Đề
Đại La

Đại Việt
Đàm Dĩ Mông
Đan Phượng
đàn dây
đảng viên gương mẫu
đạo
đào nương
Đặng Nghiêm Vạn
đất giải phóng
đấu tranh giai cấp
điển
đinh
Đinh Đình Phú
đình
đình ca
đình hát
đình môn
đình môn bi ký
đình môn sự lệ
Định
định hướng
Đoài Khê
Đồ Sơn
Đỗ Thị Luyến
Đỗ Tước
độc lập
đổi mới
đội
đồn điền
Đông
Đông Mỹ phường
Đông Ngạc
Đông Sơn
đồng
*Đồng Quê*
Đồng Tháp
đức tài
đường lối quần chúng
Gia Long
gia tộc
giá trị chung
giá trị sử dụng
giạ
giải tỏa
giải tỏa oan ức

giảm địa tô
giám đốc
gian
giao khế
giao ước
giáo phường
giáo phường nhân thượng hạ
giấy công nhận di tích lịch sử văn hóa
*Giữ gìn và bảo vệ bản sắc văn hóa các dân tộc thiểu số Việt Nam*
gợi ý
Hà Đông
Hà Lan
Hà Mạnh Trí
Hà Nam
Hà Nội
Hà Tây
Hà Tiên
Hà Tĩnh
Hạ Long
Hai Bà Trưng
Hải Dương
Hải Phòng
hàng hóa đặc biệt
hát chơi
hát đình
hát quan
hát thi
Hân
Hậu Giang
hiến đất
Hoa
Hoa Bản
Hòa Bình
Hoàn Kiếm
Hoàng
Hoàng Anh Hùng
Hoàng Trọng Tri
Hoành
Hóc Môn
Hòe Thị
Hồ Chí Minh
Hồ Đông
Hồ Quý Ly
Hội An
hội đồng bồi thường và giải phóng mặt bằng

Hội Văn hóa Văn nghệ các Dân tộc
hợp lý
Huế
Hùng
Hùng Cường
Hưng Hóa
Hưng Yên
Hương Canh
hương hỏa
Hương Tảo
Hữu Bằng
Hữu Cước
Kẻ Bàng
khẩu
khẩu phần điền thổ
Khoa
Khoái Châu
khoán
không gian văn hóa cồng chiêng
khởi nghĩa
Khu Tả Ngạn
Khuất Duy Tiến
Kiến An
kiện
Kiều
Kim Dạ
Kim Động
Kim Quang
Kim Ty
Kinh
Kinh Bắc
ký
Lam Sơn
làm ăn cá thể
làm ăn tập thể
Lan
Lạng Sơn
lao động
*Lao Động*
lập khoán xướng nhi ký
Lập Thượng
Lê
Lê Kim Quế
Lê Lợi

Lê Quang Liêm
Lê Thanh Hải
Lê Thánh Tông
Lê Tiến Thọ
Lê Trọng
Lê Văn Châm
Lê Văn Định
Lê Văn Kích
Liêm
liên khu
Linh Trung
Long Xuyên
Lộc
lợi ích của nhà nước
Lưu Kim Thái
lưu truyền vạn đại
Lý
lý và tình trong việc chấp hành pháp luật
Mạc
mãi chủ nhiệm xướng ca truyền vạn đại
mãi đình môn
mãi đình môn bi ký
mãi trù
mãi trù văn khế chi bi
mãi tuyệt
mẫu
miệt vườn
Minh Mạng
minh tân
mót
một núi cái lý không bằng một tí cái tình
Mỹ Sơn
Mỹ Tho
Mỹ Trà
Nam Định
Nam Giao
Nam Giới
Nam Kỳ Khởi Nghĩa
Nghệ An
Nghệ Tĩnh
*Nghị quyết V TW Đảng*
nghĩa vụ
Ngô
Ngô Đình Diệm

Ngô Đình Nhu
Ngô Đức Thịnh
Ngôn
Nguyễn
Nguyễn Ái Quốc
Nguyễn An Ninh
Nguyễn Chí Bền
Nguyễn Doãn Lăng
Nguyễn Kim Dung
Nguyễn Kim Khánh
Nguyễn Minh Triết
Nguyễn Ngọc Huy
Nguyễn Tấn Dũng
Nguyễn Thái Bình
Nguyễn Thái Tự
Nguyễn Thành Tuy
Nguyễn Thế Hùng
Nguyễn Thị Nhu
Nguyễn Thúc Bảo
Nguyễn Trãi
Nguyễn Trí Tuyển
Nguyễn Văn Hân
Nguyễn Văn Huyên
Nguyễn Văn Sáng
Nguyễn Văn Sửu
Nguyễn Văn Thinh
Nguyễn Văn Thuận
Nguyễn Văn Trỗi
Nguyễn Vũ Hoàng
người dân
nhà chung
Nhà Đèn
nhã nhạc
nhân dân
nhóm tiếp quản
Nhu
Ninh Bình
Ninh Thạnh Lợi
nô
nô tỳ
nôm
*Nông Cổ Mín Đàm*
Nông Quốc Chấn
nương
Ông Hai

Ông Mười
Phách
Phạm Mộng Giao
Phạm Thị Vách
Phan Bội Châu
Phan Chu Trinh
Phan Đăng Nhật
Phan Đình Phùng
Phi Vân
Phong Nha
phong phú
phong trào thi đua
phóng sự
Phú
Phú Mỹ
Phú Nhuận
Phú Riềng
Phú Thọ
Phùng Minh
Phước Long
phường
quá sâu
quan
quan họ
quan thụ điền thổ
quan viên quân tử
quan xã
*Quốc Dân Diễn Đàn*
quốc hữu thường pháp cố lập văn khế hoàn đình mãi chủ vị chiếu dụng giả
quốc hữu thường pháp cố lập văn khế vị chiếu dụng giả
Quốc Oai
*Quốc triều hình luật*
quyền độc lập
quyết định trước khi xét xử
Rạch Giá
Sa Đéc
sai lầm
Sang
sắc phong
sở địa chính
Sở quản lý điền thổ Hà Nội
*Sơn Dương*
Sơn La
Sơn Lộ
Sơn Nam

Sơn Tây
Suối Sâu
Suối Sòng
sử thi
sự hợp lý
sự mệnh lệnh
Tà Ôi
tá điền
Tạ Văn Tài
tân mãi
tân mãi đình môn trù tiền
Tân Phú
Tân Sơn Nhất
Tân Tạo
tân tạo mãi đình bi ký
tân tạo mãi đình văn khế bi ký
tân tạo trùm trưởng tự đình bi ký
Tây Nguyên
Tây Ninh
Tây Sơn
Tết
thạch bi mại đình
thạch bi thuyên tạo
Thái Bình
Thái Công Nguyên
Thái Nguyên
Thái Tổ
Thanh Hoa
Thanh Hóa
*Thanh Niên*
thanh tra chính phủ
Thanh Trì
Thanh Xuân
Thanh Xuân Trung
Thành
thành quả cách mạng về đất đai
Thăng Long
Thắng
thặng
Thị Nghè
Thiên Mạc
Thiên Mạc châu mãi bản huyện giáo phường ty
Thiết Đột
Thinh

Thịnh
thỉnh thị án
thỏa đáng
Thủ Đức
Thung
Thụy tổng mãi bản huyện phường ty đoạn mại đình trù tiền văn bi ký
Thừa Thiên – Huế
thượng hạ lão tiểu đẳng
Thượng Mỗ
tịch thu
Tiên Lữ
tình cảm láng giềng
tình yêu giai cấp
tính đa dạng
Tô Ngọc Thanh
Tô Xuân Phúc
tổ dân phố
tổ đổi công
tổ nghiệp đinh
tộc
tội ác
tôn nhân
Trà Lâm
trại
trang
Trảng Bàng
Trần
Trần Chánh Chiếu
Trần Đang Chấp
Trần Đăng Khoa
Trần Mạnh Tiến
Trần Quốc Vượng
Trần Thị Kim Anh
Trần Trọng Kim
Trần Văn Khê
Trần Văn Tuy
Tri Tôn
Trịnh
trù
trùm đẳng
trùm trưởng
trưng mua
trưng thu
Trương Vĩnh Trọng

Trường Chinh
Trường Sơn
trưởng tộc
tuần niên chính nguyệt quý xã phó quan giáp đào nương nhị nô tảo thời
Tu Lý
*Tuổi Trẻ*
tuồng
Tuy
Tuyên Quang
tư
tư ước
Từ Liêm
Từ Sơn
Tử Trầm
Tự
tự giải tỏa
tự túc
Tước
uy tín
ủy ban thẩm phán
Vách
Văn Giang
văn khế
Văn Lâm
văn minh
Văn Nhân
văn phòng tiếp dân của Trung Ương Đảng và Nhà Nước
vị quan dịch – đồng tiền
Việt Cộng
Việt Minh
Việt Nam
Vinh
Vĩnh Thuận
Võ Thanh Bình
Võ Văn Kiệt
Vũ Đức Vận
Vũ Văn Dzũng
Vụ Quang
vùng sâu vùng xa
Vượng
xa rời quần chúng
*Xã Hội*
xã hội hóa
Xuân

xử trí
xướng trù
xướng trù bi ký
Yên Sơn

## Note

1 Proper personal and place names are capitalized. Book and publication titles and scientific names are italicized. Vietnamese words are sorted according to the "ngang, huyền, hỏi, ngã, sắc, nặng" diacritical order.

# Bibliography

Agrawal, Arun and Jesse Ribot. *Analyzing Decentralization: A Framework with South Asian and West African Environmental Cases*. Working Paper, 2000.

Aikawa, Noriko. "An Historical Overview of the Preparation of the UNESCO International Convention for the Safeguarding of the Intangible Cultural Heritage." *Museum International* 56.1–2 (2004): 137–49.

Allina-Pisano, J. *The Post-Soviet Potemkin Village: Politics and Property Rights in the Black Earth*. New York: Cambridge University Press, 2008.

Asian Development Bank. "The Impact of Land Markets on the Poor: Implementing de Soto." Hanoi: Making Markets Work Better for the Poor Discussion Paper 3, 2004.

Balme, Stephanie and Mark Sidel (eds). *Vietnam's New Order: International Perspectives on the State and Reform in Vietnam*. New York: Palgrave Macmillan, 2007.

Ban chap hanh nong hoi xa va cac to truong doi cuong, nong hoi (BCHNHX). *Duoi su lanh dao cua Dang Lao dong Viet Nam nong dan Ta Ngan quyet tam tien manh tren con duong doi cong hop tac (Tai lieu hoc tap cua Ban chap hanh nong hoi xa va cac to truong doi cong, nong hoi)*. n.a.: HTX An loat doan ket, 1958.

Ban Lien lac nong dan toan quoc (BLLNDTQ). *Van dong san xuat sau Cai cach ruong dat*. Hanoi: Tien Bo, 1956.

Ban Thuy loi (Van phong). *Du thao Bao cao tong ket cong tac thuy loi 10 nam (1954–1964) cua Bo Thuy loi*. (H.s. 53 v/v).

Ban Tuyen huan Uy ban Cai cach ruong dat Khu Ta Ngan (BTHUBCCRDKTN). *Ruong ve ta (Tho ca phat dong)*. KTN: BTHUBCCRD, 1956.

Bao Dau tu. *Co dau hieu "chay" quy hoach o nut giao thong Thanh Xuan*. 2006. Online at: http://dantri.com.vn/c0/s0-137648/co-dau-hieu-chay-quy-hoach-o-nut-giao-thong-thanh-xuan.htm.

Barfield, Owen. *History, Guilt, and Habit*. Middletown: Wesleyan University Press, 1979.

Benjamin, Walter. "Theses on the Philosophy of History," in *Illuminations*, Hannah Arendt (ed.). London: Pimlico, 1999.

Berlin, Brent. *Ethnobiological Classification: Principles of Categorization of Plants and Animals in Traditional Societies*. Princeton: Princeton University Press, 1992.

Bernard, Paul. *Le Problème économique indochinois*. Paris: Nouvelles Editions Latines, 1934.

Biggs, David. *Quagmire: Nation Building and Nature in the Mekong Delta*. Seattle: Washington, 2011.

Biggs, David. "Aerial Photography and Colonial Discourse on the Agricultural Crisis in Late-Colonial Indochina, 1930–1945," in *Cultivating the Colonies: Colonial States and their Environmental Legacies*. Ax *et al.* (eds). Athens: Ohio University Press, 2011.

*Binh Minh*, 17 July 1945 and 2 August 1945.

Bo Thuy loi Kien truc (BTLKT). *Tap tai lieu ve Hoi nghi tong ket cong tac dap de chong lut nam 1955 cua Bo Thuy loi va Kien truc (27/11/1955)*. (H.s. 22)

Bo Thuy loi Kien truc (BTLKT). *Bao cao Bo Thuy loi Kien truc Phong quan ly cong trinh va cuc cong trinh thuy loi ve cong tac thuy nong de dieu nam 1956.* (H.s. 61, v/v).

Bo Thuy loi Kien truc (Quan ly cong trinh). *Bao cao cua Ban chi huy chong lut Hung Yen, Hai Duong ve cong tac de dieu, chong lut, bao nam 1956 (28/5/1956–12/12/1956).* (H.s. 74, v/v).

Bo Thuy loi Kien truc (Van phong). *Bien ban Hoi nghi kiem diem viec thuc hien ke hoach thuy loi va kien truc trong 3 thang dau nam 1956 (6/4/1956–10/4/1956).* (H.s. 28, v/v).

Bo Thuy loi Kien truc (Van phong). *Tap Bao cao cua BLTKT tong ket 3 nam cong tac thuy loi (1955–1957) phuc vu ke hoach khoi phuc kinh te (22/10/1957–2/11/1957).* (H.s. 87, v/v).

Bo Thuy loi va Kien truc (BTLKT). *Cong tac lanh dao chong han (Tong ket thanh tich, uu khuyet diem, kinh nghiem lanh dao chong han trong vu chiem nam 1956).* Hanoi: BTLKT, 1957a.

Bo Thuy loi va Kien truc (BTLKT). *Kinh nghiem cong tac phong chong ung nam 1956 va nhiem vu nam 1957.* Hanoi: BTLKT, 1957b.

Bowd, Gavin and Clayton, Daniel. "Tropicality, Orientalism and French Colonialism in Indochina: The Work of Pierre Gourou, 1927–1982." *French Historical Studies*, 28.2 (2005): 297–327.

Brocheux, Pierre. *The Mekong Delta: Ecology, Economy and Revolution, 1860–1960.* Madison WI: University of Wisconsin Press, 1995.

Browne, Malcolm W. "Scientists Hope More New Species Will Be Discovered in Vietnam." *New York Times* (3 May 1994).

Browne, Malcolm W. "Vietnam Finds First Live Example of Rare Ox." *New York Times* (23 June 1994).

Bui Duc Tinh. *Nhung Buoc dau cua bao chi truyen ngan tieu thuyet va tho moi, 1865–1932.* HCM City: TP HCM, 2002.

Bui Ngoc Son. "Su doc lap cua toa an trong Nha nuoc phap quyen." *Tap chi Nghien cuu Luat phap* (2003.4): 43–50.

Bui Trong Hien. "Khong gian van hoa—cac chuc nang van hoa xa hoi va nhung hinh thuc bieu hien cua nghe thuat," in *Dac khao ca tru Viet Nam.* Hanoi: Vien am nhac Viet Nam, 2006: 59–107.

Bui Van Thanh. "*Bao cao khai quat lich su va phuong huong bao ton, phat huy di tich lich su Can Cu dia cach Mang U Minh Thuong Kien Giang,*" in *Ky yeu Hoi thao khoa hoc: Di tich lich su Can Cu Dia Cach mang U Minh Thuong.* Kien Giang: Kien Giang, 2001.

Burawoy, Michael and Katherine Verdery (eds). *Uncertain Transition: Ethnographies of Change in the Postsocialist World.* Lanham: Rowman and Littlefield, 1999.

Callison, Charles Stuart. *The Land-to-the-Tiller Program and Rural Resource Mobilization in the Mekong Delta of South Vietnam.* Athens, Ohio: Ohio University Center for International Studies, 1974.

Cellarius, Barbara. "Property Restitution and Natural Resource Use in the Rhodope Mountains, Bulgaria," in *The Postsocialist Agrarian Question: Property Relations and the Rural Conditions*, Chris Hann (ed.). Münster: Lit Verlag, 2003.

Chi Hieu. "Chinh phu dong y nut giao Thanh Xuan!" Online at: http://vietnamnet.vn/xahoi/2008/06/787651/ (retrieved 10 June 2008).

Chieu, Gilbert. "Une bataille intéressante." Supplément du *Nong-Co Min-Dam* (23 October 1907): 1.

Clayton, Daniel and Gavin Bowd. "Fieldwork and Tropicality in French Indochina: Reflections on Pierre Gourou's Les Paysans du Delta Tonkinois, 1936." *Singapore Journal of Tropical Geography* 24.2 (2003): 147–68.

Coleman, James S. "Social Capital in the Creation of Human Capital." *American Journal of Sociology* 94 (1988): S95–S120.

Comaroff, Jean and John Comaroff. *Of Revelation and Revolution: Christianity, Colonialism and Consciousness in South Africa.* Vol. 1. Chicago and London: University of Chicago Press, 1991.

Commission permanente du 19 Juillet 1927. "L'Inspection générale du travail." *Tribune Indochinoise* (24 August 1927): 3.

Condominas, Georges. *Nous avons mangé la forêt de la Pierre-Génie Goo (Hii saa Brii Mau-Yaang Goo). Chronique de Sar Luk, village mnong gar (tribu proto-indochinoise, des Hauts-Plateaux du Vietnam central).* Paris: Mercure de France, 1957.

Condominas, Georges. *L'Exotique est quotidien.* Paris: Plon, 1965.

Condominas, Georges. "Introduction," in *Viet Nam's Cultural Diversity: Approaches to Preservation*, Oscar Salemink (ed.). Paris: UNESCO Publishing (Memory of Peoples), 2001, pp. 15–32.

Condominas, Georges. "Researching and Safeguarding the Intangible Heritage." *Museum International* 56.1–2 (2004): 21–31.

Constitution of the Democratic Republic of Vietnam, 1946.

Constitution of the Democratic Republic of Vietnam, 1959.

Constitution of the Socialist Republic of Vietnam, 1980.

Constitution of the Socialist Republic of Vietnam, 1992.

Constitution of the Socialist Republic of Vietnam, 1992 (revised 2001).

D. Tr (2004) "Cap so do va chuyen nhuong: Thu tuc ra sao, bao lau?" *Tuoi Tre Online*, 3 November 2004, http://www.tuoitre.com.vn.

Dahles, Heidi. *Tourism, Heritage and National Culture in Java: Dilemmas of a Local Community.* Richmond, UK: Curzon Press, 2001.

*Dai Viet Su Ky Toan Thu.* Hanoi: Khoa hoc xa hoi, 1998, 4 vols.

Dang Hoanh Loan. "Introduction," in *Dac khao ca tru Viet Nam.* Hanoi: Vien Am nhac Viet Nam, 2006.

Dang Nguyen Anh, Cecila Tacoli and Xuan Thanh Hoang. "Migration in Vietnam – A Review of Information on Currents Trends and Patterns, and Their Policy Implications," in *Regional Conference on Migration, Development and Pro-Poor Policy Choices in Asia.* Dhaka: 2003.

Dang Phong (ed.). *Lich su kinh te Viet Nam 1945–2000 (Tap II: 1954–1975).* Hanoi: Khoa hoc xa hoi, 2005.

Dau Tu. "Nut giao thong Thanh Xuan: Co dau hieu 'chay' quy hoach?" Online at http:// www. monre.gov. vn/ monreNet/ default. aspx? tabid= 210andidmid =andItemID=16798.

De Rhodes, Alexandre. *Dictionarium Annamiticum, Lusitanum y Latinum.* Rome: Propaganda Fide, 1651.

De Soto, Hernando. *The Mystery of Capital. Why Capitalism Triumphs in the West and Fails Everywhere Else.* London: Black Swan, 2000.

De Waal, C. "Post-socialist Property Rights and Wrongs in Albania. An Ethnography of Agrarian Change." *Conservation and Society* 2 (2004): 19–50.

Demsetz, Harold. "Toward a Theory of Property Rights II." *Journal of Legal Studies* 31.2 (Part 2), (2002): 653–72.

Devillers, Philippe. *Histoire du Viet-Nam de 1940 à 1952.* Paris: Editions du Seuil, 1952.

DiGregorio, Michael. "Things Held in Common: Memory, Space and the Reconstitution of Community Life." *Journal of Southeast Asian Studies* 38.3 (2007): 441–65.

DiGregorio, Michael and Oscar Salemink. "Living with the Dead: The Politics of Ritual and Remembrance in Contemporary Vietnam." *Journal of Southeast Asian Studies* 38.3 (2007): 433–40.

Dinh Huu Hoang and Dang Kim Son. *Forestland Allocation in Vietnam: From Policy to Reality.* National Workshop on Forestland Consolidation, Ha Long, 2007.

Dinh mon bi ky 亭門碑記, Ms. 1585–86.

Dinh mon cac le bi ky, 亭門各例碑記, Ms. 6888.

Dinh mon su le bi ky, 亭門事例碑記, Ms. 1628–29.

Dinh mon su le 亭門事例, Ms. 1634–5.

Dinh tien van khet hac bi, 亭錢文契碩碑, Ms. 2701–02.

Do Bang Doan and Do Trong Hue, *Viet Nam ca tru bien khao*. Saigon: 1962.

Do Dinh Sam. *Shifting Cultivation in Vietnam: Its Social, Economic and Environmental Values Relative to Alternative Land Use*. IIED Forestry and Land Use Series No. 3. London: International Institute for Environment and Development (IIED), 1994.

Do Quy-Toan and Lakshmi Iyer. "Land Titling and Rural Transition in Vietnam." *Economic Development and Cultural Change* 56.3 (2008): 531–79.

Do Xuan Loi. "Role of Mediation in Judgment Enforcement." *Democracy and Law* (2005): 44–5.

Doan mai dinh tru lenh tien, 斷買亭籌例錢, Ms. 6897–98.

Doan Trang. "Giai toa tren 3.800 can ho." *Viet Bao*, 28 October 2005. Online at http://vietbao.vn/Xa-hoi/Giai-toa-tren-3.800-can-ho/40105250/157/.

Duara, Prasenjit. "The Regime of Authenticity: Timelessness, Gender and National History in Modern China." *History and Theory* 37.3 (1998): 287–308.

Duc Hoa. "Ban an ach 10 nam vi mot lanh dao TP Hanoi." *Dan Tri*, 4 July 2006. Online at http://baotonghop.net/index.php?doc=/c20/s20-127270/ban-an-ach-gan-10-nam-vi-mot-lanh-dao-tp-ha-noi.htm; http://vietbao.vn/Xa-hoi/Ban-an-ach-gan-10-nam-vi-mot-lanh-dao-TP-Ha-Noi/30127270/157/.

Duc Trung. TP Ho Chi Minh mo rong duong Nguyen Van Troi – Nam Ky Khoi Nghia. *Viet Bao*, 15 September 2004. Online at http://vietbao.vn/Xa-hoi/TP-Ho-Chi-Minh-mo-rong-duong-Nguyen-Van-Troi-Nam-Ky-Khoi-Nghia-Gan-300-ti-dong-km-duong-van-chua-on/45112067/157.

Dutton, George. *The Tay Son Uprising: Society and Rebellion in Eighteenth-Century Vietnam*. Honolulu: University of Hawai'i Press, 2008.

Ellickson, Robert. "Property in Law." *Yale Law Journal* 102.6 (1993): 1315–400.

Eriksen, Thomas Hylland. "In Which Sense Do Cultural Islands Exist?" *Social Anthropology* 1.1 (1993): 133–47.

Eriksen, Thomas Hylland. "Between Universalism and Relativism: A Critique of the UNESCO Concepts of Culture," in *Culture and Rights: Anthropological Perspectives*, Jane K. Cowan *et al.* (eds). Cambridge: Cambridge University Press, 2001, pp. 133–47.

Evans, Graeme. "Mundo Maya: From Cancun to City of Culture. World Heritage in Post-Colonial Meso-America," in *The Politics of World Heritage: Negotiating Tourism and Conservation*, David Harrison and Michael Hitchcock (eds). Clevedon, UK: Channel View Publications, 2005, pp. 35–49.

Evertsz, Helen. *Popular Housing in Hanoi*. Hanoi: Cultural Publishing House, 2000.

Fabian, Johannes. *Time and the Other: How Anthropology Makes its Object*. New York: Columbia University Press, 1983.

Fall, Bernard B. *The Viet-Minh Regime: Government and Administration in the Democratic Republic of Vietnam*. Westport: Greenwood Press, 1956.

Feder, Gershon and Akihiko Nishio. "The Benefits of Land Registration and Titling: Economic and Social Perspectives." *Land Use Policy* 15.1 (1999): 25–43.

Fforde, Adam and Stephan de Vylder. *From Plan to Market: Economic Transition in Vietnam 1979–1994*. Boulder: Westview Press, 1996.

Follett, Wilbur Irving. *An Unofficial Interpretation of the International Rules of Zoological Nomenclature: As Amended by the XIII International Congress of Zoology, Paris 1948 and by the XIV International Congress of Zoology, Copenhagen 1953*. Unpublished paper distributed by the Society of Systematic Zoology.

Foucault, Michel. "What is an Author?" in *Textual Strategies: Perspectives in Post-Structuralist Criticism*, Josue Harari (ed.). Ithaca: Cornell University Press, 1979, pp. 141–60.

Gainsborough, M. "Corruption and the Politics of Economic Decentralization in Vietnam." *Journal of Contemporary Asia* 33, (2003): 69–84.

Galla, Aamareswar. "Museum and Heritage in Development: Ha Long Ecomuseum, a Case Study from Vietnam." *Humanities Research* IX.1 (2002): 63–76.

Gatesy, John and Peter Arctander. "Hidden Morphological Support for the Phylogenetic Placement of *Pseudoryx nghetinhensis* with Bovine Bovids: A Combined Analysis of Gross Anatomical Evidence and DNA Sequences from Five Genes." *Systematic Biology* 49.3 (Sep. 2000): 515–38.

Giao phuong bi ky, 教坊碑記, Ms. 1041.

Giao phuong bi ky, 教坊碑記, Ms. 1587.

Giao phuong khac bi ky, 教坊剋碑記, Ms. 6889–90.

Gilbert, A. "On the Mystery of Capitalism and the Myths of Hernando de Soto: What Difference Does Legal Title Make." *International Planning Review* 24 (2002): 1–19.

Gillespie, John. "Rethinking the Role of Judicial Independence in Socialist-Transforming East Asia." *International Comparative Law Quarterly* 56.3 (2007): 837–70.

Gotthelf, Allan (ed.). *Aristotle on Nature and Living Things; Philosophical and Historical Studies: Presented to David M. Balme on his Seventieth Birthday*. Pittsburgh: Mathesis Publications, 1985.

Gourou, Pierre. *Les Paysans du delta tonkinois: Etude de géographie humaine*. Paris: Les Editions d'art et d'histoire, 1936.

Gray, Michael. "Creating Civil Society? The Emergence of NGOs in Vietnam." *Development and Change* 30 (1999): 693–713.

Greene, Graham. "The Destructors," in *Collected Stories*. London: The Bodley Head and William Heinemann, 1967, pp. 327–46.

Grossheim, Martin. "Village Government in Pre-Colonial and Colonial Vietnam," in *Beyond Hanoi: Local Government in Vietnam.* Benedict J. Kerkvliet and David G. Marr (eds). Singapore: Institute of Southeast Asian Studies, 2004, pp. 54–89.

Ha Ke Tan. *Phat trien manh cong tac thuy loi*. Hanoi: Su that, 1964.

Ha Lan. *Cai cach ruong dat o cac nuoc dan chu nhan dan.* No. 5 Liberated Territory: Su that, 1953.

Haines, D.W. *The Limits of Kinship: South Vietnamese Households, 1954–1975*. DeKalb: Southeast Asia Publications, Northern Illinois University, 2006.

Han, Xiaorong. "The Present Echoes of the Ancient Bronze Drum: Nationalism and Archeology in Modern Vietnam and China." *Explorations in Southeast Asian Studies* 2.2 (1998).

Han, Xiaorong. "Who Invented the Bronze Drum? Nationalism, Politics, and a Sino-Vietnamese Archaeological Debate of the 1970s and 1980s." *Asian Perspectives* 43.3 (2004): 7–33.

Hann, Chris. "Property Relations in the New Eastern Europe: The Case of Specialist Cooperatives in Hungary," in *The Curtain Rises: Rethinking Culture, Ideology, and the State in Eastern Europe.* Hermine G. De Soto and David G. Anderson (eds). Humanities Press, 1993, pp. 99–119.

Hann, Chris (ed.). *Property Relations: Renewing the Anthropological Tradition.* Cambridge: Cambridge University Press, 1998.

Hann, Chris. "Introduction: the Embeddedness of Property," Chapter 1 in *Property Relations: Renewing the Anthropological Tradition*, Christopher Hann (ed.). Cambridge: Cambridge University Press, 1998, pp. 1–47.

Hann, Chris. "Postsocialism." Draft prepared for *Handbook on Economic Anthropology, 2003.*

*Hanoi Ban do hanh chinh.* Vien Nghien cuu phat trien kinh te – xa hoi Hanoi, 2007. Online at http:// www.thudo. hanoi.gov.vn/ eco/jsp/subCategoryListing.jsp? subCategoryID=3.

Hardcastle, James (ed.), *Rediscovering the Saola: Proceedings of the Workshop "Rediscovering the Saola: A Status Review and Conservation Planning Workshop."* Hanoi: WWF Indochina Programme, 2004.

Harms, Erik. *Saigon's Edge: On the Margins of Ho Chi Minh City*. Minneapolis: University of Minnesota Press, 2011.

Harrison, David. "Contested Narratives in the Domain of World Heritage," in *The Politics of World Heritage: Negotiating Tourism and Conservation*, David Harrison and Michael Hitchcock (eds). Clevedon, UK: Channel View Publications, 2005, pp. 1–10.

Harrison, David and Michael Hitchcock (eds). *The Politics of World Heritage: Negotiating Tourism and Conservation*. Clevedon, UK: Channel View Publications, 2005.

Harvey, David. "The City as Body Politic," in *Wounded Cities: Destruction and Reconstruction in a Globalized World*, Jane Schneider and Ida Susser (eds). New York: Berg, 2003, pp. 25–46.

Hassanin, Alexandre and Emmanuel J. P. Douzery. "Evolutionary affinities of the enigmatic saola (*Pseudoryx nghetinhensis*) in the context of the molecular phylogeny of Bovidae." The Royal Society, *Proceedings: Biological Sciences*, vol. 266, no. 1422 (May 7, 1999): 893–900.

Hayton, Bill. "A sharp knife, but not too sharp." *Vietnam: Rising Dragon*. New Haven, CT: Yale University Press, 2010.

Heng, Russell Hiang-Khng. "Civil Society Effectiveness and the Vietnamese State – Despite or Because of the Lack of Autonomy," in *Civil Society in Southeast Asia,* Lee Hock Guan (ed.). Singapore: Institute of Southeast Asian Studies, 2004, pp. 144–66.

Henry, Yves. *Economie agricole de l'Indochine française*. Hanoi: Gouvernement général de l'Indochine, 1932.

Hernandez-Fernandez M. and E.S. Vrba. "A Complete Estimate of the Phylogenetic Relationships in Ruminantia: A Dated Species-level Supertree of the Extant Ruminants." *Biological Review* 80 (2005): 269–302.

Hess, Carla. "Enlightenment Epistemology and the Laws of Authorship in Revolutionary France, 1777–1793," *Representations* 30 (1990): 109–37.

Hess, Carla. "The Rise of Intellectual Property, 700 BC–AD 2000: An Idea in the Balance." *Daedalus* 131:2 (Spring 2002): 26–45.

Hickey, Gerald Cannon. *Village in Vietnam*. New Haven: Yale University Press, 1965.

Hitchcock, Michael. "Afterword," in *The Politics of World Heritage: Negotiating Tourism and Conservation.* David Harrison and Michael Hitchcock (eds). Clevedon, UK: Channel View Publications, 2005, pp. 181–6.

Ho, Samuel and George Lin. "Emerging Land Markets in Rural and Urban China: Policies and Practices." *The China Quarterly* 175 (2003): 681–707.

Hoai Nam. "Gan 1.000 ha dan bi day ra duong do du an giai toa – tai dinh cu." 8 August 2006. Online at http://vietbao.vn/Xa-hoi/Gan-1.000-ho-dan-bi-day-ra-duong-do-du-an-giai-toa-tai-dinh-cu/45203767/157/.

Hoang Ngoc Khanh. "Saola Conservation in Thua-Thien Hue Province," in *Rediscovering the Saola: Proceedings of the Workshop "Rediscovering the Saola: A Status Review and Conservation Planning Workshop,"* James Hardcastle (ed.). Hanoi: WWF Indochina Programme, 2004.

Hoang Quoc Viet. "Can dam bao cho phap luat duoc ton trong trong cong tac quan ly kinh te cua Nha nuoc," in *Nghien cuu Nha nuoc va phap quyen.* Hanoi: Su that, 1964, pp. 31–41.

Hoang Tao. "Bat on trong cong tac den bu giai toa du an Dai lo Dong Tay." *Viet Bao*, Originally from Thanh Nien, 11 September 2005. Online at http://vietbao.vn/Trang-ban-doc/Bat-on-trong-cong-tac-den-bu-giai-toa-du-an-Dai-lo-Dong-Tay/45167770/478/.

Hobsbawm, Eric and Terence O. Ranger (eds). *The Invention of Tradition.* Cambridge: Cambridge University Press, 1983.

Hooker, Michael Barry. *A Concise Legal History of South East Asia.* Oxford: Oxford University Press, 1978.

HT. Thich Tri Quang. "Giai toa oan uc." Online at http://phattuvietnam.net/4/23/4778.html. 2008.

Human Rights Watch. *Repression of Montagnards: Conflicts over Land and Religion in Vietnam's Central Highlands*. New York: Human Rights Watch, 2002.

Human Rights Watch. *On the Margins: Rights Abuses of Ethnic Khmer in Vietnam's Mekong Delta*. New York: Human Rights Watch, 2009.

Huy Thinh. "Khuat tat dang sau du an doc kenh Nhieu Loc – Thi Nghe." *Viet Bao*, 28 June 2007. Online at http://vietbao.vn/Xa-hoi/Khuat-tat-dang-sau-du-an-doc-kenh-Nhieu-Loc-Thi-Nghe/70089969/157/.

Huynh Yen Tram My, Truong Vu Quynh, Nguyen Dong Hieu (eds). *Nhung di san the gioi o Viet Nam*. Da Nang: Da Nang, 2007.

International Commission on Zoological Nomenclature. *Opinions and Declarations Rendered by the International Commission on Zoological Nomenclature*. 20 vols, 1943–59. London: International Trust for Zoological Nomenclature.

International Commission on Zoological Nomenclature. Online at http://www.iczn.org/iczn/index.jsp. The ICZN Code. 4th ed., Jan. 2000.

Ivy, Marilyn. *Discourses of the Vanishing: Modernity, Phantasms, Japan*. Chicago: University of Chicago Press, 1995.

Jennings, Eric T. *Vichy in the Tropics: Pétain's National Revolution in Madagascar, Guadeloupe and Indochina, 1940–1944*. Stanford: Stanford University Press, 2001.

Jensen, Erik. "The Rule of Law and Judicial Reform: The Political Economy of Diverse Institutional Patterns and Reformers' Responses," in *Beyond Common Knowledge: Empirical Approaches to the Rule of Law*. Erik Jensen and Thomas Heller (eds). Stanford: Stanford University Press, 2003, pp. 336–81.

JICA. *Nghien cuu chung Viet-Nhat ve viec phat trien an le tai Viet Nam*. Hanoi: Supreme People's Court, 2007.

Kerkvliet, Benedict J.T. *Land Struggles and Land Regimes in the Philippines and Vietnam during the Twentieth Century*. Wertheim Lecture. Amsterdam: Centre for Asian Studies Amsterdam, 1997.

Kerkvliet, Benedict J.T. "Accelerating Cooperatives in Rural Vietnam, 1955–1961," in *Vietnamese Villages in Transition*, Bernhard Dahm and Vincent Houben (eds). Passau, Germany: Passau University, 1999: 53–88.

Kerkvliet, Benedict J.T. "An Approach for Analyzing State-Society Relations in Vietnam." *SOJOURN: Journal of Social Issues in Southeast Asia*, 16.2 (2001): 238–78.

Kerkvliet, Benedict J.T. *The Power of Everyday Politics: How Vietnamese Peasants Transformed National Policy*. Ithaca: Cornell University Press; Singapore: ISEAS, 2005.

Kerkvliet, Benedict J.T. "Agricultural Land in Vietnam: Markets Tempered by Family, Community and Socialist Practices." *Journal of Agrarian Change* 6.3 (2006): 285–305.

Kerkvliet, Benedict J.T. and David Marr (eds). *Beyond Hanoi: Local Government in Vietnam*. Singapore: Institute for Southeast Asian Studies, 2004.

Keyes, Charles F. "Ethnicity, ethnic group," in *The Dictionary of Anthropology*, Thomas J. Barfield (ed.). Oxford: Blackwell, 1997, pp. 152–4.

Keyes, Charles F. "Presidential Address: The Peoples of Asia – Science and Politics in the Classification of Ethnic Groups in Thailand, China, and Vietnam." *Journal of Asian Studies* 61.4 (2002): 1163–203.

Khanh Van. "Cai cach tu phap: Nhin tu nhieu goc do." *Tap chi Nghien cuu Lap phap* 4 (2003): 3–8.

Kien Cuong. "Duong 'ngoai giao' cua TP HCM se hoan thanh vao cuoi nam." Online at *VnExpress*, 5 March 2009. Online at http://vnexpress.net/GL/Xa-hoi/2009/03/3BA0C995/.

Kim, Annette. "A Market without the 'Right' Property Rights." *Economics of Transition* 12:2 (2004): 275–305.

Kim, Annette. *Learning to be Capitalists: Entrepreneurs in Vietnam's Transition Economy*. New York: Oxford University Press, 2008.

Kim Em and Dang Nam. "'Choi nghe thuat' cho giai toa." *Viet Bao*, 8 November 2004. Online at http://vietbao.vn/Phong-su/Choi-nghe-thuat-cho-giai-toa/40054729/263/.

"Kinh te: Quy che so huu cua chung ta," *Xa Hoi*, July 1953, 4.

Koh, David W.H. "Urban Government: Ward-Level Administration in Hanoi," in *Beyond Hanoi: Local Government in Vietnam*, Benedict J. Kerkvliet and David G. Marr (eds). Singapore: ISEAS Publications, 2004: 197–229.

Koh, David W.H. "Illegal Construction in Hanoi and Hanoi's Wards." *European Journal of East Asian Studies* 3.2 (2004): 337–69.

Koh, David W.H. *Wards of Hanoi*. Singapore: ISEAS Publications, 2006.

Koh, Priscilla. "Persistent Ambiguities: Vietnamese Ethnology in the Doi Moi Period (1986–2001)." *Explorations in Southeast Asian Studies* 2.2 (2004). Online at http://www.hawaii.edu/cseas/pubs/explore/vol5no2.html.

Kurin, Richard. "Safeguarding Intangible Cultural Heritage in the 2003 UNESCO Convention: A Critical Appraisal." *Museum International* 56.1–2 (2004): 66–77.

"La Grève des ouvriers et coolies de la Société des Dragages à Mytho." *La Lutte* (7 April 1938): 4.

"La Révolte des 'Ta-dien'." *La Tribune Indochinoise* (6 May 1938): 1.

Lampland, Martha. *The Object of Labor: Commodification in Socialist Hungary*. Chicago: University of Chicago Press, 1995.

Lan Huong. "Giai phong mat bang, thi cong duong Vanh dai 3, Quan Thanh Xuan: Cuong che dut diem them 15 chu su dung dat." Hanoi Moi. Online at http://www.hanoimoi.com.vn/newsdetail/quy_hoach/220715/c4327905ng-ch7871-d7913t-273i787-5m-them-15-ch7911-s7917-d7909ng-2737845t.htm.

Lap giao phuong bi ky, 立教坊碑記, Ms. 6400–01.

Lap khoan xuong nhi ky, 立券唱兒記, Ms. 1962.

Larson, Anne M., and Jesse C. Ribot (eds). *Democratic Decentralisation through a Natural Resource Lens*. Special issue of *European Journal of Development Research* 16.1 (2004).

Lask, Tomke and Stefan Herold. "An Observation Station for Culture and Tourism in Vietnam: A Forum for World Heritage and Public Participation," in *The Politics of World Heritage: Negotiating Tourism and Conservation*, David Harrison and Michael Hitchcock (eds). Clevedon, UK: Channel View Publications, 2005: 119–31.

Le Duc Tho. *Van de can bo trong giai doan Cach mang moi*. Hanoi: NXB Su that, 1961.

Le Duy Hung. "Some Issues of Fixed Cultivation and Sedentarization of Ethnic Minority People in Mountainous Areas of Vietnam," in *The Challenges of Highland Development in Vietnam*, Terry Rambo, Robert Reed, Le Trong Cuc and Michael DiGregorio (eds). Honolulu: East West Center, 1995.

Le Hong Hanh. *Giao trinh ly luan Nha nuoc va phap luat*. Hanoi: Cong an Nhan dan, 1998.

Le Hong Ly and Hue-Tam Ho Tai, "The Revenge of the Object: Villagers and Ethnographers in Dong Ky Village," *Asian Ethnology*, 67:2 (November 2008): 323–43.

Le Ngoc Chan. "Quan Ho Singing in North Vietnam: A Yearning for Resolution." PhD Dissertation, University of California, Berkeley, 2002.

Le Ngoc Chan. "Quan Ho Singing in Ritual-festivals in Bac Ninh Region (Vietnam)." http://home.vicnet.net.au/~aaf/quanho.htm.

Le Quang Liem. "La Vérité sur l'échauffourée de Ninh-Thanh-Loi (Rachgia)." *Tribune Indochinoise* (20 May 1927): 1–2.

Le Quy Quynh. *May kinh nghiem lam thuy loi cua Hung Yen*. Hanoi: NXB Nong thon, 1966.

Lefebvre, Henri. *The Production of Space*. Oxford: Blackwell, 1991.

Lessig, Lawrence. "The Regulation of Social Meaning." *University of Chicago Law Review* 62.3 (1995): 943–1045.

Li, Tania Murray. *The Will to Improve: Governmentality, Development, and the Practice of Politics*. Durham: Duke University Press, 2007.

Lin, Nan. "Social Networks and Status Attainment." *Annual Review of Sociology* 25 (1999): 467–87.

Lockhart, Bruce. "Re-assessing the Nguyen Dynasty." *Crossroads* 15.1 (2001): 9–53.

Long, Colin. "Feudalism in the Service of the Revolution: Reclaiming Heritage in Hue." *Critical Asian Studies* 35.4 (2004): 535–58.

Low, Setha M. "Spatializing Culture: The Social Production and Social Construction of Public Space in Costa Rica." *American Ethnologist*. 23.4 (1996): 861–879.

Luc giap lap mai le bi, 六甲立買例碑, Ms. 6557–58.

Lund, C. *Local Politics and the Dynamics of Property in Africa*. Cambridge: Cambridge University Press, 2008.

Luu truyen van dai, 流傳萬代, Ms. 1977–78.

McElwee, Pam. "The Nature of a Beast: Endangered Species Protection and Environmental Conservation in Vietnam." Unpublished paper, 1st Place, Atlantic Monthly Student Writers Awards, 1998.

McElwee, Pam. "Does Vietnam have 'Indigenous Knowledge'?" Forthcoming in *Modernities and Dynamics of Tradition in Vietnam: Anthropological Approaches*, Hy Van Luong (ed.). Singapore: National University of Singapore Press, forthcoming.

McGee, Terry. "The Urban Future of Vietnam." *Third World Planning Review* 3 (1995): 253–77.

McHale, Shawn. *Print and Power: Confucianism, Communism, and Buddhism in the Making of Modern Vietnam*. Honolulu: University of Hawai'i Press, 2004.

MacLean, Ken. "The Arts of Disclosure: Peasant-Bureaucrats, Historiography, and State Socialism in Vietnam." PhD Dissertation, University of Michigan (Ann Arbor), 2005.

MacLean, Ken. "Manifest Socialism: The Labor of Representation in the Democratic Republic of Vietnam (1956–1959)." *Journal of Vietnamese Studies* 2:1 (2007): 27–79.

MacLean, Ken. "The Rehabilitation of an Uncomfortable Past: Remembering the Everyday in Vietnam during the Subsidy Period (1975–1986)." *History and Anthropology* 19:3 (2008): 281–303.

MacLean, Ken. "Audit Regimes and the Rituals of Compliance in Contemporary Vietnam." Global Socialisms and Postsocialisms: An International Symposium, Yale University, 25 April 2009.

McNeely, Jeffrey A. and Paul Spencer Wachtel. *Soul of the Tiger: Searching for Nature's Answers in Exotic Southeast Asia*. New York: Doubleday, 1988.

Mai Khanh. "TP Ho Chi Minh: Dan hien dat, gop tien lam duong." *Viet Bao (Thanh Nien)*, 6 May 2004. Online at http://vietbao.vn/Xa-hoi/TP-Ho-Chi-Minh-Dan-hien-dat-gop-tien-lam-duong/45110836/157/.

Mai dinh mon bi ky, 買亭門碑記, Ms. 569 and 576.

Mai tru van khe chi bi, 買籌文契之碑, Ms. 2689.

Mai tru van khe chi bi, 買籌文契之碑, Ms. 3280.

Malarney, Shaun K. "Festivals and the Politics of the Exceptional Dead in Vietnam." *Journal of Southeast Asian Studies* 38.3 (2007): 515–40.

Manders, Jonathon. "Sequencing Property Rights in the Context of Development: A Critique of the Writings of Hernando de Soto." *Cornell International Law Journal* 37 (2004): 177–98.

Marr, David. "History and Memory in Vietnam Today: The Journal *Xua va Nay*." *Journal of Southeast Asian Studies* 31.1 (2000): 1–25.

Matthews, Jane Glenn and V. Belanger. "Informal Law in Informal Settlements," in *Law and Geography,* J. Holder and C. Harrison (eds). Oxford: Oxford University Press, 2003: 281–304.

Meeker, Lauren. "Musical Transmissions: Folk Music, Meditation, and Modernity in Northern Vietnam." PhD Dissertation, Columbia University, 2007.

Merryman, John. "Two Ways of Thinking about Cultural Property." *The American Journal of International Law* 80:4 (Oct. 1986): 831–53.

Merryman, John. *The Civil Law Tradition*, 3rd ed. Stanford: Stanford University Press, 2007.

Miller, Edward. "Vision, Power and Agency: The Ascent of Ngo Dinh Diem, 1945–54." *Journal of Southeast Asian Studies*, 35.3 (2004): 433–58.

Minh Duc. "Lech thiet ke hay lech ca..." Vietnam Television Agency, 2006. Online at http://www.vtv.vn/VN/TrangChu/TinTuc/VTV1/TieuDiem/2006/9/21/39406/.

Minh Nam. "Hien dat mo duong." *Thanh Nien*, 3 May 2009. Online at http://www.thanhnien.com.vn/News/Pages/200918/20090503234811.aspx.

Ministry of Culture, Sports and Tourism of Viet Nam. "Ca Tru intangible cultural heritage gradually penetrating into the current and future life." Online at http://english.cinet.vn/CultureAndInformationDetail.aspx?zoneid=2andnewsid=6761.

Mitchell, Timothy. "*Society, Economy, and the State Effect*," in *State/Culture*, George Steinmetz (ed.). Ithaca: Cornell University Press, 1999: 76–97.

Moise, Edwin E. *Land Reform in China and North Vietnam*. Chapel Hill: University of North Carolina Press, 1983.

Munjeri, Dawson. "Tangible and Intangible Heritage: From Difference to Convergence." *Museum International* 56.1–2 (2004): 12–20.

Murray, Martin. *The Development of Capitalism in Colonial Indochina (1870–1940)*. Berkeley: University of California Press, 1980.

Nas, Peter J. M. *et al.* "Masterpieces of Oral and Intangible Culture: Reflections on the UNESCO World Heritage List (with comments by HRH Princess Basma Bint Talal and others and reply by Peter J.M. Nas)." *Current Anthropology* 43.1 (2002): 139–48.

Ngo Duc Thinh and Phan Dang Nhat (eds). *Luat tuc va phat trien nong thon hien nay o Viet Nam (Ky yeu hoi thao khoa hoc)*. Hanoi: NXB Chinh tri Quoc gia, 1999.

Ngo Vinh Long. *Before the Revolution: the Vietnamese Peasants under the French*. New York: Columbia University Press, 1991.

Ngoc An. "TP.HCM: dan hien dat tri gia hang chuc ti dong." *Tuoi Tre*, 9 December 2006. Online at http://www3.tuoitre.com.vn/Vieclam/Index.aspx?ArticleID=176769andChannelID=3.

Ngoc An. "Cham giai toa, hai 'doi dang'." *Viet Bao*, 10 December 2007.

Nguyen Dao Ngoc Van and Nguyen Tap, comp. *An Overview of Plants and Animals Used in Traditional Medicine Systems in Vietnam*. Ha Noi: TRAFFIC Southeast Asia, Greater Mekong Programme, 2008.

Nguyen Duy Quy. "Land Law Problems and Resolutions." *State and Law* 1993:1.

Nguyen Huy Cuong. "Khu cong nghiep Trang Bang: Nhung dieu con lai sau 'giai toa'." *Viet Bao (theo Tuoi Tre)*, 15 May 2004. Online at http://vietbao.vn/Xa-hoi/Khu-cong-nghiep-Trang-Bang-Nhung-dieu-con-lai-sau-giai-toa/40033037/157/.

Nguyen Kim Dung. "Intangible Cultural Heritage Safeguarding System in Vietnam." Hanoi: Ministry of Culture and Information. Online at http://www.unesco.org/culture/ich/doc/src/00174-EN.pdf (accessed 12 August 2008).

Nguyen Kim Thanh. "Hon 35 nam Bac-Hung-Hai," in *50 Nam Thuy Loi – Nhung Chang Duong*. Bo Thuy Loi (ed). Hanoi: NXB Chinh tri Quoc gia, 1995.

Nguyen Ngoc Huy and Ta Van Tai. *The Le Code: Law in Traditional Vietnam*. Athens, OH: Ohio University Press, 1987, v. I–III.

Nguyen Nhu Phat. "Gop y kien ve van de: Dat dai thuoc so huu toan dan." *Nha nuoc va Phap luat* 28.4 (1979): 14–16.

Nguyen Nien. "Several Legal Problems in the Leadership and Management of Industry under the Conditions of the Present Improvement of Economic Management in Our Country." *Luat Hoc* 14 (1976): 33–5, trans. *JPRS*, 30 September 1976: 34–6.

Nguyen Quang Tan. "Forest Devolution in Vietnam: Differentiation in Benefits from Forest among Local Households." *Forest Policy and Economics* 8.4 (2006): 409–20.

Nguyen Quang Tuyen. "Land Holding Changes and Kinh and Khmer Farmers' Livelihoods in Thoi Thuan B Hamlet, Thoi Lai Town, Co Do District, Can Tho City, Vietnam." *Asian Social Science*, 6.1 (2009): 132–44.

Nguyen Quang Vinh and Michael Leaf. "City Life in the Village of Ghosts: A Case Study of Popular Housing in Ho Chi Minh City, Vietnam." *Habitat International* 20.2 (1996): 175–190.

Nguyen Sinh Cuc. *Nong nghiep Viet nam 1945–1995*. Hanoi: NXB Thong ke, 1995.

Nguyen Tai Thu, ed. *Lich su Phat giao Viet Nam*. Hanoi: NXB Khoa hoc Xa hoi, 1988.

Nguyen Thuc Bao. "Mot so y kien ve quan ly dat dai theo phap luat va trach nhiem doi voi cac hanh vi vi pham phap luat dat dai o nuoc ta." *Nha nuoc va Phap luat* (1986.2): 7–15.

Nguyen Trang An. "*Nut giao Thanh Xuan se lech to ve phia Ha Noi.*" Vietnamnet, 2007. Online at http://vietnamnet.vn/xahoi/dothi/2007/01/654651/.

Nguyen Trang An. "*Nut giao Thanh Xuan (Ha Noi): Meo da thanh can!*" Vietnamnet, 2008. Online at http://vietnamnet.vn/xahoi/2008/02/770140/.

Nguyen Van Dang (ed.). *Lam nghiep Viet Nam (1945–2000)*. Hanoi: Nong Nghiep, 2001.

Nguyen Van Huy. "The Role of Museums in the Preservation of Living Heritage: Experiences from the Vietnam Museum of Ethnology." *International Journal of Intangible Heritage* 1 (2006): 35–42.

Nguyen Van Huyen. "Une source d'étude démographique des communes annamites du Tonkin." *Bulletin de l'Institut Indochinois de l'Etude de l'Homme*, 1938.

Nguyen Van Huyen. "Le Problème de la paysannerie au Tonkin." *Collection Tendances*. Hanoi: 1939.

Nguyen Van Huyen. *La Civilisation annamite*. Hanoi: Ecole d'Extrême-Orient, 1944.

Nguyen Van Suu. "The Politics of Land: Inequality in Land Access and Local Conflicts in the Red River Delta since Decollectivization," in *Social Inequality in Vietnam and the Challenges to Reform*, Philip Taylor (ed.). Singapore: Institute of Southeast Asian Studies, 2004: 270–96.

Nguyen Van Thanh and Dinh Van Minh. *Mot so van de ve doi moi co che giai quyet khieu kien hanh chinh o*. Hanoi: NXB Tu phap, 2004.

Nguyen Vu Hoang. *Land, Livelihood, and Security: Struggling for Justice in Urbanizing Vietnam – A Case Study of Collective Action in Hanoi*. Master's Thesis, Vrije Universiteit Amsterdam, 2007.

Nguyen Xuan Dien. *Lich su va nghe thuat Ca Tru: Khao sat nguon tu lieu tai Vien Nghien cuu Han-Nom*. Hanoi: NXB The gioi, 2007.

*Nhan Dan*. "Tam chinh sach cua nuoc Viet Nam Dan Chu Cong Hoa moi cho cac thanh pho moi duoc giai phong." 1 September 1954: 25–6.

Nhieu tac gia. *Giu gin va bao ve ban sac van hoa cac dan toc thieu so Viet Nam*. Hanoi: NXB Van hoa Dan toc, 1997.

Nhom PV Chinh tri – xa hoi. "Buc xuc chuyen den bu giai toa – Ky 1: Ep dan bang cach 'thue'chinh quyen giai toa." *Viet Bao*, 22 August 2004.

Nicholson, Pip. "Vietnamese Legal Institutions in Comparative Perspective: Constitutions and Courts Considered," in *Law, Capitalism and Power in Asia: The Rule of Law and Legal Institutions*. K. Jayasuriya (ed.). London: Routledge, 1999.

Nicholson, Pip. "Judicial Independence and the Rule of Law: The Vietnam Court Experience." *Australian Journal of Asian Law* 37.3 (2001).

Nicholson, Pip. *Borrowing Court Systems: The Experience of Socialist Vietnam*. Leiden: Martinus Nijhoff, 2007.

Nicholson, Pip. "Vietnamese Courts: Contemporary Interactions Between Party-State and Law," in *Vietnam's New Order: International Perspectives on the State and Reform in Vietnam*. Stephanie Balme and Mark Sidel (eds). New York: Palgrave Macmillan, 2007.

Nicholson, Pip and Nguyen Hung Quang. "The Vietnamese Judiciary: The Politics of Appointment and Promotion." *Pacific Rim Law and Policy Journal* 1.14 (2005): 1–34.

*Nomination File: Intangible Cultural Heritage for Inscription on the Urgent Safeguarding List*. Online at http://www.unesco.org/culture/ich/doc/src/00309-Community%20consent-EN.pdf (February 2009).

Nong Quoc Chan. "Cultures of the ethnic minorities of Viet Nam: Some problems and realities," in *Viet Nam's Cultural Diversity: Approaches to Preservation,* Oscar Salemink (ed.). Paris: UNESCO Publishing (Memory of Peoples), 2001: 111–20.

Norlund, Irene *et al. The Emerging Civil Society – An Initial Assessment of Civil Society in Vietnam.* Hanoi: CIVICUS, 2006.

Norton, Barley. "Ca Tru: A Vietnamese Chamber Music Genre." *Nhac Viet: The Journal of Vietnamese Music* (Special Issue), 5 (1996): 1–103.

Norton, Barley. "Singing the Past: Vietnamese *ca tru,* Memory and Mode." *Asian Music* 36.2 (2005): 27–56.

Norton, Barley. Website *"Ca tru: Vocal music from Northern Viet Nam."* Online at http://www.goldsmiths.ac.uk/music/catru/.

Nuijten, Monique. *Power, Community and the State: The Political Anthropology of Organisation in Mexico.* London: Pluto Press, 2003.

Pelley, Patricia. "'Barbarians' and 'Younger Brothers': The Remaking of Race in Postcolonial Vietnam." *Journal of Southeast Asian Studies* 29.2 (1998): 374–91.

Pelley, Patricia. *Postcolonial Vietnam: New Histories of the National Past.* Durham: Duke University Press, 2002.

Peluso, Nancy. *Rich Forests, Poor People: Resource Control and Resistance in Java.* Berkeley: University of California Press, 1992.

Peycam, Philippe. "Intellectuals and Political Commitment in Vietnam: The Emergence of a Public Sphere in Colonial Saigon (1916–1928)." PhD Dissertation, University of London, School of African and Oriental Studies, 2003.

Pham Cao Duong. *Vietnamese Peasants under French Domination* 1861–1945. Berkeley: Center for South and Southeast Asian Studies, 1985.

Pham Hung. *Nhiem vu trong yeu cua cong tac thuy loi doi voi phong trao hop tac hoa san xuat nong nghiep – Dien van doc tai Hoi nghi tong ket cong tac thuy loi nam 1959.* Hanoi: NXB Su that, 1960.

Pham Luan. *May kinh nghiem cong tac dan cong trong Khang chien.* Hanoi: NXB Quan doi Nhan dan, 1966.

Pham Thi Thu Thanh and Tran Ha. *25 nam xay dung nen phap che Viet Nam.* Hanoi: NXB Lao dong, 1971.

Phan Dang Nhat. "The Timeless Epics of the Ethnic Minorities of Viet Nam," in *Viet Nam's Cultural Diversity: Approaches to Preservation*, Oscar Salemink (ed.). Paris: UNESCO Publishing (Memory of Peoples), 2001: 85–104.

Phan Huy Le. "Research on the Vietnamese Village: Assessment and Perspectives," in *Viet Nam: Borderless Histories,* N.T. Tran and A. Reid (eds). Madison: University of Wisconsin Press, 2006: 23–41.

Phan Ke Binh. *Viet Nam Phong tuc.* HCM City: NXB TP HCM, 1996.

Phan Khanh. *So thao lich su thuy loi Viet Nam (1945–1995).* Hanoi: NXB Chinh tri Quoc gia, 1997.

Phan Phuong Thao, *Land Equalization in 1839 in Binh Dinh Seen from the Land Records.* Hanoi: The Gioi Publishers, 2009.

Phi Van. *Dong Que: Phong su.* Saigon: Dat Nuoc, 1957.

Phung Minh. *40 nam quan ly nha cua o Ha Noi.* Hanoi: unpublished paper, October 1998.

Platteau, Jean-Philippe. *Land Reform and Structural Adjustment in Sub-Saharan Africa: Controversies and Guidelines.* FAO Economic and Social Development Paper 107 Rome: FAO, 1992.

Polanyi, Karl. *The Great Transformation: The Political and Economic Origins of Our Time.* New York: Rinehart, 1944.

Proschan, Frank. "The /saavlaa/ or Saola (*Pseudoryx nghetinhensis*)." Unpublished paper.

Quang Tuynh. *Thanh nien Hung Yen lam thuy loi.* Hanoi: NXB Thanh nien, 1962.

Quoc Phuong. *Hung Yen: La co "Lam thuy loi kha nhat."* Hanoi: NXB Pho thong, 1964.

Quoc Thanh. "Giai toa den bu: Lam sao dan dong thuan?" *Viet Bao*, 10 September 2004.

Reinecke, Andreas. "Bi-Cephalous Animal Shaped Ear Pendants in Vietnam." *Bead Study Group Newsletter* 28 (Winter 1996).

Rév, István. "The Advantages of Being Atomized: How Hungarian Peasants Coped with Collectivization." *Dissent* 34.3 (1987): 335–49.

Ribot, Jesse, Arun Agrawal and Anne M. Larson. "Recentralizing while Decentralizing: How Governments Reappropriate Forest Resources." *World Development* 34.11 (2006): 1864–86.

Robichaud, William "Physical and Behavioral Description of a Captive Saola, *Pseudoryx nghetinhensis*." *Journal of Mammalogy* 79.2 (1998).

Robichaud, William. "Summary of saola, herpetological, and wildlife trade studies in Nakai-Nam Theun NBCA and the proposed Nam Theun extension." Vientiane: Wildlife Conservation Society for IUCN, 1999.

Robichaud, William. *Saola Conservation Action Plan for Lao PDR*. Vientiane: IUCN Lao PDR Programme, 1999.

Robichaud, William and Robert Timmins. "The Natural History of Saola (*Pseudoryx Nghetinhensis*) and the Species' Distribution in Laos Based on the Workshop Presentation 'Saola ecology-the bare basics (i.e., all we know)'" in *Rediscovering the Saola: Proceedings of the workshop "Rediscovering the Saola: A Status Review and Conservation Planning Workshop,"* James Hardcastle (ed.). Hanoi: WWF Indochina Programme, 2004.

*Sai Gon Giai Phong*. "Pha duong day 'an mo'." *Viet Bao (theo Sai Gon Giai Phong)*, 29 November 2007.

Salemink, Oscar (ed.). *Viet Nam's Cultural Diversity: Approaches to Preservation*. Paris: UNESCO Publishing (Memory of Peoples), 2001a.

Salemink, Oscar. "Who Decides Who Preserves What? Cultural Preservation and Representation," in *Viet Nam's Cultural Diversity: Approaches to Preservation*, Oscar Salemink (ed.). Paris: UNESCO Publishing (Memory of Peoples), 2001b: 205–12.

Salemink, Oscar. *The Ethnography of Vietnam's Central Highlanders: A Historical Contextualization, 1850–1990*. London: RoutledgeCurzon; Honolulu: University of Hawai'i Press [Anthropology of Asia Series], 2003a.

Salemink, Oscar. "Enclosing the Highlands: Socialist, Capitalist and Protestant Conversions of Vietnam's Central Highlanders." RCSD Conference on The Politics of the Commons, Chiang Mai University, 11–14 July 2003 (2003b). http://dlc.dlib.indiana.edu/dlc/handle/10535/1787.

Salemink, Oscar. *Nieuwe rituelen en de natie: Nederland in de spiegel van Vietnam* (New rituals and the nation: The Netherlands in the mirror of Vietnam). Vrije Universiteit Amsterdam: Inaugural Lecture, 9 June 2006 (2006a).

Salemink, Oscar. "Changing Rights and Wrongs: The Transnational Construction of Indigenous and Human Rights among Vietnam's Central Highlanders." *Focaal, European Journal of Anthropology* 47 (2006b): 32–47.

Salemink, Oscar. "Translating, Interpreting and Practicing Civil Society in Vietnam: A Tale of Calculated Misunderstandings," in *Development Brokers and Translators: The Ethnography of Aid and Agencies*, David Lewis and David Mosse (eds). Bloomfield: Kumarian Press, 2006c: 101–26.

Salemink, Oscar. "The Emperor's New Clothes: Re-fashioning Ritual in the Hue Festival." *Journal of Southeast Asian Studies* 38.3 (2007): 559–82.

Salemink, Oscar. "Trading Goods, Prestige, and Power: A Revisionist History of Lowlander-Highlander Relations in Vietnam," in *Linking Destinies: Trade, Towns and Kin in Asian History*, Peter Boomgaard, Dick Kooiman and Henk Schulte Nordholt (eds). Leiden: KITLV Press, 2008: 51–69.

Salemink, Oscar. "Embodying the Nation: Mediumship, Ritual, and the National Imagination." *Journal of Vietnamese Studies* 3.3 (2008): 257–90.

Salemink, Oscar. "Where is the Space for Vietnam's Gong Culture? Economic and Social Challenges for the Space of Gong Culture, and Ppportunities for Protection." Paper for the international conference on Economic and Social Changes and Preservation of the Gong Culture in Vietnam and the Southeast Asian Region, Pleiku City, Vietnam, 12–15 November 2009.

Saola Working Group, Press release 9/3/2009, "Last Chance to Save the Saola from Extinction? Meeting in Laos Urges Prompt Action."

"Sau 30 nam hop tac hoa nong nghiep: Doi song nong dan va van de quan ly san xuat nong nghiep hien nay," in *Thuc trang kinh te xa hoi Viet Nam giai doan 1986–1990 (Tai lieu tham khao noi bo)*. Hanoi: Tap chi Thong Ke, 1989: 27–60.

Schafer, Edward H. *The Vermilion Bird: T'ang Images of the South.* Berkeley: University of California Press, 1967.

Schaller G. and A. Rabinowitz. "The saola or spindlehorn bovid *Pseudoryx nghetinhensis* in Laos." *Oryx: The Journal of the Fauna Preservation Society* 29.2 (April, 1995): 107–14.

Schumpeter, Joseph A. "The Process of Creative Destruction," and "Crumbling Walls," in *Capitalism, Socialism, and Democracy*. New York: Harper, 1976: 81–86, 131–42.

Scott, James C. *The Moral Economy of the Peasant: Rebellion and Subsistence in Southeast Asia*. New Haven: Yale University Press, 1977.

Scott, James C. *Seeing Like a State: How Certain Schemes to Improve the Human Condition Have Failed.* New Haven: Yale University Press, 1998.

Scott, James C. *The Art of Not Being Governed.* New Haven: Yale University Press, 2009.

Sidel, Mark. "Understanding Constitutional Amendation in Socialist Transitional Societies: The Case of Vietnam." *Singapore Journal of International and Comparative Law* symposium on Comparative Constutionalisms: The Remaking of Constitutional Orders in Southeast Asia, *Singapore Journal of International and Comparative Law* 42.6 (2002).

Sidel, Mark. *Law and Society in Vietnam.* Cambridge: Cambridge University Press, 2008.

Sidel, Mark. *The Constitution of Vietnam: A Contextual Analysis*. Oxford: Hart, 2009.

Sikor, Thomas. "The Allocation of Forestry Land in Vietnam: Did It Cause the Expansion of Forests in the Northwest?" *Forest Policy and Economics* 2 (2001): 1–11.

Sikor, Thomas. "Local Government in the Exercise of State Power: The Politics of Land Allocation in Black Thai Villages," in *Beyond Hanoi: Local Government in Vietnam*, B. Kerkvliet and D. Marr (eds). Singapore: Institute for Southeast Asian Studies, 2004: 171–200.

Sikor, Thomas. "The Politics of Rural Land Registration in Postsocialist Societies: Contested Land Titling in North-Western Vietnam." *Land Use Policy* 23.4 (2006): 617–28.

Sikor, Thomas. "Land allocations in Vietnam's uplands: Negotiating property and authority." In *Upland Transformations in Vietnam*, T. Sikor, Nghiem P.T., J. Sowerwine, J. Romm (eds). Singapore: National University of Singapore Press, 2011.

Sikor, Thomas and C. Lund. "Access and Property: A Question of Power and Authority." *Development and Change* 40 (2009): 1–22.

Sikor, Thomas and Nguyen Quang Tan. "Why May Forest Devolution Not Benefit the Rural Poor? Forest Entitlements in Vietnam's Central Highlands," *World Development* 35.11 (2007): 2010–25.

Sikor, Thomas and To Xuan Phuc. "Illegal Logging in Vietnam: *Lam Tac* (Forest Hijackers) in Practice and Talk." *Society and Natural Resources*, 24:7 (2011): 688–701.

Sikor, Thomas, J. Stahl and S. Dorondel. "Negotiating Post-Socialist Property and State: Struggles over Forests in Albania and Romania." *Development and Change* 40 (2009): 171–94.

Skomorokhop, Pavan. "Phap luat Xo Viet bao ve quyen loi dan su." *Tap san Tu phap* 1961.3: 42–4.

Smith, Laurajane. *Uses of Heritage*. London: Routledge, 2006.

Smith, Ralph B. "The Vietnamese Elite of French Cochinchina, 1943," *Modern Asian Studies* 6.4 (1972): 459–82.

So van hoa va thong tin Hai Hung (SVHTTHH). *Hai Hung nam thang va su kien 1945–1995*. Hai Hung: So van hoa va thong tin Hai Hung, 1995.

Solomon, Peter. "Courts in Russia: Independence, Power and Accountability." In *Judicial Integrity,* Andras Sajo (ed.). Leiden: Martinus Nijhoff Publishers, 2004: 225–252.

Sowerwine, Jennifer. "Territorialization and the Politics of Highland Landscapes in Vietnam: Negotiating Property Relations in Policy, Meaning and Practice," *Conservation and Society* (2004): 97–136.

Son Nam. *Mien Nam dau The ky XX – Thien Dia Hoi va cuoc Minh Tan*. Saigon: La Boi, 1971.

Son Nam. *Lich Su Khan Hoang Mien Nam*. Ho Chi Minh City: NXB Thanh Nien, 2004.

SRV Chinh Phu. *Quyet dinh 75/CP ve viec thanh lap quan Thanh Xuan va quan Cau Giay*. 1996.

SRV Thu tuong Chinh Phu. *Quyet dinh 597/QD-TTG/2001 ve viec dau tu du an xay dung giai doan 1 doan Mai Dich – Phap Van thuoc duong Vanh dai III – TP Ha Noi*. 2001.

SRV Uy ban Nhan dan [UBND] Quan Thanh Xuan. *Quyet dinh 728/QD-UB ve viec thanh lap Hoi dong giai phong mat bang den bu de giao dat cho Ban quan ly du an Thang Long thuc hien dau tu xay dung duong Vanh dai III giai doan 1 doan Mai Dich – Phap Van*. 2001.

SRV UBND Thanh pho [TP] Ha Noi. *Quyet dinh 4187/QD-UB cua UBND TP Ha Noi ve viec to chuc thuc hien cong tac den bu, tai dinh cu khi Nha nuoc thu hoi dat de xay dung duong Vanh dai III giai doan 1 (Doan Phap Van – Mai Dich)*. 2001.

SRV UBND TP Ha Noi. *Quyet dinh 4664/QD_UB ve viec thu hoi va tam giao 837,314m2 dat tai cac quan Cau Giay, Thanh Xuan, cac huyen Tu Liem va Thanh Tri cho Ban quan ly du an Thang Long de thuc hien du an xay dung giai doan 1 doan Mai Dich – Phap Van thuoc duong Vanh dai III thanh pho Ha Noi*. 2001.

SRV UBND TP Ha Noi. *Quyet dinh 5593/QD-UB ve viec thu hoi va tam giao 23.805m2 dat tai quan Cau Giay, huyen Tu Liem, quan Thanh Xuan, huyen Thanh Tri cho ban Quan ly du an Thang Long de dap ta luy hai ben nen duong vanh dai III*. 2001.

SRV Bo Giao thong Van tai va UBND TP Ha Noi. *Thong bao 401 Ket luan cuoc hop giua lanh dao Bo GTVT va UBND TP Ha Noi, kiem diem cong tac GPMB va Thi cong cac du an xay dung giao thong tren dia ban thanh pho Ha Noi*. 2003.

SRV General Statistics Office. *The 2004 Migration Survey: Major Findings*. Hanoi: Statistical Publishing House, 2005.

SRV General Statistics Office. *Lao dong dang lam viec tai thoi diem 1/7 hang nam phan theo thanh phan kinh te va phan theo nganh kinh te (Annual statistics data on labor working at 1st July divided by economic compositions)*. Hanoi: General Statistics Office, 2005. http://www.gso.gov.vn/.

Stark, D. and L. Bruszt. *Postsocialist Pathways: Transforming Politics and Property in East Central Europe*. Cambridge: Cambridge University Press, 1998.

Sterling, Eleanor Jane, Martha Maud Hurley, and Le Duc Minh. *Vietnam: A Natural History*. New Haven: Yale University Press, 2006.

Stoler, Ann. *Along the Archival Grain: Colonial Cultures and Their Affective States*. Princeton: Princeton University Press, 2009.

Stone, Richard. "The Saola's Last Stand." *Science* 314: 5804 (Dec. 1, 2006): 1380–1, 83.

Stone, Richard. "Last Chance to Save the 'Panda of Indochina.'" *Science* 325 (Sep. 4, 2009): 1193.

Sturgeon, Janet. *Border Landscapes: The Politics of Akha Land Use in China and Thailand*. Seattle: University of Washington Press, 2005.

Sturgeon, Janet, and Thomas Sikor. "Postsocialist Property in Asia and Europe: Variation on 'Fuzziness'." *Conservation and Society* (2004): 1–18.

Szalontai, Balazs. "Political and Economic Crisis in North Vietnam, 1955–1956." *Cold War History* 5:4 (2005): 395–426.

Ta Van Tai, "The Status of Women in Traditional Vietnam: A Comparison of the Code of the Le Dynasty (1428–1788) with the Chinese Codes," *Journal of Asian History*, 15:2 (1981): 97–145.

Tai, Hue-Tam Ho. *Millenarianism and Peasant Politics in Vietnam*. Cambridge MA: Harvard University Press, 1983.

Tai, Hue-Tam Ho. "The Politics of Compromise: The Constitutionalist Party and the Electoral Reforms of 1922 in French Cochinchina." *Modern Asian Studies*, 18:3 (1984): 371–91.

Tai, Hue-Tam Ho. *Radicalism and the Origins of the Vietnamese Revolution*. Cambridge: Harvard University Press, 1992.

Tai, Hue-Tam Ho (ed.). *The Country of Memory: Remaking the Past in Post-Socialist Vietnam.* Berkeley: University of California Press, 2001.

Tan tao bi tac van khe, **薪造碑**砟文契, Ms. 1979–80.

Tan tao mai dinh bi ky, 新造買亭碑記, Ms. 1945.

Tan tao mai dinh van khe bi ky, 新造買亭文契碑記, Ms. 1933–34.

Tan tao trum truong tu dinh bi ky, 新造長敘亭碑記, Ms. 1933–34.

Taylor, Philip. *Fragments of the Present: Searching for Modernity in Vietnam's South.* Honolulu: University of Hawai'i Press, 2001.

Tenev, S., A. Carlier, O. Chaudry and Nguyen Quynh-Trang. *Informality and the Playing Field in Vietnam's Business Sector*. Washington: IFC, World Bank, and MPDF, 2003.

Thach bi mai dinh, 石碑賣亭, Ms. 1977–78.

Thach bi thuyen tao, 石碑銓造, Ms. 1634–35.

Tham Ngoc Diep, Dang Thang Long, and Do Thuc comps. "A Luoi district, Thua Thien Hue province" in "Annex 3 Report of Survey of Saola *Pseudoryx Nghetinhensis*," in *Rediscovering the Saola: Proceedings of the Workshop "Rediscovering the Saola: A Status Review and Conservation Planning Workshop*." James Hardcastle (ed.). Hanoi: WWF Indochina Programme, 2004.

Thanh Duy. *Con rong nuoc: Truyen Anh hung Pham Thi Vach*. Hanoi: NXB Phu Nu, 1962.

Thanh Duy. "Co so khoa hoc va van hoa trong tu tuong Ho Chi Minh ve nha nuoc va phap luat." *Tap chi Cong san* (1997:1): 26–28.

*Thanh Nien*. "Hop dong cua HLV Dido: Vuong mac van chua duoc giai quyet." *VnExpress*,10 January 2001. Online at http://vnexpress.net/GL/The-thao/2001/01/3B9AD63C/.

*Thanh Nien*. "TP.HCM: nguoi dan trong khu vuc bi giai toa se duoc ho tro viec lam, hoc hanh." *Viet Bao*, 19 June 2006. Online at http://vietbao.vn/Xa-hoi/TP-HCM-nguoi-dan-trong-khu-vuc-bi-giai-toa-se-duoc-ho-tro-viec-lam-hoc-hanh/40145149/157/.

Thanh Tong. "Mo rong duong Nam Ky Khoi Nghia: 85 ho giai toa trang." *Viet Bao*, 16 September 2004. Online at http://vietbao.vn/Xa-hoi/Mo-rong-duong-Nam-Ky-Khoi-Nghia-85-ho-giai-toa-trang/10878646/157/.

Thaveeporn Vasavakul. "From Fence-breaking to Networking: Interests, Popular Organizations and Policy Influences in Post-socialist Vietnam," in *Getting Organized in Vietnam: Moving In and Around the Socialist State*, Benedict Kerkvliet, Russell Heng, David Koh (eds). Singapore: ISEAS, 2003: 25–61.

*Thien Mac chau mai ban huyen giao phuong ty*, 天幕州買本縣敎坊司, Ms. 6897–6898.

Thompson, Virginia and Richard Adloff. "The Cultural Institutions of Indochina Today," *Journal of Asian Studies*, 6:4 (1947): 414–19.

*Thuc trang kinh te xa hoi Viet Nam giai doan 1986–1990 (Tai lieu tham khao noi bo)*. Hanoi: Tap chi Thong ke, 1989.

*Thuy tong mai ban huyen phuong ty doan mai dinh tru tien van bi ky*, 睡總買本縣坊司斷賣亭籌钱文碑記, Ms. 2278–81.

TNO. "De tien do den bu giai toa duoc nhanh." *Viet Bao (theo Thanh Nien)*, 18 June 2005. http://vietbao.vn/Trang-ban-doc/De-tien-do-den-bu-giai-toa-duoc-nhanh/45159440/478/.

To Van-Hoa. *Judicial Independence*. Lund: Jurisförlaget i Lund, 2006.

To Xuan Phuc. *Forest Property in the Vietnamese Uplands: An Ethnography of Forest Relations in Three Dao Villages*. Berlin and London: LIT Verlage/Transaction Publishers, 2007.

To Xuan Phuc. "Why Did the Forest Conservation Policy Fail in the Vietnamese Uplands? Forest Conflicts in Ba Vi National Park in Northern Region." *International Journal for Environmental Studies* 66.1 (2009): 59–68.

To Xuan Phuc and Thomas Sikor. *The Politics of Illegal Logging in Vietnam*. Working Paper 5, University of East Anglia, 2008.

Toa an Nhan dan Toi cao. "Bao cao tong ket cong tac nam 2004 va phuong huong nhiem vu cong tac cua nam 2005 cua nganh Toa an Nhan dan." Hanoi, 2005.

Toa an Nhan dan Toi cao. "Bao cao tong ket cong tac nam 2005 va phuong huong nhiem vu cong tac cua nam 2006 cua nganh Toa an Nhan dan." Hanoi, 2006.

*Tong tap thac ban van khac Han Nom*. Hanoi: Vien Han-Nom, École Française d'Extrême Orient and Ecole Pratique des Hautes Etudes, 2005, vols 1–6.

Tran Duc. *Hop tac trong nong thon xua va nay*. Hanoi: NXB Nong nghiep, 1994.

Tran Manh Tien. "Su di dan cua mot lang que mien Trung voi viec do thi hoa o khu xom Nha Den (Tan Dinh, Quan 3)," in *Do thi hoa tai Viet Nam va Dong Nam A,* Ho Chi Minh City: Trung tam nghien cuu Dong Nam A–Vien Khoa hoc xa hoi TP Ho Chi Minh, 1996: 286–91.

Tran, Nhung Tuyet. "Beyond the Myth of Equality: Daughters' Inheritance Rights in the Le Code," in *Viet Nam: Borderless Histories*, N.T. Tran and A. Reid (eds). Madison: University of Wisconsin Press, 2006: 121–44.

Tran, Nhung Tuyet. "Gender, Property, and the 'Autonomy Thesis' in Southeast Asia: The Endowment of Local Succession in Early Modern Vietnam." *Journal of Asian Studies* 67.1 (2008): 43–72.

Tran, Nhung Tuyet. *Familial Properties: Gender, State and Society in Early Modern Vietnam, 1460–1783*. Honolulu: University of Hawai'i Press, forthcoming.

Tran Phuong. *Mot so y kien ve chu nghia tu ban o nong thon Mien Bac ngay sau Cai cach ruong dat*. Hanoi: NXB Su that, 1960.

Tran Quang Huy. *Giao trinh Luat dat dai*. Hanoi: NXB Cong an Nhan dan, 2001.

Tran Thi Kim Anh. "Ca tru qua mot so khe uoc va dieu luat," in *Dac Khao ca tru Viet Nam*. Hanoi: Vien am nhac Viet Nam, 2006: 36–58.

Trinh Khac Manh, Nguyen Van Nguyen and Philippe Papin. *Thu muc thac ban van khac han nom Viet Nam*. Hanoi: NXB Van hoa Thong tin, 2007, vols 1–5.

Truong Chinh. "Introduction to the Political Report." *Vietnam News Agency*, 15 December 1988.

Tsing, Anna Lowenhaupt. *In the Realm of the Diamond Queen: Marginality in an Out-of-the Way Place*. Princeton: Princeton University Press, 1993.

UNDP. *Access to Justice: Survey from the People's Perspective*. 2004.

UNDP. *Bao cao khao sat nhu cau cua Toa an nhan dan cap huyen tren toan quoc*. Hanoi: NXB Tu phap, 2007.

"Une source d'étude démographique des communes annamites du Tonkin." *Bulletin de l'Institut indochinois de l'étude de l'homme*. Hanoi: 1938.

UNESCO. *Convention for the Safeguarding of the Intangible Cultural Heritage* (17 October 2003). Paris. Online at http://unesdoc.unesco.org/.

United Nations. *Human Security Now – Commission on Human Security*. New York, 2003. Online at http://www.humansecurity-chs.org/finalreport.

Urry, John. *The Tourist Gaze: Leisure and Travel in Contemporary Societies*. London: Sage, 1990.

Uy ban Cai cach Ruong dat Trung Uong (UBCCRDTU). *Kinh nghiem chinh don cho Bo Nong thon trong giam to va Cai cach ruong dat*. Hanoi: Uy ban Cai cach Ruong dat Trung Uong, 1955.

Uy ban Hanh chinh Khu Ta Ngan (UBHCKTN). *Thong tu cua Uy ban Hanh chinh Khu Ta Ngan va tai lieu, cong van cua Khu Lao Dong Ta Ngan ve to chuc va giao duc ve chinh sach dan cong nam 1957 (30/3/1957–18/7/1957).* (H.s. 26/413, v/v).

Uy ban Hanh chinh Khu Ta Ngan (Khu Lao Dong). *Bao cao cua Khu Lao Dong Ta Ngan ve cong tac kiem tra va mot so kinh nghiem ve cong tac thanh tra nam 1957 (12/7/1957–13/10/1957).* (H.s. 32, v/v).

VNCI. *Land Tenure for the Private Sector*. Hanoi: unpublished report, 2007.

Van phong Thu tuong Phu. *Chinh sach phan dinh thanh phan giai cap o nong thon (Trich trong cac Dieu le Thong tu cua Chinh phu da luu hanh).* Hanoi: Van phong Thu tuong Phu, 1957.

Van phong Thu tuong Phu. *May chinh sach cu the de sua chua sai lam ve Cai cach ruong dat*. Hanoi: Van phong Thu tuong Phu, 1957.

Vandergeest, Peter, and Nancy Lee Peluso. "Territorialization and State Power in Thailand." *Theory and Society* 24 (1995): 385–426.

Verdery, Katherine. *What Was Socialism? And What Comes Next?* Princeton: Princeton University Press, 1996.

Verdery, Katherine. "Fuzzy Property: Rights, Power, and Identity in Transylvania's Decollectivization," in *Transforming Post-Communist Political Economies*, Joan M. Nelson, Charles Tilly, and Lee Walker (eds). Washington: National Academy Press, 1997: 102–17.

Verdery, Katherine. "Property and Power in Transylvania's Decollectivization" in *Property Relations: Renewing the Anthropological Tradition*, Christopher Hann (ed.). Cambridge: Cambridge University Press, 1998: 160–80.

Verdery, Katherine. "Fuzzy Property: Rights, Power, and Identity in Transylvania's Decollectivization," in *Uncertain Transition: Ethnographies of Change in the Postsocialist World*, Michael. Burawoy and Katherine Verdery (eds). Lanham: Rowman and Littlefield, 1999: 53–81.

Verdery, Katherine. *The Vanishing Hectare: Property and Value in Postsocialist Transylvania*. Ithaca, NY: Cornell University Press, 2003.

Verdery, Katherine. "The Property Regime of Socialism." *Conservation and Society* 2.1 (2004): 189–98.

Vicchio, Stephen J. "From Aristotle to Descartes," in *Animal Intelligence: Insights into the Animal Mind*, R.J. Hoage (ed.). Washington: Smithsonian Institution Press, 1986.

*Viet Bao*. "De nguoi dan ngheo bi giai toa mua duoc nha tai dinh cu." *Viet Bao*, 16 February 2005.

Vietnam News Agency. "Ong Nguyen Tan Dung duoc bau lam Thu tuong Chinh phu," Ministry of Foreign Affairs, 2006.

VIR. "Firm Foundation Laid to Build Land Laws." *Vietnamnet*, 10 September 2006. Online at http://english.vietnamnet.vn/biz/2006/09/610496/.

VnExpress. "Nganh toa an kho kham noi viec xu ly tranh chap dat dai," 2003. Online at http://vnexpress.net/Vietnam/Phap-luat/2003/07/3B9C9DE9.

Vo Huong. "Mo duong NKKN – Nguyen Van Troi: Bo mat cua ngo ra sao?" *Viet Bao (theo Tuoi Tre)*, 11 May 2005. http://vietbao.vn/Xa-hoi/Mo-duong-NKKN-Nguyen-Van-Troi-Bo-mat-cua-ngo-ra-sao/40077990/157/.

Volkman, Toby. "Visions and Revisions: Toraja Culture and the Tourist Gaze." *American Ethnologist* 17.1 (1990): 91–110.

von Benda-Beckmann, Franz *et al.* (eds). *Changing Properties of Property.* Oxford: Berghahn, 2006.

von Benda-Beckmann, Keebet. "Forum shopping and shopping forums: Dispute processing in a Minangkabau village," *Journal of Legal Pluralism* 19 (1981): 117–59.

von Benda-Beckmann, Franz and Keebet von Benda-Beckmann. "A Functional Analysis of Property Rights, with Special Reference to Indonesia," in *Property Rights and Economic Development: Land and Natural Resources in Southeast Asia and Oceania*, Toon van

Meijl and Franz von Benda-Beckmann (eds). London: Kegan Paul International, 1999: 15–56.
Vu Tai chinh ke toan, thong ke, Bo Thuy loi, Vu Tong hop, Tong cuc Thong ke. *Phong chong Lut bao o Viet Nam 1890–1990*. Hanoi: NXB The gioi, 1994.
Vu Van Dung *et al.* "A New Species of Living Bovid from Vietnam." *Nature* 363 (1993): 443–5.
Vu Van Dung *et al.* "Discovery and Conservation of the Vu Quang Ox in Vietnam." *Oryx: The Journal of the Fauna Conservation Society* 28.1 (January 1994).
Vu Van Dung and Do Tuoc. "The Discovery of the Saola (*Pseudoryx Nghetinhensis*) in Vietnam," in *Rediscovering the Saola: Proceedings of the Workshop "Rediscovering the Saola: A Status Review and Conservation Planning Workshop*". James Hardcastle (ed.). Hanoi: WWF Indochina Programme, 2004.
Walinsky, Louis J. *Agrarian Reform as Unfinished Business: The Selected Papers of Wolf Ladejinsky*. New York: Oxford University Press, 1977.
Weber, Max. *Wirtschaft und Gesellschaft*. Tübingen: Mohr, J.C.B., 1976.
Wells-Dang, Andrew. "Political Space in Vietnam: A View from the 'Rice-roots'." *The Pacific Review* 23 (2010): 93–112.
Wendland, Wend. "Intangible Heritage and Intellectual Property: Challenges and Future Prospects." *Museum International* 56.1–2 (2004): 97–107.
Whitmore, John King, "Property and the State in Fifteenth Century Dai Viet: Public and Private Land." Unpublished paper, 2009.
Whitten, Tony. "The Saola – Brief History," in *Rediscovering the Saola: Proceedings of the Workshop "Rediscovering the Saola: A Status Review and Conservation Planning Workshop."* James Hardcastle (ed.). Hanoi: WWF Indochina Programme, 2004.
Winter, Tim. "Landscape, Memory and Heritage: New Year Celebrations at Angkor, Cambodia," in *The Politics of World Heritage: Negotiating Tourism and Conservation*, David Harrison and Michael Hitchcock (eds). Clevedon, UK: Channel View Publications, 2005: 50–65.
Wollenberg, Eve, Moira Moeliona, Godwin Limberg, Ramses Iwan, Steve Rhee and Made Sudana. "Between State and Society: Local Governance of Forest in Malinau, Indonesia." *Forest Policy and Economics* 8.4 (2006): 421–33.
Woodside, A. B. *Vietnam and the Chinese Model*. Cambridge: Harvard University Press, 1971, 1988.
World Bank. *World Development Report: Building Institutions for the Market*. Oxford: Oxford University Press, 2002.
Writenet. "Vietnam: Indigenous Minority Groups in the Central Highlands." *Writenet Report* 5/2001, Geneva, United Nations High Commissioner for Refugees, Centre for Documentation and Research, January 2002. http://www.unhcr.org/.
Xuong tru bi ky, 唱籌碑記, Ms. 1069–1070.
Xuong tru bi ky, 唱籌碑記, Ms. 3487.
Xuong tru bi ky, 唱籌碑記, Ms. 4199–4200.
Yeh, Emily. "Property Relations in Tibet Since Decollectivization and the Question of 'Fuzziness'." *Conservation and Society* (2004): 163–87.
Yoon, Carol Kaesuk. *Naming Nature: The Clash between Instinct and Science*. New York: W.W. Norton, 2009.
Yvon, Florence. "The Construction of Socialism in North Vietnam: Reconsidering the Domestic Grain Economy, 1954–1960." *Southeast Asia Research* 16:1 (2008): 43–84.
Zbierski-Salameh, Slawomira. "Polish Peasants in the 'Valley of Transition': Responses to Postsocialist Reform," in *Uncertain Transition: Ethnographies of Change in the Postsocialist World*, Michael Burawoy and Katherine Verdery (eds). Lanham: Rowman and Littlefield, 1999: 15–56.

Zhou Xueguang. "Unorganized Interests and Collective Action in Communist China." *American Sociological Review*, 58.1 (1993): 54–73.

Zinoman, Peter. "Introduction to Vu Trong Phung's *Dumb Luck* and the Nature of Vietnamese Modernism," in *Dumb Luck: A Novel by Vu Trong Phung*, Nguyen Nguyet Cam, trans. and Peter Zinoman, ed. Ann Arbor: University of Michigan Press, 2002: 1–30.

Zottoli, Brian. "The Development of Public Land in Pre-Colonial Viet Nam," in *Localized Poverty Reduction in Viet Nam*, G.B. Hainsworth (ed.). Vancouver: Centre for Southeast Asia Research, University of British Columbia, 1999: 197–208.

# Index

Note: Abbreviation ICH is used for "intangible cultural heritage"